Emotions

Emotions

Problems and Promise
for Human Flourishing

Barbara J. McClure

BAYLOR UNIVERSITY PRESS

Cover design by Savanah N. Landerholm
Cover image: Photo by Steve Johnson on Unsplash
Book design by Baylor University Press; typesetting by Scribe Inc.

The Library of Congress has cataloged this
book under ISBN 978-1-60258-329-0.

Printed in the United States of America on acid-free paper with a minimum
of thirty percent recycled content.

To all who know something about flourishing
and encourage its pursuit.

Contents

Preface

Some stories take a long time to reveal themselves, and the narrative at the heart of this book is one of them. I knew a project about various understandings of emotions was an interesting and important one, especially for my academic field: pastoral theology. (Pastoral theologians at their best—as well as psychotherapeutic clinicians, pastoral counselors, chaplains, and others who sometimes draw on our work—use psychological theories, theologies, social theories, and attention to people's particular contexts to better understand and ameliorate their pain.[1] Emotions as expressions of human experience have often been pastoral theologians' most important tool for understanding what is going on in people's lives, and thus have been a primary focus of our work.) I knew, too, that there was much about emotions that I (and others) assumed, but also that there was much I did not know. Even so, I did not realize when I began what a vast amount of research on emotions existed across many fields and in many disciplines. Nor did I realize how much there was about emotions in each of the disciplines that studied them. In the early stages of the work I understood my job as providing a review of the most important scholarship on emotions and summarizing it for my colleagues' and students' use. I hoped, too, to bring the disparate understandings together in some meaningful way if I could, but what *was* the story about emotions I wanted to tell?

Part of the challenge was that different researchers had their own foci of study; their own idiosyncratic definitions of passions, emotions, moods, sentiments, and feelings (to name just a few terms characterizing the subjects of emotionology); and their own particular methods to answer discipline-specific questions. For example, philosophers such as the Stoics focused on phenomenology, while Charles Darwin was interested in "emotional" expressions and behaviors, caring little about experience. William James focused on physiology, while Augustine only considered it tangentially. While these differences exist for scholars working in the same discipline, they are even more pronounced between scholars studying emotions from different fields. Another challenge I faced was that when I started the project, I read unsystematically: trying to get a general sense of emotion research I started reading scientific examinations, then read some early Christian theological accounts, then I explored sociological theories of emotions, then philosophical perspectives, then cultural anthropological research, then back to science, and so on. I found little about emotions in one field that seemed to relate to anything about emotions in others. In other words, there seemed to be scant influence across disciplinary lines. The more I studied, the more deeply I understood the complexities of each discipline's understanding of emotions, but those gains did not help me find a storyline that would bring the various disciplines' contributions together. Without a guide to help me connect these different (and differing) perspectives, I often felt perplexed. In addition, I was reading widely and deeply, but without a guide I did not realize that many early theorists have been shown more recently to be incorrect in their conclusions, though they are often still widely assumed. Reconciling the many understandings of emotions was a baffling challenge.

My own vocational commitments require that I understand personal experiences within ecological, social, economic, political, and cultural contexts. With some exceptions, emotions scholars focus on either the intrapsychic or the interpersonal dynamics of emotions: for example, not yet had anyone succeeded in relating the physiological (especially neurological) dynamics of emotions to the contextual realities in which a person is embedded—at least not to my satisfaction. The position that emotions are socially constructed—a view held among the social constructionist schools of emotion and often promoted by sociologists, cultural anthropologists, and other social theorists—was fundamentally opposed to the conclusions by evolutionary psychologists who argue that emotions are heritable traits genetically tuned to support an individual's physical survival. Other categories were in opposition too: emotions as "positive" or "negative," theological views that did not relate to scientific ones, this-worldly understandings of well-being that were opposed to otherworldly ones, and so on. Nevertheless, I was convinced that each perspective was true in some way. Since part of my goal was to tell a coherent story about emotions drawing on multiple disciplines that did not often recognize each other's contributions, I realized I would have to figure out some of the meaningful connections myself. What were the possible relationships between competing conclusions in the scholarship? I struggled, uncertain that I would be able to produce something worth publishing, or a book that anyone would find useful beyond a literature review (albeit a complex, nuanced, and comprehensive one). At the same time, however, I was convinced that if each discipline knew something about emotions and their function in human life, there must be a way that these insights were integrated in human experience. And if both social scientists and evolutionary psychologists, for example, were each on to something important, then surely each had to be one part of a larger whole. I persevered.

It was not until the last three decades or so that the research on emotions in neuroscience began to breach the boundaries so heavily drawn between disciplines. It took *me* a few years more to find that work and learn the ways neuroscientific research was developing some of the critical connections I sought. Psychological construction theories have helped me relate neuroscientific and physiological insights to those from anthropologists and social theorists, aiding my understanding of the complex origins, functions, and effects of emotions. In other words, the psychological constructionist understanding of emotions has helped me bring together the personal and the social, as I am committed to doing. But what of emotions' value in relation to the good life, or people's flourishing—what pastoral theologians claim to be seeking to support? Early Christian doubts about finding happiness this side of heaven differed from Aristotle's materialism and his more nuanced and hopeful view about emotions' relationship to well-being in this life. But Aristotle's optimism about the possibility of happiness in this life differs significantly from Freud's relative pessimism about the human condition. Somehow a view of human flourishing had to bring together each of these insights and attend to both the material and the nonmaterial aspects of human life as well.

As I worked, I slowly began to see the faint figure of a story walking toward me out of the thick fog in which I had been lost. The narrative that was emerging went something like this: emotions, their origins, functions, and effects—as well as their appropriate place in the human pursuit of well-being—have captured people's curiosity for millennia. Although not everyone was interested in the question of emotions' role in well-being, many scholars from disparate fields have been—either implicitly or explicitly. The challenge is that they have come to many different conclusions. While each discipline offers important insights about the problems and promise of emotions for happiness, their differing appraisals have left people confused about emotions' proper place in human life. Each discipline contributes important pieces of the puzzle, but none has them all. However, new research has begun to clarify the image connecting the various theories, allowing the narrative arc I had been seeking to emerge: neuroscience has begun to provide the missing evidence that draws a more complete understanding of emotions as they relate to people in context. And more contemporary theologies that articulate the embodiment of the Sacred in the midst of human life bring ultimate realities and earthly realities together in ways I find meaningful. These perspectives are part of the conclusion to the story I have wanted to tell.

In the early days of the project, I often got lost in the nuances of research and scholars' intradisciplinary arguments. Once I realized that the aim of *my* book was to bring together different theorists' contributions to an understanding of emotions and their relationship to human flourishing, I knew I had to make some difficult choices. No longer writing a comprehensive summary meant that some important figures in the study of emotions would get short shrift and others could not be included at all. The contributions of Aristotle, Augustine, Charles Darwin, Sigmund Freud, and James Russell, for example, could be only cursorily explored. Other scholarly giants, such as David Hume and Friedrich Nietzsche, Paul Tillich, Catherine Lutz, Paul Ekman, Daniel Goleman, and Martha Nussbaum, get only a note. Some important figures with keen interest in emotions, such as Niccolo Machiavelli, Andrew Lester, Joseph LeDoux, Jonathan Edwards, Friedrich Schleiermacher, Soren Kierkegaard, and Leslie Greenberg, get a nod but hardly a note. Other names one might expect (for instance, Melanie Klein) do not even appear in the index. Such are the difficult choices authors must often make.

As difficult was my decision not to provide a toolkit for how, exactly, to use emotions, or how, specifically, to leverage the insights herein to cultivate flourishing within a more just, inclusive, and nonviolent world. These I must leave to other expositions I intend to write and to the imagination and expertise of those who come alongside the efforts in this book, critiquing, developing, and adding nuance to them.

What I hope this exploration accomplishes, in the end, is the telling of a story about the mixed messages we in the West have received about the proper role of emotions in human life and how various important scholars have significantly contributed to our understandings (and confusions) along the way. There are many differing opinions about and perspectives on emotions that span the long history of their study. The chapters of this book are an attempt to articulate what I have discerned to be the most salient. I review the most significant proposals about emotions over several millennia, from early philosophical and theological examinations to cutting-edge neuroscience. I put these in conversation with explorations of well-being, both theological and not. I ask what these resources offer and what they miss. I note the ways emotions (and the behaviors they engender) can be deeply problematic. I attempt to integrate insights from psychology, cultural anthropology, sociology, theology, neuroscience, and philosophy to offer a proposal—a way forward—for critically discerning the criteria by which emotions are to be understood and feelings are to be valued, interpreted, and engaged, given my understanding of human flourishing. The narrative ends with a plea to value and attend to our own and others' emotions while being analytical and appropriately suspicious of them. I deeply believe that emotions, understood and engaged rightly, can contribute to flourishing, both individually and corporately.

Methodologically, I rely primarily on written texts: I summarize key contributions to emotionology and how the thinking has developed. In the endnotes, readers will find commentary on intradisciplinary disagreements to thicken their understanding of the historical and ongoing research—including some of the debates that continue. (While the endnotes are not necessary for following the argument of the book—and can be skipped—they are interesting for the additions, detail, nuance, and important additional scholarship they provide.) I investigate what scholars and their research programs are trying to ascertain, what they share, and where they differ. For this reason, the book is a good introduction to significant figures in emotions research and their most important ideas.

While the reader might be tempted to read the volume as an overview of *all* the noteworthy scholarship on emotions, such a goal is beyond its scope. Nor is it possible to provide much detail about all the figures presented herein. I do, however, want to provide some insight about how certain perspectives on emotions developed, and how theories built on each other. In the end, I seek to highlight where there is most agreement and to build something of a cohesive and coherent view about the relationships between emotions and human flourishing among significant and foundational figures. I make some conclusions and proposals that I hope add another piece to the puzzle and help fill out the emerging picture.

Acknowledgments

My struggle to find a narrative arc for this book was born not only of multiple research conundrums, as noted in the preface, it was also the consequence of living the challenges of life. I was learning the hard way what flourishing is and is not, and how emotions both clarify and obscure its pursuit. Thus, my experience and my processes of learning are not far behind the pages of this book.

I had tremendous help along the way in the form of wise guides and conversation partners among my family and close friends in my personal work (you know who you are), as well as colleagues' and institutions' support on the research and writing front. I am grateful to the Louisville Institute, a believer in this project from the beginning, whose support in the form of a grant for researchers allowed me an extra semester's research leave to begin it. I am grateful to the Divinity School at Vanderbilt University and my many friends still there who encouraged me in dark times and who, as a body, granted me a research leave to begin to explore the enormous topic of emotions. I am grateful to Brite Divinity School and my colleagues there for affording me research leaves that allowed me time to figure out and settle into a new library system and its holdings, and to develop the story emerging from the murkiness I and the book had been wandering in together for several years.

Without the enthusiastic and unwavering support of Carey Newman, editor in chief at Baylor University Press, this book might not have made it at all. Thanks, too, to the anonymous readers who slogged through an early draft and offered useful comments.

I am thankful for the students I have had the privilege to teach and learn from at the Divinity School at Vanderbilt University and at Brite Divinity School at Texas Christian University. You have allowed me to try on some ideas with you in the classroom, you have tested my knowledge and understanding, and you have provided me immense encouragement to continue the hard work of this project. I am especially grateful to my student assistants, all at Brite: Adam Stockton, Linda Barnette, and Wendy Davidson. Your help came at critical moments. Thank you.

A huge thank you to Amy, Battle, and Zella for giving me a beautiful, quiet corner of your attic to think, read, write, and be with my daughters. You gave me so much more, too, deepening our friendship and underwriting lifelong bonds.

With deep gratitude to Anna and Miriam, who have brought such richness to my life—so much passion, joy, love, and meaning. Thanks, too, to Graham, with whom I am joined in the adventure of parenting them and, we hope, helping them flourish.

And finally, with profound gratitude to Tim, who knows what I mean.

Introduction

Confusion and Ambivalence about Emotions

The ubiquity, seeming self-centeredness, and potential vulnerability of the question "How do you feel about [fill in the blank]?" often makes us groan. However, it is also a vital question for each of us to answer, especially in relation to experiences, people, and objects that matter to us. How we feel about something is vital to the way we live our lives and can affect everything from our basic survival to the accomplishment of our loftiest goals. Our emotions order our lives, guide our decisions, and inform how we will behave. Not knowing what we feel and why we feel it hinders our ability to build deep and meaningful relationships, to engage meaningful work, and to live more flourishing lives.

Indeed, emotions are at the very heart of being alive.[1] Without emotional connection and a sense of meaningful belonging, humans do not survive: to develop, children need expressions of love and care as much as they need food, shelter, and security.[2] One need only review the studies of children in orphanages to understand the importance of these: infants often die within months when deprived of affectionate physical touch and emotional interaction.[3] Bodily expression of emotions is a primary means by which infants communicate their needs before words are possible.[4] Emotions can mean the difference between life and death beyond infancy as well: hope enables survival in the midst of devastating life circumstances,[5] and the importance of small gestures of care and the ability to imagine—in community—the end of suffering are well documented,

1

for example, by survivors of the Jewish Holocaust and by survivors of sex trafficking today.[6] Loneliness can kill (the isolation, depression as a result of moral injury, and feelings of hopelessness in war veterans are known to contribute to the high rate of death by suicide upon veterans' return home).[7] And yet emotions such as love and anxiety bind people to one another, and anger often guides people in the decision of when to speak up, protest, or quit a job, and how and when to advocate for justice.[8] Media outlets evoke viewers' emotions to help a nation celebrate (think of the iconic photo of the sailor kissing the nurse in Times Square in a show of exuberance after returning from World War II). Images also help us do the important work of grieving, and they can motivate change: the picture of a naked child after a napalm bombing in Vietnam evokes emotions of disgust, horror, shame, bewilderment, and guilt about U.S. involvement in war.[9] There are recent examples of the public effects of emotion as well: think of the ways hearing U.S. president Donald Trump's comment about grabbing women's genitalia at will, or the stories of sexual assault of women by film producer Harvey Weinstein, and reports of politician Roy Moore's assault of teenage girls evoked disgust in many—though curiously not all.[10] The feelings these narratives evoked sent viral the #MeToo and #TimesUp movements, sparking protests and turning, even if slightly or temporarily, the tide of U.S. politics. Emotions order our very lives, both personally and corporately.

No wonder, then, that emotions have commanded a great deal of attention for much of human history. Music, poetry, and literature almost inevitably invoke and explore the promise and perplexities of people's emotional lives. The coldhearted, stone-cold character in a movie gives us chills. William Shakespeare demonstrated the ways ambition, greed, love, and envy can build and destroy nations: Lady Macbeth used envy and fear to incite murderous violence for political gain—only to have it end in her destruction and her husband's, as well as that of the kingdom they had built. Shakespeare wrote too of Romeo and Juliet's love that brought them together in death. The Upanishads and other Hindu Vedas take up the potency and dangers of desire: "You are what your deepest desire is. As is your desire, so is your intention. As is your intention, so is your will. As is your will, so is your deed. As is your deed, so is your destiny."[11] Sigmund Freud offered insight about the influence of emotions such as anxiety, rage, and jealousy in both intrapsychic and interpersonal experiences as well as on the development of civilizations. For example, in his 1930s book *Civilization and Its Discontents*, Freud explores the violence that can happen when societies require conformity and the repression of people's instincts and libidinal urges.[12]

Religious leaders, too, consider the role of emotions, though their conclusions often differ: while the Buddha articulated the ways desire creates suffering, Jesus understood love as the greatest virtue. Augustine wrote poignantly of lust and temptation and the weaknesses of his will against them. John Wesley theologized about the importance of passionate emotion in conversion and for genuine religious experience. Soren Kierkegaard and Paul Tillich philosophized about the anxious life and the human condition, and Jewish and Christian Scriptures contain themes of love, anger, joy, jealousy, grief, and fear. Some of these find emotions to be guides toward the good life; others have found emotions anathema to well-being. Indeed, there is little agreement about emotions' importance and function in human flourishing. But no matter where one falls on the point, emotions have commanded scrutiny for centuries. Even the Stoics, who recommended that people extirpate emotions from their lives altogether, devoted a good deal of time to understanding emotions' effects.

This millennia-long interest in emotions endures in the twenty-first century as Facebook, blogs, vlogs, and online editorials provide public forums for sharing and expressing emotions—often very strong—with possibly grave consequences. For example, the emotionally heated insults on Twitter hurled between the forty-fifth U.S. president and the leader of North Korea threatened to involve the world in a nuclear war. There is potential danger in what feels good, too: the pursuit of the positive emotional rush derived from "likes" on Facebook can become something of an addiction, evoking the same physiological response as cocaine.[13] It is small wonder that emoticons have become ubiquitous—often replacing words altogether—underscoring what people are trying to communicate with the use of emotional symbols. Television shows, movies, and popular literature explore and provide outlets for characters' (and viewers') emotions. The popularity of soap operas and reality shows surely has to do with the dramatic displays of emotion, and their most compelling storylines often involve emotions gone awry. For instance, the CBS reality game show *Survivor*, which pits contestants against one another in a battle that is primarily about one's wits and emotions, is one of the most popular and successful television shows of all time. Popular Disney/Pixar movies explicitly about emotions, such as *Inside Out*, promote particular views of emotions and their importance.[14] This movie was designed to advance the idea that viewers should value, understand, and use their emotional experiences in helpful ways: "The real reason we have emotions is to connect us together," the director suggests, seemingly unaware of the ways emotions also divide and destroy.[15]

Indeed, as much as these media are the product of a certain fascination with the emotional life within and between literary, television, and movie characters, they also become cautionary tales about the appropriate displays, interpretations, and uses of emotions. Reading plays such as *Macbeth* and watching shows such as *Survivor* is cathartic, allowing readers and viewers to experience vicariously the strong and dramatic emotions they may not be able to express or even experience in their own lives. But catharsis is not these shows' only function. Media outlets are also laboratories for learning what is appropriate in emotional displays and how one should deal with one's own and others' emotions. These shows can be educative about cultural expectations of people's emotional lives: certain expressions and displays of emotion are dangerous and are likely to get one voted off a show just as they can lead to the loss of a job,[16] social condemnation, and even arrest, as Black Lives Matter supporters and other activists can attest.[17] Indeed, expressing too much emotion, or the wrong kind of emotion, or any emotion at all (depending on who one is and the role certain emotions have in one's sociocultural milieu) can be so threatening that what is felt and how it is expressed is often censured. There continues to be widespread perplexity about and deep ambivalence toward emotions.[18]

Nevertheless, contemporary Western cultures generally assume that emotions are a useful entryway to personal experience: one need only explore them to gain access to what is most significant in people's lives. Given this assumption, psychotherapists have long focused on emotions, for example, and this focus is of a piece with a general cultural reality. North Americans live in what some have called a therapeutic age or a confessional age,[19] or an "affective turn"[20] in Western culture. The rise of this culture, exemplified by a quick perusal of the self-help titles in bookstores and on TV shows such as *Oprah, Dr. Phil*, or *In Treatment*, demonstrates the centrality and public nature of "emotion work" in late modernity.[21] The popularity of these shows displays a persistent and growing preoccupation with expressing and exploring innermost feelings in public, revering and idealizing them for their revelation of truth. With the rise of the therapeutic and confessional culture it is not surprising that talk of emotions has overtaken many social transactions.

Emotions are a focus in contemporary life, so it makes sense that people often ask each other "How are you feeling?" or "How does that make you feel?"[22] Indeed, the task of identifying, understanding, and managing emotional states has become big business, from psychotherapy to self-help books, and from parenting guides to business leadership coaching.

In fact, often to the surprise (and some consternation) of old-guard business leaders, it is increasingly expected that emotions will be a part of business transactions and organizational cultures. Emotions as intimate and personal as love have made it into the corporate sphere and the importance of creating "positive institutions" in which people feel valued, appreciated, and cared for has been well documented—whether by providing a ping-pong table in the breakroom, allowing casual-dress Fridays, inviting pets to work, scheduling pep talks that manipulate using emotions as tools, giving gifts on Secretary's Day, or recognizing important work anniversaries. These emotions-evoking activities help employees feel valued, which increases their loyalty and, most importantly to the company, their productivity.[23] Likewise, sales trainings inevitably instruct participants to recognize and use potential customers' emotions to boost profits (examples: "That color looks great on you," "Bamboo is a very eco-friendly flooring choice," and "This product is well suited for the elite connoisseur").[24] These marketing and sales strategies count on the fact that one's feelings inform one's purchases. For-profit corporations rely on the idea that feelings about oneself as an employee—and the feelings for one's boss and the company—inform the amount of engagement one is willing to invest in one's work.[25]

There are conflicting perspectives on these trends, of course. Generations of older Americans (and sometimes those from other than Western cultures, too) are dismayed by the emotional displays of younger generations. Some critics worry about the increasingly public disclosure of emotions, which they believe are deeply personal and should remain so.[26] The unnuanced, undisciplined, and often dramatic displays of emotions on Twitter or Instagram are, for them, a case in point. Others worry that emotions are becoming too central to public life, commercial enterprise, and political endeavors. Those in this second camp bemoan the contemporary Western preoccupation with the emotional life and with giving emotions (rather than, say, duty, hard work, and careful, "rational" analysis) too much power. Some critics understand the preoccupation with emotions as continuous with the problematic rise of modern individualism with its emphasis on personal and existential experience, a focus that often ignores significant—and often oppressive—social realities. Still others see it as part of a growing trend toward an emphasis on narcissistic self-preoccupation or the sinful fulfillment of personal, selfish wishes.[27]

There are other reasons for concern. Emotions are not straightforward: they can be organizing (e.g., "I want to make a difference in the world, so I will attend medical school and join Doctors Without Borders, despite the sacrifices those pursuits will entail"). But emotions can also be disorganizing in people's lives and in collective social contexts: think, for example, of the potential danger of abusing substances to cope with unpleasant emotions, as when a person declares, "I feel anxious, so I am going to drink some alcohol to 'take the edge off.'" Surely everyone has experience with freezing in stage fright, has forgotten what they are about to say when embarrassed, or knows of a friend who has lost control in the heat of anger. Emotions can wreak havoc.

Emotions have significant effects in personal experience and interpersonal relationships, but emotions have political potency as well, and not always for good. Despite the goals of John F. Kennedy ("ask not what your country can do for you—ask what you can do for your country") and Barack Obama ("change we can believe in"), both of whom leveraged emotions such as hope to create more inclusive and equal societies, emotions also have been used to control, manipulate, and incite violence between people and groups. In other words, emotions can be tools of power used to exclude and oppress: for example, fear of the "other" has resulted in systemic xenophobia against entire groups of people that manifests in marginalization and suffering.[28] Anger and jealousy can lead to the murder of an intimate partner. Envy, arrogance, and aggression can end a professional career,[29] and the untrustworthiness of passionate sexual attraction for establishing loving mutual relationships is well established. To complicate matters, emotions are the *objects* of power as well as its tools: the heated debates about homosexuality (that is, who has a right to love or desire whom) have generated as much or more political focus and energy than the plight of starving children in two-thirds-world countries or the global ecological degradation already underway.

It is perhaps *because* of emotions' power that they can be used against individuals, groups, and whole societies. Recall the manipulations of religious leader Jim Jones in Guyana, who instilled enough fear about governmental policies in the United States that hundreds of his followers took their own lives.[30] Or consider the way German leader Adolf

Hitler preyed on the economic fears of the German people such that many participated—often knowingly and willingly—in one of the most horrific mass killings in human history. Even the forty-fifth president of the United States and his loyalists have leveraged for their own political gain emotions such as resentment, anger, fear, and a sense of entitlement among groups already divided by socioeconomic class, race, gender, and sexualities. Donald Trump's success has been attributed, in part, to his ability to incite and condone violence in order to justify the dominant class' perpetuation of oppression and suffering.[31] Emotions have the potential to lead astray and to be used as tools of violence. It is prudent to be cautious.

Nevertheless, human beings sense that emotions matter. *How* is the question. Though they were once viewed as dangerous or unwanted elements of otherwise rational actors, emotions are now considered by some—such as clinical psychologists—as integral to people's well-being. These understand that the implications of emotions are far-reaching, affecting intrapsychic health or illness, interpersonal relationships, and even people's physical growth and development.[32] Emotions affect sociocultural and political systems too, everything from economics to global warfare; in turn, those systems also elicit individuals' emotions, for example, when a person feels guilt for having too much power, or rage at having too little.[33]

The messages about emotions are mixed. Emotions such as love are extolled as virtues—even as love is also dismissed as naïve.[34] Emotions are often considered the domain of women, children, and the immature, even as they are seen as elemental to wisdom. Emotions are defended as the proper masters of reason—even as the very foundation for being in the world—while at the same time dismissed as mere personal phenomena, the result of physiology, utterly unintelligent and irrational, even subhuman.[35] Indeed, emotions have been regarded as being of "doubtful value" and "repeatedly deprecated as a burden,"[36] and some emotions such as anger and envy have even been demonized in religious traditions.[37] Emotions have been seen as "relatively unimportant in themselves"[38] and "irrelevant epiphenomena" among so-called serious scholars[39] and also ignored because of their taken-for-granted, self-evident nature. In other words, in some cases, emotions have been considered too complex to study meaningfully, and in others they have not been studied because they were assumed to be "straightforward in their operation."[40] A result of all of this confusion is that even scholars in the disciplines to which emotions' relation to the good life seems to belong—for example, philosophers, psychologists, ethicists, and theologians—have had little to say about them.[41] And so, the study of emotions—especially in relation to human flourishing—has been severely neglected in contemporary scholarship until relatively recently.[42] Thus, understanding what emotions are, where they come from, and how they function continues to be necessary work, as is exploring emotions' complex relationship to human flourishing.

The questions about emotions' rightful place in human experience—especially in relation to well-being—are not easy to answer: the struggle to understand and achieve the meaning and means of flourishing has been a part of philosophers' and theologians' investigations for thousands of years. However, while understanding flourishing itself is a complicated and elusive goal, even the earliest thinkers understood that the good life was somehow related to people's emotional lives: some thought emotions were related positively to the good life, though most determined it was a negative relationship.[43]

To make matters more complicated, emotions are not simple to access, nor are emotions straightforward in their origins or their meanings once they are identified. The energy directed to the emotions in people's lives (their expression, their censure, their dismissal, their denial, and their exploration) suggests that individuals and cultures recognize that emotions are ambiguous: sometimes life-giving and yet potentially problematic—and sometimes both at the same time. Perhaps it is the preoccupation with emotions that best indicates the collective and deep confusion about them, *dis-ease* with them, and anxiety in relation to emotions in ourselves and in others.[44]

Even given these complications, emotions have had—and continue to occupy—pride of place, especially in Western culture and its historical antecedents.[45] Human beings have recognized for millennia that emotions have fundamental significance in our lives, for good and for ill. Thus, people continue to try to understand emotions and how to rightly experience, express, understand, and use emotions—both their own and others'. Most people seem at least vaguely aware that emotions can be a source of life and that emotions can also lead to death: discerning the difference is crucial. The questions remain, however: given emotions' ubiquity, importance, problems, and promise, how ought we think about and relate to our own and others' emotions? This confusion and consequent wrestling are understandable—we are trying to understand our very *selves* in the context of our lives as they are being lived. It is an urgent challenge with significant implications. Answers to these questions have been sought by the earliest philosophers and the most recent neuropsychologists, and still there is no easy wisdom.

Exploring some of the questions about emotions that have emerged historically—and the answers to them—is the work of this book, as is offering a constructive proposal for a way forward. The chapters examine early philosophical, theological, scientific, psychological, and social theories of emotion, introducing some of the key figures and their thinking, as well as some of the internecine debates. Providing an overview of the scholarship on emotions serves in several ways: first, it introduces readers to the most significant research in the study of emotions (a valuable endeavor in its own right and useful, perhaps, for courses in psychology or histories of psychology and other related disciplines, such as pastoral theology). The book provides a framework—a scaffolding, if you will—around which other theories of emotion not included here can be positioned. Second, the overview demonstrates the different ways emotions have been understood and studied, thus illumining, I hope, some of the reasons for our current confusion and ambivalence about emotions in human life. Third, the overview of five significant disciplinary approaches provides an examination of how emotions have been evaluated for their relationship to the good life. This thread highlights the ways understandings of emotions' value (or lack thereof) for human flourishing have differed—often dramatically. Exploring the different appraisals of emotions' role in human flourishing can help in the construction of a position that integrates what each view offers, while also highlighting the limits of each. The end goal is an understanding of emotions' origins and functions in relation to flourishing that is sufficiently complex and nuanced to be a useful guide for those who do emotion work: our parents, our teachers, our friends, our therapists, our bosses, and—perhaps most importantly—ourselves.

Views on Meanings of *Emotion*

In this book I examine the most influential views on emotion from their earliest records to the most contemporary scholars. I explore perspectives across early philosophy, theology, science, psychology, sociology, and cultural anthropology, mining them for their answers to the questions about emotions' origins, meanings, functions, value, and uses. I explore the various research programs, underlying assumptions, conclusions, and the relation of these to human flourishing.[46]

Not surprisingly, as different as the understandings of emotions are, so are the views on what is "the good" for human beings. While early philosophers agreed that eudaimonia (or "happiness") is the chief end (or *telos*) of human life and is desired by all, views on how to accomplish it varied greatly.[47] The Stoics, for example, imagined the "good life" as one without avoidable suffering, while early theologians including Augustine understood the goal as life lived in relationship to God and in accordance with God's will as Augustine understood it to be revealed in the Christian Scriptures. Other are less interested in the good life and more interested, for example, in survival. Natural scientists understand emotions as functional: they help people survive in what is often a hostile natural environment. Social scientists study the ways emotions arise and function in groups, while psychologists are often most concerned with intrapsychic and interpersonal well-being. My own view of flourishing is complex and contextual, but also, I hope, more layered than others' have been. My understanding of flourishing includes attention to emotions' relationship to people's agency, identity, and intimate relationships as well as how emotions function in communities, sociopolitical structures, and ecological environments. My questions throughout the text include "What do emotions have to do with people's well-being, and what do scholars (both ancient and contemporary) have to teach us about these questions and their answers?"

Writing a book about emotions is problematic from the outset: what, exactly, *are* emotions and thus, what is the subject of study in a book about them?[48] A number of words have been used to describe what various scholars have studied, including passions, emotions, feelings, affects, sentiments, affections, moods, appetites, and so on. One dictionary entry notes that "historically, [the word *emotion*] has proven utterly refractory to definitional efforts: probably no other term in psychology shares its nondefinability with its frequency of use."[49] Readers may find true of themselves that "everyone knows what an emotion is, until asked to give a definition."[50] The answer to the question "What is an emotion?" is complicated, since a definition depends on various terms as well as "an extensive network" of social, moral, cultural, and psychological factors.[51]

Etymologically, the term *affect*, its Greek cousin *pathema* and Latin sister *affectus*, and the similarly used French and English word *passion* (all precursors to our contemporary use of the word *emotion*) indicate some sort of passivity of the person experiencing emotions.[52] Along these lines, early philosophers understood emotions as disruptive interruptions to "right" behaviors and thoughts—disruptions over which people had little or no control. The interruptions or intrusions were contrasted with reason or will, which one was presumed to be able to manage and for which one was expected to be responsible. The intrusions of the passions included thoughts, desires, and behaviors that could have "significant costs" to the person they affect.[53]

The term *emotion* is etymologically derived from the Latin root *movere*, meaning "to move," and shares similar usage with a French word containing in its meaning "riot" or "unruliness," which Rene Descartes used in the seventeenth century to supplement the meaning of the passions.[54] While the early philosophers' and theologians' preferred word *passions* and contemporary understandings of *emotions* are not entirely interchangeable, they both indicate a kind of movement within oneself over which one has little control; however, the word *passions* also connotes a religious meaning that *emotions* does not.[55] This is only one of many differences between the two terms and between these and other terms. Indeed, the two words have been used to convey fundamentally different things, and so much definitional confusion between terms abounds that from the mid-nineteenth century onward, more often than not even scholars' uses of the word *emotions* did not mean the same thing.[56] Indeed, though these (and other) words are commonly used and interchanged, their meanings are often so vague and varied that one historian suggests that there is "something of a terminological free-for-all" out of which the term *emotions* emerged as the generally adopted category to include all the terms that had gone before it.[57]

Early philosophers and Christian theologians used the terms *passions, appetites,* and *affections* most often. In fact, the word *emotions* did not come into general use until 1740 when philosopher David Hume used it in his essay *Treatise of Human Nature.*[58] The terms used in this book, then, will follow as closely as possible those used by the scholars themselves. For example, I use the word *passions* when writing about the understandings of Plato and the Stoics, but *affections* and *appetites* in the context of Christian theologians such as Augustine. I will use *expressions of "emotion"* when exploring Charles Darwin's work, and *emotions* and *feelings* when outlining psychodynamic and neuropsychological understandings. Each of these terms has a particular meaning; thus, where the use of a term is idiosyncratic, I note the particular usage in the endnotes. Despite the fact that one philosopher argues that "feelings aren't emotions," the fact is that they are often referred to as such.[59] It is important, therefore, to clarify one's usage and the meaning of one's terms.[60]

My own understanding of emotions suggests that they are not thoughts but are sometimes related to thoughts. Emotions are not behaviors but are generated by and can generate behaviors; emotions are not feelings per se, though they are a precursor to feelings; emotions are not physiological only, though emotions do depend on bodies for their generation. Emotions are deeply individual, having to do with a person's past experience, present contexts, and hopes for the future: they have the potential to reveal much about a person's deepest self. At the same time, emotions do not exist as discrete entities within us, and they are not particularly personal, but rather they involve physiological activity in the context of social, cultural, and political environments. Emotions are not merely perceptions, though perceptions often contribute to them. Nor are emotions always conscious, though attention to them through one's feelings can make them more available to conscious reflection. Emotions typically have to do with values and are related to motivation. Emotions rarely have single origins, nor are they necessarily specific in their effect; instead emotions are usually mixed in their sources and in our experiences of them. Emotions are related to time (past, present, and future), to memories and expectations, to fantasies and hopes, to interpersonal relationships, and to culture. Emotions are also developmentally indicative—being related in some ways to one's developmental phase. Emotions can be pleasant and unpleasant, adaptive and maladaptive, negative or positive.[61] Nevertheless, emotions are always indicative of something, and in the pursuit of human flourishing it will be important to consider what a particular emotion in a particular moment might be indicating.

My intention is to provide an integrative and complex view of emotions, their origins, their functions, and their relationships to human flourishing so as to advance the conversation about emotions beyond binaries such as, for example, "emotions are personal" and "emotions are constructed" or "emotions have nothing to do with flourishing in this life" and "emotions have nothing to do with anything that might transcend our individual lives." Thus, I draw on the ideas about emotions in each research program and try to bring them together in some meaningful way. I hope to offer a good introduction the reader can use to explore more deeply certain figures, ideas, themes, and debates. This will take readers through what can sometimes seem like a cacophony of ideas, definitions, and methods of study as a way to introduce the field of emotionology. Finally, though, it is my aim to offer a perspective that could be useful to questions about emotions and their value.

Each primary figure in emotions' study presented here offers an important perspective in understanding the origins and functions of emotions toward flourishing, but each is also incorrect in ways that confuse and confound those who have inherited earlier scholars' thinking, which we in the West have done. Only understanding and critically engaging the most influential work on emotions can guide us out of the morass and free us to find our way forward to a more adequate understanding of emotions and their role in human flourishing. In the end, I am convinced that emotions have heuristic and epistemological value in the endeavor toward flourishing and that life would be less rich, less meaningful, and less just without practices that can explore, understand, and interpret our own and others' emotions.[62] At the same time, emotions can be life-limiting, even death dealing. In fact, knowing how to access, identify, interpret, engage, and use emotions can be a matter of life and death and—perhaps no less dramatically—of the difference between flourishing and floundering.[63]

1

Emotions as Dangerous, Disruptive, and Symptoms of *Dis-ease*

Socrates / Plato and Early Greek Perspectives

Introduction

For the first two millennia of Western history, Greek philosophers, Jewish and Christian theologians, and the earliest physicians were among those who devoted most attention to the emotions (or, more accurately, words that are commonly translated as the passions, sentiments, affections, and appetites). This chapter explores the passions through the eyes of Socrates/Plato, Hippocrates/Galen, Aristotle, Epicurus, and the Stoics, each of whom significantly influenced various contemporary understandings of emotion. Their studies of the passions, their analyses, and their conclusions about the passions' proper place in people's lives advanced many of the core questions with which subsequent scholarship about the origins, value, purposes, and meanings of emotions has had to contend.[1] For example, these early thinkers debated the relationship between bodily appetites and reason, the origins of suffering and one's proper relationship to it, what it means to be human (including whether and how humans are different from animals), the relationships between personal, affective experience and one's social context, how truth is apprehended and understood, the dynamics and strength of one's will in relation to "disruptive" passions and behaviors, and the nature of the good life and the best means of achieving it.[2]

15

Early scholars differed in their answers to these questions, and the language they use to describe what they are studying often gives away their opinion about them.[3] For example, Plato and his followers used the term *passions* to describe all affective experience and either valued them all or valued none. Other philosophers, such as hedonistic philosopher Epicurus, distinguished among certain passions, examining whether they were directed at desires that are "worthy" or not. Still others, such as Christian theologian Augustine, used terms such as *appetites* for some (by which he usually meant bodily urges that take one away *from* what is good or salvific) and *affections* for others (by which he meant the movements of the soul directed *to* what is good or godly). The choice of terms indicates fairly clearly a particular scholar's opinion of certain passions' worth. While some early scholars (a minority, to be sure) found some passions to be useful guides to health and growth, others determined that all passions are anathema to the good life, harmful, and a general nuisance. The earliest Greco-Roman philosophers, including Plato, for example, assumed that the passions (*pathai*) are irrational, disruptive, and untrustworthy and as such should be carefully monitored and disciplined by reason.[4] They understood particular passions to be especially problematic, including anger, which they took to be a "brief bout of madness."[5] For these thinkers, the senses were untrustworthy, and reason alone was dependable. For example, Anaxagoras (500–428 BCE) argued that "through the weakness of the senses we cannot judge the truth,"[6] Democritus (460–370 BCE) asserted that the soul (which he argued includes the mind) must be without passions,[7] and Pericles (495–429 BCE) sought to prove that reason is invincible.[8] This line of thinking laid the groundwork on which a wide variety of thinkers would later wrestle, including philosophers such as Socrates/Plato, Aristotle, Friedrich Nietzsche, and Martha Nussbaum; scientists such as Charles Darwin, Paul MacLean, Joseph LeDoux, and James Russell; psychologists such as Sigmund Freud, William James, Magda Arnold, Paul Ekman, and Sandor Rado; social theorists and cultural anthropologists including Max Weber, Catherine Lutz, Arlie Hochschild, Sara Ahmed, and Theodore Kemper; and Jewish and Christian theologians from Philo, Augustine, and Origen to Soren Kierkegaard, Paul Tillich, Andrew Lester, and John Caputo—most of whose thinking about emotions is treated at least briefly in this book. Each of these scholars' conclusions about the passions/emotions and their role in the good life differs from those of others. And each has contributed to both contemporary wisdom and current confusion about the value and meaning of emotions in human experience.

Some early philosophers in particular—Socrates/Plato, Hippocrates/ Galen, Aristotle, Epicurus, and the Stoics—devoted their lives to understanding the value and meaning of passions, and they left a long record that laid the groundwork for the variety of contemporary views held today—even in popular culture—whether these early thinkers' influence is recognized or not. Each group or name identifies a distinct stream of early thought about the passions. Socrates/Plato believed the passions were disruptive, harmful, and even potentially dangerous and thus must be controlled. Hippocrates/Galen found them symptoms of physical illness and mental dis-ease and thus potentially useful guides to diagnose root causes of sickness. Aristotle believed passions can be used to guide and motivate growth and maturation and thus, he also argued, potentially be useful. Epicurus reasoned that the passions are natural and at times positive if guided appropriately, but the Stoics understood the passions as the root of suffering and thus something that should be eliminated if possible. Because the work of these philosophers laid the foundation for how the passions/emotions have been understood since, the following sections briefly explore each of these perspectives.

The Passions Are Dangerous and Must Be Controlled: Socrates/Plato

Happiness: The Aim or Goal of Human Life

In their early examinations of the relationship between reason and the passions, the philosophers Socrates (470–399 BCE) and Plato (429–347 BCE)[9] argued that knowledge of oneself and the world is accessible only when one uses reason to analyze personal experience, explicitly privileging people's cognitive abilities rather than their perceptual senses as the source of real knowledge and wisdom. In this, Socrates and Plato were students of Pericles, who had championed the unique ability of *reason* to work out the most difficult problems of justice, law, and ethics. As Socrates/Plato argued, "Knowledge does not consist in impressions or senses, but in *reasoning about them*."[10] Only reasoned reflection (which is informed by divine, pure and transcendent reason: the only source of truth—the Supreme or the Good) matters.[11]

To prove that the senses were not important in the pursuit of truth and wisdom, Socrates/Plato noted that animals have senses, as do infants, but neither *knows* truth, and neither can be *wise*. If knowledge and wisdom were dependent on the senses, Socrates/Plato argued, then when the object of sight or smell or hearing disappeared, wisdom would, too. Instead, Plato asserted, the *thinking soul* is the only capacity that can discern truth and wisdom, derived from the ability to reason about things.

One of Socrates'/Plato's chief concerns was the role of reason in relationship to the passions in cultivating the good life.[12] In Plato's dialogue *The Republic*, the character Socrates defends the fact that he encourages others to engage in philosophical reflection by saying that the unexamined life is not worth living.[13] In this dialogue Socrates argues that reflecting on what one values in life and why they value it (that is, "doing philosophy"[14]) is critical to a life well lived. However, Socrates argued, that is not enough. Individuals must become a master of themselves, using reason to reign in their passions, and doing what each can do to help promote the stability of their community; furthermore, each must *want* to do what is right. In fact, in response to Glaucon,[15] Socrates argued that living a just and ethical life (that is, living a good life) is not only about behavior, but also about the state of a person's soul, and the condition of one's soul is reflected in one's actions. Individuals and communities are responsible for guiding people to the right state of their souls.[16] Socrates/Plato, then, were concerned both with individual people and life in community—the state or *polis*—and with the passions' role in the workings of both.

Plato was convinced that all men (*sic*) seek happiness (that is, they love the good and want to possess it, and what they will gain by seeking the good is happiness), that happiness is desired for its own sake, not for the sake of anything else, and that happiness requires a life of virtue. For Plato, the happy man is the just man.[17] Happiness results from the exercise of the highest part of the soul—that is, reason—and men should aim at virtue or the good, not pleasure. Socrates/Plato thus argued that the good life (*eudaimonia*, happiness, well-being)[18] is not about a particular feeling or experience. Rather, the good life is a just and ethical one. For them, justice requires citizens to mind their own business (that is, to be self-sufficient—not dependent on external sources to figure out what is good),[19] do the best they can to discern what is right, and do what is good for one and all, according to their abilities.[20]

The Soul's Role in Happiness

As Socrates' student, Plato sought to identify and describe the soul—what he understood to be the center of being and experience—so that he could prescribe remedies for the "diseases of the passions." Plato believed the soul has three parts: the reasoning, spirited, and appetitive parts, each of which has its own function.[21] The appetitive soul, Plato asserted, is both concerned with getting immediate sensual pleasure—basic biological urges and drives, bodily pleasures, and wealth—and interested in avoiding suffering. The appetites are often misguided, Plato wrote, and he imagined them physically located away from the head, "where they can do as little harm as possible."[22]

The intermediate, noble, and spirited part of the soul is where Plato believed the passions are. This part of the soul is responsible for self-assurance and self-affirmation as well as aggressive self-assessment. This part of the soul is trainable and can be led by the bodily appetites or be guided by the head (reason). The spirited, passionate part of the soul, then, is located in the chest, separated from the head by the neck (the *isthmus*) but close enough to be used by the rational mind when needed. The spirited part of the soul serves as an intermediary between the rational and the physical, appetitive parts. In Plato's model, then, any of the three parts of the soul can initiate action, and they often struggle against each other.[23]

Ideally, in Plato's thinking, the reasoning part of the soul must guide the spirited part, and both must control the appetitive part of the soul. In a well-known metaphor depicting the relationship of reason to the passions, Plato compares the soul to a chariot guided by a charioteer and led by two horses: one horse represents the appetites or desires in the lowest, basest part of the soul. This appetitive soul is impulsive and stubborn and must be controlled. The other horse represents the spirited part of a person's soul. The spirited part of the soul is noble and can be used by the rational mind, represented by the charioteer, to guide the chariot where it ought to go. The spirited soul can be understood as the life force of the person, directable in a number of ways—some harmful, some good, depending on whether the appetites or reason are guiding the spirit. In Plato's metaphor, if one does not use reason to control one's desires, the person is as misdirected as a chariot run off course by an impulsive, uncontrolled horse.

Reason's Role in the Good Life

For Plato, behaving justly (*that is*, being controlled by reason and living ethically) is fundamental to the good life. Behaving ethically means both doing one's part to contribute to a stable society and community, which necessitates controlling oneself and one's desires. Plato's understanding of the good life restricts individual freedom for the good of the whole. Too much individual freedom, he indicates, would result in a widespread lawlessness that is not good for anyone.

In Plato's understanding, what is true, right, and good (that is, ethical and just) requires knowledge of permanent and universal principles of the world. This truth is not affected by changing appearances or perceptions. The good life, then, is the reasoned life about otherworldly things.[24] Plato asserted that knowledge of the *telos* or aim of life—the good life—exists inside each man (*sic*) in the form of reason.[25] Human reason can discover the eternal truths that are hidden within the soul: that is, they can access the eternal truths that are in individuals before birth and which survive after an individual's death.[26] What is right and good, then, must be discovered and unearthed by reasoned reflection rather than acquired or learned.[27] In other words, "the knower *has* the truth. He doesn't learn it; he merely recalls it with the aid of instruction."[28] In Plato's view, reason knows and loves what is good, and reason ideally should govern the entire person, guiding his thoughts and his actions.

Because the soul's reasoning is *pure* in some sense, Plato assumed that the passions are, fundamentally, disruptions of reason: that is, of right/rational thinking.[29] Because the passions interfere with deliberate, rational thought and behavior (fundamental to the good life), they are trouble. Plato, then, did not find much positive or valuable in the desires of the body and urged detachment from them as much as possible.[30] To Plato, the passions are the result of misguided evaluations of contingent, material matters that harmfully bind the soul to earthly existence. That is, all errors are errors in judgment and control. The desires and appetites of the body pull the spirited part of the soul toward mundane concerns, preventing the reasoning part of the soul from engaging more valuable, transcendent truths. The passions, then, can be dangerous. They must be controlled by constant evaluation since they will almost inevitably lead to suffering and harm if not carefully disciplined.

The Relationship of What Is Pleasant and Unpleasant to the Good Life

Plato argued that one of the challenges for the appetitive and spirited parts of the soul is that they evaluate experiences and desires on the basis of whether inner stirrings *feel pleasant or unpleasant*, as well as on what the body *anticipates* as future pleasure and pain. In contrast, the highest part of the soul (reason) strives for knowledge and right understanding and is not interested in what is pleasant.[31] The reasoning part of the soul is only interested in what is true, right, and good—what transcends life on earth. Because of the appetitive part's natural tendency to pursue what is pleasant and avoid what is unpleasant—whether or not those pursuits are wise—the spirited part of the soul must be schooled to become a servant of reason, learning indifference to earthly things such as appetites, pleasure, and satisfaction in order to lead people to right thought and action. According to Plato, detachment (*apatheia*) from earthly desires or strivings is the only way to develop the higher, rational soul properly. Because the spirited part of the soul can be habituated to help in the rational soul's struggle against one's bodily desires and strivings, it has some value (even though it is not as valuable as reason), but without strict guidance, the movements of the lower parts of the soul distract from the truth that the highest, rational soul knows: that nothing in mortal life is worthy of real concern.[32]

The metaphor of the stallions and charioteer functions in at least two ways for Plato: first, it regards the passions as inferior and dangerous—more primitive and bestial and less intelligent and dependable than reason. Second is the distinction between the passions and reason itself as if they are two different natural kinds of human experience. Reason is natural, right, and true; reason will guide one to the good life. Appetites and passions, on the other hand, are disturbances to be disciplined or at least guided. The wise man knows the difference and is in control of both.[33]

Failures of Reason to Control the Passions

As committed as Plato was to this schema, he observed that the reasoning part of the soul is not always able to control the passions, especially when people experience conflicting desires and interests; thus, Plato had to explain people's failure to control the movements of their souls. In order to explain the reasons people did not always choose what was right or good (that is, what is reasoned), Plato developed the idea of *akrasia*—knowing what is right but not following one's own reasoned wisdom toward it. This, Plato argued, is the result of a weak will, which he attributed to poor education, "mental retardation," or disease.[34]

The means for achieving the good life and avoiding *akrasia*, in Plato's view, was the improvement of the intellectual and immortal part of the soul in order to strengthen its control over one's appetites and passions.

How to develop a strong and properly formed will? Through the study of philosophy and particular practices.[35] Such study should be aimed at developing one's ability to reason and to change one's beliefs, so as to align oneself with Truth. Plato also recommended participation in symposia, choir singing, and controlled dancing to learn self-discipline and control; each requires controlling one's own desires for the good of the whole.

Though dominant, this perspective was not the only view of the passions in ancient Greece. Other views emerged alongside those of Socrates/Plato. For example, in contrast to the position that privileged reason over experience that dominated earliest Greek philosophy was the view of "physician of the soul" Hippocrates, and later Galen, who understood the passions both as causes and as symptoms of sickness in the body.[36]

The Passions Are Both Causes and Symptoms of Dis-ease: Hippocrates and Galen

A Socratic philosopher and physician (he understood himself to be a healer of the soul as well as the body), Hippocrates (ca. 460–377 BCE) was interested in healing people's suffering, and he found in the passions both the cause and symptoms of disease and of dis-ease.

Though a near contemporary of Socrates and clearly informed by him, Hippocrates had different interests than Socrates, disagreeing with Socrates' methods and his conclusions. Of utmost importance to Hippocrates and the corpus of scholarship that developed out of his work was *the body and its senses* and what wisdom they might yield. Not being particularly religious, Hippocrates was less interested in understanding what was outside embodied experience than he was in what was happening physiologically. Hippocrates was a philosopher, but he was even more a scientist who argued that the "empirical methods of fact-gathering were suspended only at the peril of those who wished to learn and understand."[37] Hippocrates and those who followed him argued that the appetites, misled passions, and consequential suffering are not the result of punishments of the gods or superstitious dealings, as commonly believed in the early Greco-Roman world. Nor is suffering the result of the misdirected relationship between reason and the body (as Socrates had postulated). Rather, the passions in Hippocrates' view are generated from natural causes.[38] Rather than having religious or philosophical sources, Hippocrates asserted, bodily disturbances expressed in the form of the passions are the product of environmental factors or lifestyle habits. In this sense, he understood the passions as natural—or at least to be expected—in cases where there is something wrong physiologically or socially.[39]

Several centuries after Hippocrates, the philosopher and one of the most influential physicians of ancient Rome, Galen, revived Hippocrates' interests and methods.[40] The Platonist Galen (ca.130–216 CE[41]) understood that psychological and physical health are fundamental components of the good life since they relate to the physical embodiment of the soul.[42] As both a philosopher and physician in the tradition of Hippocrates, Galen considered the study of philosophy to be essential to a physician's training: philosophy enables the physician to discern between truth and illusion, or between reality and mere surface appearances, which Galen found critical to accurate diagnoses. Philosophical reflection is also necessary, Galen argued, for putting treatment on a sound ethical foundation.[43]

For Galen, the balanced, harmonious, and optimal functioning of all the systems of the body—especially the organs—is the goal of life. Building on earlier Hippocratic conceptions, Galen believed that human health requires an equilibrium among the four main bodily fluids, or "humors": blood, yellow bile, black bile, and phlegm. Each of the four humors is made of particular elements and displays two of the four primary qualities: hot, cold, wet, and dry. Unlike Hippocrates, however, Galen argued that humoral imbalances can be located in specific organs, as well as in the body as a whole, and he sought to situate each in a particular physiological system.[44]

Galen favored Plato's tripartite model of the soul, whose various functions he assigned to specific organs. For example, Galen placed reason in the brain, emotion in the heart, and desire in the liver. Galen gave each organ a special role, imagining that each produced particular energies (he sometimes called them spirits, or *pneuma*) that governed specific biological functions. For Galen, then, passions are the result of physiologically experienced *movements* in and between the systems of the liver and the heart, which affect other functions in other organs. These movements can be caused by cognitive acts but can also be initiated by bodily changes—and they incline people to form corresponding passions.[45] The passions, or the "pathologies of the soul" such as delirium, mania, lethargy, epilepsy, and melancholy, originate in the humors or bodily fluids, Galen argued, and just as excessive passions can influence the humoral system, changes in the humors have effects on one's passions.[46]

In summary, Galen argued that there must be balance for proper functioning of the whole body. Disease occurs when a crucial physiological function is blocked and disturbs the balance between the humors. Losing appropriate balance between humors in the body will produce a specific temperament, which can be diagnosed and treated depending on which characteristics and qualities are dominant in a person and the relation of those relevant humors to their respective organs. Galen developed treatments for curing "excessive" or "incorrect" passions by bringing the humors and affective qualities back into balance; these treatments included diet, changes of climate, and bloodletting.[47] Longer-term therapies included habituation to the right lifestyle (including exercises such as gymnastics), being part of a healthy social/political environment, and right belief—practices through which he thought the relevant physiological functions are eventually reorganized, and balance maintained.[48]

Socrates/Plato, Hippocrates, and Galen agreed with other earlier philosophers that the unexamined life is not worth living and that individuals must know themselves in order to achieve the good life. However, Socrates/Plato trusted the rational mind to accomplish such a goal, whereas Hippocrates and Galen gave close attention to the body and the nature of embodied experience.

Hippocrates' and Galen's interest in the materiality of the passions represents a new emphasis in the methods of their study. Both Hippocrates' and Galen's work would shape the study of and conclusions about the passions for many centuries, especially in the High Middle Ages.[49] Galen's work also informed Christian theologians' interest in and struggle with the body.[50]

With Socrates/Plato and Hippocrates and Galen, then, two distinct ways of approaching the passions emerged: one in which the passions are problematic, and the other in which the passions are natural and can be used as tools to understand one's life experiences, especially those of the body. These divergent paths dominated much of what was to come in terms of method, starting assumptions, and conclusions about the passions and their value. Many other philosophers and theologians would develop these varied views, though not all would agree with them. For example, Plato's student Aristotle disagreed with the wholly negative view of the passions, understanding the passions as integral to human development and maturation and the cultivation of civic life. Whereas Plato was not particularly interested in individuals' overall well-being, Aristotle was concerned with people's growth so that they might achieve it.

Where Plato diminished the importance of the material world, Aristotle valued lived experience and reflection on it. Whereas Plato imagined truth as transcending life on earth and eschewed what perception and the senses might offer, Aristotle thought that the senses and passions had something important to teach about life and its final aim, or telos. Despite these differences, however, Plato, Hippocrates, Galen, and Aristotle all agreed that philosophical reflection was important to examine what one values, why one values it, and the effects on one's life in valuing such things.

Passions Are Tools to Be Used: Aristotle

The Value of Human Experience

Aristotle (384–322 BCE) inherited many core questions (and their answers) about human being and the good life from those who preceded him, though he offered a different evaluation of the passions.[51] Although he was a close follower of Socrates/Plato, both extending and adding nuance to their thinking, Aristotle was also influenced by Hippocrates. In fact, Aristotle sought to reconcile the two perspectives.[52] Like Hippocrates, and unlike Socrates/Plato, Aristotle did not separate the soul from the body and did not posit psychic activities independent of the body (although he did not believe the soul is always involved in physical responses). In fact, a notable feature of Aristotle's approach to passions is his interest in the phenomenology—the feeling, subjective part—of human experience.[53] By so valuing the subjective, embodied qualities of experience, Aristotle eschewed the early philosophical dismissal of everything *but* ideas as irrelevant.[54] Aristotle did this by suggesting that the knowledge gained by experience (by the actions of the senses, including the passions) is important and real, and since it is real, that "the world of sense is also and necessarily real."[55] In fact, for Aristotle, the passions, or movements of the soul, are an important, constitutive part of human being. Because he approached the passions from this perspective, Aristotle did not share Plato's body–soul dualism, nor did he accept Plato's goal of detachment from life and exclusive value of reason as a way to the good life. Rather than detachment from life, Aristotle understood the good life to be deeply embedded in the earthly realm.[56]

Like philosophers before him, Aristotle sought to identify the highest good for human beings, and his understanding of happiness was that it is the activity of the soul according to virtue, accompanied by pleasure, when provided with sufficient external goods and "fair fortune."[57] Like Plato, Aristotle presumed there is a highest good or *ultimate end* that is to be pursued in action, and that this good is eudaimonia, or happiness, as it is commonly translated.[58] But according to Aristotle, happiness is not a state of mind or being, but rather, an activity: the cultivation of virtues and a state that can support the good of its citizens.[59]

For Aristotle, the good life is one in which one's most important interests are safeguarded, and it is also one in which citizens can be self-sufficient—that is, knowing what is right and good without external influence. Nothing and no one can make it better: once one has achieved the highest good, life is complete.[60] Aristotle argued that while most people would claim that wealth, the pursuit of honor, or the satisfaction of bodily pleasures is the highest good, these are, in fact, deficient. For example, Aristotle pointed out, wealth is usually acquired for the purpose of attaining something else, honor has little to do with the person but rather others' perception of the person, and the satisfaction of bodily pleasures is not a good unique to human beings. In this Aristotle gives insight into his understanding of the highest good: it must be consistent with the maximization of people's abilities as human beings.[61] Because Aristotle understood it as the integration of the soul and the material, eudaimonia belongs to the work of both, rather than being solely the purview of the goods of the body or the world or only pertaining to the hereafter.[62] Eudaimonia is a matter of the activity one engages in and the ways one engages. Eudaimonia is less about the *results* of one's engagement than the *pleasure one attains in actively pursuing what matters.*[63]

The Relationship of Virtues and Eudaimonia

Echoing Socrates/Plato, Aristotle argued that what separates human beings from animals is humans' capacity for reason. A life bent only on satisfying immediate, bodily desires or passions is not a life fit for humans but is for animals only. But Aristotle did not eschew the importance of the body. Instead, he saw the good life for humans to be focused on contemplation and learning, acquiring important virtues, and accruing wisdom, all of which incorporated both reason *and* the body. To this end, Aristotle identified two kinds of knowledge and modes of being (what he called "virtues") that human beings should cultivate.[64] First, people should seek the knowledge of first principles (that is, scientific knowledge, or knowledge about nature and truth), and second, people should seek the knowledge derived from applying these first principles—character or moral virtues. In other words, a life of contemplation and learning is not enough. To live the good life, Aristotle claimed, a person must act rightly, by which he meant in accordance with the "appropriate" state of character from which right actions come. Intellectual virtues are acquired as a result of learning, while character virtues such as generosity, courage, kindness, and honesty are acquired as a result of life experience and habituation.[65] For Aristotle, happiness consists of perfect fulfillment of the potentialities of both the irrational and the rational sides of human nature.[66]

The cultivation of intellectual and character virtues makes up the highest good and leads to eudaimonia:[67] one achieves eudaimonia if one cultivates all the intellectual and character virtues.[68] However, this is not an easy task. For Aristotle, acquiring virtues requires more than studying or habituation: it requires a kind of practical reason. This practical wisdom informs people so that their responses to circumstances are rational. Practical reason enables people to deliberate well about what to do in a situation on the basis of the highest good, and it helps them articulate and justify a valid conception of the highest good.[69] Aristotle understood the good life to require that people both live up to their own potential and find happiness, but he also argued that eudaimonia requires that each person contribute to a just and well-functioning community and society.[70] Thus, the good life for Aristotle had everything to do with people's character development and meaningful participation in the state, or polis, to support the *well-being* of others.

Certain external conditions must be present for the virtues' cultivation, though they are often out of the full control of individuals. People must live in a state (or polis) that allows them to live well. More specifically, the state—namely, its organizations, institutions, and laws—should be designed to help citizens improve their characters, which tend to fall on a spectrum between vicious and virtuous.[71] For Aristotle, moderation in the virtues and other qualities of life is key.[72] Because individuals possess reason and know the difference between good and bad behavior, they can *learn* to be virtuous. However, while some people do the right thing even though they do not want to, the virtuous person both *wants* what is right and *does it*. The role of the polis, Aristotle argued, is to help individuals progress from a vicious, primitive state to a virtuous, mature one. Laws help citizens choose the right actions, and as people habituate to what is right, they develop an affinity for what is good and right, and they will choose the good in the future.[73]

The Soul's Relationship to Eudaimonia

In Aristotle's schema, the soul is a critical component of living the good life. Aristotle understood the soul to be the life principle of human beings: he viewed it as a single entity with different capacities that guides people's pursuit of what is good. In Aristotle's view, the soul is holistic and includes the passions—which Aristotle understood to be less about disturbances or diseases but rather "composites" of beliefs and one's expectations about situations—as well as physical, bodily sensations. Because it is holistic, the soul functions together with the body,[74] and the passions are often embedded in a rich cognitive structure of beliefs rather than being associated with one single desire. In addition, Aristotle argued that though the passions can exist only through the body, they are "sensations as conditions of the soul,"[75] meaning that passions are experiences that allow elements of the soul to be observed. As indicators of what is happening in the soul and in the polis, Aristotle asserted, the passions are valuable and educative elements of human life.[76]

Thus, for Aristotle the passions are more complex than Socrates/Plato proposed: he wrote that people should "feel [the passions] at the right times, with reference to the right objects, towards the right people, with the right motive, and in the right way."[77] In Aristotle's view, the passions are not only focused on immediate gratification but can also include the imagination and are often future looking, striving for what is good but not yet achieved.[78] In Aristotle's understanding, then, each capacity of the soul has a vital, significant part in achieving the good life, which consists of participation in the various activities of "civilized society." The good life is not just the goal of an individual's life but the purpose of the law, politics, and civic institutions as well.[79]

Despite his more temperate view of the passions, Aristotle accepted Socrates'/Plato's negative opinion of bodily pleasures and characterized pleasure as a "first movement" of the soul, akin to the physical appetites, or passions in their most simplified form. While the bodily pleasures (such as "licentiousness") can lead someone away from eudaimonia, Aristotle argued that some bodily pleasures can have some positive function. First, when satisfied, as in the case of thirst, bodily appetites help direct the organism to the restoration of a static normal state; and second, positive sensations or even pleasures arise when an organism exercises its "unhindered" natural capacities: bodily pleasures are a sign that the organism is functioning as nature intended.[80] Thus, the passions can be used as a *means* to eudaimonia and as *signs* one has achieved it.[81]

However, there *are* "false pleasures" in Aristotle's view. These include the overestimation of future pleasures, mistaking a neutral state for pleasure, and experiencing what should not be pleasurable as something desired. Furthermore, Aristotle understood that the passions are not as discrete as Socrates/Plato suggested: there is often a mix of both pleasure and pain in each. For example, a person can feel anger by being belittled. But he can turn that into an occasion for pleasure—the pleasure that comes with the thought of revenge and the restoration of one's value.[82] In other words, some passions, such as anger and the decision to make right a wrong, can be used for good if directed rightly. Indeed, Aristotle was convinced that some passions can be a moral force that can and should be cultivated, though always directed by reason and philosophical rhetoric.[83] Aristotle even included anger in a list of virtues, arguing that only fools do not get angry, for example, if they have been offended in some way. However, one must know the circumstances in which it is appropriate to get angry and what amount and intensity of anger is justified: sometimes one should release an emotion.[84] Forgiveness may be a virtue, he thought, but only sometimes.[85]

Aristotle argued, then, that passions are not some foreign substance alien to proper human being; rather, they are natural. The passions, appetites, and behaviors are also related to social contexts, personality, values, desires, beliefs, and the situation of the individual, and ought to be assessed in ways that include reflection on whether a passion is appropriate to the context, whether it takes into account the facts of the situation, and whether the perceptions generating the passion are fair.[86] In Aristotle's schema, then, because the passions are an integral part of humans' natural makeup, not to have any passions at all—or only to a small degree—may be a sign of mental illness: those who fear nothing are mad, insensitive, or "idiots."[87]

In contrast to Socrates/Plato and other early Greek philosophers, then, Aristotle was less interested in seeking the meaning or chief end of life outside of this world. Aristotle did not recommend avoiding contingent, material things and the passions associated with them. Instead, Aristotle argued not only that finding pleasure in this life and in the relationships and processes that are a part of human existence is important to the good life, but also that people are social *by nature* and that a good human life involves developing human rational abilities, cultivating relationships, valuing certain passions that support personal development and nurture life together, and participating in various forms of social life, including the development and maintenance of a polis that supports the well-being of its citizens.[88] Because a great variety of passions are generated by social institutions and human practices, Aristotle argued, it is worth assessing human collectives for their effects on individuals. To this end Aristotle identified and catalogued the passions he observed—including anger, courage, and desire—as well as the contexts in which people experienced them.

In sum, Aristotle understood the passions to be fundamental to human being and essential to the good life, and the analysis of passions' nature to be part and parcel of ethical analysis and the development of wisdom.[89] Aristotle thought that the key to the good life is people's ability to control and direct the passions toward the development of right character and engagement in the polis.[90] While some passions can mislead a person, in general Aristotle argued that the passions can be edified and guided in the same ways as other human capacities and can be turned into virtuous habits.[91] One of the best ways to do so is through guided participation in carefully planned activities to educate and form children and youth.[92] Aristotle's final assessment of the passions, then, is mixed: the passions are vital to human being and to the good life, but because the passions can disrupt humans' capacities for reason and right behavior, they must be carefully controlled. The passions are not themselves virtues or vices but states of being, and can become habitual, and so—since they influence people's states of being and character formation—the passions are morally significant. Because experience of the passions is intrinsic to humans' life in this world, Aristotle thought that any account of the good life must give the passions their due. For Aristotle, this had both phenomenological meaning (that is, something feels good or not) as well as moral significance (that is, is conducive of or an impediment to the good life). Aristotle understood the importance of ethics and one's community to support people's well-being and provide helpful checks on individuals' baser impulses, encouraging the state to support the good of the whole. While Aristotle was interested in a fairly complex view of human nature, motivation, and the good life, others were less so, and consequently evaluated the passions more negatively. For philosophers such as Epicurus and the Stoics, experiences of suffering and their views on what is pleasant and unpleasant were paramount, deeply informing their understanding of the good life.

For example, Epicurus was less interested in cultivating the polis than was Aristotle, though he agreed with Aristotle's view that motivation is informed by what is pleasant and what is unpleasant. In fact, Epicurus built a philosophical system based on the differences between the two. Epicurus claimed that pleasure is not only the highest good, but the *only* good, though he did not offer much clarity about what being a hedonist amounts to, or whether he was a fully committed one.[93] Epicurus' view was nuanced: he wanted to be clear what pleasures were positive and which were not, building on Aristotle's belief that some passions were important and conducive to the good life and deepening the classification and examination of particular desires in order to separate the positive from the negative. Epicurus detailed the proper or "worthy" pleasures, and their right direction, proposing that the good life is one full of worthy pleasures and the avoidance of suffering.

Passions Can Support and Guide Well-Being: Epicurus

Epicurus (341–270 BCE) was, along with the Stoics, the founder of one of two primary Hellenistic (that is, after Aristotle) philosophical systems. Epicurus, like Socrates/Plato and their followers, was interested in the differences among common man, the philosopher, and the sage, and was especially interested in what it took to become a sage. For Epicurus, being a sage and achieving the good life had everything to do with learning to rid oneself of bodily and psychic distress by training oneself to *desire only what is necessary*. For Epicurus the *necessary* was the equivalent of the *good*.[94] Epicurus echoed Socrates/Plato and Aristotle when he argued that happiness is the end all humans seek, but he defined happiness slightly differently than did Socrates/Plato or Aristotle: Epicurus argued that all things are done for the pleasant feelings associated with them, and that this is reasonable and right.[95] Epicurus wrote, "Pleasure is our first and kindred good. It is the starting point of every choice and of every aversion and to it we always come back, inasmuch as we make feeling the rule by which to judge every good thing."[96] Despite the contemporary appropriation of his name for a hedonistic lifestyle, Epicurus advocated not the general pursuit of pleasure but the pursuit of *right* pleasures and the reduction of pain and distress. Epicurus maintained that people are miserable because they desire things that they need not desire. In Epicurus' thinking, the philosophers who learn to habituate themselves to desire only what is necessary and "natural" to human beings are able to bathe in the "pure joy of being," meaning they learn to appreciate the sheer pleasure it is to exist.[97]

Epicurus defined pleasure as absence of pain in the body and trouble in the soul. Given his understanding of the good life as a pleasant life free of suffering, Epicurus distinguished between necessary and unnecessary desires: necessary ones are those required to produce happiness, specifically freedom from bodily pain or an inner tranquility.[98] To accomplish this, reason must search the motivations behind particular choices and avoidances and rid the self of beliefs that lead to tumult in the soul. Epicurus examined specific passions, such as desire for honor and fear—especially fear of death and of the gods—to demonstrate how they are baseless and destructive of the good life: such passions rest on desires that are unnecessary and empty, he said. However, some pains are useful, as they move one in the direction of pleasure: for example, sadness moves a reflective person (that is, a *philosopher*) to appreciate life or friends and to have compassion for others. Other pleasures, such as copious amounts of wine, create unnecessary and unhelpful pain. Wisdom is needed to discern which pleasures and pains are genuinely necessary for happiness and which are not. Simple food, drink, and friendship are the chief goods because they satisfy natural needs and are pleasant, and, Epicurus argued, they are fundamental to survival.[99] Thus, valuing these simple things in life is most important. To the contrary, putting stock in external things, such as money or good looks—or the desire for passionate sexual intercourse with particularly special people—will create distress when one loses them.[100] These "unworthy" pleasures will drive one to anxiously to hold on to them and constantly try to acquire more.[101] For Epicurus, then, the highest form of pleasure is the state of *ataraxia* (the freedom from disturbance, trouble, or anxiety—the mental equivalent of the absence of bodily pain or distress), though some immediate, embodied pleasure is valuable as well, Epicurus acknowledged—especially if it enables the person's physical survival, like the fullness one feels after a feast. The good life is one in which worthy pleasures are maximized and unworthy pleasures are not pursued.[102]

In Epicurus' view, unworthy, unnecessary, and misguided passions arise from many places. For example, Epicurus believed that the values and practices of social life are largely unnatural and wrong, forced upon the citizenry. From infancy, he noted, people learn socially enforced beliefs and behavioral expectations that distract them from pursuit of the good life. Nevertheless, he too believed that citizens are most likely to find genuine happiness in the context of a community where each is supporting others' happiness as well as their own, as friendship is a basic human need.

In summary, then, whereas the natural, base appetites are simple and easily satisfied, cravings for culinary delicacies and material comfort are learned in cultures and are "unworthy" because they obscure simple, natural, positive desires.[103] Because unending longing and the unlimited desirability of external things (including wealth, honor, and respect) are fostered by mistaken beliefs and encourage empty attachments, one should eschew them. Epicurus understood himself as a doctor of souls (literally, a *psychiatrist*[104]), and developed a set of practices that included confession of weakness and poor choices, and frank criticism from others as means to uncover unhealthy desires and unwise commitments.[105] Epicurus thought that by disclosing one's desires to another, one could ensure that one was pursuing only the right pleasures for the good life.[106] The Stoics—whose footprint on the history of philosophies of the passions is deeper and wider than any others'—disagreed and recommended eliminating both pain and pleasure from human experience entirely, if at all possible.

Passions Are Sources of Suffering and Must Be Rooted Out: Stoics

Apatheia as the Goal

The legacies of Socrates/Plato, Aristotle, and Epicurus influenced Stoic philosophers whose work spanned three centuries.[107] The Stoics (ca. 330 BCE–180 CE), who became one of the most influential groups in the early thinking about the passions, continued earlier philosophers' positive valuation of reason and emphasized the negative qualities of experience and perception—both key elements of the passions. The Stoics also weighed in on the question of whether pleasure was positive or negative, though they differed from Epicurean thinking in one especially significant way: where Epicurus recommended training oneself not to desire what is not worthy, Stoic philosophers such as Seneca the Younger (4 BCE-65 CE) advised eschewing desire altogether, and just accepting what is, no matter how difficult.[108] In contrast to Epicurus, the Stoics argued that because there are many things people cannot control in life that create suffering for them—for example, death, poverty, loneliness—the philosopher seeks to passively accept the many troubles he will experience. The goal is not to cease desiring things that are "unworthy," but rather to cultivate courage, strength, and wisdom to bear the tragedies that befall one with calm, refraining from acting on the desires to change one's situation or exact revenge. For the Stoics, happiness—or the good—is found in "tranquil acquiescence," understood as submission to nature and usually the status quo.[109] In *Letters from a Stoic*, Seneca writes the following:

> The difference here between the Epicurean and our own school is this: our wise man feels his troubles but overcomes them, while their wise man does not even feel them. We share with them the belief that the wise man is content with himself. Nevertheless, self-sufficient though he is [in the Epicurean system], he still desires a friend, a neighbour, a companion. Notice how self-contented [a man is in the Stoic schema]: on occasion such a man is content with a mere partial self—if he loses a hand as a result of war or disease, or has one of his eyes, or even both, put out in an accident, he will be satisfied with what remains of himself and be no less pleased with his body now that it is maimed and incomplete than he was when it was whole. But while he does not hanker after what he has lost, he does prefer not to lose them. And this is what we mean when we say the wise man is self-content; he is so in the sense that he is able to do without friends, not that he desires to do without them. When I speak of his being "able" to do this, what I am saying in fact amounts to this: he bears the loss of a friend with equanimity.[110]

Stoic understandings were deeply informed by Socratic/Platonic thinking about the existence of some supraworldly (though not divine per se) rational principle from which originated all eternal truths.[111] However, like Hippocrates and Epicurus, the Stoics were also materialists: they proposed that matter is neither created nor destroyed, and that all matter distributes itself according to natural law. For the Stoics, then, the soul is a substance: the *pneuma* in Stoic thought meant the vital spirit and creative force of a person, entirely mixed with the body. The center of the soul is the governing faculty that reaches out like tentacles of an octopus or like a spider's web, serving as the center of the sensations and other psychic functions. In other words, in Stoic philosophy the soul is a centralized system that distributes the pneuma through the body to energize and sensitize it, just as blood is distributed through the veins to benefit the body.[112] Because of their commitment to materialism, the Stoics did not accept the idea of a transcendent soul or an afterlife: one must be concerned only with life *as it is today*. Contemplation about what is real (that is, physical, material) is the means to true happiness, they suggested, the only thing that will bring comfort in the midst of trouble.[113] For the Stoics, the good life consisted of believing and behaving in accordance with reason; they sought the purification of soul through likening oneself to the immaterial reason, which, in their understanding, is completely free from the passions. The good life, in the Stoic perspective, is composed of a calm and strong disposition in which one is unbowed by the vicissitudes of life. For the Stoics, there are three assumptions: *eudaimonia* will be the ultimate end of rational deliberation, happiness and virtue consist of living in accordance with nature and accepting calmly what is, and moral virtue is *chosen* for its own sake and is *preferred* above anything that has nonmoral value.[114]

Relationship Between the Passions and Misguided Judgments

Whereas Socrates/Plato and Aristotle believed that passions are natural capacities that need only to be disciplined, the Stoics idealized a rational soul without any passionate part at all, asserting that one could learn to live without any movements of the soul and its passions whatsoever. In other words, the Stoics prescribed eradicating the passions altogether in order to achieve the good life: if Socrates'/Plato's ideal philosopher is in full control of his passions, the Stoic sage has no passions at all.

The Stoics analyzed the passions and their relationship to reason more systematically and in more detail than any others. According to the Stoic view, the passions are forms of false judgments. Stoic philosophers placed strong emphases on the will and developed the idea that freedom is limited to the degree to which peoples' wills are reconciled to their material destiny; Stoic philosophers argued that "destinies of nature" are to be obeyed, not violated.[115] Letting go of what cannot be controlled is the means to comfort in a troubled life, the Stoics maintained.[116] They reasoned that both cognitive judgments and the passions are voluntary and that people can choose how they feel about the world and their place in it: people do not have to accept certain "value propositions" that bring misery.[117] Contemplation on "natural law," and dispassionate acceptance of what is and will be, is the means to the good life, defined by the Stoics most simply as the avoidance of anxiety and psychic pain inevitably caused by the passions.[118]

Whereas Aristotle believed passions to be essential to the good life if they lead to the formation of character and right, the Stoics understood the passions as conceptual errors and conducive to misery: for them, passions are mistaken judgments about the world and one's place in it.[119] Stoic philosophers argued that only higher reason could help one avoid the "vanities and vagaries" of the world, and they therefore urged people to abandon the idea that anything that they cannot control really matters, including the passions.[120] The Stoics' goal was to overcome their passions—or the "feeling life"—and realign their defective beliefs in order to understand what was of real value, namely the development of one's rationality and virtuous—that is, unattached and dispassionate—character.[121]

Because the Greco-Roman world "was not a happy or rational place," the Stoics experienced their world as out of control and beyond reasonable expectations and the passions as misled hopes that cannot be realized, leading only to frustration and misery.[122] For example, anger carries with it a moral judgment about something that may or may not be true and a demand for rectitude that may or not be possible. Likewise, love makes people vulnerable and hopeful; it creates attachments that bring loss, grief, and misery. Fear arises from the belief that one should be safe, which is never guaranteed. Furthermore, the Stoics argued, mistaken attachments and beliefs such as these are based on the "childish habit of regarding oneself as the center of things."[123] Rather than give in to this habit, people would be better off if they followed "cosmic reason," and saw themselves as nothing but "singular moments" of reason in the rational universe.[124]

What Is Preferred and Dis-preferred in Relation to the Good Life

Stoic philosophers distinguished genuine good and evil from what is preferred or not preferred. For them, the only good is virtue: that is, approaching life with calm, courage, and concern for others. The only evil is vice: being deceived by one's beliefs and material attachments and being distracted by one's own needs and desires. They came up with a system to help in the distinctions: death, sickness, loss of property, and friendlessness are "dis-preferred" but not evil, while continued life, health, and friendship, while preferable, are not *good*. While death and friendlessness may *appear* evil to the "unwise," who thus respond with passions of fear and distress and with the inordinate desire to avoid them, they are not actually evil, just dis-preferred. These are examples of the ways the Stoics define passions as "*assent* to *false* impressions of good and evil that engender *inordinate* impulses"—that is, giving in to them.[125] Real happiness in Stoic thinking, then, does not depend on things that are conventionally good, such as long life, health, pleasure, beauty, strength, wealth, reputation, noble birth, or their opposites. Instead, happiness is achieved as one grows from a natural tendency of self-love to self-objectification—that is, seeing oneself, one's life, others, and all that is objectively and with dispassion: living in accordance with transcendent reason and without attachment to earthly things. The Stoics believed that human beings are born with self-concern as well as a naturally given other-concern; however, attachments to one's self are misguided and should be let go.[126]

The Stoics, then, understood the passions (*pathai*) to be the result of people's beliefs about external events, things outside people's control, akin to disease.[127] To be prey to one's passions is to violate a fundamental capacity of humans' reasoning nature and the rational nature of the universe, to which all people should submit as both law and fate. In addition, the Stoics argued, the passions are not just the result of evaluative judgments that something is good or bad; they also include the (incorrect) assessment that *it is right to react passionately.* The better way to deal with the passions' movements, the Stoics proposed, is to achieve psychic indifference, being clear about the "ultimate pointlessness of emotional attachments and involvement."[128] Rather than be tossed to and fro like a ship on stormy seas, a genuine Stoic sage would achieve a state of *apatheia*, or the absence of any foreign, unwelcome *pathai*. The state of *apatheia*, then, is the highest virtue and the only means to the good life.[129] In fact, *apatheia* defines the good life in Stoic philosophy.[130]

Stoic conceptions of the good life (as bleak as it may seem) had in mind a healthy, well-functioning organism that lives in accordance with its nature and the nature of universal reason. In order to achieve this, the Stoics argued, therapy for the soul was as important as medicine for the body; in fact, it may be more important because the "diseases of soul are both more dangerous and numerous than those of body."[131] Unfortunately, few people treat their "illness" because sick souls cannot realize they are sick, for they have not achieved the self-objectification and self-examination that comes with the state of *apatheia*. Similar to Platonic thinking, Stoic philosophers understood that nature has given humans the ability to discern what is right through the natural order of things. However, like Epicurus, the Stoics believed the "faint inborn light" of nature is quenched by false beliefs, hedonism, and bad practices. People learn these wrong beliefs and behaviors during development through the influence of parents, caregivers, and teachers—and this wrong thinking is strengthened by poets, public opinion, and political leaders who infect citizens with erroneous views and the prejudices of society.[132]

The Role of Assent in the Good Life

Like others before them, the Stoics had to account for people's experiencing passions and the behaviors that accompany them—that is, people going against their nature or rational wisdom. In fact, the Stoics observed more of this among their fellow citizens than they found examples of sages who were in full control of themselves. In the face of this reality and the charge by other philosophers that *apatheia* is impossible, the Stoics accepted and further developed the Aristotelian doctrine of the so-called first movements or "pre-passions," going so far as using it to explain why there can be something similar to feelings—even in enlightened philosophers. On this point, Stoics argued that first movements, or pre-passions, are sometimes felt as urgings or longings in the body: first movements are transient and not real passions *as long as they are not assented to*.[133] First movements are involuntary, a *preparation* for real passions and action, but suggest at minimum an initial evaluative interpretation of the situation. *Assent of the mind* is the second movement and is voluntary. The third movement is the blind insistence that one must react come what may, the sense of having little or no control over oneself. Even sages experience first movements or physiological "natural affects" because they share in a common human nature: all people are disposed to experience them. Furthermore, though therapies may weaken them, first movements cannot be stopped by reason. This natural tendency is not curable, but passions as assent to feeling and acting on them can (and should) be eradicated. A sage may experience pre-passions, even suffering, but does not behave in response to them. In other words, a sage can feel pain and even show signs of suffering but not actually form or feel the *experience* of distress.[134]

Stoic philosophers' negative views of the passions and the superiority of the rational mind did not die with them and their highly influential philosophy, though their views did undergo significant changes.[135] A legacy of the Stoic philosophy was the emphasis on individual responsibility: because each material entity has its "natural purpose" and is punished if it deviates from that purpose, later philosophers saw commitment to individual control of one's passions and one's behavior as highly significant.[136] The primary legacy of the Stoics' study of the passions is the belief that the passions are primitive, base, bestial, undependable, and dangerous and that it is best to be rid of them.[137] These views influenced subsequent philosophers and Jewish and Christian theologians who would wrestle with similar themes, often pitting body against mind, will against passion, the material against the immaterial, and soul against spirit.[138]

Conclusion

Although early philosophers thought much about the passions, they did not agree on their origins, function, or value. The differences in early scholars' questions, methods, and conclusions about human experience eventually led to very different understandings of the passions, their relationship to the good life (which was, itself, a contested notion, as has been noted), and how to achieve it. Five dominant strands of thought about the passions' relation to the good life emerged in the earliest Greco-Roman scholarship. First, the passions are disruptive of reason and must be controlled (Socrates/Plato) so that one can live the good life of reason. Second, the passions are natural, can be understood as the result of disease, and they are causal in the sense that they also create dis-ease (Hippocrates and Galen); thus, attending to and balancing the passions is central to well-being. Third, the passions are natural and can be used to help people mature and grow in the virtues that support individual and communal well-being (Aristotle). Fourth, the passions are good when rightly directed toward what is worthy in pursuit of the good life but not valuable when directed toward what is not worthy (Epicurus). Fifth, the passions are anathema to the good life, and one must try to extirpate them entirely (the Stoics).

These and other themes shaped emotions scholarship for many centuries. For example, Christian theologians continued to assert the superiority of reason, the dangers of the passions, and the importance of will to control them for the purposes of living the good (that is, the saved) life. Others disagreed, arguing that the passions are useful insights into the state of the soul and the condition of the state (polis). Other arguments waged as well: philosophers debated whether truth is a metaphysical reality or not. They debated about whether the body was to be valued or not. And they asked how one articulates the uniqueness of human beings—especially in relation to animals—and whether sense and perception are trustworthy or valuable. Each of these questions significantly informed and added complexity to later discourse about emotions, and later thinkers were heavily indebted to these earlier figures.[139] Indeed, few areas of early modern philosophy were untouched by at least some theory of the passions.[140]

In the eighteenth century, however, philosophers largely lost interest in the relationship of the soul to the body or the physiology of emotions, and even the role of the passions toward the goal or goals of life.[141] Because the passions increasingly became relegated to bodily causes as empirical methods rose in prominence, the "anatomists" took over passions' study from philosophers and theologians.[142] In short, the influence of philosophical and theological perspectives on the passions/emotions waned under the rise of science and the emphasis on logic—but not before Jewish and Christian theologians developed their own perspectives.

As I will argue in chapters 6 and 7, an adequate view of emotions will understand them as more complex than any of these philosophers did. A more adequate understanding of the relationship between emotions and well-being (or—even better—flourishing) will recognize some kind of ultimate, transpersonal reality as Plato and his followers did, but not see it as only otherworldly. A more adequate view of the emotions will recognize the importance of reason, cognition, and perception, as the Stoics did, but not in opposition to the passions'/emotions' role in the good life. A more adequate understanding of emotions will also recognize the importance of the body as Hippocrates and Galen did when they encouraged attention to one's physical health and lifestyle choices. Such an understanding will also encourage constant reflection about what is worthy, or what really matters, as Epicurus did, and it will recognize that happiness/flourishing is an activity, not a state. A more adequate understanding of emotions' relationship to the good life will recognize flourishing as a developmental achievement without making the mistake of assuming women and people of color, for example, are not capable of it (though Aristotle is correct that enslaved peoples cannot flourish, though for reasons other than those he assumed). A more fulsome understanding of emotions and flourishing will include attention to those who have historically been disadvantaged—excluded from what is good because they were presumed to have something ontologically wrong with them. A more adequate view of eudaimonia will challenge the unjust systems that exclude and oppress, attending to the polis as Aristotle urged. Unfortunately, Jewish and Christian theologians did not help in this endeavor as much as one might hope.

2

Emotions as Sinful, Signs of the Fall, and Impediments to Salvation

Philo and Early Christian Theologians' Perspectives

Introduction

Early Greco-Roman philosophers established predominantly negative evaluations of the passions, and Jewish and Christian theologians developed their themes. Early Christian theologians especially were deeply interested in the passions, or more specifically the "appetites" and "affections," overlaying philosophical understandings with the burdens of sin and salvation, as depicted in the Jewish and Christian Scriptures, and articulating the passions' role in both. And while some took seriously Aristotle's thinking that the passions can have a salutary effect, much of the early Christian thinking about emotions was most heavily informed by Socrates'/Plato's cautionary view and the Stoics' negative assessments of the passions and their results.[1] Christian theology took early philosophical ideas about the passions, infused them with biblical themes, and disseminated them far beyond the bounds of the Greco-Roman world. The distinction between the passions and the affections (indeed, the categories themselves to some degree), as well as the idea that people can—and should—control their passions, was "well suited to a Christian understanding of the human person in which a free and active will was a particularly important faculty."[2] Christian theologians argued that "the only really *human* life . . . is one in which devotion, experience, action, and contemplation are combined"

41

to effect salvation in God.[3] Thus, the seeds of a particularly potent set of perspectives were sown. Where the earlier philosophical understandings of the good life had more to do with either resisting the passions' (mis)leadings or extirpating them altogether, by relating the passions to sin and processes of salvation, Christian theologians shifted the emphasis from the philosopher's good life to the life saved in Christ. And, informed by the Greco-Roman philosophies, they examined the passions in light of that goal.

Commitment to the superiority of reason over the passions had been strongly advocated by pre-Socratic and Socratic/Platonic philosophers from Anaxagoras to Seneca the Younger (a Stoic).[4] The sage, these early thinkers argued, judges rightly that only what transcends earth (that is, Zeus, divine reason, "world-mind") is worth caring about—all else is to be held with indifference.[5] Informed by this perspective, the Stoics (whose views dominated understandings of the passions for several centuries) argued that the telos of human life is to live according to human nature, in contemplation of the "truth and order of all things," and thus in conformity with humans' place in the natural, material world, giving up hope for something better.[6] For the Stoics, life is not about gritting one's teeth but rather about learning to see, experience, and understand things differently so that one can remain detached, calm, and unperturbed.

The Stoics held strong positions on the passions in general, and on specific passions as well: for example, they derided ambition as a result of the fear of death,[7] fear they interpreted as the anticipation of misfortune and wrongly held hope for something different.[8] They excoriated love for anything but reason, and extolled the virtues of accepting what is natural as creating unnecessary suffering.[9] Stoic thinking set the foundation for more than three centuries, but by the second century CE, Stoic views had waned in their prominence. So, too, waned unwavering trust in reason to control the negative impulses in people as the answer to early philosophical problems. In the aftermath of significant social and political upheaval, it became clear that "reason could not deter the barbarian," nor could pleasure or the absence of pain solve the problems of life in turbulent and violent times.[10] The challenges to and limits of *apatheia* signaled the end of the pre-Christian era and ushered in the Age of Faith.[11]

The "Age of Faith" was the result of Latin scholars who sought to find value and meaning in the aftermath of the fall of Rome. And while these scholars would take up many of the same questions that had occupied Socrates/Plato, Aristotle, Epicurus, and the Stoics, because Christian theologians' starting positions differed from those of the pre-Christian era philosophers, so did the questions Christian theologians asked, and the reference points they used to answer them. As Christianity was being established and began to spread, its leaders sought to understand the human condition, human experience, and passions' relation to the divine life—that is, God's will as revealed in Jesus Christ.[12] Whereas earlier philosophers such as Aristotle were interested in the good life on earth (that is, attending to control and development of oneself, the development of other-concern, and the establishment of the polis and ethical living in community so as to cultivate happiness), early Christians tended to be more Platonic. That is, they were less interested in this-worldly experience and added a new element: the problem of sin and the hope for salvation in the life hereafter. Christian theologians accepted early philosophers' opinion that the passions were signs of a misdirected spirit as well as their reasons for it. Early Christian thinkers understood themselves as perfecting Greek philosophy: however, while philosophers imagined the telos of life in relation to the gods or transcendent reason, Christians were advancing their understandings and developing practices toward salvation in relation to the Jewish and Christian God as found in Scripture. Less interested were early Christian theologians, then, in establishing the polis or state than they were in salvation in God, and salvation (as opposed to ethics or the "good life") became the primary teleological aim of the region and the era. Not surprisingly, these shifts had a significant effect on Christian theologians' understanding of the passions, and contemporary thinking about emotions in the West is deeply indebted to their work, developing, refining, and adding to it.

For example, to early philosophical understandings of the passions, Jewish and Christian theologians added the concept of evil. To philosophical recommendations of therapies that control or excise the passions, Christian theologians added carefully detailed means of curing one's soul.[13] Attention to the human condition as fallen and sinful required confession, forgiveness, asceticism, and reconciling practices, for redemption and salvation could be accomplished only in relation to and through the mercy of the God they found in the Jewish and Christian witness. For this reason, Christian theologians did not find as much to build on in Aristotle.[14] Instead, the Stoic ideal of *apatheia* and doctrines of spontaneous first movements were qualified and Christianized.[15]

Christian theologians, including Augustine of Hippo, Anselm of Canterbury, Peter Abelard, and Thomas Aquinas, debated in great detail whether and in what ways the passions were related to sin and salvation; whether the passions were natural or not; just how much control one had over one's passions; the importance of exerting the power of one's will to control or extirpate them; whether passions such as desire were inherently sinful; and whether or not Jesus (and by extension, God) experienced any passions. Christian theologians studied Christ's experiences and practices to reveal what they indicate about the human condition, the purposes of life, and the passions' relation to both. They wondered whether Christ had achieved *apatheia* while on earth and debated whether *apatheia* differs from salvation. They wrote much about the role of people's will in their own salvation, and Christian theologians developed practices to support converts' salvation, many practices of which addressed the passions.

Jewish and Christian theologians found the Hebrew Scriptures useful (Genesis had particular importance), as well as the earliest witnesses to Jesus' life and work. For Christian thinkers, the New Testament emphasis on matters of the heart (which its authors assert contains both clean and unclean desires) led many writers on the subject to make distinctions in their terminology between *passions* (such as envy, lust, and jealousy, which lead one *away* from God) and *affections* (such as love, awe, and humility, which lead one *to* God). On these matters Christ's emotional experiences were especially significant. There was much speculation about what it meant that Christ wept over Jerusalem,[16] and at the death of Lazarus,[17] or whether Jesus actually felt fear when he prayed that the cup of crucifixion pass from him.[18] Jesus Christ's passions in the Garden of Gethsemane, turning over the tables of the moneylenders in the temple, and crying out on the cross complicated any view of Christ (and thus of God) as being without the passions—unperturbed and in a state of perfect *apatheia* (as they imagined God, having been influenced by Plato). Indeed, while the biblical accounts provided models of *apatheia*, they also created challenges for early Christian theologians, giving them much with which to contend.[19]

Early Christian thinkers, then, parsed the passions more carefully than the early Greek philosophers: they distinguished between appetites and affections and introduced the language of sin and grace to the analysis.[20] Thus, although they borrowed Plato's use of the term *passions* to refer to bodily instincts or appetites, Christian writers added the new connotation of sinfulness to the ancient term.[21] Much of Christian theology—both early and contemporary—promotes, at least implicitly, the idea that people's passions are not of God, and so must be subject to the control of one's will.[22] Tracing the development of Christian perspectives on the passions requires briefly revisiting the first-century BCE thought of "bridge" figures who connected early philosophers' work and Jewish and Christian theologies. One such figure is the Jewish philosopher of Alexandria, Philo (20 BCE–50 CE). Philo, the first-century Jewish Platonist who had clear Stoic sympathies, developed ideas found in Plato and the Stoics, significantly informing the Christian thinking about the passions that came later. Philo was convinced that the passions were a sign of the fallenness of human nature, and thus a sign and symptom of original sin.

Emotions Are a Symptom of the Fall: Philo

One of Philo of Alexandria's most significant contributions was his thinking about first movements, which he took up from the Stoics, and about which he wrote a treatise directed to a semi-anchorite community outside Alexandria.[23] To guide his thinking on first movements and their relation to the good life, Philo, like other Jewish thinkers, examined the Hebrew Scriptures: Philo carefully studied biblical characters' experiences and their reactions to those experiences as significant sources for understanding the passions and right response to them. For example, in Genesis 23:3 where Abraham is described as bewailing the death of Sarah, beating his breast and standing on her corpse, Philo wanted to make clear that Abraham was experiencing a pre-passion, not a passion, as demonstrated by the fact that Abraham left the corpse, thus not giving assent to the pre-passion.

A related question about the ideal of *apatheia* was central to Philo's inquiry. Philo studied the Hebrew Bible for models of sages and how they dealt with the passions, and there he found four: Aaron and Moses (in Exodus 32 Aaron is almost executed for making idols, but his brother Moses intervenes) and also Abraham and Isaac (in a story found in Genesis 22, God commands Abraham to sacrifice his son, Isaac, and Abraham agrees to comply). Philo argued that Aaron and Moses represent control of the passions, and Abraham and Isaac their eradication. From this, Philo concluded that not everyone could achieve *apatheia* (though it was always the goal and should be pursued by all), but that *metriopatheia* (moderation) was all some could hope to achieve—and for many was a step on the way to *apatheia*. Philo even proposed that some passions, such as gluttony, lust, anger, and other "natural" appetites, could be helpful as reminders of humans' fallen nature; however, even if some passions are natural, they can (and should) still be denied if possible.[24] Philo modeled a close examination of the Jewish Scriptures as a way to understand human experiences of the passions, and Christian theologians including Clement, Origen, Evagrius, and Augustine followed Philo's example, finding much in the Hebrew and Christian Scriptures about the passions and their proper role in human life.

Emotions Are Unnecessary But Inevitable Given Original Sin: Clement and Origen

Accepting much of what Philo had concluded, Clement of Alexandria (150–215 CE) added his own perspective, arguing that while *apatheia* was the ideal, it could not have been achieved before the resurrection of Christ because of the Fall.[25] Clement distinguished himself clearly from non-Christian philosophers with his work on the difference between reason and revelation, emphasizing revelation as seen in Christ (rather than reason) as the absolute truth, far removed from and far superior to what could be learned from philosophy.[26]

Clement accepted the Stoic ideal of *apatheia* but argued that its achievement requires God's grace and is accomplished through faith. However, Clement did not imagine that *apatheia* could be accomplished before Christ's return, since only then would the bonds of sin be broken. In a view congenial to Stoicism, Clement understood the Christian life to mean obedience to the divine Word and believed that detaching oneself from earthly things was a first step to perfection, and thus salvation. The goal, Clement argued, is to detach from the values that are embedded in and give rise to the passions, focusing instead on the values of God as revealed through Christ.

Clement described passions as excessive and runaway impulses that are disobedient to reason and to revelation. One's first task, then, is to moderate and control them; the final goal is to achieve *apatheia* in order to become more like the impassible God. Because Clement related the detachment from earthly things to love for God, he advocated for the mortification of the passions.[27] Nevertheless, in Clement's thinking, evil can aid the process of perfection by allowing the increasing influence of God's grace. Origen (184–253 CE) accepted Clement's assertions, but in Origen's thought, Clement's understanding of the passions took a significant turn.[28]

Origen's work focused on the pre-passions (or first movements), and he expanded earlier Platonic understandings. Origen was the first to argue that pre-passions are not just physical appetites but also include bad thoughts and suggestions. The pre-passions of the mind are imposed on individuals by the devil, demons, or evil angels, and it is up to individuals to resist.[29] Like Philo and Clement before him, Origen studied Jewish and Christian Scriptures as the source of wisdom about the passions and as a model for how to handle them. For example, Origen understood Christ's sadness in Gethsemane as a pre-passion and Christ's temptation in the desert as the same. Jesus had first movements (pre-passions) that were sinless because Christ did not let them develop into the real passion of sadness, and it is only in giving assent to a passion that one sins. Origen argued that the fact that Christ did not *assent* to these thoughts of sadness and fear demonstrates that passions are both a sign of the Fall and also unnecessary. The Scriptures, Origen argued, illustrate Christ's impassible divine nature but also, because of the incarnation, show what is possible for humans. Like Christ in the desert, both Clement and Origen argued, individuals should practice asceticism and aspire to detach from all but God and God's Word. Christians should try to achieve *apatheia* by fasting, observing vigils, and practicing humiliation of the affective soul (all of which weaken the tendency even to form sinful thoughts).[30] While the passions are negative according to Origen, some—such as guilt—might prove useful if one pays attention to their message with the goal of salvation in mind. Thus, Christians should work diligently to eradicate the passions, and at the same time they should recognize that full detachment from worldly things cannot be realized, and thus the consequences of the Fall cannot be escaped until Christ returned, bringing full redemption to the world.[31]

In a series of what some call misinterpretations of earlier philosophies of first movements, these pre-passions were no longer to be considered neutral.[32] Christian theologians' understandings of first movements came from the Stoics, who considered them pre-passions. The Stoics had posited two kinds: first, mental "bites" (that is, affective responses) that arise in the soul from the appearance of something without one's assent to the response, and second, physical movements, such as one's pallor (that is, face flushing), or a man's erection. The Stoics did not consider these kinds of movements genuine passions because they are involuntary and not—at this stage—given consent, and they did not consider thoughts to be passions. Christian thinkers would continue to explore the questions about what is "natural," what is "necessary," and what is controllable and by what means. While for some the first movements, or pre-passions, were natural, unavoidable, and not true passions, Evagrius would shift this thinking, demonizing the pre-passions and categorizing thoughts as dangerous. Evagrius strongly informed Augustine's thinking, thus explicitly leaving a mark on Christian theology for many centuries—and, at least implicitly, Western views of emotion.

Emotions Are Sinful: Evagrius

Evagrius of Pontus (ca. 345–399 CE) significantly influenced Western thinking and practice around the passions through his system of monastic spirituality.[33] Whereas the Stoics and others had imagined *thoughts and initial bodily urges* as pre-passions and did not worry much about them, Evagrius was very concerned. He believed even thoughts to be dangerous: for Evagrius thoughts are genuine passions if entertained and thus, even thoughts, once considered pre-passions, can be sinful as well.

Evagrius was particularly interested in how, exactly, to work toward *apatheia*. In light of this, Evagrius proposed that eight thoughts especially can assail human beings: merely the thought of gluttony, the thought of fornication, the thought of avarice, the thought of distress, the thought of anger, the thought of listlessness, the thought of depression, the thought of vanity/pride, are passions dangerous to the Christian soul. And while these thoughts are not passions per se,[34] they are temptations to sin, often injected into one's head by demons (though also sometimes by people's own natural inclinations: that is, from one's sinful heart, natural constitution, or character). Because of the demons' work, people cannot control whether thoughts disturb their soul; however, it is up to each person whether to linger on a thought, and whether to allow the thought to stir up actual passions. Thoughts, then, are only temptations, but they can lead to evil things if entertained.[35] One must be on constant watch for demons who "play dirty tricks," and the timing of spiritual practices is crucial. For example, the "noonday demon" regularly arrives at midday and stays for four hours, bringing with him *akedia* (boredom and impatience, listless depression), while the demon who leads one astray at dawn can affect a whole day.[36] Evagrius urged constant vigilance.

For Philo, Clement, Origen, and Evagrius, then, the spiritual life requires a constant fight against both the pre-passions and the passions in a battle for the salvation of one's soul. While *apatheia* is the goal, active resistance is also crucial. Resistance to evil, however, requires a mortification of one's human will: only God's will as it is exercised by human beings can fight the demons that humans experience. Fasting (which, in the Eastern tradition, includes abstaining from sex),[37] holding vigil, and playing off one pre-passion or passion against another can help. For example, anger is needed to fight demons, and the appetites both demonstrate one's sinful nature and provide the motivation to grow in virtue: they remind people of their fallen nature and help develop humility and provide motivation to change.

The question of original sin especially came into play for theologians who agreed with Clement, Origen, and Evagrius that the passions were signs of the Fall. Church father Jerome (347–420 CE) emphasized the notion of original sin, which became increasingly relevant because the faithful were finding that they could not achieve *apatheia*. Jerome confirmed that because of original sin none could achieve the stated goals without God's grace. In fact, Jerome posited, people should not even *hope* for *apatheia* since imagining it and hoping for it denies the stain of original sin; humans should only hope for *apatheia* after the resurrection.[38]

Under the influence of these theologians came heightened attention to particular pre-passions, what was achievable in a person's time on earth, and practices for achieving the goal of salvation. For example, the writings of the Cappadocian Fathers (Basil the Great, Gregory of Nyssa, and Gregory of Nazianzus)—which were some of the most systematic and widely disseminated treatises—were an eclectic combination of Neoplatonic themes and religious thinking about perfection of the soul through asceticism and *theoria* (or contemplation of the divine). They focused on controlling the passions but also on the mortification of earthly desires and hopes. In fact, the Cappadocian Fathers were not much bothered by anything outside the soul's relation to God. Like Nemesius, Origen, and Jerome, these church fathers understood the Fall to mean that no human is without sin; in the Fall, Adam and Eve lost their godlikeness and were "dragged" down by their desires—their passions. Because of the Fall, then, human beings cannot avoid having passions and must pay careful attention to their tendencies.

These thinkers understood the restoration of people's souls to godlikeness as the *process* (though perhaps not the final achievement) of salvation. While *apatheia* was the goal, the Cappadocian Fathers also allowed for *continence* (or suppression of demons' suggestion of an evil thought or pre-passion) and *metriopatheia* (moderation) of the passions, understanding that the goal could not easily, if ever—at least on earth—be reached. Consequently, salvation required gradual progressions full of attempts and failures to control one's passions.[39]

Emotions Are God Given but Often Misdirected: Augustine

The idea of pre-passions was one of the early medieval contributions that modified ancient philosophical ideas and left a significant mark on Western thought until the modern period. Theologians such as Augustine (354–430 CE) and others who read widely on the topic (including Origen's work, which was translated into the Latin) perpetuated the view that the spiritual quest was necessarily strictly separated from earthly passions.[40] They drew from earlier sources' doctrines of first movements, focusing on the differences between pre-passions and sins, studying with minute investigations the voluntariness and involuntariness of the passions.[41] In addition, Augustine's and other Christian theologians' understanding of what is good is firmly rooted in ancient theories of eudaimonia. Like the Greek philosophers whose work he engaged, Augustine "takes it as immediately evident" that all men (*sic*) want to be happy and that eudaimonia is achieved through the "stable possession" of the supreme good, which, for these Christian theologians, meant God as revealed in Jesus Christ.[42] For Augustine and others, the ultimate object of desire (*that is*, God) is chosen for its own sake, not for any other reason. Because Augustine spent a great deal of energy combating pagan philosophies and cults popular in the Roman world in the fourth and fifth centuries, his Christianized understanding of happiness or the good was radically different from theirs.[43] For Augustine, the ultimate object of desire is God; in God everything is complete, since in God every desire is satisfied, and God is independent of all bodily and external circumstances. Christian theologians did not always agree on the role of the passions in the pursuit of God, however.

Two of the most influential Christian philosophers—Augustine and later Aquinas (1225–1274 CE)[44]—distinguished between *lower animal appetites* such as hunger, thirst, and sexual desire, which were of the lower soul found in the body, and the *affections*, including love, joy, and sympathy, which they understood to be movements of the higher, rational soul that could, if directed properly, lead one toward God.[45] For both Augustine and Aquinas, the lower soul and its appetites are both a sign of and punishment for the original sin of Adam and Eve, while the affections are responses to God and are signs of grace and wisdom. They argued that the passions are involuntary and not cognitive judgments; in some cases, Augustine and Aquinas thought the passions could be used by God for various purposes and with particular ends. In their view, the appetites are unruly and disturbed, driven ultimately by a love of self. In contrast, they argued, the affections are holy: in them lies the hope and possibility of reunion with God.

Augustine understood the theory of first movements from many sources, and his misunderstanding of the Stoic position altered the course of Christian thinking about emotion.[46] Unlike the Stoic view of first movements as pre-passions, Augustine interpreted all first movements to be appetitive passions, though uncontrolled ones; for this reason, he took them to be indicative of original sin. Whereas the Stoics exonerated first movements but condemned passions, Augustine was "blind to the Stoic distinction" between involuntary first movements and genuine passions.[47] Influenced by Origen, who included in his understanding of first movements thoughts and suggestions—thereby obscuring the distinction earlier thinkers had made between thoughts and passions—Augustine followed this idea to its logical (to him) conclusion: passions do not have the permission of reason. In fact, Augustine argued, all passions—including first movements or pre-passions that do not yet engage reason—are acts of one's will *against* reason and thus are potentially, though not necessarily, sinful.[48] Nevertheless, Augustine understood the passions as part of the fallen human condition. Because the aim of human life is unity with God, Augustine allowed that there might be a positive function toward that aim for all passions—both affections and appetites: for example, Augustine thought proper examination of the passions can show one's depravity. However, while some passions such as anger *can be useful* for illuminating the fallen soul, they are *not necessary*, and one is better without them.

Augustine's starting point is that only God is to be enjoyed (that is, loved for God's own sake); all else is to be used.[49] It matters, Augustine argued, what people set their hearts on, and people should set their hearts on God.[50] For Augustine, then, true happiness lies beyond this world; happiness (or the ultimate good) is in salvation, understood as full union with God in eternal life.[51] Until then, individuals are responsible to live according to God's design. Because of original sin and its relationship to the passions, living according to God's will requires God's grace, given as a gift. As such, Augustine viewed the Stoic emphasis on self-sufficiency and the ideal of *apatheia* as wrongheaded from the start. Neither goal recognized humans' complete dependence on God for their salvation. Thus, Augustine disagreed with the Stoic Cicero's belief that eudaimonia could be achieved on earth, or strictly through human effort. Virtue and well-being are utterly dependent on grace, though personal endeavor is required to contemplate God's will and align one's own toward it.[52] For this reason, Augustine examined the passion of love and its relationship to salvation more extensively than almost any other theologian and prized it (rightly ordered) above all else. For Augustine, love refers to a person's commitment to a set of godly values,[53] and he argued that *"reason should be master of these in human life,"*[54] used to guide people's experiences of these toward the Divine by guiding one's rightly aligned will.

Unlike the Stoics, who viewed love as a misguided attachment to earthly things, then, Augustine believed that love can make people experience desire, joy, fear, or distress in ways that can be salvific if willed in the right direction by God's grace. If the direction of one's love is toward God, the occurrent passions will be good, and if one's love or desire is directed toward evil, the passions will be evil. What is most important, then, is the quality of one's will, because if one's will is wrongly disciplined, it will have wrong passions, but if it is right, the passions will be "not only blameless but even praiseworthy."[55]

Rather than eschew the passions entirely, then, Augustine recognized the human condition as fundamentally flawed and passions as inevitable, though not necessary, for achieving salvation. Because of this, Augustine argued that people should use the will to guide their desires and energies toward God. Reminiscent of Plato's thinking, Augustine developed the view that because God is ultimate truth, the inborn will (and reason, which guides it) seeks to know God: this goal is a primary factor in right human living. For Augustine, a right will can direct one toward divine love, and a wrong will turns an individual toward the love of earthly things.[56] The will is potentially both salvific or dangerous and is involved in the rise and direction of all passions or, more accurately, "all passions are acts of one's will."[57] For Augustine, then, the will is ideally led by God's grace. In fact, Augustine argued, each person is endowed with an interior, *"nonsensory* awareness of truth, of error, of the moral right, of personal obligation, and of personal identity."[58] The rational mind is the *judge* of perception and is therefore above it. Under the guidance of God's grace, reason is a useful tool for discerning Truth and must be used for that purpose as it guides the will.[59]

Augustine's theological anthropology depended on a Platonic separation of human beings into multiple parts. One part of the self, Augustine proposed, is driven by the base and bodily appetites, which require control by the other part, composed of the more superior intellect, will, and rationality.[60] Both parts of a human being are accompanied by different kinds of souls (the higher and lower souls), and because of the Fall of Adam and Eve, people struggle as "houses divided against themselves" in which the reasonable self no longer has control: after the Fall the will has to work to control the bodily appetites.[61] The corrupted human will is unable to resist the impulses of the lower soul fully; as exemplified by Eve, a misguided will gives in to earthly pleasures and seeks satisfaction of them rather than seeking godly ones.[62] Furthermore, the will is never in complete control. The will is unable to repair the broken soul itself; only God, through grace, can restore a person's right orientation and help the will in the struggle against evil. The most important guide for the good life (that is, salvation in God), then, is love rightly directed—to God—by the grace of God enacted by the will.

In summary, then, Augustine understood the passions to be signs of the Fall; however, they are not wholly negative. Augustine divided the passions into appetites and affections: whereas he understood the appetites as negative by definition (leading one away from God), he considered the affections to be positive—even potentially God given—since they lead one toward God.[63] Augustine eschewed the Stoic commitment to passions' complete extirpation on at least two grounds, then: first, passions' effacement denied the fallen nature of human being, and second, eliminating the passions did not allow God to work through the human condition to achieve salvation.[64] Because Augustine understood the passions to be signs of the Fall with potential salvific function, he disagreed with the Stoic's understanding of them as diseases or defective judgments. For Augustine, the passions become problematic only when they fail to take their "proper place in the order of things."[65] The passions can play an important role in the Christian life as long as they are controlled and directed appropriately.

Furthermore, Augustine argued, not only are the passions potentially good, but they are all, finally, expressions of God's love. With proper guidance of the will, the passions could be saving movements toward God, and while Augustine considered uncontrolled appetites as sins, even they could be useful reminders of the fragmented, broken, fallen self and good reminders of the consequence of deviating from the

Divine will.[66] Even the appetites could be helpful reminders of humans' inherent sinfulness and a check on hubris. Thus, accepting the fact of the Fall and its effects on the human condition, Augustine gave some potential positive value to all passions—both affections and the appetites—as long as individuals allow God's grace to illuminate and guide them.[67] Augustine's position was that it is important for people to use their God-given and innate capacities for reason to guide their will to control the "rebels" and "tyrants" of the appetites, turning them into affections and thus unifying the different parts of the self and protecting the "sovereign virtues" of God's salvific desires.[68] Because of his lifelong struggle to control his own appetites, Augustine understood the passions, while potentially good, to be primarily dangerous: unruly forces that are involuntary and sometimes impossible to control, no matter how hard one wills it.[69]

Continuing the trajectory of Socrates/Plato and the Stoics but also adding nuance to their thinking, then, early Christian theologians such as Augustine introduced important distinctions between worrisome, possibly sinful movements of the soul (appetites, lusts, desires, passions) and the higher, more rational will that directs one toward God through love and other affections. Augustine made psychological, moral, and theological distinctions that had not previously existed in classical discourse of the passions (*pathe*). Most significantly, early Christian theologians were committed to understanding the human experience of passions in relation to God. Their view was that while the passions are inevitable in this life—and some can even be proper and necessary to the process of salvation—the ultimate aim is to be in union with God and finally to be rid of passions (and the need of them) since God, the angels, and perfected humans are free from the turmoil and perturbations of sin and the passions. The legacy of this model is a hierarchy of feelings that, at least implicitly, still pertains today: some would say love, joy and other "positive" emotions are of God, while "negative" emotions such as anger or sadness are not.[70] Indeed, negative emotions—including those appetites listed among Augustine's passions—have long been maligned in Western Christian traditions, in which the dominant view of emotions is of "unruly instincts erupting with blind and selfish force" and the historical view was of "wild animals that must be domesticated and controlled."[71]

Conclusion

As the review in the last two chapters shows, the prevailing view of the passions for the first two millennia was mostly negative.[72] Although philosophers such as Aristotle and Christian theologians such as Augustine allowed for some passions' importance for the growth and spiritual maturity of an individual, the view of the passions as negative was far reaching.[73] The legacy of early theological reflection on the passions has meant that human passions (and later "emotions") have become subject to moral evaluation: emotions are good if they are in accord with reason and a will directed toward God and salvation, bad if they are not.

Besides the largely negative view of the passions, early medieval philosophical and theological reflections on first movements had an "enduring effect" on theoretical and practical discussions of the passions.[74] Under their influence, later philosophers and theologians held the commonly accepted view that spontaneous movements (pre-passions) toward sin could (and should) be controlled by avoiding situations that might invoke them and by *replacing* thoughts that lead to (wrong) passions with those passions and forms of will that are of God. These themes—especially the notion that sins can be committed simply by experiencing first movements, or pre-passions, by gaining pleasure by thinking about a sinful feeling or act, as well as consenting to a sinful thought—became widely accepted.[75]

Early Jewish and Christian theologies of the passions gave rise to a variety of practices to manage them. In some cases, practices were designed to accomplish the passions' extirpation and the humiliation of the soul; in other cases, they were designed to help individuals discern a particular passion's value. In the latter case, methods were designed to direct, control, and discipline passions properly.[76] Their view that reason and will should be the masters of human beings' lives, used to direct people toward God, was widely accepted.[77]

Differing views of the passions and their value have contributed to contemporary confusion about emotions.[78] So, too, have the different understandings of the telos (or aim) of human life and the passions' role in that, the nature of ultimate reality ("God," "world-mind," "Reason," etc.), and reason's and the passions' relationship to the good life. While early Greek philosophers such as the Stoics sought to guide their fellow citizens toward a more peaceful and contented life by ridding themselves of all passions, Christian theologians sought to guide their neighbors toward salvation in God by directing passions and behaviors in accordance with the divine life.[79]

The Christian theologians paid little attention to Galen's views, for example, or other more sanguine views on the passions. Thus, despite some positive opinions of the passions and their potential usefulness for a life well lived, positive views did not prevail.[80] In other words, although the negative view (especially of the "unpleasant" emotions) is not the only strand present in the early philosophical and theological traditions, it has been the dominant one. While the studies of passions remained a central focus in later medieval philosophy and theology and beyond, little new scholarship emerged. Philosophers and theologians tended only to study and comment on earlier views rather than to develop new perspectives.[81] The first real revolution in the study of emotions would come with the rise of science and its emphasis on empiricism. And with the rise of the Age of Science, interest in exploring philosophical and theological questions waned. At the dawn of the Age of Science, the philosophers' and theologians' understandings gave way to the views wrought by scholars of different sorts.[82] "Mentalists," natural scientists, social scientists, and brain scientists would change the questions about human emotions, the methods used to answer those questions, and the conclusions at which they arrived. Natural scientists would return to the empirical and this-worldly commitments of Hippocrates and Galen and emphasize the "natural" quality of emotions. Although Western culture is largely informed by early Greco-Roman philosophy and Christian theology, modern scientists such as Alexander Bain, Joseph Breuer, Charles Darwin, William James, and Paul MacLean would challenge earlier philosophical and religious conclusions about the passions/emotions and turn the investigations to the scientific and psychological spheres. Interest in passions' relation to the good life and Christian salvation gave way to scientific interest in emotions' function for survival.

As I will argue in the chapters ahead, an adequate understanding of the relationship between emotions and flourishing will recognize the importance of the will and intention as Augustine and his followers did, and attend to an ultimate reality without making the mistake of bifurcating the Good from the material, embodied world. An adequate view of emotions will recognize that people sometimes have impulses that need to be critically examined for their worthiness without making the mistake of viewing all passions as anathema to the good life. These distinctions were, however, not of particular interest to the scientists that took up emotions' study as the Age of Faith waned.

3

Emotions as Functional for
Physiological Survival

Darwin and Evolutionary Science

Introduction

At the dawn of the nineteenth century, philosophical and theological interest in the passions was waning. In the Age of Reason and empiricism that dominated after the Middle Ages, the voices of theologians and philosophers became muted in passions/emotions scholarship, and science became one of the few disciplines that studied them with much new insight.[1] Early scientific study of emotions was based on ethology, or the study of animals, and demonstrated that human beings are more creaturely than earlier philosophers and theologians had imagined. Furthermore, scientific research demonstrated that people have less will and control over their emotional experiences than the Stoics, for example, had thought. One man's experience in particular helped disabuse philosophical and theological assumptions about human being and the relationship of the self—including the soul—to the body. That man was Phineas Gage (1823–1860 CE). Gage's case was an impetus for and lent support to the scientific study of emotions, their origins, meanings, and roles in humans' lives.[2]

In 1848 Gage was a popular twenty-five-year-old construction gang foreman working on a stretch of railroad in Vermont. In preparation for blasting a section of rock to make way for the rails, Gage poured gunpowder into a hole and tamped it down with a thirteen-pound iron tamping rod more than three feet long and an inch and a quarter in diameter. The act of tamping the gunpowder created a spark, and the powder exploded, blasting the tamping rod through Gage's left cheek and through his skull. The rod landed a good distance away, covered in blood and brain tissue. Gage was thrown to the ground in the explosion, but witnesses reported that he was awake, even alert, and though his limbs convulsed slightly, he was soon able to speak. His men put him on an ox cart and transported him, sitting upright, to a nearby hotel where a doctor helped him mount a flight of stairs before dressing his wound. Gage suffered an infection, but he recovered from the terrible injury—at least in some ways. Although his body healed, Gage's mind and his personality were irrevocably altered. Indeed, Gage could not remember significant events or people in his life, and while he had been a friendly and popular person before the accident, he was now impatient, easily angered, and impulsive. His friends and family reported that Gage was "no longer Gage." He could no longer work a steady job and spent the rest of his life exhibiting his scar and the tamping rod in the circus, wandering to the West Coast and even to South America for a time. Eventually he made his way to San Francisco, where he died in 1860. Upon his death, the doctor who had treated Gage immediately after the accident prevailed upon his family to donate his skull and the rod, which he used to illustrate an academic paper on the brain that the physician delivered to the Massachusetts Medical Society in 1868.[3]

Gage's case made clear that, contrary to popular belief, the immaterial parts of a person's character—including the soul, reason, and the passions—are entwined with the material, physical body. This notion was an affront to many: the idea that human beings are not quite as unique as philosophers and theologians had made them out to be created something of a crisis. In fact, Gage's case reignited earlier scientific convictions that humans are evolved from, and in many ways similar to, "lower" animals. To theologians committed to their understanding of the *imago dei*, the idea that the essence of a person is materially embodied was a direct attack on the view that God had created each person in God's image. However, Gage's case and the research it inspired made it clear that to be a *self*, to have a unique personality, experiences, and expressions, each human being is utterly dependent on a body—especially the brain. Gage's well-publicized experience helped pave the way for acceptance of scientific research and explanations for the origins and functions of emotions. Scientific research changed the understandings of emotion forever. Whereas earlier philosophers and theologians were committed to the notion that humans' uniqueness was directly related to their capacities to reason and to exercise will, the account of Gage's experience further eroded confidence in philosophy and religion to ascertain the truth, especially in relation to the soul and the good life. The message was clear: people's souls, passions, abilities to relate, and so on are formed by what was in one's body, and the most important battles for the *body* are not good vs. evil or righteousness vs. sin, but survival over extinction. Further, early scientists argued, human beings are distinct from other animals, not because humans have a soul or the ability to use reason but because they are the pinnacle of evolution.[4] Human beings are like animals in many ways, only more evolved.

Empirical scientists such as Charles Darwin, William James, and Paul MacLean accelerated research in emotions' relationship to physiology, and their work spawned thousands of subsequent research projects. Both Darwin and James studied emotions using the best tools they had: direct observation, peoples' self-reports, rudimentary nerve science using manual and electrical stimulation, and comparative studies between different cultures and between typical and "atypical" people.[5]

"Emotional" Expressions Are Evolutionary Adaptations: Charles Darwin

Charles Darwin (1809–1882 CE) helped shift the thinking about the passions/emotions from philosophical and theological modes of thinking to those of empirical science: he was convinced that something seemingly natural and unavoidable could not be as problematic as many had claimed. Although he had intended to attend seminary and become a pastor, Darwin's life took a different turn, and he spent four and a half years traveling around the world aboard the HMS *Beagle*, collecting specimens of rocks, birds, plants, insects, fossils, and mammals. Darwin sent many of his collections, illustrations, and notes back to his mentor at Cambridge University, Reverend John Stevens Henslow, professor of botany, and upon his return to England, Darwin was surprised to learn that his reports had impressed the scientific community and that he was already a well-established and well-respected scientist.[6] Despite this, Darwin's first book, *On the Origin of Species* (1859) was highly controversial and heavily criticized for its emphasis on science over theology. However, it established his views of evolution and natural selection that would inform his study of emotional expressions in animals and humans.[7] In fact, Darwin developed one of the first explicitly nonphilosophical or nontheological explanations for emotions, in which he claimed that "emotional" expressions are an ancient part of the evolution of human beings.

Darwin read widely in the research on the passions available to him, including early philosophers such as Plato and Aristotle, though he found most of it "of little or no service," since it had made "no marked advance" on the subject of the emotions.[8] Darwin set out to find his own answers to the questions about emotions' origin, meaning, and function.[9] Darwin became convinced that certain expressions in the body and face, which he took to be signs of physiological and phenomenological experience and intent, though they did not originate as such, were an evolutionary adaptation that increases an organism's likelihood of survival.

Darwin's book on emotions demonstrated his interest in body language, or the *bodily expressions of emotions*, rather than the *experience* of emotions, as early philosophers and theologians had done.[10] In it, Darwin described and illustrated his and others' observations of emotions' expression in humans and animals, demonstrating many similarities between human and animal expressions.[11] For example, using illustrations, Darwin famously argued that a particular monkey species, when being caressed, makes an expression that looks remarkably like a human smile. Darwin also illustrated how alike the snarling of a dog or cat is to the angry expression of a human and detailed the similarities in expression including the withdrawn mouth, narrow eyes, and bared teeth in both dogs and humans.

Darwin recognized that evolution would apply not just to anatomy and physiology, but also to an animal's "mind" and behaviors.[12] He based his studies on animals, human infants, and human adults in various cultures, concluding that expressive behaviors serve adaptive functions. Darwin's work thus expanded the study of the passions. He set their expressions in a physiological and evolutionary context, changing the mode of thinking about them, the language used to discuss them, and the methods used to research them. Because of Darwin, it became legitimate to ask the question "In what way does a particular emotion or behavioral pattern function in aiding survival?"[13] For Darwin, the terms *welfare* and *the general good* are more appropriate terms than *happiness*, and he defines the general good as "the rearing of the greatest number of individuals in full vigor and health, with all their faculties perfect, under the conditions to which they are subjected."[14]

The Principle of "Serviceable Associated Habits"

Darwin's theory of emotion was that emotional expressions *did not evolve for the purpose of expressing an inner feeling*, but for other purposes more closely related to survival: it is only because they consistently accompany other actions associated with strong emotion—such as biting an attacker—that observers consider certain expressions or bodily movement to be "emotional."[15] As Darwin put it, "Distinct uses, independently of expression, can indeed be assigned with much probability for almost all the facial muscles."[16] He noted that the "distinct use" was physical survival. Survival is the primary function of bodily expression, Darwin asserted, though other uses might well develop later.

Darwin called the emotional expressions that accompanied bodily actions such as pulling one's ears back or baring one's canine teeth "serviceable associated habits," by which he meant actions that were intended to increase the survival chances of an animal, but which later evolved to be associated with any expression related to the original situation. Serviceable habits are those that serve an important function and are inherited by offspring. Darwin proposed that over time, complex and repeated habits evolve—over the course of many generations—into inheritable actions:

> Certain complex actions are under direct or indirect service under certain states of the mind in order to gratify certain sensations, desires, &c.; and whenever the same state of mind is induced, however feebly, there is a tendency, through the force of habit and association for the same movements to be performed, though they may not then be of the least use.[17]

In fact, the less functional a habit is for humans in the modern era, the more evidence Darwin found for evolutionary inheritance: otherwise, why would people perform "disserviceable habits," or habits that do not seem to have any meaningful function?[18] Darwin found no other plausible explanation than that disserviceable habits had originally served to protect the individual and species but no longer had any useful purpose. Darwin suggested that people's attempts to control disserviceable emotional expressions or behaviors did not nullify his theory of natural selection and serviceable habits, but rather showed that consciousness and will can play a part in emotional expression, though not fully. In fact, Darwin suggested, it is the facial muscles (which he argued are most difficult to control) that reveal the traces of disserviceable patterns.

Of particular interest to Darwin on this score was the expression of weeping.[19] Usually associated with deep pain and sadness, it nevertheless confused Darwin: why should the production of tears accompany mental anguish? What was the survival function of weeping? Since Darwin was committed to his idea of "associated habits" that were derived from some nonemotional function, he set out to discover what physical and material purpose it would have had originally, no matter that it had come to signify emotional anguish. At first Darwin thought weeping might have a cleansing function: that is, having the literal purpose of washing debris from the eye. Only later did it come to be associated with the emotion of sadness, he thought. In his observations of the production of tears in animals and in humans, Darwin found that the muscles around the eyes were active during periods when the animal or person was engaged in some kind of "violent activity." Darwin became convinced that tears had something to do with the actions of screaming. He wrote, "There can, I think, be no doubt that the contraction of the muscles around the eyes during violent expiration or when the expanded chest is forcibly compressed is, in some manner, intimately connected with the secretion of tears."[20] The original function of tears, then, according to Darwin, was to protect the eyes during times of violent screaming, which was accompanied by "engorged" blood vessels in the eyes, and the subsequent contraction of the muscles around the eyes to guard them against harm. The contraction increases pressure on the eyes, stimulating the lachrymal glands, which produce tears. Darwin was convinced that weeping became associated with suffering because suffering is often accompanied by screaming and other behaviors that create intense pressure on the eyes, making them tear.

Committed to his idea that emotional expressions are evolved from actions that once served a direct, physical, survival-related purpose for the organism, Darwin interpreted all emotional expressions within this basic framework of serviceable associated habits. Even something like weeping, which has no obvious survival function, could be explained as a byproduct of the intense pressure put on the eyes during the "intense exertion" associated with screaming and crying.[21] However, emotional expressions that could not be easily understood in his theory of serviceable associated habits were more challenging to Darwin, and he added two other related principles he hoped would explain these: the principle of antithesis and the principle of overflow.

The Principle of Antithesis

Darwin recognized that his principle of serviceable associated habits did not explain the origin or function of all emotional expressions, and he sought to augment his theory:

> Certain states of the mind lead to certain habitual actions, which are of service, as under our first principle. Now when a directly opposite state of mind is induced, there is a strong and involuntary tendency to the performance of movements of a directly opposite nature, though these are of no use; and such movements are in some cases highly expressive.[22]

In other words, some emotional expressions developed as direct opposites to the initial serviceable habit. Darwin's theory of emotion, then, also provided for a mode of emotional expressions that, while not serviceable associated habits, were closely related as their direct opposite. He called this proposal "the Principle of Antithesis."

Emotional expressions that fall into the category of *antitheses* to serviceable associated habits are only mechanical, Darwin thought; they are related to serviceable associated habits through simple association. As an example of this in cats, Darwin argued that the arched back, erect tail, and pricked-up ears is often a sign of affection. This is in contrast to the crouching position in which the tail is extended horizontally, which, he observed, usually accompanies anger. For the actions in opposition to anger, such as affection, Darwin proposed that the expressive movements were originally done voluntarily or by will, and later through repetition they became habitual, involuntary, and inherited by successive generations.[23] Through these repetitive and inherited behaviors, "even insects express anger, terror, jealousy, and love" when they rub their body parts together to make sounds, Darwin asserted.[24]

The Principle of Overflow

Though these first two principles helped Darwin explain many different expressions in both animals and in humans, there were some emotional expressions that did not seem to be explained by either principle, and Darwin was not convinced he had offered explanations for all emotional expressions. In fact, for some expressive bodily movements—such as trembling of muscles due to cold or fear or muscle exhaustion, screaming with rage, and sweating as a reaction to fear or pain—he could find no physical or material function, but he was nonetheless committed to explaining them.[25] Eventually Darwin explained these with his "Principle of Overflow." In Darwin's words, this principle asserts that "certain actions, which we recognize as *expressive of certain states of mind*, are the direct result of the constitution of the nervous system and have been from the first independent of the will and, to a large extent, of habit."[26]

Darwin's explanation for these otherwise unexplainable forms of emotional expression drew upon a "very old idea of Western culture":[27] "the notion that the energy that is produced within animals', including humans', nervous systems in response to various kinds of events in their environment at certain times simply 'overflows.'"[28] As Darwin put it, "When the cerebro-spinal system is highly excited and nerve-force is liberated in excess, it may be expended in intense sensations, active thought, violent movements, or increased activity of the glands. . . . Great pain urges all animals, and has urged them during endless generations, to make the most violent and diversified efforts to escape from the cause of suffering."[29] Darwin thought that this led to the development of a variety of stereotyped expressive reactions in both animals and humans. For example, Darwin wrote that shaking a limb when injured is an attempt to shake off pain "though this may obviously be impossible."[30] It is, Darwin thought, an effort to shake away the pain by reducing the energy in one's overexcited body part. Crying out in pain is not necessarily directly associated with alleviating one's pain but rather begins in the young who need to call their parents to come offer comfort.[31] Both vigorously shaking a limb and having caregivers come to one's aid function to release nervous pressure associated with pain.[32] Darwin returned to the subject of weeping in his discussion of this principle, arguing that the harder we weep, the greater the relief because of the pressure it eases.[33]

Darwin had developed a threefold explanation that, in his mind, answered most of the vexing questions about emotions; however, he was still not entirely happy with his classifications. He wrote, "It is . . . impossible to decide how much weight ought to be attributed, in each particular case, to one of our principles, and how much to another; and very many points in the theory of expression remain inexplicable."[34] Despite Darwin's reservations, he nevertheless remained convinced that there are universal facial expressions of emotions, suggesting that at least a small set of emotions—usually identified as happiness, sadness, fear, disgust, anger, and surprise—would be exhibited, recognized, and interpreted in the same way by people everywhere.[35]

The Role of the Will in Emotional Expression: "Disserviceable Habits" and Display Rules

Influenced by the philosophers before him who considered self-control and the role of the will in their relation to emotions, Darwin undertook his own study of human will. He found that in some cases the will had little influence on the expression of emotions, while in others, it did inform them. Darwin believed that all emotional expressions are genetically inherited and not fully under individuals' control by reason or will, even if they were disserviceable. That they cannot be controlled by reason was proof for Darwin that they were encoded in humans' genetic makeup and not easily resisted or changed. The example he gave is of pressing his face against a thick glass window at the zoo:

> I put my face close to the thick glass-plate in front of a puff-adder in the Zoological Gardens, with the firm determination of not starting back if the snake struck at me; but, as soon as the blow was struck, my resolution went for nothing, and I jumped a yard or two backwards with astonishing rapidity. My will and reason were powerless against the imagination of a danger which had never been experienced.[36]

Although Darwin's reaction of fear was understandable, it is nevertheless disserviceable (that is, unnecessary given the glass) and not under control of his will. Thus, Darwin challenged the faith in people's ability to control much related to emotions and their expression with one's will.[37]

Darwin's contribution to the scientific study of emotions can hardly be overstated. His most significant contributions are five: his *scientific*—rather than philosophical or theological—interest in emotional expressions and the emotions that came to be associated with them; his use of theories of *evolution and natural selection* for understanding the origin of emotional expression; his *documentation* of the "general principles of expression," or what he claimed were universally recognized expressions of emotion, which he recorded and drew; his *identification* of what he thought were basic and universal emotions; and finally, his *empirical method* for studying emotional expression in humans and animals.[38] Darwin's work in *Expressions* established in his mind that animals and humans share universal essences of emotion, that emotions are expressed in the face and body for the purposes of survival and to expel excess energy, that "emotional reactions" are triggered by the outside world, and that emotional reactions are largely outside of creatures' control.

Darwin's research spawned a new set of assumptions about emotions, their origin, and their purpose. Evolutionary psychologists, among others, continued and added complexity to his work, contributing to the development of an entire field for which emotions and their expression is a critical subject. The work of evolutionary psychologists will be engaged later, but first it is important to note the contributions of William James, another of the most significant figures in the twentieth-century psychology of emotions.

Emotions Are the "Name and Interpretation" of Physiological Activity: William James

Like Darwin, American philosopher and psychologist William James (1842–1910 CE) is one of the most influential figures in the study of emotions in the nineteenth and twentieth centuries, and his understanding of emotions has inspired an approach to emotion studies that continues today. However, James' work differed from Darwin's in important ways. Specifically, although they used the same word ("emotion") for the subject of their examination, what Darwin studied was fundamentally different from the focus of James' work. In some ways, James' work is reminiscent of the work of Galen: both asked about the bodily origins of emotional experiences.

Although James examined a different facet of emotions and spawned research in distinctly different directions than did Darwin, his work was at least as influential as Darwin's, and maybe more so.[39] Darwin and James defined emotions differently from each other, and these differences shifted their questions, their research, and their conclusions. The primary difference can be described as the difference between emotions as expression and emotion as experience. Darwin's research focused on the first view, James' on the second. However, although James emphasized *emotional feeling* or *experience* rather than *emotional expression* as Darwin had, their research was closely related. Like Darwin, James was interested in the origins of emotions for their own sake, though James was less interested in their relationship to survival than was Darwin.[40]

Several questions motivated James' work: "What is the origin of the *experience* of emotion?" "How can we understand the different emotions that people experience in similar contexts?" "Are there universal autonomic specificities in emotional experiences?" It was James, often considered the first psychologist of emotion, who formulated what feelings are and how they are different from but related to the emotions and their expression.[41] James was primarily interested in which comes first, the feeling of an emotion or the bodily changes associated with it. James believed that for the "coarser" emotions such as fear and anger, the bodily changes—such as increased beating of the heart or increased blood pressure—come first, and the *feeling* of an emotion was based largely on a person's recognition of these changes.[42]

For James, emotions are merely the *perception and interpretation of physiological changes.*[43] He wrote, "If we fancy some strong emotion, and then try to abstract from our consciousness of it all the feelings of its characteristic bodily symptoms, we find that we have nothing left behind."[44] James was convinced that prevailing understandings of emotions—including Darwin's—got the sequence of emotional experience wholly wrong. In James' view, people do not first encounter a stimulus, then experience an emotion, and subsequently express it. Instead, individuals first *experience the bodily changes* that have been elicited by the perception of an event in the environment, *interpret* those changes, and then *experience* the emotion—or what might be called a *feeling*—and then finally express and/or respond. For James, the physiological arousal itself *is* the emotion. As James said in "what may be the most frequently quoted statement by any psychologist ever,"[45] "bodily changes follow directly the perception of the exciting fact, and . . . our feeling of the same changes as they occur is the emotion."[46] Indeed, James' research convinced him that "'a purely disembodied human emotion is a nonentity.'"[47] That is, *physiological changes* are the *automatic responses* of people's bodies to the *perception* of something important to them in their environment, and it is these *bodily changes* that a person experiences and then interprets as an emotion.[48] The physiological changes are also the body's way of *preparing for some kind of action*. For example, when one sees something threatening, the rush of adrenaline, increased heart rate, and so on prepare one to run. It is these physiological changes, James argued, that one experiences as a feeling—in this case, fear.[49]

Clearly, James differed from Darwin in the way he defined emotion: in James' view, emotions are the *physiological reactions to an event* rather than a particular expression in the face or body, as Darwin had proposed. James wrote the following:

> The more closely I scrutinize my states, the more persuaded I become that whatever moods, affections and passions I have, are in very truth constituted by, and made up of, those bodily changes we ordinarily call their expression or consequence; and the more it seems to me that if I were to become corporeally anesthetic, I should be excluded from the life of the affections, harsh and tender alike, and drag out an existence of merely cognitive or intellectual form.[50]

Where Darwin was explicitly interested in inherited bodily expressions (which evolutionarily became associated with emotions), James argued that emotions cannot be divorced from their physiological event and the experience of it; indeed, they are one and the same. For James, emotion is a *perception* of a physical response to something in the environment, and often this response is internal, including heart rate. This is in contrast to the bodily expressions of something felt internally—for example, fear—that is then expressed in the body, which was the focus of Darwin's study. For James, then, *emotions* are the realization of physiological activity while *feelings* are the experience of how one interprets that activity.[51]

James was interested in what he called the "science of mental life" and promoted the idea that emotions are merely passive "mental feelings of movements of the viscera."[52] In his book *The Principles of Psychology* (1890) James' aim was to understand the brain as the organ of the mind: he wanted to establish a psychology rooted in neurophysiology and his discoveries in an experimental laboratory. James became a spokesman for the "new psychology," insisting that psychology take into account the structure and function of the nervous system and the brain, especially in psychology's account of human experience.[53]

The most important idea in James' theory on emotions, then, is his assertion that bodily changes follow directly the *perception* of the exciting fact, and that our *experience* of the same changes as they occur is the emotion.[54] Prior to James' work, scholars in the Darwinian tradition had devoted themselves to *describing* the emotions and their expression and exploring the meaning and function of those. But James began a new angle of investigation by suggesting that emotions could be used as a basis for a study of *causality* in the body, and the effects of physiology on human experience.[55] He wrote, "we now have the question as to how any given expression of anger or fear may have come to exist; and that is a real question of physiological mechanics on the one hand, and of history on the other, which [like all real questions] is in essence answerable, although the answer may be hard to find."[56]

In other words, although James was deeply indebted to Darwin and his pioneering work, James deviated from Darwin's strict focus on the *expression* of emotion for survival, studying instead the *conscious experience* of emotions (that is, *feelings*), and the physiological origins of them. Like Darwin, James assumed a close relationship between emotions and the physiological events (the emotions) that accompany them, but he turned the order of the two around, arguing that the physiological events preceded the emotions, rather than, as Darwin had it, the "emotional response" (e.g., the one that came to be called fear) preceding the physiological response (e.g., baring one's teeth). On this point, James concluded that "the neural machinery is but a hyphen between determinate arrangements of matter outside the body and determinate impulses . . . within its organs."[57] For James, feelings are the result of physiological movements that are interpreted in particular ways: "we feel sorry because we cry, angry because we strike, afraid because we tremble, and not that we cry, strike, or tremble, because we are sorry, angry or fearful, as the case may be."[58]

Like philosophers, theologians, and Darwin before him, James was interested in the will's ability to control emotions and their expression, but James offered a more positive view than others had. Specifically, James argued that the body's posture, facial expression, and movement can directly affect how a person feels—which means, said James, that people have some control over their emotions (physiology) and feelings (the interpretation and experience of physiological change) by changing their posture. For example, James wrote, "The sovereign, voluntary path to cheerfulness, if our spontaneous cheerfulness be lost, is to sit up cheerfully, to look around cheerfully, and to act and speak as if cheerfulness were already there. If such conduct does not make you soon feel cheerful, nothing else on that occasion can."[59] Whereas the Stoics and others had recommended changing one's *thoughts* to change or rid one's emotions, James suggested changing *one's face, posture, and other physical elements* to change one's emotions.[60] He said as much in his article "What Is an Emotion?" in which James wrote:

> Refuse to express a passion, and it dies. . . . Whistling to keep up courage is no mere figure of speech. On the other hand, sit all day in a moping posture, sigh and reply to everything with a dismal voice, and your melancholy lingers. There is no more valuable precept in moral

education than this, as all who have experienced it know: if we wish to conquer undesirable emotional tendencies in ourselves, we must assiduously and in the first instance cold-bloodedly, go through the outward motions of those contrary dispositions we prefer to cultivate. The reward of persistency will infallibly come in the fading out of the sullenness or depression, and the advent of real cheerfulness and kindliness in their stead. Smooth the brow, brighten the eye, contract the dorsal rather than ventral aspect of the frame, and speak in a major key, pass on the genial compliment, and your heart must be frigid indeed if it does not gradually thaw![61]

James was clear that if people are feeling down and wish to be happy, they should act as if they are happy, and they will become happy.[62] He was convinced that "the face can help the heart to change."[63]

What was most striking in James' theory was the primacy he gave to the viscera, rather than the soul, as the origin of emotions. Whereas Plato and others had suggested that the spirited passions/movements of the soul acted on the body, specifically the brain or nervous system, James argued, as Galen had centuries earlier, that emotions start in the body and then affect the brain. The emotions, James proposed, are not first a psychic act that then affect the body but are a bodily state called an emotion, which is subsequently experienced as a feeling. James, like Darwin, then, did not view the emotions as negative, but as natural, biological processes that are related to an organism's functioning.[64] Also like Darwin, James sought to place emotions within the context of natural science and the processes of evolution.[65] Both Darwin and James considered animals' behavior to be adaptations of the organism to its environment, carried through by natural selection. Furthermore, Darwin and James understood the nervous system to be simply the ways animals respond to the "evolutionarily important" events in their environments.

James' work "unambiguously reduced emotions to products, even epiphenomena, of physical processes" and this view coincided with the foundation of university departments and professional journals of psychology in both the United States and Europe and influenced much of the subsequent scientific study of emotions.[66] Thus, James' theory of emotion became the primary emotion theory of the emerging *science* of psychology.[67] Indeed, James made one of the earliest contributions to the psychological tradition and its understanding of emotions, establishing a legacy that is "one of the liveliest debates in the field of emotions": the relation between physiology and emotion that put physiology first.[68]

James' work, which was in response to Darwin's propositions, influenced thousands of subsequent studies of emotions.[69]

An important legacy of both Darwin and James is that they convinced empirically minded researchers that emotions could be studied insofar as they could be observed and measured. This led to significant studies of the face as the source of emotions.[70] Darwin's and James' interest in the physiological bases of emotions also led to emotions' examination by researchers interested in emotions' neurological basis, especially in the brain: they wanted to know just where in the brain emotions existed. Neuroscientist Paul MacLean took up these questions in the early twentieth century and, like both Darwin and James, spawned decades of research in attempts to locate emotions in the brain.

Emotions Are in Evolutionarily Derived Sections of the Brain: Paul MacLean

Scientists such as Scottish "moral psychologist" Alexander Bain had tried, as early as the nineteenth century, to map the parts of the brain, their relationships to one another, and the various roles they play in the functions of the body and personal experiences, including the emotions.[71] For example, based on extensive studies on animals, certain parts of the brain—particularly the hypothalamus, which was considered the "seat" of emotions—were thought to be the integrating center for emotional feelings as well as behaviors. Gage's experience justified similar research in humans, which eventually led to significant attempts to understand the various roles different parts of the brain have in determining emotions and their displays.[72]

Bain and mid-nineteenth-century physician Paul Broca also claimed to have discovered the area in the brain responsible for human language—known now as *Broca's area*—countering the "prevailing belief" that language was given to humans by God at the Tower of Babel.[73] Other scientists, too, were studying brain anatomy in search of "emotional sites." In the 1940s, physician and neuroscientist Paul MacLean proposed that the human brain was in reality three brains in one, positing a "reptilian brain," a "limbic brain," and a "rational brain," or neocortex.[74] More specifically, MacLean argued that the human brain is composed of a system of layers that are a direct result of the evolutionary process: increasingly complex brains are built on top of simpler, older ones, though they all continue to function and interact. The oldest, most primitive part (the reptilian brain) is the deepest layer, MacLean proposed, with the limbic brain developing in a layer on top of it, and the neocortex (which he thought to be in charge of rational thought, consciousness, and conscience) being the last to develop, making up the outermost layer.[75]

MacLean suggested that animals have undergone a series of evolutionary, developmental phases that have provided neural circuits both essential to and responsible for the changing needs of the organism. MacLean argued that the three phases relate to the particular functional needs and capacities of reptiles and all mammals, including the highest mammals—primates and humans. In the first phase, MacLean believed, the inner, older parts of the brain developed. This layer (often called the striatum) is present in all vertebrates: lizards, birds, and mammals, including humans. MacLean suggested that these circuits are responsible for the instinctive activities of these creatures, including establishing a nest or home site, defending territory, fighting or fleeing, finding food, forming some social groups, greeting, mating, flocking, and migrating. In modern lizards, the striatum is the largest part of the brain, and, MacLean argued, other more advanced parts of the brain are conspicuously missing in them.[76]

The next layer MacLean called the limbic system (building on Broca's work), which, he asserted, developed with the evolution of mammals.[77] The limbic system, MacLean proposed, allows mammals to do three things that reptiles cannot do: mammalian young can attach to and be nurtured by their mothers, mammals make vocal signals to communicate to each other, and they engage in rough-and-tumble play, especially when they are young, which helps them develop social bonds and hierarchies. Mammals with a well-developed limbic system are able to survive socially in ways that are very different from anything seen among reptiles. In addition, MacLean and those who followed him argued,[78] the new structures in mammals not only allow for increased and different social actions, but are also the seat of the emotions.[79] (In recognition of this, the limbic system has often been called the "emotional brain," first by MacLean, and then in much of the twentieth-century literature on emotions that is indebted to his work.)

MacLean theorized that the third and last (evolutionary) layer of the brain to develop is the neocortex.[80] This part of the brain may exist in some lower mammals, is most developed in primates, and is most highly complex and refined in humans, MacLean argued. In language reminiscent of the early philosophers and theologians, MacLean believed that it was the job of the cortex to think and control the lower, "unruly" parts of the brain.[81]

A significant move forward in the attempts to locate emotions in the brain occurred when research suggested that each emotion is based on a particular system of brain circuitry.[82] By stimulating distinct areas of the brain, researchers found that they could induce distinct emotions. For example, late-twentieth-century psychologist and well-known emotions researcher Keith Oatley wrote, "For each emotion, [one's neural circuitry] makes ready a particular set of brain processes, somewhat appropriate to the events that triggered them. Among the processes that each circuit generates is a particular form of consciousness that we probably share with other mammals: of happiness, of fear, of anger, and so on."[83] This research shifted the understanding of emotions in two significant ways: first, one of the implications was that human beings are not the only creatures to experience emotions, and second, it helped answer the century-long question about the origins of *different, discrete* emotions that William James had explored. MacLean's and Oatley's research suggested that different parts of the brain may be responsible for the generation of different emotions and for the particular bodily reactions people commonly have during an emotion (e.g., blushing when embarrassed) and that these different sections of the brain and the neural patterns within and between them are evolutionarily related.

Early neuroscientists, then, were convinced that the sympathetic and parasympathetic systems are responsible for many of the bodily reactions that James, Darwin, and their followers understood to be the essential components of emotion. They argued, for example, that the sympathetic nervous system initiates the fight-or-flight response when one sees a bear.[84] Further, they demonstrated that feedback from the body plays an important role in the experience of emotion, supporting James' work. However, whereas James proposed that the visceral and other bodily changes were of primary importance in emotional life, subsequent recent research demonstrated that the *face* may be the most important area in providing the physical feedback that influences humans' emotions. In fact, for some emotions, feedback from the face can and does help determine the experience of particular emotions, and some researchers went so far as to say the face is a primary differentiator in the experience of different emotions.

Following this trajectory, emotions researchers and psychologists Antoinette Feleky and Paul Ekman argued that emotions are communicated universally in the human face, and Ekman has spent his long career arguing that the evolutionary function of emotions as expressed in the face means that the same emotions can be traced across all people, cultures, and historical periods.

Emotions Are Basic, Physiological, Standardized, Universal, and Functional: Antoinette Feleky and Paul Ekman

Darwin had assumed that certain emotional expressions such as the teeth baring—which came to indicate the emotion *fear* and the intention to strike—have a fundamental functional purpose: to support survival.[85] Darwin assumed then, that some emotional expressions came to be universal.[86] Some of the most significant researchers in the study of emotions continued Darwin's interest in the facial expression of emotions, and some of them greatly influenced psychological understandings of emotions.[87] Thus, scientists of emotion in the twentieth century continued to explore a number of questions about the origins and functions of emotions begun centuries earlier, and each wrestled with a variety of conceptual and methodological issues, especially in regards to the experiential and context-dependent dimensions of emotional expression. Many researchers, including Hungarian Antoinette Feleky (1875–?)[88] and American Paul Ekman (b. 1934), focused their attention on the face.

Feleky took as her starting assumption Darwin's assertion that emotions and the expressions that accompany them are the products of evolution. In fact, Feleky wrote that she was interested in the "expressive movements characteristic in certain emotional states, or rather, to show what emotional states certain facial expressions do signify."[89] In a famous experiment, Feleky showed eighty-six photos to "one hundred reliable persons."[90] The photos were the same in every way (background, clothing, pose, distance from the lens, and so on) except in the subjects' emotional expression. She asked those one hundred people to identify the emotion in the photo based on a list of almost one hundred names of emotions. She then asked the volunteers to write down the name of the emotional expression the photograph suggested to them. Feleky concluded that there were, indeed, a series of universal and identifiable emotional expressions and sought to catalogue them.[91] Her work was interpreted to "prove" the evolutionary and universal reasons for emotions.

Other researchers took the early scientific research in similar directions. One of the best-known scientists researching emotions as physiological, basic, and universal is American psychologist Paul Ekman, whose work is heavily indebted to Feleky's.[92] In 1971 Ekman set out to test Darwin's claim about the universality of facial expressions in humans across cultures. Ekman focused on the face and its expression of emotion with the intent to "vindicate"[93] Darwin's understanding of emotions as universally significant for survival, as well as to confirm and extend it.

Ekman and his colleagues undertook a research method similar in some ways to Darwin's and Feleky's, though what Feleky studied locally, Ekman and his group took global.[94] They took photographs of people displaying facial expressions of happiness, sadness, anger, surprise, disgust, and fear and presented them to people in a variety of cultures, intentionally including members of some groups that had never encountered people from the West. They even visited a group of people who had had little contact with Western culture, the *Fore*, an isolated preliterate group living in the highlands of New Guinea. The researchers showed both adults and children several pictures of facial expressions of emotion and asked them to match a face with an emotional description. For example, researchers were expecting the phrase "Her friend has come, and she is feeling happy" to be matched with a picture of someone smiling. The studies demonstrated a high degree of similarity in the ways the facial expressions were interpreted universally.[95] Ekman and his colleagues concluded that the six emotions they studied were present across cultures, had recognizable facial expressions, and were universal and biological in origin.[96] As a follow-up, Ekman and his collaborators also did the experiments in reverse: they asked people from the *Fore* group to make expressions and took pictures of them. Then they asked American college students to identify the emotion each expressed, which they claimed their subjects were able to do. Ekman also repeated his original research about a decade later: he and his colleagues published a significant study in 1987 that replicated the studies with the *Fore*. In this follow-up study, they explored emotional expressions in ten different cultures from Estonia to Hong Kong and from Sumatra to the United States and found that people native to each interpreted accurately the facial expressions shown to them.[97]

In an effort to explain cultural differences in the expressions of emotion that they *did* find, Ekman and his collaborators developed Darwin's theory of "display rules," or guidelines that are a part of a particular culture that determine how particular emotions will be displayed, or expressed.[98] They proposed that in every culture there are social norms that define and regulate people's expression of emotion.[99] These rules govern the range of possible meanings and knowledge that can be invoked about the situation and its applicable emotion. In this way, Ekman and his collaborators argued, different cultures inform emotions and their expression by providing a "convention for feeling, a guidebook for what is legitimate in the circumstance, with sanctions provided for not feeling what is prescribed."[100]

Ekman's understanding of the function of emotions and their expression is that they communicate to those around them what is being felt, what is needed, and what action should be anticipated. Emotions and their expression, Ekman argues, have evolved to facilitate survival in social contexts when life in collectives requires the capacities to communicate and read subtle cues in thinking and to anticipate behavior. The display rules Ekman proposed are ways for each particular social group to define and refine their communicative tools.

Convinced that facial expressions are—as Darwin proposed— evolutionarily developed and important to the survival of both the individual organism and the species, Ekman sought to demonstrate "conclusively" that the facial expressions for happiness, surprise, sadness, fear, disgust, and anger—often referred to as the big six, though Ekman now wants to add to the list a seventh, contempt—are correctly identified by people from vastly different cultures and that other emotions are combinations or modifications of the basic emotions.[101]

The fact that there is "no known validity" to these particular facial poses, and that studies using more objective methods such as facial EMG and facial coding "do not find evidence that people routinely make these movements in real life during episodes of emotion,"[102] has not deterred Ekman from arguing that "the evidence now for universality is overwhelming."[103] In other words, despite evidence to the contrary, Ekman continues to maintain that there are basic, universal emotions, shown in common expressions on the face, that function to enable communication between individuals, and thus increase the chances for survival. The focus on universality of emotions and their connection to the face funded a great deal of interest in neuroscience and the "location" of emotions in the brain. However, cultural anthropologists, sociologists, and other social theorists have thrown into Ekman's conclusions a monkey wrench, as explored in chapters 5 and 6. First, though, to understand how these early scientific assumptions became so well accepted, it will be important to explore the ways psychoanalysts and psychologists adopted the case for universal, basic emotions and built a system of identification, interpretation, and healing based on it.

Conclusion

The theories of emotions that developed out of the work of early scientific approaches have had an incalculable influence on contemporary understanding of emotions and their relationship to the goal or telos of life. Whereas philosophers and Christian theologians, for the most part, understood the passions as anathema to the good life and maintained the goal of the passions' control, discipline, or eradication, many empirical, scientific studies on the emotions and their expressions presented a different conclusion. Scientists such as Darwin, James, Maclean, and Ekman promoted the view that the passions/emotions and their expression are natural and biological: human beings are born with ancient, inherited "emotional" structures in the brain. Emotions are expressed in the face, which establishes the foundation for emotions and people's experience of them—and for understanding emotions' primary function: in their view, communication. The conviction that the "newest" part of the brain (the neocortex) sets humans apart from their animal ancestors and represents a significant evolutionary achievement contributed the generalized assumptions about the emotional lives of human beings: that is, emotions are identifiable, interpretable, and functional for survival (Darwin) and for communicative (Ekman) purposes in humans. This view of the evolution of the brain and of human emotions assumes that certain "basic" emotions are inborn and universal and that understanding them is fairly straightforward. All "typical" people, no matter where they come from in the world, are said to display and recognize them. Subsequent challenges to the universal experience and recognition of emotion—as well as difficulty finding any patterns of circuitry for particular emotions—led a new generation of researchers to propose that the brain inserts an appraisal or judgment about a situation and decides whether and what emotion is required; this work will be presented in chapter 4. The assumption that there are basic, fundamental, universal, and straightforward emotions inherited to support the survival of mammals—primarily through their bodily communication to predators and others in their social group—has been both accepted and challenged by twentieth-century psychologists. For example, Sigmund Freud accepted that emotions are natural, but he disagreed that they were easily accessible or positive in their function. Others, such as behaviorists, however, argued that emotions are too subjective to study empirically and ignored them. In general, though, psychologists (often unknowingly) adopted many of the views that had come before, from the philosophers and the scientists especially, adapting them for their clinical work.

An adequate understanding of emotions' relationship to flourishing will accept the idea that emotions are natural without assuming they are all life-giving. Such an understanding will also incorporate the view that emotions are important for survival, as Darwin and his followers knew, but not for physical survival only. It will understand emotions as having physiological bases, and also recognize that feelings as we know them are entirely constructed. An adequate understanding of the function of emotions will maintain the importance of display rules as Ekman does, but not make the mistake of assuming that emotions are genetically inherited or universal features whose expressions alone are variable. An adequate view of emotions will understand that emotions are significant means of communication without making the mistake of assuming that any of them mean the same thing to all people in all times and all places. In other words, subsequent research, including that by sociologists and cultural anthropologists, disputes some of the assumptions Darwin, Ekman, and others held. In addition, the role of what is pleasant and unpleasant for motivating behaviors will also be challenged. First, though, an examination of psychological perspectives on emotion will be important, both for the differing views such perspectives offer, and also for the ways clinicians adopted—sometimes uncritically—the perspectives that had come before, popularizing them as psychotherapeutic theories and practice gained traction.

4

Emotions as Pathological, Signs of Dysfunction, and Indicators of Need

Sigmund Freud and Depth Psychology

Introduction

When philosophy and theology gave way to empiricism in the eighteenth century, science rose to prominence; not surprisingly, the study of emotion followed that trend.[1] Despite William James' interest in the phenomenology of emotion, scientific researchers tended to be skeptical of the study of the *experience* of emotions because subjective experience is difficult to quantify or explain. Philosophers in the nineteenth and twentieth centuries even "scoffed at the idea that the study of emotion was an important part of their job,"[2] and some scientists' views were congruent with this dismissal: what Charles Darwin, Antoinette Feleky, and Paul Ekman found worthy of study was the *expression* of emotions, not one's internal experience of them.

In fact, although he may not have intended it, Darwin's work generated a theory of emotions and their expressions fairly narrowly focused on survival and natural selection. In studying animal behaviors, Darwin recognized that the process of evolution applies to animals' expressive behaviors as well as to their anatomy. Expanding his research to human infants and adults in various cultures, Darwin concluded that expressive behaviors serve an adaptive function in the lives of animals and surmised that those functions continued to operate in humans' lives.

According to him, emotional expressions evolved to function as signals and preparations for actions, communicating information from one animal, including humans, to another about what is likely to happen next.[3] Thus, Darwin and his followers argued, emotions and their expressions increase the chances of survival of the individual demonstrating the behavior and perhaps of the one being communicated to as well.[4] Darwin's work shifted the study of emotion from the study of the *experience of* the passions and responses to them (which had been the primary focus of philosophers and theologians) to the study of behavior within a biological, evolutionary context. Darwin made it scientifically appropriate to ask, "In what way does a particular emotion or behavior pattern function in aiding survival?" Scores of researchers responded to the challenge of answering that question.[5] Two strands in emotions research emerged in the early twentieth century: one in which emotions were not considered worthy of study, and the other in which emotions became a primary focus in treatment for a host of psychopathologies.

Emotions Are Not Worthy of Study:
John Watson and B. F. Skinner

Because the field of psychology began as a quasiscientific and academic discipline, many of its earliest students tended to study behaviors, as those are quantifiable in ways that subjective emotions are not.[6] For example, behaviorists such as John B. Watson (1878–1958 CE) and B. F. Skinner (1904–1990 CE) were among those who distrusted the introspective approach being led by those interested in the unconscious, dreams, and the dynamics of the internal, psychic world. Instead, behaviorists were convinced that only what could be observed and repeated in experiments was truly reliable and objective. They eschewed the study of subjective feelings, and like Darwin, they restricted their work to the study of behavior, and the simpler or more basic the behavior the better.[7] Behaviorists' research "reduced psychology to the study of behavior" rather than the mind or experience, leading to a preoccupation with conditioned responses, simple habits, and automatic reactions to stimuli and reactivity.[8] Behaviorists' understanding of emotions' function was limited, then, though they did provide a large body of scholarship about the ways pain and other unpleasant sensations help direct choices, behaviors, and motivation. Their conclusions are reminiscent to those of the Epicureans and Stoics: the good life is the pleasant and pain-free one, and animals and human beings are prone to behave in accordance with such tendencies.[9] Using reward and punishment to effect certain behaviors became the focus of their work.

Nevertheless, despite the recognized difficulties in studying people's subjective experience and the challenges of the meaning of "emotional" behaviors beyond reactions to pleasant or unpleasant stimuli, those in the emerging field of psychodynamic psychology did not share the concerns of the behaviorists. Josef Breuer, Sigmund Freud, and other "mentalists"[10] understood themselves as bridging philosophy, psychology, and science, and they studied people's subjective experience using what they believed were credible research methods. Like the earliest medical doctors such as Galen, Freud and other early twentieth-century researchers believed that homeostasis is the body's desired norm—the automatic response to sustaining a constant, normal state within the blood and throughout the body.[11]

Darwin's commitment to the strictly expressive and behavioral aspects of emotions, then, gave way to more-complex perspectives and understandings. Indeed, emotions and their study proved more complex than either James or Darwin—or Plato, Galen, the Stoics, or Augustine, for that matter—had proposed, and emotions scholarship began moving in new directions. In the early twentieth century, the commonalities in an individual's emotional responses to *different stimuli* as well as the differences between different individuals' emotions to the *same stimuli* became the focus of interest again—as they had been in early scientific examinations such as William James'. While some empirical researchers stayed close to Darwin and his interest in "emotional" expressions and behaviors, others deviated from studying only what could be directly observed. Cognitive psychologists studied the beliefs and appraisals involved in emotional experience, developmental psychologists explored the ways emotions are related to the goals and motivations that influence people's decisions, and psychodynamic theorists outlined the ways relationships engender deeply entrenched emotions that affect people throughout their lives. Researchers in these groups were convinced that emotions are informed by people's beliefs, their needs, their goals, their relational histories, and current contexts. Three significant trajectories in the psychological study of emotions emerged in the twentieth century, then: psychoanalytic/psychodynamic approaches, cognitive/appraisal theories, and psychoevolutionary understandings. Perhaps the most significant early psychological theory, however, was Freud's classical psychoanalytic view, in which emotions are understood as pathological, needing to be discharged, interpreted, or tamed.

Emotions Are Pathological: Sigmund Freud

Against the empiricists' concern that emotions were too subjective to be studied in any meaningful way, psychoanalyst Sigmund Freud (1856–1939 CE) was influenced by nineteenth-century philosopher Friedrich Nietzsche's existentialist anthropology.[12] In a view directly opposed to the early philosophers' and theologians' view of the passions, Nietzsche (1844–1900 CE) had argued for the importance of the non-rational and nonconscious elements of human experience, asserting that the more chaotic side of human being was worth analysis, acceptance, and guidance.[13] Freud agreed.

Over the course of his life, Freud, who established the framework of psychodynamic theory and practice, developed at least four theories of emotion—more specifically, of anxiety. Heavily indebted to physiological understandings of emotions (he read Darwin's work with great interest), Freud understood the need to take into account the physical and chemical forces that are active in humans.[14] Freud became convinced that when physical energy gets strong enough, the tension is transformed into "psychical affect" or anxiety.[15] Informed by Darwin's theory of overflow, Freud argued that emotions (in his language, "affect") are the *result* of the accumulation and blocking of tension.[16] Emotions or affect are also the *symptom* of distress or anxiety. Affect is the result of a physiological disequilibrium, and it is often felt as a distinct subjective experience, though this understanding develops later in his work.[17] However, especially early in Freud's thinking, affect is both physical and psychical energy that needs to be released.[18] In his later work, Freud posited a fourth possibility. Each of his perspectives will be reviewed briefly here.

In Freud's first theory about anxiety, formulated in 1915, he proposed that affects are a form of energy that demand some kind of expression, either directly or indirectly. If affect is not expressed but repressed or inhibited in some way, the energy of that repressed emotion will manifest in the form of "neurotic overflow mechanisms" such as phobias, obsessions, or compulsive rituals.[19] Freud, then, understood affects such as anxiety as the consequence of the inhibition or repression of emotions.[20] Along with his colleague Josef Breuer, Freud theorized about the neglected, denied, or repressed emotions that had to do with past experiences, particularly the sexual molestation Freud believed many of his patients had experienced in their childhood. Freud argued that the effects of those sexual traumas were so painful that even the memory of them had been repressed. However, in Freud's thinking, the emotions resulting from and signaling that trauma could not be fully repressed and were often acted out through "hysterical" affective symptoms. These symptoms included "inappropriate" crying, sudden changes in facial expression, muscular or sensory losses of function, or other neuroses. In other words, unpleasant affective "symptoms" are symbols of other past events. Freud, then, imagined that affects such as anxiety are the result of an inability to cope with an overwhelming stress—often from one's past.

In his second theory of anxiety, Freud argued that anxiety first occurs during the trauma of birth, which results in what Freud called *primary anxiety*.[21] Primary anxiety serves as the prototype for auxiliary anxieties later in people's lives,[22] so that anything that triggers or evokes the feelings one had during birth would result in subsequent feelings of anxiety.[23] In his third formulation of anxiety, Freud argued that anxiety is the result of the ego's evaluation of dangerous aspects of the external or internal environment. These dangerous experiences include birth, hunger, absence of the mother, a loss of love, castration, a conflict of conscience, and death. The primary anxiety of birth could never be overcome, Freud thought, and so being rid of anxiety altogether is not an option in his view. In Freud's fourth understanding, anxiety is the *reason for* the repression of emotions, not the *result of* repression.[24] Accepting the thinking that humans fundamentally seek pleasure and avoid suffering, Freud shifted his theory once again. Because people are driven by the desire for pleasure (what Freud called the "pleasure principle"), he argued, the unpleasant feelings of anxiety or rage are repressed in favor of more pleasant feelings of fitting in, being accepted, or being loved.[25]

Freud, then, identified several different forms and etiologies of affect—in particular, anxiety—but he was especially interested in what he labeled *signal anxiety*, the anxiety that results from a conflict between internal wishes or drives and constraints that come from either internalized inhibitions or external reality. A song, for example, through a chain of associations, can bring up ("trigger") strong feelings of anxiety because old affect resides within. In Freud's understanding, the fact that a song triggers anxiety or other affective experiences is evidence of its link to emotions that one has been unable to accept and process successfully. For this reason, Freud encouraged free association in his patients to facilitate their recall of past material and to release intense feelings, thus returning the patient to some level of homeostasis.[26] Freud argued that triggering affect must accompany the recall of past experiences in order for people successfully to get rid of the related affects—or to understand and work through the importance those experiences have for them.[27]

Thus, there is a double usage of affects such as anxiety in Freud's work: affect as an *expressed physical state*, the result of a chemical imbalance in the body, and affect as an *experiential state*, which can be the result of and the signal for dis-ease. Affect is both physical and psychical, and in both cases must be released. Armed with this understanding, Freud—in concert with his patients—developed the practice of catharsis as a primary way to eliminate symptoms. In the process of their work together, the practice of emotional catharsis in the practice of psychoanalysis was born.[28]

For Freud, emotions such as anxiety are "irrational" events: "intelligent and civilized adults" can together join forces and deal with the "recurring marauder" who intrudes into natural homeostasis.[29] Reclining on the couch encourages regression, fantasy, and open revelation of thoughts, imaginings, feelings, and bodily sensations.[30] Freud argued that his psychoanalytic treatments were like "the opening up of a cavity filled with pus, the scraping out of a carious region . . . to remove what is pathological."[31] Removing what was negative allowed Freud's patients to change their psychoses to ordinary neuroses, enabling them to "love and work," the supposed goals of Freud's practice and an implicit peek into his understanding of the good life.[32] At the very least, in most cases, a reduction in patients' neurotic affective symptoms was Freud's goal. In post-Freudian understandings, however, affects such as anxiety are not understood to be wholly pathological. Psychologists who followed Freud's approach and developed his theories expanded Freud's focus from anxiety to other affective experiences, broadened his assumptions that anxiety is usually generated from traumas including birth or childhood sexual experiences to a wider range of life events, and added nuance to Freud's conclusion that affect is a symptom of and contributor to pathology.

The psychodynamic models that were developed after Freud generally adopted his thinking about the nature of emotions, understanding them as both the reason for repression and the result of repression, as Freud had. But new models also began to view them as helpful signals for what has happened or what is happening in a person's intrapsychic and relational life.[33] The view developed that emotions are inevitable and are not wholly negative—and can be either functional or dysfunctional depending on how they affect people, their interpersonal relationships, and their ability to function in the world. Key to this line of inquiry is understanding the ways one's thoughts and evaluations inform one's emotions.

Emotions Are the Natural
Result of Cognitions and Appraisals:
Stanley Schachter/Jeremy Singer and Magda Arnold

Although he was committed to the physiological origins of emotion, William James had left open the possibility that beliefs or appraisals are an important part of emotions' generation when he suggested there is a gap between an event and the physiological arousal—or what James considered an emotion—that came in response to that event.[34] However, while James' theory opened the door for the role of cognitions (including beliefs or "appraisals") in the generation of emotions, James did not develop the possibilities of that gap that others found so significant. Subsequent theorists such as Stanley Schachter and Jerome Singer took special note of the lapse between event and arousal.[35] That gap, they suggested, was the place where beliefs about the event occurred, and they emphasized the role of belief in the generation of emotions.

Cognitive Precursors to Physiological Changes:
A "Two-Factor" Theory of Emotion

The "two-factor theory" of emotions incorporated both *physiological arousal* and *beliefs about* the situation in the experience of emotion. Researchers working to resolve some of the challenges to the theories of Darwin and James began to notice that beliefs play a significant role in whether and how people experience emotions. The two-factor theory was developed as researchers set out to explain why different people experience different emotions in the same situation with the same event, why different situations and events generate the same emotion in different people, and how individuals figure out the "appropriateness" of an emotional response to a situation.[36] It had been established that the sympathetic nervous system was not as wholly implicated in the generation of emotions as had been proposed by early neuroscientists.[37] Just as important as the nervous system, it became clear, is some form of cognition that is related to a person's immediate context. Researchers understood these beliefs to be the links between the arousal of the bodily changes associated with the nervous system and the experience and expression of a particular emotion. Among other things, they showed that the physiological ("visceral") changes that James had presumed to be critical to emotional experience could not account for the differences in emotions that people felt: for example, did crying indicate sadness or joy? Do flushed cheeks indicate embarrassment or a fever? Visceral changes that purportedly accompanied different emotions were essentially undifferentiated, and thus something else had to be the factor in emotions' differentiation. Cognitive theorists proposed that beliefs and interpretations are the differentiating factors between physiological arousal and emotions. In contrast to other theories that posited that emotions are the result of the events themselves in a stimulus-response sequence—that emotions are fundamentally understood as physiological processes located in the brain—cognitive theorists argued that particular emotions are elicited by the perceptions, beliefs, and evaluations of the events and situations in which people find themselves.[38]

Some of the earliest proponents of the importance of cognitions for emotions were American researchers Stanley Schachter (1922–1997 CE) and Jerome Singer (1934–2010 CE), who developed the role of beliefs and interpretations of a situation that was only nascent in James' physiological understandings of emotion. Schachter and Singer were persuaded that people's *beliefs* about a situation could explain much of what strictly physiological theories could not, and their "cognitive arousal" theory became one of the most influential theories of emotion in the twentieth century.[39]

Schachter and Singer agreed with James that physiological arousal was important in the creation of an emotion, but they were also convinced by research demonstrating that the physiological arousal was not specific to a particular emotion and could not alone account for different emotional expressions or experiences. Rather, Schachter and Singer proposed a sequential process in which a stimulus is encountered, a physiological arousal occurs, and then the individual interprets the stimulus and arousal, making meaning of both. Together the arousal and the interpretation of it determine the emotion, its expression, and the behavioral response that follows.[40] Their research included a number of studies in which they demonstrated that people use "contextual cues" to interpret their arousal, including injecting subjects with adrenaline and giving them different information about what would happen. For example, some subjects were told they could expect to feel aroused just after the injection; others were told the contents of the syringe were vitamins and would have no immediate physical effect. A representative mix of the two groups was then put into a room with a person who was acting excited and happy, while some were sent to a room where the coconspirator was behaving annoyed or angry. Schachter and Singer found that though subjects had been injected with the same amount of the same adrenaline, reports of their emotional experience varied significantly depending on what they had been told and with whom they shared the room.[41] Their research clearly demonstrated that what the subjects *believed* about what was happening to and around them significantly influenced their emotional experience. Schachter and Singer showed that emotions are formed when a cognition—any cognition—is joined to physiological arousal. And since the arousal was supposedly physiologically identical for any emotion, the true *differentia specifica* for emotions must be the result of subjects' beliefs, understandings, or interpretations of a situation—their cognitions.[42]

Schachter and Singer's two-factor theory of emotion, then, consisted of two elements: the physiological arousal, which they understood to be autonomic feedback from stimulation of the viscera or other parts of the body, and the situationally appropriate belief, which differentiated these arousals into the different experiences of emotion.[43] In their view, physiological arousal was not enough to generate experiences of emotion or to differentiate between different emotions, and they proposed the formula that physiological arousal plus belief leads to an emotion.[44] In addition, Schachter and Singer suggested there are "evaluative needs" that are aroused along with the physiological arousals, and these needs, described as "the need to explain one's bodily state" would lead to the interpretation of the event and the experienced emotion.[45] The implication of the two-factor theory is that individuals' ability to interpret a situation and the stimulus they are experiencing allows for a more flexible and adequate response by that person in that context. Furthermore, because survival is most ensured when the chosen reaction to a stimulus is the one that allows the individual to meet her most salient needs, such as safety, the two-factor theory enhanced the understanding of evolution's wisdom in emotional responses.

In Schachter and Singer's view, beliefs "label" the physiological arousal one is experiencing.[46] That is, subjects had one response to a stimulus when they believed all was well because the researchers seemed happy, but subjects had very different responses to stimuli when the researchers seemed angry. It is reasonable to imagine that, had their theory been sufficient, controlling one's beliefs would be enough to control one's emotions. However, this did not always bear out in subsequent tests. Schachter and Singer had missed another important element of emotions: appraisals. Appraisals have an element of evaluation, or *assessment of value*, an element that did not play a prominent role in Schachter's and Singer's theory. Early nineteenth-century psychologist Magda Arnold, however, demonstrated the roles appraisals play in affective experiences.

Emotions Are the Result of Appraisals: Magda Arnold

Although the two-factor theory would come under heavy criticism in the latter part of the twentieth century, it heavily influenced researchers who followed in their path. Hungarian-American researcher and psychologist Magda Arnold (1903–2002 CE)[47] developed the first full-blown appraisal theory, contributing enormously to the understanding of emotions and their place in flourishing. Arnold agreed that a belief occurs very early in the genesis of an emotion, but she proposed that an appraisal was *also* required.[48] In Arnold's model, a stimulus (or arousal) occurs, and almost immediately—and often unconsciously—the person appraises the situation, event, or arousal stimulus as *good or bad* in relation to his or her needs, goals, or values. That is, an individual not only forms a *belief* about a stimulus as Schachter and Singer proposed, but also assesses the *value* of that stimulus for well-being. Although the appraisal is usually unconscious—as are the beliefs—the person experiences the combined stimulus plus appraisal as an emotion (stimulus + beliefs + appraisal of value + physiological response = emotion).[49] For Arnold, too, the physiological response follows the stimulus and cognitions about it. She wrote, "in emotions proper (as distinguished from the desire that accompanies instinctual actions) the physiological changes follow upon perception and appraisal instead of preceding them."[50] The action tendency follows so that: "An object or situation is perceived, appraised, and liked or disliked; and . . . this liking or disliking arouses a tendency to approach or withdraw, to deal with this thing in some particular way."[51]

Arnold continued the trajectory of Darwin's and James' thinking, though she turned James' order of events leading to an emotion on its head in favor of Darwin's model. Arnold proposed that what initiated the physiological changes, emotions, feelings, expressions, and behaviors accompanying each emotion was the judgment about whether an event or situation was positive or not—that is, for example, whether it is threatening or not. Thus, Arnold reversed the order of the relationship between thoughts and physiological changes: whereas James had proposed that physiological changes come first and one's interpretations of them follow, Arnold argued that interpretations about a situation precede the physiological responses.[52]

Although she considered herself working in the same trajectory as Darwin and James, Arnold was an ardent critic of both, finding their theories inadequate for explaining the complex physiological and psychological interplay that produces an emotion in a particular person in a particular situation. She was especially critical of James' idea that bodily changes equal emotion and argued that his theory does not address the question of what initiates the physical changes in the first place.[53] Arnold argued that it was insufficient to say that simple "associations" with stimuli produced particular emotions (as James had suggested),[54] and she set out to develop a more adequate theory of emotion that could take into account both the physical changes and the interpretations of the relative *value* to a person of the stimulus or event. She, too, concluded that emotions are evolved events that contribute to the survival and well-being of an individual and a species, though her understanding went beyond Darwin's strict focus on expressions.[55]

Arnold defined emotion as "the felt tendency toward anything intuitively appraised as good (beneficial), or away from anything intuitively appraised as bad (harmful)."[56] She asserted that the attraction or aversion to a stimulus is accompanied by a pattern of physiological changes organized toward approach or withdrawal and that the patterns differ for different emotions.[57] Arnold agreed with James' commitment to the idea that bodily changes in a situation are important to the experience of emotion. And, like Darwin, she believed that emotions serve to enhance the possibilities for survival of the organism. In fact, Arnold argued, emotions can be considered "impulses to action," or "readiness to respond to the environment in a particular way": for example, fear leads to the desire to fight or to flee.[58] Similarly, she was convinced that each emotion has its own pattern of physiological activity, as earlier researchers had proposed; she was convinced these differences support survival. Arnold wrote, "since different emotions urge us to different actions, and the physiological symptoms are relieved when we give in to this urge, we might expect that the physiological changes, taken by and large, will be as different as are the emotions, and the physical sensations we feel are different in different emotions."[59] Different physiological responses to stimuli (e.g., running from a bear or fighting a weaker member of the group for territory) supported the overall survival and other salient goals of an organism, she believed.

A core element of Arnold's theory extended James' understanding of the possible perceptions of a bear as a bear (that is, something that looks threatening), or Darwin's "associations" of past experiences with a bear (that is, the fright from an actual encounter with a bear in the past informed the desire for survival in this instance). She argued that both Darwin's and James' use of words such as *perception* and *associa-tion* conceals the fact that one's perceptions or associations cannot be separated from evaluations about "the bear's *intentions* towards me or mine towards him."[60] Arnold suggested that "mere perception" is differ-ent from "emotional perception" in the way in which the latter "always involves a judgment of how the object of perception affects one person-ally."[61] As Arnold put it,

> To perceive or apprehend something means that I know what it is like
> as a thing, apart from any effect on me. To like or dislike it [that is,
> to perceive it emotionally] means that I know it not only objectively,
> as it is apart from me, but also that I estimate its relation to me, that
> I *appraise* it as desirable or undesirable, valuable or harmful to me, so
> that I am drawn toward it or repelled by it.[62]

This appraisal, as Arnold came to call it, is at the heart of every emotion: it is "the direct, immediate sense judgment of weal or woe."[63] Without appraisal of something's effect on a person and how it will affect one's situation, there can be no emotion. Arnold argued that to arouse an emotion, an object must be appraised as affecting one personally, as an individual, out of one's own particular experience and aims.[64] She wrote, "If I see an apple, I know that it is an apple of a particular kind and taste. This knowledge need not touch me personally in any way. But if the apple is of my favorite kind and I am in a part of the world where it does not grow and cannot be bought, I may want it with a real emo-tional craving."[65] What makes seeing an apple an *emotional* experience rather than a mere fact is whether and what kind of personal choice one makes about the apple in relation to oneself. That appraisal of value helps explain why a green apple might arouse desire to eat it in one person but not in another.[66] The knowledge about which fruits one prefers—or which fruits are edible and which are toxic—supports survival and emotional well-being.

For Arnold, then, the more adequate understanding of the events that generate all experiences of emotion is better expressed thus: stimulus + belief/perception + appraisal + physiological arousal = emotion.[67] She often referred to appraisals as *sense judgments* to indicate their "'direct, immediate, nonreflective, nonintellectual, [and] automatic' nature."[68] With this she emphasized her view that while appraisals are judgments about the meaning of a situation, they are not necessarily intellectual or *rational* judgments; that is, they are not *mere* cognitions. They cannot be conscious, intellectual judgments, she reasoned, in part because of the speed with which individuals make them.

This theory, then, imagines emotions as part of a complex, circular feedback system that engages "stimulating events"—whether external or internal, such as dreams—which act as primary triggers that begin the process of emotion.[69] However, the events need to be *interpreted* and be *meaningful* for them to have an effect on the individual.[70] Sometimes the interpretation is obvious; occasionally it is less so.[71]

Arnold's legacy in the understanding of emotion casts a long shadow. Her research inaugurated decades of interest in the relationship between emotions and cognitions and in the difference between beliefs and appraisals. Generations of scholars after Arnold spent many hours in the lab trying to confirm or dispute her conclusions.[72] Schachter's/Singer's and Arnold's research was a serious blow to strict physiological understandings of the processes that generate emotions. However, as significant as it was, their assumptions that beliefs and appraisals are sufficient for emotion are now considered flawed.[73] (For example, subsequent research—and common sense—has shown that people use "far more" sources of information in generating their emotional explanations than their analyses of beliefs and appraisals suggested).[74] Nevertheless, Schachter/Singer's and Arnold's work is enormously significant, and their focus on the evaluative components of emotions led to evolutionary psychologists' contention that the content of emotions is the evaluation about what is pleasant or unpleasant, or supportive or limiting of one's goals (e.g., survival), as Arnold seemed to suggest, but what would also increase one's—and one's species-survival, or even well-being, to reintroduce a more complex term. The appraisal of a situation's good or harm, based on one's goals and values, remained a prominent theme in the study and uses of emotion—especially among evolutionary psychologists—and the idea that beliefs and appraisals are a significant part of emotions is now well accepted.[75]

Emotions Are Important Indicators
of Need: Sandor Rado

Darwin had presented a functional view of emotions in his book *The Expressions* (1872), which was widely read by scientists. In fact, Darwin's theory that "emotional" expressions had evolved to support individuals' and species' survival was the dominant view for almost a century, and subsequent work has refined and developed his thinking.[76] Nevertheless, Darwin's ideas were largely ignored by psychologists until a decade after World War II, when evolutionary thinking gained more influence in emotions scholarship. James had followed Darwin closely (though, as noted, James deviated from Darwin significantly), Schachter/Singer and Arnold developed what was nascent in both, and other well-known scientists followed. In 1963, for example, early neuroscientist Paul MacLean concluded that emotions direct an organism's behavior with respect to the two basic life principles of self-preservation and the preservation of the species.[77] He argued that emotions have biological functions and that these functions are related to the survival of the individual as well as survival of the group of which the individual is a part.[78]

Evolutionary psychologists took MacLean's theory of the tripartite brain seriously and developed a new psychological theory of emotions that supported these assumptions: that to survive—as individuals, as species, and as phyla—all organisms need to perform certain life-sustaining functions, and that this is as true of the lowest organisms such as amoebae as it is of the most complex organisms, commonly understood to be humans.[79]

Adaptive behaviors found in all individuals, species, and phyla include, evolutionary psychologists argue, ingestive behavior (eating), shelter seeking and home building, fight-or-flight behaviors to avoid injury, sexual behaviors (for both reproduction and for relationship maintenance),[80] care-soliciting behaviors (usually from young animals toward mother), caregiving behaviors (usually from adults to young), excretory behaviors to expel toxins and waste, imitative behaviors for learning and bonding purposes, and exploratory behaviors and mimicking capacities, both of which are significant in learning.[81] However, these are carried out in different ways by different classes of organisms because each organism has certain capacities but not others, and the environments in which organisms find themselves create particular functional challenges for survival. For example, organisms must be able to distinguish between potential mate and potential enemy *for them*, and prey and predator *for them*, and take in information about the beneficial and detrimental aspects of their immediate context *for their own survival*.[82] Evolutionary psychologists, then, argue that organisms' simplest and most common emotional behaviors include automatic mechanisms to maintain life processes such as immune responses and basic reflexes, as well as metabolic regulation to maintain hormone and other chemical imbalances.[83] In addition, however, they focus on emotions' function in particular contexts that are significant to the organism.

Evolutionary psychologists generally assume that emotions exist in all animals and that the various forms of expressions of emotions in different animal groups—including humans—reflect the operation of evolutionary forces acting on the same fundamental survival mechanisms. However, the levels of emotion and response vary by organism and evolved to support the survival and functioning required by each in its own context.[84] While all of the mechanisms required to maintain homeostasis—such as the urge to eat and, eventually, the urge to copulate—are present at birth, more-complex systems require learning to engage them in more-complex organisms.

A psychoevolutionary view of emotions, then, holds the conviction that emotions are closely related to drives or motives in even simple organisms such as amoebae, and it suggests that emotions and their expression are especially important in more-complex organisms such as mammals.[85] Even the very young experience the need or drive for nurturance, safety, power, curiosity, control, and autonomy—and their emotions are the methods by which such drives are satisfied.[86] Emotions as understood by evolutionary psychologists, then, are complex chains of events that involve stabilizing positive and negative feedback loops that attempt to produce some level of physiological homeostasis and increase the likelihood of survival. This chain of events includes the cognitive elements in emotion, appraisals in relation to value to an organism's well-being, as well as the impulses to action and the inhibiting forces that operate to control action.

Hungarian-American psychoanalyst Sandor Rado (1890–1972 CE), for example, developed a multilevel theory of emotion based on these evolutionary needs.[87] Rado defined *emotion* as the "preparatory signal that prepares the organism for emergency behavior, the goal being to restore the organism to safety."[88] Rado hypothesized that there are four psychological levels of control that organisms at various levels of evolutionary development can exercise to maximize their survival. These four represent increasing levels of complexity in the pursuit of pleasure and avoidance of pain, the needs to be met, and goals and motives an organism pursues.[89]

Rado hypothesized that the first, the *hedonic* level, refers simply to the effects of pleasure and pain in organisms and selecting forms of behavior. He argued that this primitive mode of control is present in all organisms, even the very lowest, such as amoebae. The dynamics of pleasure and pain work in concert to ensure getting needs met and thus to support survival: the sense of pleasure leads to "incorporation or ingestive" behaviors—or eating and drinking. For example, they direct amoebae toward food sources and away from toxic ones. In humans, it might go something like: "Apples taste good, so I eat them." Pleasurable or life-sustaining activities lead to the repetition of those activities: an amoeba is attracted to foods that help it survive, and a human being might think, "Eating apples also makes me feel good, both because I know like them and also because I know it increases my physical health." The obverse is also true: a behavior that results in discomfort and pain leads to "riddance behavior," or avoidance of toxins—for example, "Eating rotten eggs makes one sick, so it is wise not to bite into them." Unpleasant stimuli—such as a full bladder—also help in the elimination of waste, as in urination. The hedonic level of control, then, moves organisms toward sources of pleasure and away from what causes pain.[90]

The second level of control, what Rado called the *brute-emotional level*, is present in organisms that have evolved higher central nervous systems that can *process* and *respond* to events in their environments—both internal and external—with more complexity. Newly evolved capacities to organize and select patterns of behavior result in simple emotions such as fear, rage, love, and grief (research demonstrates higher mammals such as elephants and whales exhibit behaviors that can be interpreted as emotions such as grief, and they engage in behaviors that can be interpreted as mourning).[91] In the same ways pleasure and pain move an organism toward or away from stimuli in the environment, Rado proposed, these emotions provide a more controlled way to do the same thing. For example, anger organizes patterns of combat or attack, and grief signals the desire for reconnection with the lost loved one. At this level, emotions also create the possibility of anticipating future events, because an organism that has experienced a certain stimulation previously can evaluate or appraise an event as threatening or against one's best interests and may fearfully run away or angrily attack.

Rado's third level of response developed with the increased complexity of the brain. At this level of control, *emotions are more reflective and less reactive* than basic reactions such as fight or flight. In addition, emotions at this level are more mixed. In other words, with this third level of emotional capacity, an organism can have a variety of emotions about a particular situation and can also consider a variety of responses; thus, appraisals factor more significantly into responses. For example, a hungry feral kitten being offered a dish of milk by an eager youngster will evaluate whether to let fear of a strange human or the need for food and affection take over. Rado argued that at this level "derivative" and more-nuanced emotions such as apprehension, annoyance, jealousy, and envy begin to appear. With increasing social complexities, this added nuance becomes more important. For example, in humans the goal of managing oneself and others through rules or manipulation replaces the goal of destruction associated with anger. And it is at this level, Rado asserts, that defense mechanisms such as repression and splitting begin as people seek to minimize the often unpleasant effects of feelings.[92]

Rado's fourth level of control and regulation of action is the *unemotional thought* level, which he argued developed in higher organisms that could master events by rational, intellectual means alone, possible only in organisms that possess a neocortex. Humans have the largest neocortex relative to brain size among mammals.[93] Having rational, intellectual means—some might say, echoing Plato and Augustine, one's reason and will—is sometimes successful for controlling one's emotions, but often it is not. Thus, a person who experiences pain resulting in fear, rage, or other "emergency" emotions will try to eliminate the stimulus with behaviors such as withdrawal (e.g., avoidance or denial of emotions, or low affect), submission (e.g., depression), combat (e.g., anxiety or rage), or distraction (e.g., emotional eating or alcohol/drug abuse).[94] These emergency reactions often do not work to address the *real* need or needs and consequently are enacted over time in futile efforts, creating sometimes extreme, rigid styles of behavior that are fundamentally an overreaction and lead to disordered behaviors.[95]

Rado's research on emotions, then, demonstrates the ways emotions support organisms' survival. From this perspective, emotions are conceived as basic adaptive patterns that can be identified at all phylogenetic levels. These adaptive patterns have "functionally equivalent" forms through all phylogenetic levels.[96] Emotions are defined in this theory as communication and behavioral processes that serve individual and genetic survival.[97] The scientists and psychologists introduced thus far have each contributed insights that the psychological construction theory of emotions (considered the "gold standard") supports.[98] Darwin was correct as far as he took his research: "emotional" displays act as signals of intentions of future action that function to influence the interpersonal relations of the interacting individuals. By appropriate reactions to emergency events in the environment—for example, by fight or flight—individuals can increase their chances of survival. James was also correct, in that emotions are physiological events which are then interpreted as "feelings". Schachter and Singer offered insight into ways beliefs function in the generation of emotions, and Arnold deepened understanding of the ways one's appraisals (considerations of value) inform emotional responses. In different ways, and with different complexities, then, emotions are factors in organisms' survival, from the simplest amoebae to complex mammals.[99]

Psychoevolutionary theories of emotion in particular relate the simple, reactive emotional functions of amoebae to those of more-complex emotions of whales and humans, asserting that emotions are "relevant to all living organisms and have highly adaptive purposes, in particular to communicate information and intentions from one individual to another, regulate social interactions, and increase the survival in the face of life's adversities."[100] As such, emotions are considered to have universal relevance. For complex mammals, emotions' relevance is more complicated than it is for amoebae, of course: they must negotiate social situations with other complex beings. Indeed, especially for complex mammals such as apes and humans, creating and maintaining the attachments to caregivers is crucial. Researchers studying ape and human attachments see emotions as *strategies for negotiating interpersonal relationships*. Implied in this view is the idea that attachments to caregivers and others in the group are required for survival.

The Role of Attachment in Survival

Attachment theorists' argument goes that because human and ape infants are notoriously vulnerable to the dangers inherent in their environment and take a long time to mature relative to, say, foals or puppies, newborn apes and humans have various signals, communication patterns, and behaviors to influence the actions of caretakers and increase their own survival. Evolutionary psychologist Robert Plutchik put it this way:

> Because the problems of survival exist from the moment of birth, certain mechanisms must exist both in the child and the caretaker to help ensure survival. If young infants had to wait until they learned how to attract their parents' attention and support, and if the parents had to learn how to provide it, the chances of species survival would be small. Communication patterns have to work the first time they are used. From this viewpoint, emotions may be thought of in part as communication signals by the infant to caretakers that help increase the chances of survival.[101]

Emotions and their expressions, in this view, are critical for the survival of the young of complex mammals.[102] But the need for interpersonal connection and care is not limited to infants: this interpersonal dynamic continues through life, since all relationships are built on constant and mutual interplay "in order for positive affect to be maximized and negative affect minimized" in social situations.[103] For example, love and respect maintain good relationships, and anger prevents exploitation, whereas "anxiety and guilt . . . motivate people to fulfill their commitments, to abide by the social contract, and to stay loyal to their friends."[104] In fact, "reasonably correct" interpretations of other people are critical to successful adaptations.[105] This is because social interactions affect the survival of individuals, species, and, ultimately, phyla. The emotional indications of needs and goals and the behaviors of a person, then, must be recognized and related to the goals and behaviors of others and in the context of their social environment.[106] Psychological theorists and practitioners further developed understanding of emotions and practices related to people's feelings, assuming that feelings (that is, the conscious awareness of and reflections on emotions) are windows into a person's thoughts or beliefs, values, motivations, and deepest needs. As such, emotions came to be valued as signs, sources, and remedies of pathologies, indicating when physical, emotional, and relational needs have not been met, and providing the tools for diagnosis and healing.[107]

It was theorists and clinicians such as Joseph Sandler and Carl Rogers who moved beyond Freud's view of affect as the result of symptoms and/or causes of repression to the view of relationships as the primary motivator and organizer of human experience in psychoanalytic thinking, and emotions as the signal for when people's relationships provided what they needed and when they did not.[108] Self-psychologist Heinz

Kohut (1913–1981 CE) and object-relations theorist D. W. Winnicott (1896–1971 CE) also highly valued affect and focused on feelings as a primary tool in curative, or "restorative," processes.[109] Whereas Freud's psychoanalytic theory emphasized analysis and redirection or working through of affective experience, Rogers and many clinicians who came after him have emphasized the *relationship* between therapist and client as critical to the process of healing. So-called "relational theorists"—such as Kohut, Winnicott, Otto Kernberg, John Bowlby, and those who followed them, including contemporary psychoanalytic thinker Peter Fonagy—focused on the "corrective emotional experience," the importance of empathy for establishing the therapeutic alliance, and the need for empathy and relationship as a primary motivator for an individual's development and the achievement of a cohesive self.[110] In a newly developing view in the second half of twentieth century, then, emotions were understood to serve as an effective organizing structure for understanding the self because emotions bring together complex patterns of thinking, appraising (evaluating), and behavior.[111] These thinkers argued that the therapist's function is to help clients recognize and clarify what emotions they are feeling. In a notable return to people's *experience* of emotions, then, humanistic and relational psychologies helped bring the focus of emotion in people's lives back to the forefront.

Emotions Are Useful Tools for Understanding and Healing: Humanistic and Relational Psychologies

Psychologists and clinical practitioners, particularly in the second half of the twentieth century, created something of a meld of the four scientific perspectives presented here, although often intuitively and from their own clinical experience and not because they read Darwin or Arnold (although some did: as noted previously, Sigmund Freud read the work of Charles Darwin), but because of their own clinical observations and popular assumptions. Psychologists generally accepted the prevailing views as correct. They accepted Darwin's and evolutionary psychologists' thinking that emotions are evolutionary inheritances designed to enhance the survival of organisms. They seemed to accept that emotions are the result of beliefs and appraisals, as Schachter and Singer and Arnold had proposed, and they adopted Rado's view that emotions are indicators of need, though they would add nuance to his understanding. Against the empiricists' concern that emotions were too subjective to be studied in any meaningful way, psychoanalysts and clinical psychologists' observations and subsequent wisdom about emotional experience and meaning took hold in the middle of the twentieth century. For psychologists, emotions do not just support surviving but also well-being—which also includes psychological and relational health.[112] Attending to emotions (or more accurately, feelings—the conscious reflections on emotions) became the primary focus of their work.

For example, although clinician Carl Rogers (1902–1987 CE) did not have a well-developed academic theory of emotions per se, it can be argued that his valuation of emotions has informed contemporary psychotherapy as deeply as has Freud's. Rogers made emotions an important focus of treatment. In a statement that sums up his approach, Rogers wrote, "Experience [as known through feelings] is, for me, the highest authority. The touchstone of validity is my own experience. No other person's ideas, and none of my own ideas, are as authoritative as my experience. It is to experience that I must return again and again, to discover a closer approximation of truth as it is in the process of becoming in me."[113] Effective therapies begin with a certain "warmth of relationship" between counselor and counselee and a genuine interest on the part of the therapist in the client's inner world.[114] In a successful therapeutic alliance, the client is free to see himself without defensiveness, and gradually to recognize and admit his "real" self with its (normal) childish patterns, its (expected) aggressive feelings, and ambivalences, as well as its mature impulses, and rationalized exterior.[115] Rogers' understanding of emotion was primarily based on anecdotal reflections and his clinical observations: through his therapeutic commitment to what he called *experience near* encounters with people, Rogers developed a view that, while not theoretically detailed, was nevertheless phenomenologically and therapeutically sophisticated.[116] He understood the *relationship* between the clinician and client to be the primary mode of healing.

As the work of humanistic psychologists such as Rogers developed and gained popularity, the view of emotions as dysfunctional or even pathological waned. Followers of Rogers began to argue for dysfunction as arising from the *suppression* of the healthy emotion, from lack of awareness of positive or growth-promoting experience.[117] In this view, disowning emotion—and difficulty in tolerating painful but "necessary" emotions—is what leads to disease. Indeed, it is more common now for contemporary clinicians—especially those working out of the psychodynamic psychotherapeutic tradition—to see emotions as playing a healthy role in people's lives if they are experienced, understood, accepted, and used as reliable guides. In large part this is because of emotions' role in creating and sustaining healthy attachments to others. Following this vein, attachment theorists such as Bowlby and relational psychologists such as Kohut and Winnicott understood positive interpersonal attachments as one of the fundamental requirements in the development of a healthy self.[118] As a consequence, their view of emotions gave rise to the importance of the *interpretation* of the patient's ability to explore emotions as they arise in the context of relationship with the therapist. The therapeutic relationship reveals much about the patient's interpersonal and intrapsychic dynamics, which are often the source of distress that began in the dynamic of early childhood relationships.[119] One of the core characteristics of the work of interpersonal theorists and clinicians is that they seek to help people become better attuned to their interpersonal needs and to express them in a spontaneous fashion while also building relationships that can provide "corrective emotional experience."[120] In this view, emotions both provide insight into intrapsychic and interpersonal deficits and also are a tool for healing.

In relational therapies, then, attending to the conscious affective experience of patients (their "feelings") is the best way to understand the challenges they are facing. Treatment typically focuses on exploring a client's subjective experiences and meanings, thus enabling the clinician to enter into the client's relational and feeling world.[121] In other words, fully experiencing affective responses in the context of a therapeutic relationship is seen as a "prerequisite for correcting distortions of the object world."[122] Like Rogers, Kohut believed that the therapist should take a nurturing role, emphasizing active and open listening and providing acceptance, understanding—especially of the client's feelings—and explanations or interpretations to facilitate the unfolding of the client's subjective world.[123]

These psychotherapeutic approaches assume, though they do not always articulate, that beliefs and evaluations have something to do with the feelings a client has: Freud argued that one's experiences of early childhood were recorded in the recesses of subconscious memory and could be accessed by attending to one's feelings. Relational psychologists such as Kohut attended to the feelings that arose particularly in relationship to the clinician—as signals of the past—as well as the beliefs and values those feelings indicated. In these clinical models, the goal is to increase clients' awareness of their emotions and feelings so that it is available as orienting information to help them deal with their environment and the challenges they are facing.[124] Psychopathology often arises when emotions and feelings are not experienced, identified, expressed, and understood. As one clinician puts it, "It is that inability to know their feelings (to be aware of and use the information of emotions) integrated with ideas as guidance that puts people in trouble with themselves."[125] Thus, psychotherapeutic practitioners accept much of what came from scientists' and psychologists' studies of emotions: they typically accepted that beliefs, appraisals, needs, values, and goals are implicated in a person's feelings and that those should be explored in the process of treatment.

Conclusion

When philosophers' and theologians' interest in emotions waned at the end of the nineteenth century, animal biologists, psychologists, and other scientists took up the task of analyzing and theorizing emotions and their place in human life. Although early examinations such as Freud's assumed emotions to be largely pathological, perspectives shifted under the influence of Darwin's evolutionary thinking and its development toward the middle of the twentieth century. Scholars asserted that emotions have to do with survival of individuals, species, and phyla: emotions are adaptations for survival of both individuals and collectives. In the natural-scientific schools, certain assumptions perdure—including the belief that emotions have a genetic base, are evolutionarily adaptive, are universal, and because they have a communicative function, are universally recognizable and interpretable. Across various schools of psychology, these assumptions were largely accepted, but the goal is usually a more nuanced (if unarticulated) one of well-being rather than mere survival. Together these theories suggest that especially in complex organisms, emotions involve a complex interplay of beliefs, appraisals, values, impulses to action, and need- and goal-directed behaviors. Understood this way, emotions are attempts by individuals to navigate their personal and social environments. Although theirs is a discrete field that does not seem to engage psychological theory, social theorists enriched the idea that emotions have social, relational functions, adding to the mix cultural and political qualities of emotions. What social theorists would add is that emotions are geared to survival *in a particular social and cultural context*, rather than being universal in their experience or expression.

An adequate understanding of emotions and their relationship to human flourishing will need to account both for the fact that emotions are unconscious, and that they communicate something about people's past and present experience without assuming that all relevant material is sexual and traumatic. An adequate understanding of emotions' function will also need to understand the ways emotions are often related to what a person is imagining for their future. An adequate theory of emotions will recognize that emotions indicate needs and values and that they also motivate behaviors, without assuming that all values are worthy and all desires must be met. An adequate understanding of emotion will also need to account for how emotions can be the causes and signs—as well as remedies—of distress and disease. An adequate understanding of emotions, then, will need to recognize the ways emotions can mislead and deceive, that they can be difficult to access, and that to explore them requires close and intentional examination. An adequate understanding of emotions will recognize that emotions bind people to one another without assuming these relationships are primarily familial or intimate. In other words, an adequate understanding of emotion will need to account for the ways they are intrapsychic, interpersonal, and also sociocultural. Finally, an adequate understanding of emotions and their relation to human flourishing will need to address more fully than psychologies usually do their cultural origins and their wider social functions—for good and for ill.

5

Emotions as Relational and Sociocultural Artifacts

Challenges to Natural Scientific Understandings

Introduction

Natural scientists' influence on the study of emotions reached its peak in the early twentieth century, and until the last third of that century, scientists' work on emotions was largely ignored or dismissed, in part because interest in emotions as a subject of scholarly study waned more generally, but also because emotions are more complex than natural scientists had proposed, and their theories did not satisfy those who studied emotions from different perspectives. Emotions scholarship was moving in different directions, and in the middle of the twentieth century, psychologists were the ones who attended to emotions and their function in human life most closely. When interest in emotions began to gain momentum again in the 1970s by scholars in fields such as anthropology, history, and sociology, increased attention was paid to cultural differences in emotional *expression* as well as emotional *experience*. These emotions researchers shared the conviction that emotions are not a universal and generalizable category, common to all people everywhere and in the same ways, as natural scientists and even some psychologists had assumed.

Natural scientific research on emotions had led to the conclusion that emotions are universal (in the sense of being part of the repertoire of all living things) and that there are some basic, fundamental emotions that help individual organisms and their species survive. First, in natural scientists' view, emotions communicate possibilities of danger or threat, and they lead an organism to what is pleasurable (and thus likely life supporting) and away from what is toxic or dangerous (and thus, life diminishing or limiting). Second, emotions motivate an individual to accomplish important goals: from the simple, such as obtaining food, to the more complex, such as earning a degree. Third, emotions enable bonding and facilitate social interactions critical to survival. Finally, emotions can function as guides for one's own behavior, and they also influence the behavior of others. But psychologist Sandor Rado had argued that emotions are geared to organisms' survival *in their particular context*, even if he did not explore this idea much beyond the goal of physical survival. Historians and sociologists did explore it, however (although there is no evidence that their work was explicitly informed by that of Rado or other evolutionary psychologists): they demonstrated the ways emotions are informed by historical contexts and help meet needs beyond physical survival. Where natural scientists assumed a set of basic emotions (fear, surprise, happiness, sadness, disgust, and anger) that exist in all people in all cultures, the results of anthropological, cultural, and historical studies showed much more variation than that.

Paying attention to the ways emotions vary by historical period, historians, for example, demonstrated a burgeoning new emotional life among the peasantry in France which led to the French Revolution,[1] and how the rise of manners and class hierarchies in deeply class-conscious Europe were enforced by the emotional regimes of that time and region.[2] Others traced the emergence and the retreat of emotional trends that have significantly shaped history itself, such as "sentimentalism" or the "cult of sensibility"—a "loosely organized set of impulses" that played an influential role in "the rise of cultural currents as diverse as Methodism, antislavery agitation, the rise of the novel, . . . and the birth of Romanticism."[3]

Whereas natural scientists studying emotions were primarily interested in emotions' role in physical survival, social historians and theorists have focused on the *social origins and functions* of emotions, especially the adaptive capacities that emotions allow within interpersonal relationships, social groups, and political environments that enhance both individuals' and groups' survival. Not unlike Aristotle, contemporary social theorists of emotion have argued that emotions have much to do with the establishment of the collective, polis, or state. How communities form, what keeps them together, the beliefs and norms people develop and adopt, and the behaviors they display all have to do with emotions and their expression (or lack thereof). And, social theorists of emotion argue, these adaptations are both learned from and contribute to the social, cultural, institutional, and political dynamics of one's contexts. It could be argued, then, that social theorists of emotions understand—at least implicitly—that emotions function to enable the social survival of individuals.

However, emotions are also leveraged to *benefit sociocultural systems* rather than the people in them, and people are taught to manage their emotions under pressure from their wider contexts. Perhaps this is part of the reason emotions often make people uncomfortable, and they dismiss people who express their feelings, for example, by remarking "she is so emotional!"[4] With this kind of censure, people are taught not to feel or express certain things. Think, for example, of the familiar admonishment that "big boys don't cry," directed at guiding young males to manage their emotions in particular ways.[5] There are other means of emotional training as well: emotions such as fear and anxiety are powerful tools for encouraging certain kinds of behaviors and discouraging others. Parents use these emotions to manage emotions and behaviors in their children ("if you want something to cry about, I'll give it to you"), but emotions can be used as cultural tools too. For example, the differences between shame-based cultures and guilt-based cultures have been the subject of much interpretation. Emotions are powerful bonding agents, and the need to bond is a fundamental human need. For this reason, emotions can be used as powerful tools for control.

Emotions Function for Social Survival

Emotions tie people together into groups. Moving together to a shared beat—and the deep feelings it evokes—has been a powerful force in holding human groups together and enabling both people and communities to survive. From the records of ancient peoples to the latest findings of the life sciences, there is evidence that collective, coordinated rhythmic movement (or what historian William McNeill calls "keeping together in time") has played a profound role in creating and sustaining human life.[6] From festival village dances to the morning exercises of Japanese factory workers, from the ecstatic dances led by shamans to the drill of military formation, coordinating to a common beat keeps people and groups alive. To understand this phenomenon, it helps to understand the fellow-feeling McNeill calls "muscular bonding."[7] Muscular bonding is the embodied and emotional effect of keeping together in time; it is a "sense that the group is one," McNeill suggests.[8] This muscular and emotional bonding endows members with a capacity for cooperation, it makes collective tasks far more efficient, and it increases individuals' investment in and commitments to one another. Whether ambushing a deer in the hunt, attacking an enemy in battle, or sustaining communities of enslaved peoples through song, the groups who have stalked or drilled or sung and danced together are more likely to be successful than those who are fragmented, whose individual members are isolated and on their own. The point is that humans need to keep together and march to a shared beat in order to survive and that they depend on emotions to band together and stay together.

This thinking is supported by the earliest dependence of infants on caregivers for their survival. Attachment and human development theorists have argued that human infants' physiologies are "open loop" feedback systems, dependent on caregivers' bodies in ways not previously understood.[9] Their research suggests that in utero the sound of the mother's heartbeat helps regulate the electromagnetic pulses of the infant's heart, training it, in effect, to pulse with the rhythm that will sustain its life. Babies' physiologies do not mature enough to regulate themselves dependably until they are several months old, and they depend quite literally on the proximity of caregivers to stay alive after birth. One example of this is that the very young need to hear the rhythm of another's heartbeat to learn to beat their own.[10] Babies learn to call caregivers by crying and will put a great deal of effort into keeping caregivers close. Thus, babies use emotional expressions to manage their relationships with others and to call attention to their needs. While critical for babies, the need for the proximity of others' bodies is a lifelong need. Even insects such as bees and ants know this.[11] But the proximity of others in groups has other implications for emotions as well: emotions are *generated* both *in* and *by* groups, as early sociologists observed.

For example, sociologist Emil Durkheim explored the ways emotions both generate and are generated by collective practices and ritual in the creation of communities. Durkheim noted that rituals that generate particular emotions in individuals magnify and intensify the feelings shared by the participants practicing the performance.[12] For Durkheim, strong emotions lie at the root of all life and are created by and create participation in group activities; emotions arise most often not in the solitude of the human heart, but in collectives—especially ritualized (e.g., religious)—gatherings.

Durkheim suggested that feelings generated by the collective process are "amplified" by being echoed by others and create a feedback loop that builds to a crescendo. One of Durkheim's "most enduring" contributions is that "emotion, regularly re-enacted, and recalled in between times, forms the basis of social solidarity."[13] The joint participation in religious ritual, then, creates a sense of solidarity that plays a crucial role in the establishment of sociocultural worlds. The relationship between people, their social contexts, and emotion is seen clearly in this interactive dynamic because social ritual literally brings people together by generating and enhancing emotion, evoking an overarching sentiment that unites those who share the emotion, and binding the group together. In the account Durkheim gives, emotions are essentially social, just as society is essentially emotional.[14] These are positive uses of emotions in groups that increase the likelihood of survival for groups and their members. Staying together matters.

There are also more insidious social uses of emotions—for example, to create and support economies. Uses of emotion for economic gain become obvious when one notices the ubiquitous advertising, for example, that appeals to fear, love, and envy. In developed countries, neoliberalism[15] capitalizes on individuals' sense of achievement and entitlement and convinces people that one of the most personal acts in which they can engage is consumption; indeed, consuming—shopping and eating, for example—is often promoted and used as a way to ameliorate anxiety and to promote the admiration and envy of others. These basic survival behaviors can take on intense emotional resonance in one's social milieu.[16]

Emotions, then, are used as tools in consumer-driven economies that depend on sales staff to push a company's wares. Companies seek to control their employees' emotional lives as part of the goal to create "emotionally intelligent" workforces and increase customer satisfaction and loyalty.[17] Thus, people's emotions have become part of the economy.[18] Concern about the uses of emotion for social control contributes, no doubt, to cultural ambivalence about emotions in Western cultures. Emotions, it seems, have social and political functions, and these are not always positive.

From the outset, social theorists of emotion have resisted the understanding of emotions as innate, basic, and universally shared, arguing instead that emotions and people's experience of them are socially derived and meaningful only in context. While they understand emotions as fundamental to human life, social theorists' interest in them has more to do with the ways they facilitate functioning in particular social groups, institutions, and cultures. This interest is fueled by research on the variability of emotions—and their expression—in different historical periods and in diverse contexts.

Emotions Are Generated within Social and Cultural Milieus

Emotions Are Culturally and Historically Variable

Natural scientists posited that emotions are evolutionary inheritances adapted to increase the survival of individuals, species, and phyla. They assert a set of basic emotions that serve to meet basic needs and are expressed in universally communicable ways. Nevertheless, some natural scientists also recognize the influence of social context in the generation of a particular emotion. For example, Charles Darwin, as committed as he was to the universality of emotional expression, allowed for contextual factors—for example, context-dependent social "rules" for what could be expressed and when—in which an individual's social environment helps determine how people are to express their emotions in any particular situation. Though he did not elaborate on this, Darwin acknowledged that certain context-dependent, socially derived rules can regulate when, how often, and how intensely certain emotional expressions are shown. In research that followed Darwin's, the body—and especially the face (particularly its muscles that are not under people's complete control)— becomes "the site of contestation" between innate habits and cultural scripts.[19]

However, while natural scientists and psychologists allow for the influence of environment for the *expression* of an emotion, the influence of social context on emotions' expression goes far beyond what Darwin and Paul Ekman called display rules, which overlay and regulate "natural" emotional displays. Rather, social theorists of emotion argue, emotions are the *products* of social context;[20] in other words, emotions are not something innate whose *expression* is determined by environment. Nor are the differences in emotions experienced by different people in different circumstances merely the result of the variety of biological needs needing to be addressed in varying circumstances; rather, the differences in emotions experienced by different people in different circumstances are the result of varying *social needs under socio-political-cultural influence*. The assertion is that instead of there being a set of universal, basic, and fundamental emotions and their expression as Darwin, Ekman, and others proposed, emotions' generation depends on the nature of the social context in which the person is, both in that moment and as influenced by the person's wider sociocultural milieu over time. Social theorists agree that emotions are related directly to the goal of survival in the *particular context in which one finds oneself at a particular moment*. For social theorists, then, the focus is not on the good (ethical) life or the saved life (in God), or even physical survival (though that is assumed); rather, the goal of emotions is to aid survival and functioning in particular social and cultural contexts.

Cultural anthropologists have long been interested in the role of culture in the experience and expression of emotions and have challenged the basic assumptions promoted by natural scientists. In fact, after reviewing evidence that he and other anthropologists had collected about the cultural relativity of emotional expressions, one early nineteenth-century researcher concluded that "there *is* no 'natural' language of emotional gesture."[21] Another anthropologist, in the course of his own study of expressive bodily and facial movements (attempting to replicate the studies of Darwin and Ekman), argued that he could find no universal words, no universal sound complexes that carry the same meaning "the world over," no body movements, facial expressions, or gestures that provoke identical responses.[22] In fact, he noted, "A body can be bowed in grief, in humility, in laughter, or in readiness for aggression. A 'smile' in one society portrays friendliness, in another embarrassment, and in another still may contain a warning that unless tension is reduced, hostility and attack will follow."[23]

Indeed, the work of researchers who had followed closely in Darwin's footsteps came under fire. Critics argued against Darwin's interpretation of emotional expressions as "leftover" evolutionary habits. Others resisted Darwin's (and later Ekman's) claims that there is an identifiable set of universal, basic emotions and emotional expressions. As noted earlier, Ekman argues that there are certain facial expressions for a basic number of emotions that are recognized across all cultures, which he interpreted to mean that people share a universal set of basic emotions. However, it did not take long for Ekman's critics to take issue both with Ekman's findings and with his interpretation of the data.[24] There were stringent challenges to the methods Ekman and his associates used, to Ekman's choices of subjects, to the facial expression stimuli that Ekman and his associates presented, to the *ways* stimuli were presented, and to the format the subjects were given for responses.[25] The assumptions that emotions are universal, that they communicate universal messages, and that they function in similar ways across cultures were roundly criticized.[26]

Display Rules and Emotional Management: Social Context as Guide to Emotional Expression

Proponents of the view that display rules explain the differences in emotions in different social contexts argue that groups and societies depend on the cooperation of their members to function. Consequently, no human society can tolerate much deviation from normative behavior expectations. Rather, human beings must live and act within defined limits, and to venture outside those limits is to invite some kind of retribution. The character and severity of the retributive response will depend on a cultural definition of the event and its significance, as well as on the particular features of the one who strays: for example, black and brown people and women are known to suffer harsher social repercussions and stricter punishments in the courts.[27] Thus, members of a society are "encouraged to be afraid of departing from what is expected of them and what is tolerated."[28] This has been shown true for cultural members as a whole (though particular people and members of certain groups may have to adhere to different rules), even within the same general cultural milieu.

To test the assertion that different groups (e.g., African Americans, women) are socialized or "allowed" particular emotions and not others, numerous studies of the socialization of emotions by gender, race, ethnicity, and age have been conducted, and they demonstrate clear differences in the kinds, degrees, and locations of emotional display that people in different demographics experience. For example, a large study of gender differences in emotions has shown differences in how male medical residents and female residents responded when handling a corpse. Women often cried or seemed uncomfortable, while men either laughed or showed little emotion at all.[29] Other studies have examined the "feminization" of jealousy and the "masculinization" of anger and violent behaviors.[30] Even the manifestations of clinical disorders such as Tourette's syndrome seem to be under some social control such that the expressions or manifestations of the condition take the shape of the surrounding culture.[31] In fact, some people living with Tourette's express certain tics only in certain situations or around particular people.[32]

By following display rules and the emotional scripts provided to people by their cultural environment, members of any group are able to allay guilt, deflect others' potential disapproval, and maintain a sense of belonging to that group. These benefits are so powerful that people are motivated to maximize them, dutifully learning emotional scripts from the moment of birth and for the rest of their lives.[33] As one pair of researchers describes it, in the process of development and socialization, "children learn to distinguish bodily sensations evoked in particular contexts as emotion. Their feelings are shaped by reinforcements, role modeling, imitation, identification, and instruction until they become skilled emotional performers in social dramas."[34] People learn to be happy at weddings, sad at funerals, serious at the office, and tender in intimacy.[35] Eventually, certain emotions are felt and others are not, although the social influence on this is hidden, and emotions are experienced as "natural" and "personal."

In the end, critics of the display-rule position argue that while there is certainly social censure against expressing certain feelings, neither the evolutionary perspectives nor the evidence for the universality of emotions is strong.[36] Various cognitive structural models of emotions (such as Schachter's/Singer's, and Arnold's) that attempted to identify the relationships between particular cognitions and their attendant emotions came under attack. What these models have in common is the assumption that the beliefs about a situation generate emotions and that different beliefs about an event explain the differences between people's affective experiences of the same event. But subsequent researchers have had difficulty specifying *what* beliefs are important for *which* emotions;[37] they found that a number of the cognitive emotion-structural relationships did not bear out in subsequent investigations. Furthermore, these critics found, emotions sometimes change even when cognitions remained the same. In other words, despite cognitive psychologists' important contributions, different beliefs about something did not necessarily result in differences of emotions related to it.

Critics of the cognitive approaches, then, argue that cognitions alone are unreliable sources of differentiation in emotions. There are literally millions of situations that might evoke any emotion, they suggest. "Moreover," one researcher points out, "there are far fewer emotion categories than the almost infinite number of social content situations that can be used to predict each of them."[38] The idea that in certain situations—and given particular beliefs and appraisals—a particular emotion will be generated has been shown to be false.[39] For one thing, beliefs and appraisals ("cognitions") are constantly evolving: people take "continuous account" of their context and social environments. Second, cognitions are often mixed—including those that are both supportive and not supportive of one's well-being at the same time. (For example, a person might assess that it will *feel good* to eat a pastry and doing so may restore some level of physiological and emotional homeostasis, but that the pastry will not contribute to his or her overall health. Whether a person chooses to eat the pastry depends on which evaluation sways the person in that particular moment.) A third sign that beliefs and appraisals cannot reliably predict what emotion will be generated is that emotions do not necessarily change with new cognitions. Researchers investigating the cognition-emotion relationship, then, have come to understand cognitions as a *process*—that is, "as an ongoing series of evaluations of and reactions to environmental events that include a person's more or less continuous *re*-evaluation of his or her environment based on his or her responses to it."[40] In other words the cognitive process is constantly operative, a dynamic in which beliefs, appraisals, and assessments of goals in the situation are being "continuously performed."[41] This process continuously updates a person's information about an event or situation, including her needs or goals in the moment, which can and do change as the situation does. These fluctuations change one's beliefs and appraisal of whether it will feel good to eat a pastry and whether, in the end, it is the best thing to do. There are other objections to the cognitive-structural approaches as well. For example, emotions occur when no explicit cognitive activity has taken place, or, equivalently, before any cognitive activity has had the chance to take place. In other words, emotions are often generated without the benefit of cognitions—and certainly emotions do not require *conscious* cognitions and appraisals.[42]

Social constructionists take the social factors in emotions' generation and their experience even more seriously, arguing that emotions are not just *influenced* by culture in the accepted norms of their display, as Darwin, Ekman and others would have it. Instead, psychological constructionists of emotion argue, emotions are a *product* of culture. Emotions are social constructions, and emotions can only be understood fully if one's actual *experience* of them (as opposed to the mere *expression* of them) is analyzed in relation to social contexts.

The Experience *of Emotion Is under Sociocultural Influence*

Social constructionist theories of emotion go beyond display rules. They contend that *cultural habit* and *expectations*—rather than biology—generate particular emotions, denying that any "basic" or "essential" emotions are universal across time and cultural situations. Cultural anthropologists' research has found, for example, that "the same social content producing the emotion labeled anger in one culture-specific social situation might not in another."[43] Thus, they argue, certain social relationships give rise to particular emotions as well as the ways they are expressed. The language used about and for emotions plays a significant role in this.[44]

Cultures differ in what they value and the *selves* (that is, the kinds of people) they expect, develop, and sustain. It should not be a surprise, then, that members of different cultural systems would experience, express, and understand emotions differently. Researchers who study emotions across cultures suggest that different language about emotions eventuates in different experiences of emotions. Because historians and anthropologists have established conclusively that there are historically and culturally diverse emotion vocabularies, "it follows that there are *culturally diverse emotions*."[45] For this reason, the usual language one uses to talk about emotions can be an important tool in discovering the structure and contents of one's "emotion concepts," and in addition, the emotion concepts one has can reveal a great deal about one's experiences of emotion in social context.[46]

In the United States, for example, people describe being "gripped" by fear, "seized" by anger, or "paralyzed" by anxiety, and they tell the story of how they "fell" in love—all passive experiences of emotion. The metaphors used for anger in the United States are also illuminating: Americans "blow their top," they get "hot under the collar," and images of cartoon characters with steam coming out of their ears helps illustrate this.[47] Indeed, people in the West often think of anger as an "opponent against which [one] must struggle."[48] These and other expressions represent emotions as affective events that happen outside one's control.[49] The point is, language and metaphors used for emotions inform the behaviors that people engage in relation to their emotions (in this case, anger). For example, if one continues to think of anger as "fluid under pressure" (a model inherited from the early Greek medical doctor Galen and adopted by Freud), one will act in ways consistent with that metaphor and find ways to safely "vent" anger to release the unpleasant tension it creates. Furthermore, to the extent to which one thinks of anger as an opponent against which one must "struggle," a person will likely try to avoid becoming angry or try to control it in others. By speaking of emotions in this way, "it is as though emotions were alien forces which 'overcome and possess' a person."[50] This way of speaking about emotions is primarily metaphorical, revealing widely shared cultural ideas of them.[51] In short: *how cultures talk about emotions has a major influence of how their members experience emotions.*[52] In addition, the ways people talk about their emotions reveals significant qualities of these emotions; consequently, the language used for emotions (what is often called "emotion talk") reveals the importance a particular culture gives them, people's relationship to their emotions, and how people feel about their own feelings.[53] From the perspective of behavioral scientists interested in display rules, human and animal expressions of emotions are always communicative and are best considered as tools to meet social goals.[54]

Linguists suggest that "the language of emotions is woven out of the fabric of a culture's more general discourse about social life."[55] In other words, "emotion talk does not exist in isolation from other domains of knowledge."[56] Emotion talk, then, is never simply about emotions: it is about all of the complex issues associated with interpersonal relations within a culture—this is why it is appropriate to think of emotions as the *lingua franca* of the politics of everyday life.[57] To complicate matters further, however, it is not always easy to identify what is a culture's "emotion talk." Some cultures do not use language about emotion explicitly, making it difficult to get a "satisfactory" answer to the question, "Does [X] refer to an emotion?"[58] This challenge led Ekman's critics to argue that emotions scholars must be careful not to define emotions entirely by the way they are defined by people in North America, and then look for the way the same concepts are used in other cultures as Ekman and his colleagues did.[59] Rather, researchers must find what words for affective experience are used in other cultures, what they mean, when they arise, and how they are expressed and study those in their own context. Emotion talk is never simply about emotions, then, it is about all of the issues associated with interpersonal relations and dynamics of power within a culture.[60]

To illustrate the point, cultural anthropologists have shown that there are words in non-Western cultures that have no direct translation in English. In many situations where this is the case, certain emotions and their accompanying words and descriptors suggest the valuation of different kinds of social relationships than are typically found in the Western cultures. For example, among the Ifaluk in the South Pacific there exists an emotion called *fago*, which suggests a combination of sadness, love, and compassion associated with being away from one's community, not something deemed particularly significant in the dominant (white, bourgeois, highly mobile) North American culture.[61] Another example is the Japanese word *amae*, used to describe a kind of dependent, "almost childlike" relationship with another—a highly valued and positive relational concept in Japan, though it is often viewed negatively by Western observers who tend to prize independence and self-sufficiency. Originally depicted in a Chinese ideograph with a mother's breast, Americans have interpreted the behaviors associated with *amae* as childish and even embarrassing. However, Japanese researcher Takeo Doi suggests that *amae* expresses the bonds that are vitally important to the maintenance and functioning of Japanese society.[62] There are other examples from different cultural contexts, too: Pashtun women in Pakistan are expected to express *gham*—a particular and especially intense form of sadness—in public, especially once they are married. *Gham* is shown to other women in gatherings where they weep and wail together, especially when a person close to them, for example a son, is injured.[63]

Even in European languages there exist words that do not have exact translations in English. And as one group of researchers observes, words such as *Schadenfruede* and *Heimatlich* in German, *simpatico* in Spanish, and *hygge* in Danish enable native speakers to *feel* different emotions (and to feel particular emotions differently) than do English speakers. These differences make clear that various ways of conceptualizing emotion in different societies highlight the cross-cultural variations. Members of modern Western cultures experience emotion as embedded in their psyche, whereas members of other cultures—past and present—may associate emotions with certain bodily organs (such as the heart and the liver), experience them as external forces, or assume emotions are the result of spirit-play or are even divine or demonic.[64] These examples and many others have led to the conclusion that "societies can shape, mold or construct as many different emotions as are functional within the social system."[65] Clearly, people's experiences of emotions are influenced by language about them which is, of course, largely determined by culture. In addition, emotions are produced in the context of particular social hierarchies and have political implications.

Emotions Have Political Origins and Functions

Fitting in to one's social context is critical to survival, and sociological interest in the relations between power, sociopolitical structures, and the generation of emotions (and, implicitly, the well-being of members of certain groups and societies) can be traced to sociologists such as Karl Marx, Max Weber, and Theodore Kemper. Marx's interest in emotions had two levels: Marx was concerned first about the ways human needs and hopes can be manipulated to further the system of capitalism and, second, how social organizations and structures determine the emotions in masses of people, often for the good of those organizations and structures but to the detriment of individuals.[66] In the second case, Marx was particularly concerned with the feelings of alienation, chagrin, bitterness, and resentment those who were separated from ownership of the products of their labor experienced. Separating the laborer-producer from the product led to a state of "immiseration," Marx argued, an emotional condition so difficult it sometimes threatened life itself. This, he worried, is compounded by the alienation and loneliness of people from one another, the isolation of people in increasingly individualized society as communities began to break down under the pressures of modern life. Marx worried, too, about the boredom and mental and emotional numbness that resulted from the repetition of tasks that serve an industrial economy. As opposed to the creative and challenging work and self-ownership of pre-industrial farming or craftsmanship, Marx saw work in modern economies as increasingly mechanized, rote, and alienating in multiple ways.[67] Thus, Marx's interest in emotions focused on the powerlessness and anxiety generated when one's life is controlled by others, the sense of meaninglessness and estrangement when one's work is driven by outside forces, and the alienation and isolation that occurs when others become "enemies" or "competitors in a zero-sum game."[68] Marx obviously understood emotions not just as personal experiences of individuals but rather as products of social structures with significant social consequences. Marx, then, was one of the first to theorize about the relationships between emotions and social position, power, and status.

Max Weber had a slightly different interest in, and take on, emotional control than Marx, though he, too, related the generation of particular emotions to specific social systems. Weber was especially interested in the ways emotions both contributed to and are controlled by religious doctrines and practices and how those supported particular economic systems such as capitalism.[69] Though he agreed with Marx about the historical contributions to the control of emotions wrought by changing localized economies into industrialized capitalism, Weber understood religion—specifically Calvinism—to be largely responsible for the emotions that emphasized those values, feelings, and behaviors. John Calvin's Protestantism, Weber thought, offered such a deterministic and bleak view of the human condition and its salvation that it "yielded emotions that led to an entirely unintended set of consequences, namely, the undergirding ethos of modern capitalism."[70] Marx's analysis of emotions included the dismissal of religion altogether; religion is necessary only as a "working-class anodyne," an opiate against the pain of living and working under the regime of capitalism. Weber, too, saw only ill effects of the influence of religion on people's emotions in modern life.

Another example of sociocultural contexts' negative effects on and use of emotions is the way manipulating emotions has shown economic payoff. As early as the eighteenth century, manufacturers began to appeal to their customers' emotional sensitivity to sell products that elicited potential consumers' emotions, thereby influencing their purchase of goods.[71] However, researchers have shown that economics drive the very experience of certain emotions as well as particular forms of their expression.[72] As one cultural historian put it, the "diversification and refinement of emotion in eighteenth-century discourse, for example, was in part an effect of the proliferation of the kinds of objects that people could have feelings about" and just how they were expected to feel about them.[73] This last point suggests that the management (or, more pessimistically, the manipulation) of emotions can regulate social norms, control people's behaviors, and direct consumer activity, whether or not it is the best interest of the person or the long-term well-being of the polis. Nevertheless, emotions can be tools of power used to establish, maintain, and promote certain social, economic, and political arrangements in a society.

Social theories of emotion, then, assume that emotions are not only personal, nor are they context-free. Display-rule proponents try to account for differences in how certain emotions are expressed or repressed in different contexts by various people or groups. Anthropologists demonstrate differences in emotions' experience and expression in different cultures and various social locations within cultures (e.g., gender and race). Historians point to the ways different historical periods not only guide what emotions are "appropriate" or "acceptable," but actually determine what emotions are felt, as well as how they are named and understood. The display-rule approach to emotions' variability assumes that everyone feels the same emotions but expresses them differently or not at all, depending on the rules governing that emotion within that person or group. In contrast, the social constructivists' position takes the idea of emotional influence (or control) even further when they argue that different contexts actually *produce* different emotions. Like the ways different language about emotions eventuates in different *experiences* of emotions, social constructivists lay bare the ways emotions are *generated* by context.

Hence, there are no emotions (either the origin, experience or expression of them) that are not rooted in a specific history, or social environment. Emotions, then, can be understood as functioning to adapt to one's particular environment, and emotions both respond to that environment and contribute to the maintenance of it.[74] The generation of specific emotions in particular social hierarchies is one field of research that seeks to understand these dynamics.

Specific Emotions Are Created by Particular Social-Cultural-Political Structures

Social constructionist theories of emotion can be considered outgrowths of the cognitive views of Schachter/Singer and Arnold's work, but as an identifiable tradition of emotion research and theory in psychology, social constructionism is relatively young.[75] However, a sizable body of literature now exists on the topic.[76] As noted, the social constructionist view of emotions holds that no emotions are "natural" or inevitable; rather, "emotions are determined by social and cultural fiat."[77] The example of fear is illustrative on this point, since it is almost always included in researchers' lists of basic, fundamental, and universal emotions. The argument natural scientists make is that the fight-or-flight impulse is evolutionarily "hardwired" in human beings. However, studies have shown that *whether* people feel fear, *when* they feel it, *how* they experience it, *what* people fear, and *how* they express that varies by social context.[78]

For example, in an oft-cited study, anthropologist Catherine Lutz demonstrated that it is not just how people display fear that is culturally informed, but also whether or not they actually *experience* fear in universally predictable situations. In her work among the Ifaluk, a small cultural group indigenous to islands in remote Micronesia, Lutz found that what members of that group found fearful was different than what Americans in the twentieth century generally find fearful. Rather than feeling afraid of the dark, for example, the Ifaluk feel and express fear when they arrive at the home of someone of higher rank without food, and for good reason: in a social system that depends on hierarchies, cooperation, and sharing, understanding this emotional system and how it works, and willingness to participate in it, is critical for survival.[79] Thus, while expressions of fear may have some function for physical survival, as Darwin proposed, they have important functions for survival in social groups as well. Lutz's work demonstrated that the objects of fear may be culturally determined and that what is understood as an object of fear can be a means of regulating social behavior.[80] In fact, many of the objects of fear in Western contexts, such as people with AIDS,[81] vaccines, or black teenagers in hoodies "have significant cultural content" and are of recent origin and have specific cultural effects.[82] As one anthropologist notes, "some of the kinds of social objects that children are taught to fear are 'instrumental in sustaining social values,'" and what people are taught to fear (such as the consequences of not doing one's homework, or taking candy from strangers, or protesting unjust conditions too loudly) "have the effect of keeping us safe but also about keeping us in our place."[83] Emotions, then, can have a powerful function in regulating the social order.

As noted, contemporary social theorists of emotions are interested in "socially derived" elements of emotions, or those emotions produced by historical period, cultural context, or sociopolitical structures. They are also interested in the ways emotions function to maintain social and political hierarchies. As Lutz's work among the Ifaluk showed, the experience and display of emotions can maintain the social order by maintaining hierarchies. Thus, social theorists suggest that social and cultural understandings of emotion show that while emotions are undoubtedly experienced by discrete individuals, emotions are also a collective property of sorts, whether dyadic or societal in scope, and are often used as tools to maintain the status quo.[84] Emotions are generated by social and cultural structures, then, and help to maintain those structures. The power at play in the creation and "allowance" of certain emotions is particular focus: how do emotions come into being, bidden by social arrangements? And how are emotions used to support and maintain the sociopolitical status quo? Social-structural perspective on emotions combines cognitive perspectives and the constructionist views with unique attention to issues of power and political agendas. The assumption in political models is that emotions emerge from the interpersonal interactions that result in the context of relations of power and status.

One such model, the social-structural perspective, assumes that all members of a society are situated within some matrix of power and status. Participants in social interactions have different forms and amounts of power and status, ranging from deficient to adequate to excessive, and the social-structural model of emotionology proposes that the amount of power or status a person has will be "universally predictive" of the emotions they are likely to experience.[85] Thus, in this view certain emotions can be predicted given certain social and political realities.[86] For example, a person's possession or exercise of "excessive power" will cause guilt, sociologist Theodore Kemper argues. Those who have "adequate power" share a feeling of security, and the experience of having "inadequate power" will cause fear and anxiety.[87] Likewise, an agent's experience of having appropriate status conferred by the other will result in happiness, of having excess status conferred, shame, and of having insufficient acknowledgement of status, depression.[88] Other examples of these "predictable emotional experiences" related to social arrangements include shame—which results from someone withholding deserved status—and guilt, which arises in the context of one's use of excessive power against the other.[89] Social structural perspectives fundamentally assume, then, that the source of many emotions is the social, historical, and cultural context in which the individual finds himself or herself. In this view, context is the social transaction that *preceded* the emotion's occurrence.[90] If people want to understand why certain emotions are experienced at all, Kemper asserts, they must look primarily at prior incidents (or anticipation of the occurrence) of the social relationships.[91]

Social-structural theorists propose that there are "normative components" to emotions and that individuals change their emotions to stay in tune with the prevailing normative order. This means that interactions on a spectrum between power and status determine emotions, but so do social expectations.[92] In this way, then, social regulations within cultures lead to "uniformity" of emotional experience and expression.[93] An implication of the understanding of emotions as generated by social-structural hierarchies is that the options and "normative requirements" for emotions change by historical period and by geographical and cultural location. As variations in relational structures and hierarchies change, the argument goes, so do emotional experiences. As Lutz's research showed, for example, the Ifaluk are taught that showing up to an elder's hut without a gift or offering is a shameful thing and results in the experience and expression of shame.[94] Feeling shame motivates a group member to rectify the situation in some way, and expressing shame demonstrates to the other that one is aware of having transgressed a social hierarchy and will likely behave differently next time. The expression of shame after a breach of protocol allows for forgiveness and a return to the expected set of relationships and power dynamics in social arrangements, thus maintaining the status quo. Emotions, then, are understood to be related to particular social contexts and situations, and they change as new relational practices and accompanying mental constructions and social contexts do, making previously common emotional expressions seem "personally and socially dysfunctional."[95] In this model, then, emotions are deeply embedded in the social fabric and political structures of a particular time and context, and these valences of power affect the experience and expression of emotion.[96] This may be especially clear in the examination of emotions within underrepresented groups, especially in relation to dominant, middle-class, and white expectations.[97] (One way to dismiss the resistance of minoritized groups to their oppression is to say they are "too angry" or "just envious of us" in dominant groups.)[98]

This social and political research on the ways emotions function to maintain social hierarchies illuminates the ways emotions are useful windows both into people's needs, goals, and values, *and* into the ways their historical, political, cultural, and institutional contexts are deeply entwined in those personal features. As useful as the social-structural models of emotions' generation and function are, however, they are structural models, meaning that they assume that certain circumstances and certain social arrangements will give rise to predictable emotions. However, recent neuroscience challenges cognitive and social-structural models and show that emotions are *constructed in the moment* given what is happening physiologically and what one has learned socioculturally.

Conclusion

The work of social scientists demonstrates that emotions vary by cultural context and historical period. For example, social historians have shown differences across time in the relationships between emotions and historical epochs. Cultural anthropologists have studied differences in emotional displays, documenting cultural variances in expressions of emotions and of "socially appropriate" intensities of the expressions of them. Others have provided insights into the gendered natures of some emotions, such as the feminization of jealousy and the masculinization of competition and physical violence, and political theorists of emotion have asserted that emotions are generated according to positions of power and status. All of these analyses expand the understanding of the origins and meanings of emotions and people's experiences and expressions of them beyond the natural sciences' and psychologies' understandings. Indeed, social theorists of emotion argue that most natural scientific and cognitive theories fail to appreciate fully the *social* nature of emotions; that is, they obscure the ways many emotions (such as guilt, shame, embarrassment, and joy) take into consideration *other* people, *others'* needs, *others'* opinions, and *others'* situations in important ways.

Social theorists' understandings of emotion assume that emotions are social, relational, and interpersonal and that emotions are generated by what is happening in the contexts of social, cultural, and political dynamics. In other words, emotions are created in one's milieu: they are not innate, nor are they confined to intrapsychic and interpersonal relationships as psychologists often imagine.[99] Rather, emotions also serve a group's or society's goals and needs even when those are not supportive of individuals' (or even groups') well-being. Thus, social theorists argue, to understand emotions adequately requires an analysis of their social context; it simply makes no sense to understand emotions outside of that.

The many mixed messages about emotions and their origin, value, and function pose challenges for understanding emotions' role in human flourishing. Early philosophers and theologians worried about the passions and their role in the good life, often recommending their elimination or at least their careful control. In contrast, natural scientists accept emotions as natural, and assume that emotions evolved for the purpose of physical survival and propose a set of emotions that is basic and universal, shared among all people regardless of social, cultural, or historical context. While accepting that emotions support physical survival, and accepting emotions as natural and inevitable, social theorists argue that emotions also function for social survival and are specific to environment: understanding social and political hierarchies, having a place of belonging in the social order, and knowing one's place in the pecking order helps society function. However, the structural models assumed by the natural, psychological, and social sciences presented here have been shown to be too rigid. People's emotions do serve survival in a number of ways, but the predictive, structural models have not been confirmed by subsequent research: there is no set of core or basic emotions, and particular emotions do not reliably emerge in all instances of a particular social arrangement.

Human beings *are* attuned to their environment and their closest relationships, adapting to them to maximize their sense of well-being. In fact, because human beings are so dependent on others for their survival, they are exquisitely tuned to the dynamics of those relationships. But how are social contexts related to the physiological factors in emotions' generation and experience? Social theorists seem not to have been particularly interested in this question. But those of us who might wish to relate the most important contributions from the various research programs on emotions might be. Fortunately, there are recent developments that can help in this effort. Contemporary neuroscience helps explain the relationships between physiology, interpersonal relationships, social contexts, and culture in the generation, experience, and expressions of emotion without falling prey to the structural theories that have garnered so much criticism.

Understanding how emotions are both physiological *and* social, as is explored in the next chapter, will aid in finding a way to imagining emotions' promise for well-being. However, most natural scientists, social theorists, and neuroscientists do not prescribe what *should* be to effect human flourishing: they usually seek only to *describe what is*.[100] Emotions' relationship to human well-being and even flourishing (not just surviving)—which was a keen interest of the earliest philosophers and theologians—will need to be reincorporated for a more adequate understanding of emotions' functions, effects, and value in human life for flourishing. First, however, a psychological constructionist understanding of emotions' origins will help bring together many of the previously discrete, "classical" views of emotions, including both the natural and social scientists' perspectives. Psychological constructionist theories of emotion help overcome the deep divides that have, until now, existed between various research programs on emotions.

6

Emotions as Psychological Constructions in Context

Recent Neuroscientific Discoveries

Introduction

Human beings experience emotion as a central and often defining aspect of their lives. Every day, at least in North America, people ask and answer the question "how does that make you feel?" over coffee or in a therapist's office: it is assumed that experiencing and exploring an emotion gives one access to something inevitable, inside, real and true in some way. But this is only partly correct: emotions are not something a person "has" inside.[1] Nor are particular emotions inevitable in the ways we often take them to be. As chapter 5 demonstrated, emotions are neither physiologically automatic nor necessarily predictable in their origin, expression, or in people's experience of them: recent structural theories of emotions that predicted particular emotions would arise in specific sociocultural-political contexts do not always bear out. This is, in part, because researchers' starting assumptions were not correct.

The dominant paradigm in studies of emotions has assumed that emotions are entities that exist in particular parts of the brain (e.g., Paul MacLean and the limbic system) or in the "deep structure of the situation" (e.g., Theodore Kemper's social hierarchies) that are just waiting to be "triggered" by a particular event.[2] Until recently, the most prominent scientists assumed that each different subjective experience is the

125

result of separate and distinct "emotional" locations and processes in the brain—for example, those related to emotion, cognition, memory, and perception. In fact, neuroscientists have been trying to map these faculties to specific locations in the brain for more than a century.[3] The research programs that followed this thinking assumed that emotions are discrete, basic categories of physiological and psychological phenomena; basic emotions such as fear, anger, happiness, sadness, and so on are discrete expressions of particular emotions, irreducible and universal;[4] that the discrete emotion types are localized in distinct areas of the brain, whether these are single brain regions or discrete networks; and that specific emotions are communicated bodily in particular ways and result in predictable behaviors.[5] Early studies of emotions—which led to general assumptions about emotions that continue to prevail—suggested that people experience emotions because people "have" emotions inside them that arise given the right circumstances. This model assumes there are predictable physiological systems that are activated and predictable emotions that are "triggered," resulting in subsequent and predictable experiences of feeling. These beliefs have a long history: seventeenth-century philosopher Rene Descartes believed that emotions emerge from the pineal gland (a small gland in the middle of the brain), while physiologist Walter Cannon argued that the thalamus is the neural center for emotion.[6] As noted in previous chapters, both James Papez and Paul MacLean argued that emotions emerge from the limbic system, as a set of phylogenetically "old" subcortical and allocortical structures.[7] More-recent scientists have carried on in that tradition, seeking evidence for emotion modules in the brain for specific emotions such as fear and disgust.

However, many studies—both in the twentieth and twenty-first centuries—have tried and failed to find the "site" or "fingerprint" for particular emotions. They have failed to identify a basic set of emotions or universal expressions of them, and they have been unable to identify situations that give rise to certain emotions across all cultural and social contexts studied.[8] Even relatively recently (and with the benefit of increasingly sophisticated tools), neuroscientists have looked for these universal emotions and their locations, but they still have been unable to find them.[9] Their research could not confirm that emotions exist in evolutionary physiology alone as Charles Darwin thought, that they exist in certain parts of the brain as Paul MacLean argued, that they are reliably activated when certain appraisals are evoked as Magda Arnold proposed, or that they emerge when particular social relations were experienced as Theodore

Kemper asserted. Twenty years of neuroimaging research has revealed that the brain "does not respect common-sense emotion categories or any commonly held faculty psychological views,"[10] and cultural studies agree.[11]

Thus, although these assumptions that emotions originate in particular organs (e.g., Galen and Descartes), or parts of the brain (e.g., Paul MacLean and Antonio Damasio), or even in particular social contexts and political hierarchies (e.g., Karl Marx and Theodore Kemper) have been held for millennia, they are not entirely correct. Furthermore, these beliefs have created fundamental puzzles that, until about the last thirty years or so, have been unsolvable. For example, if emotions are evolutionarily hardwired, how can they be context-specific? Why do the same beliefs result in different emotions at different times in the same people? And why do different contexts give rise to the same emotions? Recent neuroscience has begun to provide answers to these and other conundrums the classical models posed.

Instead of these "classical" models, contemporary neuroscientists have suggested that the emotions' generation requires a complex interplay of multiple factors, including physiological, cognitive, and social ones.[12] Thanks to contemporary neuroscience, it is now known that emotions are fullbody events (not located just in the brain) constructed moment to moment and that emotions are entirely dependent on immediate stimuli—both physiological and social, and informed by past experience—to emerge.

In addition, there are no "emotional" sites in the brain: emotions are constructed from *domain-general operations* in the body and the brain.[13] Meta-analyses of brain activity for emotions show that there are networks that support general operations in the brain, such as the generation of expression, thought or conceptualization, memory, imagination and representation, perception, and attention and that these are also active during episodes that are commonly identified as "emotional."[14] In other words, there are no intrinsic, anatomically defined functional networks for distinct emotion episodes in the brain; instead, general neural networks support basic functions across all mental states—including those typically categorized as analytical and perceptual as well as those that are "emotional."[15] In addition, there is a growing body of neuroimaging evidence demonstrating that when individuals experience emotions and other mental states, those feelings emerge from the "dynamic interplay of [widely] distributed neuronal assemblies across the brain" and that the same neurons that code for one psychological event "flexibly code" for another.[16] In other words, brain mapping cannot find the "structures" for particular emotions because they do not exist.[17] To complicate matters, cognitive processes alone do not lead to specific emotions. Something else is going on, and it has to do with the interplay of input from the entire body and one's experience—both past and immediate—in context. Complex mammals such as humans, it seems, are exquisitely tuned to survival, both physical and social. They are "wired" to learn what will ensure survival in any given moment and in their particular context at that moment and over time, and they are working consistently on a number of levels to effect it.[18] Flexibility in the construction of emotions is a crucial part of that fine tuning.

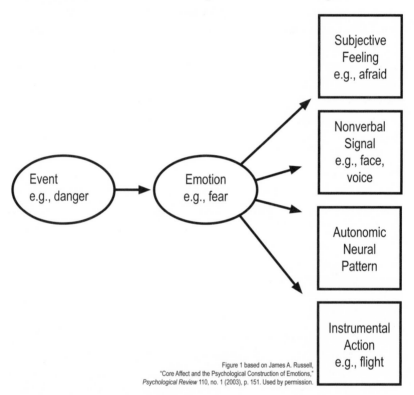

Figure 1 based on James A. Russell, "Core Affect and the Psychological Construction of Emotions," *Psychological Review* 110, no. 1 (2003), p. 151. Used by permission.

Figure 1: Classical Emotions Theory[19]

Arguments against Classical or "Natural Kinds" Models of Emotions

The emotions theory captured in Figure 1 is a depiction of commonly held classical, or "natural kind," models. The assumption in these frameworks is that when a particular kind of situation is encountered (such as a snake in the grass), it triggers an emotion (such as fear) from a discrete module in the brain that has developed through the process of evolution to protect the organism. The person seeing the snake feels the emotion which results in a distinct kind of feeling state—that of being "afraid." Thus, the emotion of fear is assumed to be the "veridical sensory detection" of an object that causes one's experience of that emotion: for example, seeing a snake in the grass equals fear.[20] In other words, in this understanding, seeing a snake in the grass "makes" one feel fear. Figure 1 also suggests that there is some objective, universal indication of a person's experience of emotion: that an emotional response (e.g., physical responses such as a facial expression or a particular behavior, such as jumping back—even when the snake is behind a glass window) is directly related to the emotion (fear) generated by encountering the object (snake). This correspondence is assumed in schemas such as Charles Darwin's, in more recent structural programs such as Paul Ekman's, Robert Plutchik's, and Charles Kemper's, and in everyday parlance about emotions. But emotions are more complex and more elusive than that.[21]

Thus, although these common beliefs about emotions are among the "most compelling ideas" in the psychology of emotion, they have been shown not to be true.[22] For example, while some parts of the peripheral nervous system respond to threat and challenge[23] and register certain levels of arousal experienced as pleasant or unpleasant sensations,[24] these processes do not figure clearly in all emotional events, even among all those assumed to be basic, such as anger, sadness, or fear.[25] Nor do these neurological processes necessitate certain actions in response: there is no "fear response" to certain situations. Behavioral responses to fear are on a spectrum from freezing to fighting to vigilance to flight. In fact, not only are different behaviors associated with the same emotion, the same behaviors can be associated with different emotions. For example, attack behaviors can be associated with different situations that are assumed to engender fear or anger. Jealousy and guilt can also lead to violence, just as fear and anger can. Research strongly suggests, instead, that expressive behaviors are specific to *context-determined* attempts to deal with a situation: people learn what is an "appropriate" response to a particular emotion within their socio-political-cultural context in a particular situation. Furthermore, people's past experiences and their immediate context inform both what they feel and how they behave in the moment. Thus, one's *subjective* experience of a particular emotion and the ability to recognize an emotion in others—as well as their responses to both—are highly varied and depend on what they learn about what is happening physiologically in their bodies and in context.

Rather than taking a classical approach that assumes emotions exist in localized regions of the brain, then, psychological construction theories of emotion do not believe that any particular emotion (e.g., fear) is a unitary phenomenon. Rather, psychological construction models map each emotion as a *category* that is composed of the interaction of various components and multiple dynamic processes in the brain. Experiences and expressions of emotions are socially derived, as are the feelings of which people become aware, their interpretations of them, and their responses to them. All emotions depend on context—both of the one having an emotion and of the one observing it.[26] Emotions, and one's experience of them, then, are indicative of one's particular physiology, past experience, and the socio-political-cultural context of which one is a part. People *learn* emotions.

Emotions Are Constructed Moment to Moment

Component Models of Emotions' Generation

Recent psychological construction models of the mind propose that emotions are constructed moment to moment from *multiple components* that are derived from both intrapsychic and environment-specific elements.[27] For example, neuroscientific researcher Lisa Feldman Barrett suggests that the process is analogous to ingredients that are in recipes, which, when put together in certain amounts, with certain processes, and in certain contexts, create a cake.[28] The cake, in Barrett's analogy, is an emotion.[29] The *feeling* of an emotion is the conscious interpretation of physiological experience based on past events, current experience, and future imaginings. Because different ingredients are available to different people (because of, say, their cultural location or because of their personal history), or to the same person at different times (because of, say, their relational context at any particular moment), an infinite variety of cakes might be made for a variety of particular occasions. The differences between a person's (and people's) emotions and the way they interpret them—that is, the *feelings* one experiences, reports, and reflects on—depend on the *conceptual categories* one is using.

In a neuropsychological construction model of emotions theory (described as the current "gold standard"), an emotion word such as *fear* corresponds to a "conceptual category" rather than a discrete entity or actual "thing."[30] An *emotion category*—or the experience of an emotion, often identified as a *feeling*, such as fear—is not something that has a physical essence; rather, it is a collection of instances that vary in their physical manifestations that have come to be labeled "fear" by a particular social and cultural group.[31] Further, emotions are constructed by certain categories and concepts that are themselves socially constructed out of learned categories and concepts. This idea likely needs further explanation.

Recent research has shown that processes of categorization are fundamental to all cognitive activities.[32] To *categorize* something is to recognize a class or group of people, things, or events that are treated as sharing similarities. To categorize something is to determine what it is, why it is, and what one should do with it.[33] A *concept* can be thought of as "a collection of mental representations for a category that people draw on during the process of categorization."[34] And once conceptual knowledge is brought to bear to categorize something as "one kind of thing" and not another, the *thing* (which is then given a name) becomes meaningful, allowing people to make reasonable inferences about that thing, predict about how best to act on it, and communicate the experience of one particular thing in relation to others.[35] For example, the category "apple" invokes concepts that one relates to apples. Apple is a category, and *concepts* about that category (apples are healthy, apples are related to the Fall, green apples remind me of my mother) relate to other mental processes. A category identifies a round, firm, fruit with a stem in the middle of it as an apple, with a shape distinct from that of a pear and a size distinct from a pumpkin. A concept includes ideas about the value of apples, what one *does* with an apple, whether it is good for people to eat apples, and so on. *Concepts* also relate to whether one likes apples in general or only green apples in particular, how one feels after eating green apples and remembering one's mother, and so on. Categories and concepts relate closely to one's feelings, or one's conscious awareness of, identification of, and articulation of an emotion. Categories (the way of identifying what objects are) and concepts (understandings or beliefs about them) help generate emotions; for example, whether one feels happy about eating an apple or not.

Processes of categorization and conceptualization are happening constantly. This helps people navigate the world without having to assemble new concepts or understandings in every second of their lives. Concepts and categorizations help human beings make assumptions that organize what might seem unfamiliar, random, and chaotic at every turn into a world in which one can develop habits of thinking, feeling, and behaving.

Such organization is, of course, a social construction out of unconnected events, but it streamlines the processes of experience through prediction. In fact, because people's bodies are constantly registering myriad data points through their senses (sight, smell, touch, hearing, taste), the brain must have a way to sift through the chaos for what is meaningful; it cannot register everything. Human brains (as well as those of other animals) use the categories and the prediction of categories as an efficient way to respond to the constant barrage of data through the senses. Emotions are the results of categories and concepts, and the predictions of these that are "taught" by one's past experiences and one's social-cultural-political context.[36]

Instances of an emotion, then, are not random but are "functionally linked" to the immediate situation or environment in which they emerge.[37] In other words, emotions are a result of the categories and concepts learned about the world. An *emotion word* such as *fear*, then, names a set of diverse events (or *instances*) that emerge from multiple causes; an emotion word does not refer to a single process that produces a set of similar instances or events, as the classical models hold (e.g., a snake in the grass = fear). An emotion such as fear is not "triggered" as if it is lying dormant waiting to be activated by seeing a snake or some other stimulus. Rather, psychological construction models hypothesize that an emotion is created *in a particular moment* and *within a particular context* out of a *particular past* given the *components* involved in the immediate sensory data processing. The process includes *neutral physical changes* (such as the dilation of one's pupil or that a person's mouth begins to water) which are interpreted and given meaning based on the person's context (again, immediate and past) as she sees a snake or imagines eating a green apple. Information from past experience about psychological meaning and the utility or functionality, say of a green apple, is given to those physical changes, and if enough of the components—including beliefs about apples, whether one likes them or not, whether one is hungry or not—are added, an emotion is created (looking at a green apple she remembers her mother and is aware of feeling lonely without her).[38] But that (or any other) emotion is not predicted when one sees a green apple (not everybody's mouth waters when she sees or imagines a green apple). Sensory data can be taken in—shape, smell, size—but not enough components are present to create an emotion. There must be more that goes on for an emotion to be created.

Contemporary research neuropsychologist James Russell has proposed a model to describe a componential process of emotion creation using four terms (core affect, affect quality, attributed affect, and Object) that bear brief definition.[39] The generation of an emotion requires a number of components including the experience of a *core affect*. This Russell defines as a neurophysiological state that is consciously accessible as a simple, "primitive," nonreflective experience that is an integral blend of hedonic (pleasure vs. displeasure) and arousal (sleepy vs. activated) values.[40] Core affect is physiological, primitive, universal, and simple—and can exist without being labeled, interpreted, or attributed to any cause.[41] Russell offers this schema to help explain the constructionist model of emotions, which imagines emotions as constructed out of components. Core affect is just one:

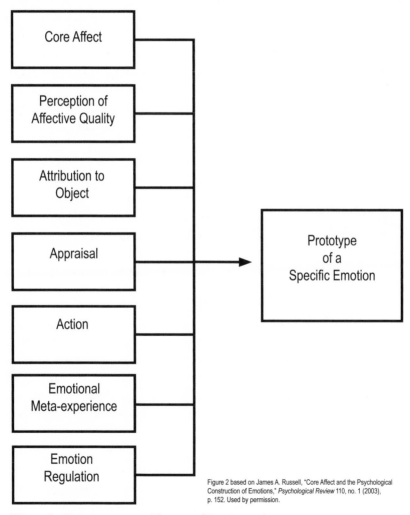

Figure 2 based on James A. Russell, "Core Affect and the Psychological Construction of Emotions," *Psychological Review* 110, no. 1 (2003), p. 152. Used by permission.

Figure 2: Constructionist Theory of Emotions[42]

Core affect is always present, like body temperature, and is just as fundamental and critical. Nevertheless, like body temperature, core affect is usually part of the background of a person's conscious world.[43] Core affect is the experience of a subconscious but continuous assessment of one's current physiological state, and it affects all other psychological processes. People do not always have direct access to the reason for changes in their core affect; rather, they often *make attributions and interpretations* of their current affective state and noticeable changes to it. Sometimes the cause for a particular state of core affect is obvious (for example, "My blood sugar just dropped and so I don't feel well"). At other times, however, a change in one's core affect "evokes a[n] [often subconscious] search for its cause" and thus facilitates attention to and accessibility of "like-valenced" material, or another time—imagined or real—when the person's core affect felt the same way.[44] For example, if, unbeknownst to him, a person's blood sugar has dropped, he experiences physiological change, which he interprets as agitation, anxiety, and anger because it feels like other times he has been angry. He may lash out at his friend as a result. (In fact, the word *hangry*—a mash-up of physiological and attributed feeling states—has become a common neologism.)

Core affect guides cognitive processing and perceptions and is directly related to *affect quality.* The more positive one's core affect is, the more positive the events encountered or remembered or imagined—their affective quality—seem (unless the core affect is attributed to something else, as in, "I enjoyed my date with that person, but upon reflection, I think it was more about the delicious cake I had for dessert than it was about the company.")[45] Similarly, the more negative one's core affect is in a given moment, the more negative events appear.[46] Furthermore, because most people usually (though not always) seek to maximize pleasure and minimize displeasure, their goals and motivations to pursue them involve predictions of future core affect, and the affective quality ascribed to Objects (which can be positive, negative, or mixed).[47] And past experience of affect quality can guide one's interpretation of core affect and attributed affects. For example, one might say, "I feel a gnawing in my stomach. I usually feel that when I am hungry. It is about the time I usually eat. My body must need food."[48] However, dehydration (which changes one's core affect) is often mistaken for hunger. This error is unfortunate, especially in countries such as the United States where food is readily available to most of its population and where food is often used to regulate changes in core affect regardless of physiological need for calories or nutrients. These changes in core affect are often interpreted as feeling-states—such as anxiety.[49] Indeed, rather than address the need for hydration with water, people often eat or go shopping in an attempt to relieve their vague sense of anxiety.[50] Interpretations of core affect thus direct specific behaviors even when a specific behavior will not necessarily address the changes in core affect one has just experienced ("I always feel good when I eat cake. I had a bad day, so I am going to go buy some cake for dessert so that I will feel better"). For example, one might feel good immediately after eating a piece of cake—partly because of the rise in blood sugar and partly because of past associations—and then later wish she had eaten a green apple instead because she feels nauseated after so much sugar, because she knows that apples are healthier than cake, and because she remembers getting green apples from her mother, who loves her, and the pleasant feelings and positive emotions that arise when she remembers her mother help her feel better.

Core affect is a physiological and a mental process, but it is not a cognitive or reflective one. Cognitive events such as beliefs, assumptions, or values (as in the preceding examples) are intrinsically *about* something, but core affect is not. In other words, core affect is free floating: it has to do with the homeostasis of the body or the departure from its resting point, usually on the pleasure/arousal axis. One's homeostatic point is ideally, though not always, pleasant and not much aroused.[51]

Changes in core affect can happen without any direct object. However, through *affect attribution*, core affect can become directed at an object: "My feeling of happiness and my arousal/interest goes up when I think of green apples because I have past experience feeling good when eating them." Russell defines anything that has the ability to cause a change in core affect the *affective quality* of that object.[52] Like cognitive theorists before him, Russell argues that emotions are *about* something: they arise in relation to "Objects."[53] Russell defines an *Object* (capital *O*) as any person, condition, thing, or event at which a mental state is directed. *Any* object can have affective quality and change the core affect (in the same hedonic and arousal values noted previously) for any person, thus becoming an Object for that person. *Attributed affect*, then, is the attribution of the core affect one "gives" to an Object.[54] Attributed affect is isolated from the "objective reality" of the object and is typically quick and automatic. However, attributed affect can also be deliberate: a person might be taught to dislike apples because it is the fruit that resulted in the Fall in Christian mythology but choose to learn to like apples because they are healthy. She might even develop an affinity for a certain kind of apple—for example, green apples—because her mother used to pack them in her school lunch; thus, eating green apples will become the occasion for a sense of happiness and contentment for the rest of her life. Green apples, then, have become an Object for her.

Human beings are in a constant state of what Russell calls the process of "affect regulation," which aims directly at altering core affect. If there is a change in their core affect, they will try to return to core affect homeostasis, as in the example of eating something (anything) when their stomach gnaws (thus raising their blood sugar), or eating a green apple to recall a mother's comforting presence when feeling anxious.[55] Changes in core affect are the result of many things, from a change in body temperature, to low blood sugar, to encountering an object to which one attaches meaning (in other words, an Object). Some of the changes in core affect are outside of one's ability to detect, such as ionization in the air, subtle shifts in body temperature, barometric pressure, and infrasound.[56] Other shifts in core affect are more conscious, especially if one is connected to an Object one has given meaning to, such as a particular kind of apple.

The meaning of an Object is the appraisal one gives it: for example, "I like green apples; they remind me of my mother, and I feel warm and comforted when I eat one." Russell argues that this "meaning" is experienced as pleasant or unpleasant and is linked to some level of arousal, either very mild or extreme. In this last case, core affect depends on and responds to all the information available to an individual about an Object, from its initial sensory registration to full cognitive processing. Core affect is especially responsive to information being provided by consciousness, whether it is based in objective reality (e.g., "there is a snake in my path," "my loving mother fed me green apples") or virtual reality (watching a movie with snake in it or seeing an ad for green apples on television). Core affect influences one's behavior, ranging from reflexive behavior to complex decision making, and it affects the subsequent behaviors. Most often, changes in core affect are the result of a combination of events: for example, not getting enough sleep combined with the cumulative stress of one's job and the stress of a volatile intimate relationship provides core affect influence (unpleasant, high arousal) so that when one sees green apples in a grocery store at the end of a difficult day, one feels compelled to buy one. However, even the pleasant, high arousal one experiences when *imagining* eating green apples helps restore the core affect to a more positive, balanced equilibrium. Just seeing an *image* of the fruit can help downregulate the high-arousal state of desire to a more desired, homeostatic state if green apples are an Object for an individual.[57]

Core affect, then, is the result of the *affective quality* of a situation, and it also has an influence on the *estimated affective quality* of a situation. In a process called *mood-congruent priming*, feeling happy leads a person to process more-positive information about an affective Object and estimate its pleasantness: her now-favorite cake tasted great the first time she had it because she was already happy in that moment, not because a renowned pastry chef made it for her.[58] In fact, *misattribution of affect quality* leads one, if one is feeling happy, to attribute the happy feelings to an Object and perceive it as more pleasant than one otherwise might—for example, "Cake makes me happy since I was happy the last time I ate some."[59] In other words, if one is experiencing enormous stress on the job, eating a piece of cake or a green apple will briefly alleviate the stress, but will only do so to the extent that one believes it will. Cakes and green apples have nothing objectively to do with alleviating stress on the job or managing conflict in a relationship, but one might *believe* they will help, based on past experiences of them. So if one associates eating one's favorite cake with alleviating stress, one will, in fact, accomplish a reduction in the unpleasant feeling of stress—at least for a short time—when one eats some.[60] To perceive the affective quality of an Object is to *attribute* or *represent* rather than *experience* core affect. In other words, the affective quality of something is not inherent to it, but rather given it by a person and then perceived as inherent to it. Cake and green apples do not have automatic or universal affective qualities, and they cannot reduce stress in everyone; however, this does not limit their capacities to do so for some people who *give* them that power.

These fundamental components in Russell's framework (*core affect, attributed affects*, affective *Objects*, and the perception of *affective quality*—or affective attribution) define everything else. In the creation of an emotion, a change in core affect is attributed to its perceived cause, or Object—which can include a person, place, event, physical object, or a situation. Sometimes the cause of homeostatic disruption is obvious (e.g., "I have not eaten in a long time and am hangry"), but at other times an immediate mental search is required to identify the cause of the change. Frequently, mistakes are made: for example, low blood sugar is interpreted as being angry at one's friend.[61] Nevertheless, whatever cause is *identified* as the reason for the usually unconscious experience of one's core affect change becomes the affective Object in that moment. Thus, a change in core affect, an Object, and the *attribution of the core affect to the Object* are the necessary and sufficient features of an emotion.[62] Because attributed affect is the *perception* of the causal links between events in a person's state and the situation, the idea of affective Objects and attributed affect allows for individual and cultural differences.[63]

Attributed affect has two primary functions: first, it guides attention and behavior to affective Objects (thus focusing people's attention). Second, it is the main route to the *attributed quality* (that is, the level of pleasantness/unpleasantness and arousal/sleepy quality) ascribed to the Object. To put it more simply, the attributed affect that a person assigns an otherwise random object makes it an Object to him. Thus, an individual gives an Object its affective quality and turns one's selective attention to it. Attributed affect is phenomenologically simple and common: fear associated with snakes, sadness with loss, empathy for a friend. Affective qualities are attributed when one's core affect changes.[64] These processes are primary for the generation of an emotion, but more than these are required for an *emotional episode*, or *feeling*, and one's *behavioral response* to that feeling.

Recall Barrett's ingredients, recipe, and cake analogy: an emotion (cake) is an *episode* that consist of *multiple components* (ingredients), and in psychological construction models, the particular components and their number vary depending on the person, the person's history, and the immediate situation. In addition, the *order of sequence* (recipe) of how components are mixed can vary. In Russell's model, the components and processes of an emotional episode are complex, as Figure 2 shows. There is no set sequence of the activation of the components (that is, no particular order is necessary for the generation of an emotion), and no set number or formula of components' mixture for any one emotion or its attendant feeling. Rather, the emotion and the feeling that subsequently emerges have everything to do with what one has been taught about certain circumstances or events.[65]

Following the interaction of components, then, action may be directed at the affective Object, depending on whether it is experienced as a problem or an opportunity: for example, the "pleasure-displeasure" spectrum influences the choice one makes in the moment, as in approach or withdrawal.[66] A person may choose to eat a piece of cake rather than an apple for dessert because she remembers that eating cake makes her feel good (or, more accurately, she remembers that she felt good when she ate cake once and has come to believe that eating cake will make her feel good). In addition, this emotion leads to behaviors: her facial expression, voice, and other changes can occur and are part of the experience of the emotion, or as preparation for—or recovery from—the behavior the emotion elicited.[67] In the experience of a feeling, all these components come to consciousness: changes in core affect, the affective quality of an Object, subsequent bodily changes, and behaviors and what these components together mean.

Accompanying the *conscious experience*, including the interpretation of the feeling, is also a flood of "metacognitive judgments" including a sense of urgency, an evaluation of what is socially appropriate, feelings of uncertainty, incredulity, and so on, so that the emotional event can seem beyond one's deliberate control.[68] That is, emotional events and one's interpretation of them (that is, one's *feelings*) seem outside one's reason, rational capacities, or will: "I feel anxious. Eating cake makes me feel good. I want to eat a piece of cake."[69] Finally, then, an *additional* and *separate* subjective and conscious experience occurs: the person experiences a particular *feeling* such as "fear" or "anger" or "desire." Russell calls this the "emotional meta-experience" of an event to indicate that it is not an introspection or naming of an event; rather it is a *self-perception*, the *categorization, explanation, or interpretation* of one's state of core affect in the moment.[70] People's *categorization* of their particular state, or their experience of and articulation of a feeling, is based on the other components of the episode. In other words, their feelings include the immediate or imagined stimulus, a change in core affect, the attributed affect, the affective Object, and the context in which they find themselves, both immediately and culturally. One's categorization of a particular feeling also depends enormously on what one has experienced in the past. In other words, *emotions* and their articulated experience as *feelings* are entirely context- and history-specific, based on the categories one has been taught ("Cake is for dessert; dessert comes after a main meal") and the concepts one has developed out of one's own experience: "I feel good when I eat cake. Sometimes I eat it for dessert and other times I eat it when I feel anxious." The categories and concepts of Objects and their affective quality are "given" by social-cultural contexts in concert with personal experience through the teaching of categories and concepts.

Emotions Are the Result of Learned Categories and Concepts

The categories involved in an emotion episode (that is, whether one feels "fear" or "anger" or "desire"), as well as how that episode is experienced and expressed are specified (and simplified) by the "folk concepts" that underlie a particular culture's words for emotion such as fear, anger, and so on.[71] Those who speak the same language likely have some *categories* and *concepts* that are in some ways similar (although they may also differ, given their own particular socialization within geographic regions and families of origin). *Emotion categorization* allows an individual to put the current state and situation within a broader body of knowledge, including social norms and expected roles.[72] Nevertheless, it is important to remember that *no one component* defines or is even essential for a particular emotional episode. In addition, no component is, by itself, an *emotion*, much less a *feeling*. Rather, the more components resemble the "script" or expectations of a specific emotion in a particular social or cultural context, the more likely that episode is to be categorized as a particular "emotion," and the more likely it is that people describe what they are feeling using culturally prescribed and taught "folk" (that is, commonly used) words such as *fear, anger, love* or *jealousy*. These words streamline, simplify, and categorize the experience one attributes to an Object. They help the brain function quickly and efficiently, and they help individuals communicate more effectively so that their friends understand, for example, when one says "I am hangry."

Components do not necessarily occur in a fixed sequence but instead are processes, many of which are components unfolding over time, changing in each moment as the various components interact with each other, with other processes, and with the surrounding environment.[73] Components interact collaboratively with other componential processes of the brain, and they interact with other psychological processes—such as cognitions, memory, and "reason"—in the context of the external world. In addition, components and the ways they come together in an emotion are dependent on prior conditions, both moment to moment and over time.[74] Furthermore, no possible components can be excluded from the construction of emotion, though some have more weight than others in categorizing an episode as emotional or as a particular type of emotion, depending on what is learned in one's social or cultural context. For example, whether one feels "anger" at being "disrespected" in a social hierarchy or feels "shame" for violating a hierarchy of power and status has everything to do with how one is socialized and the structure of the socio-political-cultural context: one must be *taught* that one deserves respect, and how and when to show it to others, and this lesson often comes from one's earliest experiences in childhood.[75] In other words, there are no *necessary* ingredients for any particular emotional episode, and none that exist in all episodes. Nothing is fixed: not the list of ingredients, the order in which they occur, or how they are mixed. This means an emotion and one's experience of the feeling that attends it cannot be fully or accurately depicted in any flow chart. The brain is continuously processing sensation from external stimulation, such as what one is seeing or imagining, what is happening in one's organs and limbs, and what one is perceiving, thinking, planning, expressing, acting, remembering, or hoping for. These processes in the human body never cease. All of these components are constantly lit up on the switchboard of the brain, and they are conscripted into emotional processes when socially learned categories and concepts call on them. It is only the *particular events* in a specific social context that define when a particular combination of these components will be identified as a particular feeling.[76]

Emotions and the Experience of Feelings Are Often the Result of "Predicted" Categories and "Simulations"

That human beings actively contribute to their own mental processes such as perceptions and cognitions is well accepted. In fact, the brain is a "predictive organ" that creates mental life by a process called predictive coding (which is the way the brain typically functions—it is an exceptionally efficient way of operating). Through predictive coding, the brain continually generates *hypotheses* based on past experience in a "top-down" fashion and tests them against incoming data.[77] These predictions are based on the categories and concepts developed out of previous encounters with a similar object, event, person, or situation and what one has been taught about it. For example, when one takes in sensory information about a green apple through the eyes to the visual cortex, neurons are processing the lines, edges, colors, and relative size of that apple. The neurons and clumps of neurons in the amygdala are firing rapidly, possibly changing one's core affect (arousal levels increase in the experience of something new, or familiar but exciting, and it is context that determines whether it is felt as "anxiety" or "excitement").[78] As the core affect changes—either in response to what, for a particular person, is an Object or, say, because of a subtle change in one's blood sugar or body temperature—multiple regions of the brain try to explain the reasons for the change to itself. The brain sifts through past experiences to determine whether one has ever encountered anything like this round green object with a stem before, and "converses" with the body to prepare it for a yet-to-be-determined action: "What is that object?" "What does one do with green apples?" "How do I feel about green apples?" Whatever the brain decides about past experiences with that object—whether learned in direct encounters with it or learned virtually in photos, movies, or books, for example—gives meaning to the present situation in the current context. Recognizing the category of "apple," then, invokes a concept of the apple (in this case, the green apple evokes memories of the school lunches the person's mother used to pack). The brain registers the color, shape, and size of the apple, and even if the person does not pick it up and take a bite, the brain adds information from prior experiences and *constructs* an emotional experience in the moment, creating a *simulation* of what one is seeing or experiencing based on a hypothesis.[79] The brain then compares its prediction to the barrage of actual data still coming in from the senses to confirm or disconfirm its expectations.[80] If the person perceives that it is a green apple and associates green apples with warm memories of his or her mother, the person will likely experience a pleasurable association, begin salivating, and may choose to eat it. If the person takes a bite and the apple is rotten, the warm feelings fade quickly: the simulation has been disconfirmed by additional incoming data (the apple is rotten, which is incongruent with past memories of eating perfectly ripe green apples during lunch), and the happy memory dissipates in that moment.

From the brain's perspective, then, the "commotion" from the heartbeat, breathing, digestion, and so on (the core affect) is the source of sensory input, as are those data (sight, smell, touch, hearing, taste) coming from the outside world.[81] In other words, the sensations from the organs, one's metabolism, changing body temperature, hunger, sleep deprivation, and so on are *affectively neutral*: they have no objective psychological meaning. It takes *categories* and *concepts* for them to take on meaning. And these are contextually dependent: for example, if a person feels an ache in his abdomen at 5:00 p.m., he might experience it as hunger. If a person ate something that did not taste fresh, she might attribute the feeling in her gut to that food and experience the same ache as nausea.[82] From an ache in one's abdomen, a person's brain constructs an instance of hunger, nausea, or dread, depending on the context. The same is true of emotions: an emotion is a person's brain's *creation* of what his or her bodily sensations mean, in relation to what is going on around him or her in the world and what he or she has experienced in the past, which has been categorized and conceptualized. "In every waking moment" the brain uses past experience and learned categories to guide actions and to give sensations meaning.[83] When the concepts involved are *emotion concepts*, the brain may then construct an instance of an emotional event. The human brain constructs out of that emotional event a particular feeling, or the awareness of an interpretation of an emotion episode. For psychological construction theorists, then, an instance of an emotion is a series of brain states that includes representations of the body (core affect), responses, *and* the additional information (categories, concepts) necessary to combine the components that make an emotion.[84]

The constructive process for emotions is invisible and constant, and it does not only represent what is being encountered in the moment but also fills what is not there based on prediction. In an emotion episode, the brain changes the firing of its own neurons in the absence of incoming input: the brain *fills in* information from the past and from the current environment to create an emotional episode. Human brains feel the sensory changes in people's bodies (changes in core affect) but give different meanings to those bodily sensations depending on past experience (and learning/coding) and on context. Barrett writes, "If you went on a run and your heart started pounding, you wouldn't be too alarmed. But as you're reading this [chapter], if your heart began racing and you began sweating, you might be concerned and call your doctor."[85] Context matters, because the *brain fills in information* that might be missing, predicting what is happening and what makes most sense given past experience. Perhaps one has heart disease in one's family and starts to feel anxious about sensing tachycardia while reading and calls 911. However, it may not be a heart attack at all; rather, the changes in heart rate—a contributing factor in core affect—may be the result of increased blood sugar after eating a piece of cake before settling down to read, and will pass once the body produces enough insulin to bring the blood sugar down.

This process of "filling in" information is the process of *simulation*—again, believed to be the default mode for all mental activity. Simulation is the brain's predictive function that applies categories or concepts that, in the process, *construct* the world out of an overwhelming amount of data. The brain simulates what is predicted because these processes streamline the input of data and allow for perceptions, cognitions, and actions that *make sense* given what has happened in the past and

what is happening in the moment in that particular context.[86] Categories and concepts are a primary tool for the brain to guess or *predict* the
meaning of incoming sensory input. Every moment one is alive, one's
brain uses categories and concepts to simulate the outside world, based
on learning through experience or exposure. The constructions *feel* like
they are arising naturally from within because they seem automatic and
the processes are invisible, but the reception of data from inside one's
body is given meaning in the context of the external world and is really
an interpretation *created in the moment* from immediate and past sensory
input.[87] The construction of an emotion, then, is based on immediate
sensations inside the body combined with (not usually conscious) memories of experiences that have been given categories, concepts, value, and
language from social contexts.[88]

In summary, then, psychological constructionist models of the mind
propose that emotions and feelings are mental states constructed out of
more basic, domain-general psychological processes. Researchers have
not found these mental events in specific areas or networks of the brain
but rather understand them as emerging from the constant, dynamic
interaction of large-scale distributed networks that support basic physiological and psychological processes (the "switchboard").[89] According to
a psychological constructionist view of the mind (which implicates the
generation of emotions and feelings), the brain is engaging in three kinds
of basic mental processes at any given time: (1) it is representing basic
sensory information from the world (incoming data from the eyes, ears,
notes, skin, and so on, called "exteroception"); (2) it is registering basic
"interoceptive" sensations from the body (that is, core affect); and (3) it is
making meaning of internal and external sensations by activating stored
representations of prior experience and socialized categories, values, and
expectations (or "categories" and "conceptualizations").

Barrett and her research team have learned that the only consistency
to emotion is its variability, so how do people (individually and collectively) know what "anger" is? The answer, they propose, is through learning, prediction, and creation in the moment, not through evolutionary
inheritance. In fact, the *only* thing human beings' brains have inherited
is the *capacity* to bond with others, which enhances safety and learning,
to take in sensory information, and to wire categories and concepts in
neural networks.[90] Barrett argues that although people "see" emotion
in a smirk or a furrowed brow, "hear" it in the pitch of a voice, or feel
emotions in one's own body, human brains are not actually programmed

by nature to recognize facial expressions or other "emotional displays" and then react to them.[91] Rather, the emotional information is in interpretation, which is learned in social relationships and cultural contexts. Nature provides the raw materials to wire the brain with categories and a conceptual system that is constructed by other people who speak emotion words in deliberate and culturally specific ways.[92]

The *capacity to learn* emotions is so fundamental and so critical to physical and social survival that it is given at birth. Research has shown that babies begin statistical learning at very early age, which means infants, and even those in utero, start to learn simple concepts, to group objects in categories, and to notice patterns.[93] (Newborns respond to words and linguistic patterns in their mother's language but not to words and patterns found in other languages.) Children learn emotion categories in other ways, too, such as being asked if they are angry or afraid in different situations and associating their bodily sensations and perceptions in that moment with the word *anger* or *fear*.[94] In other words, people use their acquired, context-specific knowledge to categorize and conceptualize the "bottom-up" information that is provided via the core affect.[95] More specifically, the experience of feeling an emotion—or seeing one in another person—occurs when the *conceptual knowledge* of that emotion learned from others categorizes the person's internal state. The experience of "having" an emotion or "recognizing" emotion in someone else happens when that person's behavior is categorized as "emotional"—or rather it "fits a category that [one's] social group or culture deems *emotional*."[96] This is what happens in the construction of an emotion episode and then in one's experience of a particular feeling.

In sum, then, psychological construction models of emotions propose that the human brain captures every instance of core affect that is culturally labeled and interpersonally taught. For example, the "folk concept" *anger* is learned over the course of one's life (but especially when learning is at its peak, between one and five years of age). The information is captured and coded in the networks of the brain as it occurs in a child's perception of exteroceptive data, actions, and interoception (which is represented as somatovisceral information—or core affect).[97] When the category "anger" is first being learned, the brain records all of these occurrences, later to be drawn on to represent knowledge of "anger," including the articulation of what it feels like, when it occurs, how a caregiver describes it, how one should express it (or not), respond to it, and so on. Subsequent occurrences of "anger" are then produced by a set of simulations that have developed as particular sensory, motor, and somatovisceral features that have been integrated across instances and settings when those experiences combined and were identified and labeled as "anger."[98]

The properties that are pointed out by early caregivers, or those that are functionally relevant in everyday activities in one's sociocultural context, will bind to core affect to represent an emotion episode of "anger" in that particular instance.[99] As instances of "anger" accumulate in the brain, creating a pattern, the category and brain simulation for "anger" develops, and conceptual knowledge about the experience and meaning of "anger" accrues.[100] Once the brain has created a simulation for the emotion category "anger" (or a mental cookie cutter shaped like "anger"[101]) through simulation, the brain can reenact smaller subsets of its content as specific simulations are needed to help make sense of one's experience in a situation and to help determine the action to take in response.[102]

A folk term such as *anger*, then, or *anxiety* is used to describe an emotional episode in a variety of situations: certain core affects that are related to attendant beliefs and appraisals and to the behaviors associated with them can be categorized as walking calmly away or eating a green apple. Similarly, in rage a person may yell, shake a fist, sit quietly fuming in a boardroom, or throw a tantrum on the playground.[103] In each case, the situational context (meaning both the physical and the relational context) will, in part, determine what behaviors will be performed and how they are interpreted when they are engaged. In this way, one's context—both immediate and past—is an intrinsic element of any episode of "fear."

This model helps explain why the somatovisceral (that is, core affect), cognitive, and behavioral patterns for "anger" and thus the emotion concepts of "anger" vary by context and situation. "Packets of conceptual knowledge" about an emotional concept will vary by person, context, situational demand, and so on. Thus, the experience, interpretation, and expression of an emotional episode will also vary, depending on context. There is not one "script" for "anger"; there are many. As Barrett notes, in any moment, the content of a "situated conceptualization" for the folk concept of an *emotion* will be constructed to contain those properties of emotions that are *contextually relevant*. Therefore, any emotion category (e.g., the cookie cutter shape for "anger" formed through learning processes in a particular context) contains only a small subset of the knowledge available about that emotion category.[104]

As noted, the simulations that give rise to "emotions" and "feelings" are learned through experience, whether actual or virtual—such as through television shows, movies, or electronic games. Each time someone labels a child's behavior with a folk emotion term—such as *anger* or *fear*—or every time the child watches the term being used to label someone else's behavior, the child's brain extracts a complex set of information about that instance and integrates it with past information associated with the same term already in memory. And the brain codes this information in its neural networks. Thus, people learn to represent emotion episodes in the same way they learn about other abstract concepts for which there is no biological basis, such as language or the concept of God or the value of justice.[105] In this view, then, language plays a strong causal role in the development of categories and concepts of emotion knowledge.[106] For this reason, children acquire emotion categories that conform to their culture: there is no *biological pattern* for anger or fear, only sociocultural patterns.[107]

Categories and Concepts as Contextually Functional

The categorization and conceptualization of emotions is socially functional. Barrett suggests that "the emotion words for *anger* (e.g., *angry*, *hostile*, *irritated*, and so on) serve as the glue that integrates a variety of different sensorimotor states into one category called *anger* in ways that others in one's group can understand and relate to."[108] Language and learning, then, determine the emotion categories and concepts people acquire as well as which simulations their brains generate for emotional categorization and conceptualization. This helps in novel situations as well as more familiar ones, since simulations "fill in the gaps" of sensory perception in a core affective experience.[109] It is an efficient and effective method of cognition that human brains have evolved.

Different cultures have different norms that drive which "recipes" of ingredients are experienced as common concepts for "anger," "fear," or "happiness." This is why people from different cultures will have varying emotional concepts and consequently, different emotional experiences. It also helps explain the similarities: for example, most people learn that snakes are dangerous—because objectively speaking they can be life-threatening for humans—although some learn to handle them as collectors or in religious ritual, demonstrating that socialization regarding and beliefs about them can be altered. While core affect is universal and "psychologically irreducible," the affective quality and attribution to particular objects (thus making them Objects) vary within a person over time,[110] and across people,[111] groups, and cultures.[112] In other words, when people identify and describe an emotion they are feeling, they are communicating their core affective experience in a particular moment in time as categorized and conceptualized by their sociocultural environment.[113] The *processes* of relating core affect, attributed affect, perception of affective quality, and emotional meta-experience are universal processes, but the specific *categories* and *concepts* of emotional episodes—that is, whether and when an emotional episode occurs, how it is expressed to others, and the emotional meta-experience (what it *feels* like)—vary by social and cultural context.[114] Emotions, then, are a window into a particular culture in a particular time and place, as well as into one's personal experiences of the past and present, and expectations of—including hopes and goals for—the future.

What is an "emotion," then? Each emotion episode bears a resemblance to other neurological episodes, but the only thing "emotions" have in common is that *a particular language community calls them emotional.*[115] Particular psychological events are *categorized* as an emotion within a particular social context.[116] An emotion is an emotion, then, if one is *taught* that it is.[117] The same is true of feelings.

Emotion Categories Organize the World and One's Life and Simplify Functioning in One's World

The scientific study of emotion has undergone a "revolution" in the last thirty years as technology has become more precise and as theories about emotions' etiologies and functions have developed increasing sophistication. Nevertheless, there are some assumptions that these new understandings share with earlier research programs. First, any theory of emotions—including the psychological-constructionist understandings—must be an evolutionary account, even if it is not the specific evolutionary account proposed by the basic emotion view.[118] Second, emotions must be understood to communicate people's values, beliefs, and appraisals. Third, all theories of emotion and feelings (except those of the early philosophers and theologians) assume that emotional episodes are functional in some way, either to regulate social relationships or to regulate one's own equilibrium, even if the functionality is not viewed in the sense of being life-giving in the long run, but instead is defined by "collective intentionality."[119] Emotions help human beings navigate their particular cultural and social worlds.

Emotions, then, are closely linked to organisms' survival—both physical and social—and, more complexly, to well-being in humans.[120] Emotions can signify needs, values, and goals to the one experiencing them and the ones observing them. Emotions and the experience of feelings draw attention and energy toward what individuals and groups hold important to their well-being, and they warn against what is life-limiting (understood physiologically, psychologically, and socially).[121] In fact, while the core of emotional episodes (core affect) can have noncognitive causes such as hormonal changes, pharmacological agents, satiety, or hunger, changes in core affect can also result from the process of valuation.[122] Indeed, valuation (that is, "what is good/what will harm me") is so critical to survival and well-being that people constantly and automatically evaluate situations and the Objects they encounter for those Objects' relevance and value in relation to survival or well-being,[123] for whether they are significant to that individual within a certain milieu,[124] for whether they are relevant to goals,[125] and for whether and how to engage them.[126] These processes are finely tuned to particular environments: cultural influences often define what is understood as valuable or meaningful such that each emotional episode is a "highly specialized package of conceptualized knowledge" that is situated in a social context and tailored to meet the needs of the person in that context.[127] Emotions, then, are the result of constant and ongoing assessments of what is happening around and inside oneself, in conjunction with what one has learned from others and through experience. Emotions—as experienced and as observed—bind individuals together; act as signals to oneself and others; act as clarifiers and motivators for the pursuit of needs, goals, and values; serve as regulators of self, others, and situations; and guide action, thus enabling survival and even well-being, at least in a particular context.

The challenge of what to do with emotions is that emotions are both culturally scripted and transpersonal, and yet they are also deeply personal and moment-specific. Emotions are scripted in the sense that they are the result of categorizations and conceptions "given" by one's significant caregivers' mediation of sociocultural scripts to each individual and each group. They are personal and deeply subjective because each emotional episode—and each experience of feeling—is wholly one's own, created out of the long list of available ingredients one could use in any recipe, from what is happening in one's body at the time, and from the beliefs, values, goals, history of relationships, and neurological wiring in that moment. Knowing how to use emotions and feelings in the pursuit of well-being is a complex task. Figuring out how emotions and feelings both limit and support well-being will require a nuanced understanding of what exactly flourishing is.

Conclusion

Emotions and the feelings that sometimes attend them are less reactions to specific events and more a part of a compilation of ingredients emerging from the everyday ebb and flow of the sensory input that is made meaningful in the moment. Emotions are not the result of neural networks that are hardwired in the brain, ready to be "triggered" by a particular (and specific) stimulus. Rather, evolution has given the human newborn the capacities to learn (especially categories and concepts), to develop (cognitively, functionally, relationally, emotionally), to bond (first to primary caregivers, then to others), to learn, to register core affect, to compute valuation, and to code these in the continuous capacities of the brain. These raw capacities are given and not constructed, but in the case of emotions and feelings, everything else is constructed. Human beings' *capacities* for emotions are hardwired and evolutionary because these capacities simplify processes of living through categorization, conceptualization, and organization of the world. However, each emotion is caused and organized, a "one-time event built on the fly." Emotions are not something that just happen to people: people create them. Perhaps, then, people are freer in relation to their emotions and their feelings than they might have thought, and they can actively seek and steer their emotions to cultivate well-being. It also means that emotion and feeling work has moral dimensions, as the earliest philosophers and theologians thought; emotions can support people's well-being and they can impede it.

An adequate understanding of emotions' origins and functions, then, will recognize the ways they differ depending on context—in people's experience of them, expressions of them, and interpretations of them, as cultural anthropologist Catherine Lutz and others have shown. An adequate understanding of emotions will recognize that they are utterly physiological, as William James did. But in accepting that emotional episodes are fundamentally rooted in the body, we must not make the mistake of essentializing emotions' origins or functions, as, for example, MacLean did. Nor ought we accept that certain emotions emerge in the context of particular social structures, as Emil Durkheim, Karl Marx, and Theodore Kemper argued. It is a mistake to believe that certain systemic structures *inevitably* produce certain emotions. Rather, an adequate understanding of emotions will investigate *why* certain emotions arise in certain contexts and at certain times in particular people. I have argued that psychological constructionism offers tools for such an investigation. However, as useful as psychological constructionism is for integrating the until-now discrete and separate research programs (the "classical" views) on emotions, it does not promise to answer the question of emotions' role in human flourishing. What is still needed is a view of flourishing that can be used as a standard against which emotions' origin, experience, value, and use can be measured. Returning to the interests of the early philosophers and theologians will help us close the circle, though the perspective on flourishing in chapter 7 differs from what was explored in chapters 1 and 2.

7

Emotions as Crucial

Emotions and Human Flourishing

Introduction

The integral relationship between individuals' emotional lives and the social-cultural-political environments in which they find themselves underscores the need for critical analysis of emotions. Having clarity about what is life-giving in relation to one's emotions—as well as what is a life-giving social system (what the early Greeks called the polis)—is more important than ever. Psychological construction models of emotions offer hope for emotions' use in both personal and systemic improvements. Individuals construct emotions in the moment, in context, and people can develop the capacity to reflect on their core affect, on the affective attributions that are given to Objects, on the goals, needs, and values their emotions indicate, and on how individuals' personal experiences interface with their world.

Historical and sociological accounts suggest that emotions function to keep people together in groups where individuals are safest and in which they can cooperate to enhance resources, thereby promoting their survival. Neuroscientific research affirms this view: staying close, moving to a shared rhythm, and being synchronized to the emotions of others is what keeps human beings alive. Keeping together, then, is fundamental to flourishing.[1] The challenge, however, is that not all rhythms are life-giving; some groups breed death.[2] Adolf Hitler set the beat for a

153

march designed to create a national solidarity which targeted and eliminated millions of people. The world watched as ISIS moved in formation across Syria—murdering and pillaging as it went—and accounts of the devastation wrought by groups engaged in racialized or sexualized violence dominate headlines around the globe. Such realities are haunting, and they serve as a helpful check on an overly optimistic view of emotions and their uses. When individuals surrender their own will and agency to the command of another, or when people merge into a group of fellow human beings for a sense of security, they often suspend their critical judgment and begin making choices that may meet immediate needs but impede human flourishing. Keeping together can serve purposes of life or it can serve evil and death. It is important to know which groups to join, which rhythmic movements to share, what beat to follow. Knowing the difference is critical in the effort to cultivate humans' well-being.

Thus, while emotions such as love and the desire to belong bind human beings together and support their survival, the same emotions can be manipulated, leading people to commit heinous crimes in the name of their group.[3] There are other ways emotions and the choices they motivate are not life-giving, too.[4] Some behaviors and attempts to address emotions and the feelings that attend them are life-limiting: for example, consuming material goods or overeating—both of which can change one's emotional state, or core affect, in the moment—do not ultimately alleviate anxiety. It matters what people individually and collectively "set their hearts on," as early Greek philosopher Epicurus and early Christian theologian Augustine noted.[5]

In the context of early Greco-Roman philosophy, eudaimonia—usually translated as "happiness" but sometimes as "well-being" or "flourishing"—meant the good life, and in exploring eudaimonia, philosophers were interested in the passions' relationship to ethical living, the development of one's character, and one's contribution to the polis.[6] Early Christian theologians were interested in the passions' role in salvation, which they understood as aligning one's will with God's (happiness, most thought, could only be achieved in the afterlife). Natural scientists seem less interest in questions of eudaimonia; for them, it seems, it is enough to communicate with other organisms in order to survive physically so that genes will be passed on and the species can continue. Psychotherapists are implicitly interested in well-being, though they do not always articulate clearly what they mean by the term: the ability to love and work well (or to be self-actualized) seems the primary goal. For social scientists, belonging to a group helps afford security. Finally, although they may not be explicit about it, contemporary neuropsychologists' work could be interpreted to suggest that the entire human organism is geared toward *life* in complex ways and that emotions are crucial to being fully alive: they relate in ways previously not possible the intrapsychic, interpersonal, social-contextual, and neurological components at play in emotional episodes. This chapter attempts to integrate these views into a more explicit, holistic understanding of flourishing and its cultivation—and emotions' role in that.

Because there are life-limiting responses to and uses of emotions, having some way to adjudicate what *is* life-giving and what is life-limiting—both individually and in the social order—is important. An understanding of the difference will allow for a more positive and careful approach to emotions than a quick dismissal of emotions' value— so common in Western cultures—allows. While pastoral theologians such as myself—as well as philosophers, theologians, ethicists, and psychologists—often understand well-being as the goal of our work (at least implicitly) and have thought hard about how to achieve it, the actual features of flourishing, or what it might require, have not gotten as much sustained attention as the goal warrants.[7] Understanding how emotions can be useful for flourishing will require overcoming some of the either/or thinking that has dominated thought about emotions—for example, that they are *either* personal *or* socially constructed, that they are *either* positive *or* negative, and that the good is *either* of this world *or* in the next. Psychological-construction models help overcome some of the classical models' divisions that have perplexed for over a century. A more refined understanding of human flourishing can help overcome some of the challenges posed by early understandings of eudaimonia.

The good news is that, despite the challenges of controlling emotions with the will, people have more control in relation to their emotions than is often thought; change for the better is possible. This suggests that human beings can harness their emotions toward well-being if they understand what some of the features of well-being are. But positive change will also require developing disciplined practices toward exploring emotions and willingness to intentionally work toward engaging what leads to more flourishing.

Early Philosophers' and Theologians' Understandings of the Good or Saved Life

Despite centuries of study, there still seems to be little consensus on the appropriate relationship of emotions to a good or desired life. Indeed, there is little agreement about the nature of the good life or human flourishing itself. For example, while Plato understood the passions to be anathema to the right and desirable life, Aristotle found them critical to the development of virtuous character and meaningful participation in a life-sustaining polis. Where the Stoics understood the passions to be the cause of suffering, philosopher and medical doctor Galen understood them as a useful diagnostic tool. Although Augustine and Aquinas considered the passions to be signs of the Fall and human brokenness, Charles Darwin understood emotional expressions as natural and critical to survival. And indeed, since Darwin's time, emotions' importance for survival, both physical and social, has enjoyed a place in both popular culture and psychotherapeutic practice. In fact, I have argued that each of the perspectives on emotions' functions, effects, and value informs contemporary confusion about emotions' appropriate place in people's lives. But survival is a narrow and basic requirement for the telos (aim or goal) of life. While necessary to life by definition, survival does not say much about the nature of and means toward flourishing.[8]

In most cases, examinations of emotions have been more descriptive than prescriptive. Although the scientist Paul MacLean mused at the end of a seminal article that "we are witnessing the evolution of a spirit with a concern for the future suffering and dying of all living things," many scientists shy away from making normative statements about the good life and what it entails.[9] Psychoanalyst Sigmund Freud dared suggest that his aim was to enable analysands to love and work, and psychotherapeutic practitioners use emotions to support life-giving relationships—to oneself and others—and self-actualization, even though they seem loath to be prescriptive about what genuine flourishing might entail.[10] Because recent neuroscience has helped connect the intrapsychic, interpersonal, and social-political-cultural contexts with the physical, embodied aspects of emotions, a normative vision of well-being will need to address its manifestations at the personal or individual level as well as the interpersonal, group, institutional, organizational, and societal level.[11]

In other words, while it is a worthwhile pursuit, loving or working "better" only *implies* a value system: What does it mean to love "better"? What does it mean to work "better"? What does self-actualization look like and how does one achieve it given the very real constraints, especially on targeted and oppressed people's lives? Answers to these questions are deeply significant for understanding what "human flourishing" might mean and what it will require. Constructive additions to the conversation about emotions and flourishing from philosophers and theologians—including pastoral theologians—then, are crucial.[12] Pastoral theologians—whose work ideally draws on many disciplines, including psychology, social and cultural theories, science, and theologies—are well suited for the task of proposing a vision of flourishing. Indeed, although pastoral theologians are not always explicit about what they mean by it, people's flourishing is, fundamentally, the goal of our work. Pastoral theologians' efforts are informed, explicitly and not, by the earliest thinkers on the matter, but we also seek to critically analyze and augment the thinking of those who have come before.[13]

Early philosophers' interest in eudaimonia was framed as the "happy" or "good" life, with emphases on ethics and moral action. For example, Socrates and Plato, the Stoics, and Aristotle all reacted strongly to what they perceived as the increasing materialism and acquisitiveness of their fellow citizens. They feared that the "race for material aggrandizement, personal honors, martial recognitions, and literary awards were dwarfing the search for truth and virtue."[14] Athenians, they feared, were trying to attain happiness through gymnastics, pleasure, and even the mere study of philosophy (instead of genuine contemplation) rather than through the proper channels of cultivating right thinking and virtuous living.

Socrates and Plato understood happiness (or well-being) to be the result of a calm character that flows from a right relationship to the passions; they assumed that if one controlled the passions with reason, one could achieve an enduring sense of "happiness." Plato's view of well-being had a "decidedly mystical and otherworldly" quality—a telos predicated on a vision of the good that transcends life on earth.[15] Because embodying pure reason was the ultimate goal for Plato, happiness is an intellectual virtue, and happiness achieved through reason is an objective condition of the soul. To refer to happiness as an objective condition as early Greco-Roman philosophers did suggests that it is not just a matter of a person's experience or belief that one is happy; rather, well-being must be a state confirmed by others based on some generally agreed-upon criteria established by wise members of one's community, both contemporary and historic.[16]

Because of his tripartite view of the soul, Plato defined happiness as the harmony of the soul such that reason, the highest level of the soul, moderates and controls aggressive appetites and desires.[17] In Plato's view, one's passions are not inherently bad, but they must be assiduously controlled. Likewise, health, wealth, physical beauty, friends, love, honor, and so on are not viewed as *inherently* good in Plato's schema, though they may be *instrumental* goods if used wisely in the pursuit of wisdom and dispassionate living. However, Plato took pains to emphasize that no instrumental good is sufficient or even *necessary* for happiness. Consistent with his perspectives on the passions, then, Plato privileged the soul over the body and argued that human beings must rise above the material realities and vicissitudes of the earthly realm if they wish to find happiness. And individuals *should* wish so, for happiness thus defined is the ultimate goal of human life, early philosophers agreed.[18]

Philosophers who followed Plato's thinking, such as the highly influential Stoics, took Plato's work further than Plato had perhaps intended when they dismissed the importance of the passions for happiness or well-being. The Stoics declared that the passions create suffering and people should resist and even extinguish all desires. By minimizing their passions, the Stoics believed, people can be happy as they nurture the virtues of "negative freedoms" including *freedom from* need, want, desire, personal or social success, and material well-being.[19] The radical asceticism that the Stoics argued leads to happiness requires self-control, poverty, and a repudiation of societal conformity. Thus, well-being is cultivated by internal discipline and the dismissal of conventional morality,[20] patriotism, pursuit of wealth, courtesies and refinements, fame, honor, reputation, and sexuality.[21] Even valuable endeavors such the arts and sciences or the pursuit of knowledge should be treated with indifference. People who seek well-being should be indifferent to both joy and grief, accepting with calm the vicissitudes of life. The Stoics argued that common things people desire, such as love, honor, good health, avoiding maltreatment from others, "congenial" family life, and personal freedom, all depend too much on external circumstances beyond individuals' control and should be held with indifference.[22] By living according to nature, by elevating reason over the passions, and by nurturing good habits—especially of self-control, right belief, and right behavior—people can free themselves from the desire to change the unalterable and be indifferent to both pleasure and pain. In other words, the Stoics understood well-being as freedom from the passions and achievement of inner peace (*apatheai*).

The Epicureans took a different tack than the Stoics: the passions, including pleasure, are not evil. Instead, pleasure is the highest good. However, only *certain* pleasures are worthy, namely the simple, life-sustaining ones. Worthy pleasures do not include the "tortured trinity" of wine, sex, and song.[23] Rather, right pleasures prevent pain and produce a serene spirit: these "pleasures" include health, self-control, independence, moderation, simplicity, cheerfulness, friendship, prudence, intellectual and aesthetic values, peace of mind, and conscience. The calm, tranquil, and harmonious life, then, is the happy or good life for the Epicureans.[24] However, because humans are beset by a condition of wanting more and more, humans can become addicted to pleasure and not practice self-control, allowing themselves too much of the wrong things. Because Epicurus' goal was to avoid pain (especially mental suffering), he did not advise being invested in politics, marriage, or family. These and other passionate pursuits produce excessive and inexhaustible desire, as well as anxiety, and thus should be avoided.[25] Epicurus advocated for the development of the virtues that bring peace, especially restraint and denial. Epicurean philosophy promoted an individualistic, egoistic hedonism that seemed grounded in withdrawal from public life.[26]

Aristotle's position differed significantly from those of the thinkers he followed. Aristotle understood happiness as an activity of the soul in accord with *excellence in the pursuit of one's highest capacities*. Aristotle heralded well-being (eudaimonia) as the greatest good because it is desired for its own sake, not for the sake of anything else, and because it is the end toward which all other goods aim.[27] For Aristotle, eudaimonia is not simply a mental state or disposition: because Aristotle was not a dualist like Plato, he did not believe the soul can be a separate entity from the body. Thus, he argued that well-being requires, among other things, fulfilling the needs of the body.

Aristotle argued, then, that happiness requires living well and faring well. *Living well* consists of understanding and acting on the intellectual and moral virtues: the pursuit of truth, understanding, prudence, courage, temperance, and generosity.[28] These virtues are predicated on the rules found in practical and moral wisdom—"the judgement of the enlightened."[29] Thus, Aristotle believed that living virtuously out of the discerned wisdom of careful reflection is the highest value and necessary for well-being. However, living well, while necessary for well-being, is not sufficient to achieve it: Aristotle's understanding of eudaimonia also requires *faring well.*

For Aristotle, faring well encompasses a host of practical matters: a measure of material stability, a good family life, friends, leisure time for contemplation, personal freedom, health, and a "not repulsive physical appearance."[30] Aristotle also thought that a well-ordered and stable state (polis) was necessary to provide the opportunities and preconditions for happiness. Thus, Aristotle's understanding of eudaimonia was more complex than others': well-being requires contemplation on what is the highest good, the development of intellectual and moral virtues to support personal and social well-being. Eudaimonia also requires a society that supports the faring well of its citizens (though Aristotle privileged contemplation and virtuous living above all else).[31] As Aristotle defined it, then, eudaimonia requires knowledge, wisdom, courage, temperance, justice, and the pursuit of truth. Happiness (well-being) is neither a mood nor an emotion. Rather, it is an activity that accompanies virtues in action. Eudaimonia is understood to be an objective condition—a state—that arises from leading a certain type of life, achieved only through the development of a virtuous character and the establishment of social and political systems. Though Plato had imagined true well-being as fully achievable only when one eschews earthly matters, both the Stoics and Aristotle understood happiness in earthly terms. This view did not last, however.

Christianity overtook Stoicism as the dominant philosophy of life in the West, and the Stoic and Aristotelian this-worldly understanding of well-being gave way to an otherworldly view. Early Christian theologians co-opted Plato's transcendent vision and "remedied his penchant for abstractness," offering the masses ultimate hope and a transformed world.[32] For example, Neoplatonist philosopher-theologian Plotinus, who wedded Platonism and Christianity, argued that human beings are defined by their immortal souls. Perfect happiness is achievable only in the otherworldly realm and consists of the everlasting merging of the soul with God, the One.[33] Only through a mystical experience given by the special grace of God can people temporarily glimpse perfect happiness. Plotinus argued that the goods and experiences of this world are unimportant and may distract from the primary telos of human beings: moving people's souls toward the One. Thus, Plotinus disagreed with Aristotle, arguing that salvation does not require good fortune, material success, positive personal relationships, or a state that supports well-being for its citizens. Rather, happiness as salvation, and the preparation for it, requires only the proper training of the soul for its highest destiny: people must live virtuously and practice fortitude, prudence, wisdom, and temperance. In short, happiness requires nurturing reason and practices that move the soul toward God.[34]

Augustine agreed with Plotinus that salvation is the telos (or end goal) of human life and added that people's desire for salvation is an instinct "implanted" by God to draw them toward God. For this reason, Augustine argued, salvation really *is* the greatest good.[35] Augustine defined happiness/salvation as the satisfaction of desire, though because only union with God could finally satisfy ultimate desire, it matters which desires one is talking about. Happiness cannot involve a "treadmill" of satisfying desire after desire; rather, happiness comes with the satisfaction of *all* desires and liberation from the cycle of desiring.[36] The logic of happiness/salvation for Augustine, then, suggests that only *freedom from* need and want can produce genuine happiness; humans are created to desire God alone, and thus are naturally drawn to the extinction of all otherworldly desires. Because happiness is the fulfillment of all desire and can be found only in God, real happiness cannot be attained in this world, nor can well-being/salvation be destroyed by the contingencies of life. Augustine's revisioning of desire and happiness suggests that the Stoics' prescription for inner peace cannot succeed in this life; nor is Aristotle's appeal to a measure of material success or meaningful relationships on earth correct. For Augustine, right desire is God-given and leads the saved out of this world and into union with God. While this understanding of happiness/well-being/salvation was the dominant one among early philosophers and theologians, it was not the only one.

Other early Christian theologians were more interested in the human experience of life as lived. For example, Boethius (480–524 CE) and Aquinas directly confronted the tragic quality of life on earth, acknowledging that suffering is difficult and deprives people of finite goods but that it can offer an opportunity to reaffirm what is the ultimate good: that is, God. Boethius believed that if one allows it, the tragedies of one's life can highlight what should matter most and help people realign their perspectives from earthly suffering to heavenly grace. Aquinas agreed and argued that a modicum of suffering is part of a saved life because individuals define themselves not *only* by the amount of pleasure they experience but also by the amount of suffering they bear and the ways they engage it.[37] Pain is not evil as such, then, Aquinas argued. In fact, he thought, Christ's experience on the cross shows the ways suffering can be a necessary part of the saved life. Thus, creative and virtuous human beings can turn suffering into benefit if they respond in ways that bring them closer to God. These theologians understood the connection between pain and a good life, pointing out that a pain-free life is not a human life: humans are not rocks, or islands. Part of being human is the experience of loss and pain, and people naturally grieve.[38] And ideally, Boethius and Aquinas argued, individuals grow through their experiences of pain.

Theories on Human Flourishing

On Not Being Well: "Happiness Is Overrated"[39]

Contemporary philosophers have again taken up the question of eudaimonia and its pursuit as proposed by Plato, the Stoics, and the Epicureans—especially the use of reason to avoid pain—and early understandings have come under fire.[40] If either the minimization of suffering or maximization of pleasure genuinely determines well-being, contemporary philosophers point out, then such a life would be universally enviable. One might ask whether one would be willing to trade one's life for that of an oyster that is in a continuous state of pleasure (imagine it at the bottom of the sea in the perfect conditions).[41] If something holds one back from eagerly agreeing to be an oyster, then something else must be at stake in the good life.[42] Perhaps, then, happiness understood as an enduring pleasant and contented state is not the highest good. It may be that freedom from pain and distress—the dominant view in Greek thought for centuries—is not enough. It is conceivable that freedom from pain and distress, as some early philosophers understood it—or even a subjective feeling of happiness, as contemporary popular culture might have it—is not the ultimate goal of human life.[43]

Many theories of "happiness" as bases for understanding well-being, then, are inadequate in at least five ways. First, the dominant connotation of happiness is being in a cheerful mood.[44] Second, life satisfaction—the measure of *how good one feels* in the particular moment rather than *how well one judges one's life to be going* more generally—holds too privileged a place in popular understandings of happiness.[45] Both are tied too closely to the subjective experience of feeling happy.[46] Third, the idea of happiness as a subjective feeling does not take into account the importance of meaningful engagement in something larger than oneself and the importance of meaning making, especially in the face of suffering. More specifically, the focus on pleasure in early philosophers' and contemporary under-standings of happiness do not account sufficiently for the fact that people often eschew pleasure and comfort for the purpose of achieving a higher, more meaningful goal. Fourth, happiness cannot sustain people in the midst of the losses, grief, suffering, pain, and disappointments that come in the quotidian experiences of human life. Finally, theories of happiness do not attend sufficiently to oppressive social, political, and economic systems that impede well-being for most of the world. Something more than a feeling of completely satisfied desire or freedom from desire or pain altogether is needed for a more adequate understanding of flourishing.

On the Meaningful Life

Desire and the pursuit of its satisfaction are a part of being human. With-out desires, without strivings, without incomplete projects to address and a future to work toward, human beings would be "saturated sponge(s) of desire"[47]—oysters at the bottom of a sea—which is not, evidently, a life most people would choose.[48] Most people need desires to pursue lest they be taken over by boredom and anomie.[49] Contentment—at least if it is understood as inactivity, a final termination, or merely savoring the past without moving actively toward the future—ends in boredom or retreat from the world.[50] However, contentment and satisfaction understood more robustly are compatible with ongoing creative activity and thus flourishing. In a revised view, happiness and contentment are not resting points but part of a positive self-appraisal that acknowledges one is on the right path. In this view, happiness/well-being includes savoring the past while working toward a hopeful future, and a sense of satisfaction in the life one is engaged in creating.[51] In this view, happiness includes high levels of robust meaning-making, the attainment of goals that mat-ter, and the conquest of challenging obstacles.[52] These are elements of a meaningful life that have been found critical to flourishing.

However, a meaningful life without the subjective experience of happiness can be a difficult one. In other words, the feeling of being happy is not everything, but it is *something*.[53] The annals of history are full of the names of people whose lives were deeply significant, even valuable, in terms of their contributions to culture—literature, music, art, politics, intellectual resources—but who cannot be said to have been happy. As meaningful as their lives were, those of musician Ludwig van Beethoven, president Abraham Lincoln, prolific author Emily Dick-inson, and theorist of moral development Lawrence Kohlberg (to name a few well-known figures) were difficult, beset with crises and pain. In each of their lives, there are indications of dark depressions and suffering. Lincoln almost killed himself in the depths of his depression, and biographers believe Kohlberg *did* take his own life.[54] Despite the fact that their lives were enormously valuable and eminently worth living, surely it would have been better if these people could have been happy *as well as* being some of the world's greatest creators.[55]

Flourishing's opposite comes in many forms, and it is often recognized when it is seen or experienced. Boredom, anomie, and a sense of listlessness are the opposite of zest.[56] Loneliness and depression can kill. Descriptors of "unflourishing" include chronic and debilitating anxiety or depression, stagnation, rigidity, despair, cynicism, hopelessness, disintegration, a sense of fragmentation, and contempt.[57] This sense of "deadness" can come as a result of many things, and it can affirm and complicate some earlier thinkers' views: I would argue that life is diminished in the midst of deprivation but also in over-indulgence. One's humanity is deadened through a sense of entitlement but also through extreme self-sacrifice and self-abnegation.[58] The deadening of enthusiasm can be wrought both by overcommitment and overextension and also by alienation from oneself, others, and God (or "Goodness Beyond Being"). In an effort to "thicken" the understanding of well-being beyond feeling happy or creating value, then, it is important to distinguish between happiness, well-being, and flourishing.

In common usage, the word *happiness* refers to a personal, subjective experience, but this differs from the understanding of eudaimonia or flourishing. Well-being and flourishing are composed of multiple components—including participation in creating what is good for the whole, not just for oneself (although that is important, too). Happiness as touted in contemporary popular culture, then, is too shallow, this-worldly, and individualistic to be the ultimate aim of life. There must be something more. It is possible that happiness as a subjective experience *and* a sense of well-being *and* participation in what is good for oneself and others are required for flourishing. Furthermore, while happiness is difficult to measure (one can only *say* whether one feels happy or not), well-being and flourishing have several measurable elements, though none fully defines well-being or is sufficient for flourishing.[59]

Experiencing Well-Being

Well-being and flourishing are found in the balance of various qualities of human life: too much or too little of any one thing, including pleasure and pain, diminishes a person's capacities to flourish.[60] In addition, most people would not want to extirpate unpleasant emotions just because they are unpleasant; sometimes depression, anxiety, or anger can be important indicators of unjust systems.[61] Both "unpleasant" and "pleasant" (or "positive" and "negative") emotions, then, can be important for well-being. It seems that well-being is found somewhere in the mix and balance of multiple elements and in emotions' indication of them. A fulsome understanding of flourishing must be the bar against which emotions, feelings, and people's responses to them are judged.

Aristotle argued that at the individual level, components that comprise well-being include some level of physical and psychological safety and security and some measure of material stability, which implies equal access to required resources. *Well-being* also includes some freedom of choice, satisfying and life-giving intimate relationships with friends and family, and time to reflect on what matters most.[62] Well-being includes opportunities to pursue forms of engagement that express one's most compelling values at a particular moment and across one's life span.[63] It implies being treated with dignity and respect by oneself and others, being valued by oneself and others, maximizing one's capacities, and having a sense of satisfaction, even pride, in one's accomplishments. Well-being also requires a polis, or society, whose organizations and institutions encourage and support the good for all its members.[64] It also suggests participation in the development and nurture of such a society, including commitment to justice and inclusion.[65] Flourishing has many components that support faring well, living well, and being well. In addition, flourishing adds the element of joy or zest to the features of well-being.[66] Flourishing can be recognized when it is seen in others and when it is experienced subjectively: the descriptors that come to mind include creative fullness, liveliness, responsiveness, passion, compassion, zest, awe in the wonder and mystery of life itself (all life), some measure of freedom, and participation in systems that support the good of the whole. In other words, when people are flourishing they are more able to live with dynamic faith; hope; a sense of deep connection to themselves, others, and the earth; profound love; and even joy.[67] (In fact, when they are flourishing, people are more resilient and are more likely to engage.)

A more-nuanced understanding of flourishing, then, suggests that a subjective response—a conscious condition of contentment, a sense of meaningfulness, satisfaction, and at least occasional joy—is also necessary, and distinguishes flourishing from well-being. However, as noted, one's feelings of joy—while a necessary part of flourishing—are not sufficient for it. An objective assessment that one is pursuing activities that *matter* for the good of oneself, others, and the whole must be included in an adequate understanding of human flourishing. In other words, people can meet (and know they had met) all the culturally accepted conditions of happiness and still be sad or highly anxious. (Think of the wealthy businessman constantly anxious about maintaining his preferred standard of living.) Thus, flourishing cannot be only about meeting external, objective, culturally prescribed conditions. It objectively matters *what* a person contributes to; thus, flourishing has moral implications. Furthermore, it should be clear that as important as feeling happy is, *pursuing* happiness or joy as a subjective feeling will inevitably fail: genuine joy comes only as a *result* of meaningful and robust engagement in objectively valuable pursuits. In fact, flourishing is best understood as a by-product—not a final goal. Flourishing accompanies ongoing activity; it is not an end state. This assumes that being engaged in something that truly matters (is worthy) is fundamental to being human.

Humans and the Creation and Discernment of Value

Human beings are, by nature, valuing creatures. To value something is to make it an object of concern and to want to engage it, and the desire for engagement and participation in something larger than oneself is a fundamental part of being human.[68] Human beings cannot be stonily indifferent to themselves, others, and the world around them and retain their humanity.

Human beings naturally create, and sometimes discover, value in the world. And because human beings *value* people, things, or experiences, they inevitably experience loss. Because of the losses one inevitably endures in life, because of the frustration one experiences in the process of pursuing one's grandest projects and highest values, because human beings suffer illness—and any number of other challenges—pain cannot be avoided.[69] And grief is the appropriate responses to the exigencies of life.[70] Rather than being inherently evil, then, pain—people's emotions in response to it, including also frustration, anger, and fear—confirms that certain things matter and reminds people that they care.[71] The challenge of creative living, however, is to use one's painful experiences for practical advantage, as a springboard for the pursuit of robust meaning and grand hopes for life—in efforts toward a life of flourishing.[72]

Both the subjective experience of happiness and a life of meaningful engagement are required for flourishing, then:[73] feelings of happiness alone are too thin a gruel to sustain it. (Indeed, "happy" people should be interrogated for their level of depth, engagement, and positive engagement in the world; their happiness may have been purchased at an "unacceptable price."[74]) Human flourishing, then, requires rich and complex criteria. Flourishing, as it is being defined here, assumes a connection to what is identified as valuable, either by objective standards or by human appraisal that has accumulated over time by people whose lives history has deemed positive and meaningful.[75] Because human beings naturally find and help create value, flourishing requires, in part, human experience and expression of creative power. People often achieve flourishing by confronting and overcoming sometimes formidable challenges and pain.

In this process, as noted, pain is not always negative: it can provide opportunities for the only happiness worth pursuing.[76] If human beings naturally perceive and create value and care about certain things, life without pain and grief is not a human life. Instead, it is like the life of an oyster at the bottom of the sea under perfect conditions, it is a life most people would not want even if it were possible. Furthermore, no single accomplishment—nor series of accomplishments—will satisfy a person once and for always. Human life requires continuous activity, self-transformation, and engagement in what is objectively meaningful. Flourishing is experienced in exertion; it is not a state of perfection that ends the journey.

Flourishing, then, is in part the result of choices, actions, and direct confrontation with the ordinary realities of human existence. The sense of having defined what matters to oneself and to others and of having worked toward what matters raises one's spirits (engenders joy) and is an important component of flourishing.[77] Flourishing is not something anyone fully accomplishes; rather, flourishing is something one seeks with intentional daily practice.

Conditions That Support Flourishing

It is important to identify the elements of flourishing, but it is also true that genuine flourishing can be achieved only if it is cultivated by and nurtured in both individuals and the collective (the polis). Furthermore, what flourishing looks like has qualities that are contextualized and particular to each case. At the individual level, flourishing presumes positive, meaningful relationships, engagement in valuable activities, the accomplishment of significant goals, and a subjective experience of joy. Flourishing is something of a developmental task that is experienced—at least to some degree—by having significant needs met, living into one's deepest values, setting meaningful goals, and developing capacities to meet them.[78] One's goals ideally include both self-interest and other-interest and can be used to build life-giving communities and social orders.[79] "Choose life," readers of Jewish and Christian sacred texts are admonished in Deuteronomy 30:15-20, not death.[80] But how? No one lives an unconstrained life. No one makes choices as freely as he or she might wish. Opportunities to build meaningful relationships, to choose life-giving work, to achieve relative safety, to realize some measure of freedom and creativity, and to pursue other means to and signs of "self-actualization" are always constrained by the "givenness" of the worlds in which we all live. Some of these constraints are given in the finitude of humanness. Some are the results of decisions people make—singly and together—moment to moment, in their own lives: indeed, some limits on flourishing are the result of personal and collective election.

For example, all people participate in hierarchies that divide, rank, and exclude certain people and groups. These oppressive hierarchies are built into the structures of legal systems, encoded in global economic strategies, and built into environmental policies.[81] These destructive hierarchies are the results of members of advantaged groups—often in step with one another and with deep fellow feeling[82]—working together to define, target, oppress, and exclude others on the basis of race, age, gender expression, class, physical ability, sexuality, or religious belief. These destructive systems are often unconscious and usually well hidden, yet they significantly shape a person's life chances and sense of possibility. Limits on flourishing are embedded in societies and enacted in interpersonal and intergroup relations. The decision to pursue a life that allows flourishing cannot be only an individual one. Nor can it be achieved without some attention to an Ultimate Reality, the *Force for Life* that helps define what is "good." As the earliest philosophers and theologians believed, it is helpful to put emotions and feelings in the context of one's understanding of ultimate reality, though the view of ultimate reality presented here will differ from that of Plato, Augustine, and others presented in chapters 1 and 2.

Christian theologians understand well the challenges of the human condition and living as constrained creatures, and yet they suggest this is not all there is. For example, philosophical theologian John Caputo imagines all life as lived between the *Unconditional* and the *conditional* in which the conditional is what is done in the service of or for the purpose of something else, and the Unconditional is without reason or purpose; it simply is because it is.[83]

Jewish and Christian theologians, for example, understand that the Unconditional (that is, the Sacred) gift of life is always juxtaposed with the experience of the conditional material realities of life, and human beings live between the two: they are "dust and breath, matter and spirit, divine and clay, finite and infinite, insignificant and of estimable significance, body and self, brain and mind."[84] Life is lived between the conditional and the Unconditional reality. Flourishing, then, must lie somewhere between what is current, conditional reality and what is Goodness Beyond Being, integrating the otherworldly with the here and now.

Caputo argues that the Unconditional Sacred depends on the conditional for its realization on earth. That is, what is conditioned (meaning everything that exists in the material world, as on earth) is invited to be the fullest expression of itself by what is Unconditional.[85] In other words, the Unconditional invites the conditional/material/human to self-realization. Everything is encouraged to maximize itself to its highest form. And because only human beings can be human beings, Caputo suggests, they are invited—or rather urged—by what is Sacred to be the fullest expression of humanness that they can be within the constraints of finitude.[86] In fact, this may be all that is asked of creation: to embody Sacredness and express the best of itself within the condition to the fullest extent possible. This is the orientation of one's life that is foundational and necessary for flourishing. Humans' response to the Sacred Invitation is to live as fully as possible toward flourishing, and to rejoice in their time in the world. This, however, depends on whether each individual can cultivate the virtues, values, and motivations that express the values and hopes of "God." Because the values of Goodness Beyond Being depend on the conditional to exist on earth, human beings are urged in the direction of love and justice, to value oneself and also what is beyond oneself, and to engage meaningfully for the good of the whole. Because what is Good needs people and societies to be given its conditional existence in the world, flourishing requires humans' creative and intentional effort to bring it into being.

The Telos (Aim) of Life

There is no objective, predetermined *purpose* to life that can be proven, and even believing that life has meaning takes a certain leap of faith. Similarly, there is no objective, set *meaning* for human life that can be discerned. There are, however, *ways to create* the meaning of life through the pursuit of what is worthy. Human beings need not begin the quest for what is genuinely valuable from an ideal, transcendent, otherworldly vantage point, however. They can begin with the values already present in themselves and in their contexts: highest-order values that are visible over the course of history, in the best of religious traditions, and built into traditions and conventions that have currency because they are "right."[87] Virtues of love, justice, patience, kindness, and wisdom are time-tested, and they fund flourishing as it is being defined here because they contribute to individual flourishing as well as collective well-being. In this view, the Holy Other is not wholly other.

The understanding of flourishing being proposed here, then, is based on an understanding of life and the universe that describes a highly interconnected, deeply interdependent system of everything that is.[88] Thus, while the arc of justice is long, often sputters, and even loses ground at times, the full inclusion of all[89] toward flourishing is crucial.[90] Working to achieve flourishing for all people is a creative and meaningful endeavor worth pursuing, for by the definition being proposed here, as long as some are excluded from pursuing flourishing, none can fully achieve it.

While the virtues extolled by Aristotle can be discerned in the best (that is, the most just) moments of human history and its leaders, it helps to have a clearly articulated sense of the value system that is embodied in these virtues and which guides their application.[91] Most beliefs and practices related to Jewish and Christian traditions, for example, are committed to the idea that human flourishing requires awareness of the ways all of life is a response to the invitation of the Unconditional (or the Sacred, "Goodness Beyond Being," or "God") toward love and justice. And the Jewish and Christian traditions recognize that individuals' and communities' ability to respond to the Insistence of the Sacred has something to do with capacities that must be cultivated: Aristotle and the philosophers and theologians he informed were right that no person is *born* wise.

The Sacred Insistence urges creation into being—indeed, it invites the world into existence in every moment. The name scientists usually give to the force of "cosmic allurement" is evolution, contained by the forces of gravity,[92] but from a theological standpoint this understanding is limited: gravity describes only the attractional force and does not accommodate the whole-making nature of evolution. The concept of love may be a better word, and it is one employed to describe both cosmologists and theologians.[93] Yearning for wholeness through love, then, is at the heart of all creation from some cosmologies and from a Jewish and Christian perspective. The experience of wholeness is the awareness—at some level—of belonging to another, the awareness of being part of a whole. Love is the means to and the result of this awareness. The degree to which people and societies are (and are aware of being) part of this whole is fundamental to flourishing.[94]

The expectations of flourishing, then, include an evaluation that one's life is meeting one's internal standards (succeeding at what genuinely matters, both to oneself and objectively), realizing significant goals, developing one's capacities for complex tasks such as love and justice, establishing self-esteem, developing self-respect, and attending to what matters for the flourishing of others. Because everything on earth is interconnected, none can fully be well until all are.[95] One's motivating values must be affirmed by objective criteria grounded in history and by the best of what societies have achieved thus far: the Sacred can be materialized only when love, justice, and care are.[96] These virtues can provide guidance for handling moral situations in which self-interests are at odds with others' interests.[97] In fact, right action must be evaluated while also holding flourishing of the individual and the whole in tension. Those who seek flourishing must seek to know what is right, moment to moment, in their context and circumstance. Sometimes that will mean being motivated primarily by love for another, sometimes by love for oneself, sometimes by respect or principle, and sometimes by likely consequence or outcome. These discernments require wisdom, defined as knowing what is best when joined with motivation to act on it. In other words, wisdom and virtuous action require at least an intuitive understanding of what lies under each circumstance, insight into how things hang together and what makes individuals and societal systems tick, as well as the practical know-how to apply to concrete situations and determine how best to proceed.

Thus, while the promise of flourishing is a deeply personal experience that invites each individual to examine his or her life moment by moment, it is also a collective endeavor. Flourishing requires a democratic and inclusive effort. It is participatory, affirming the ontological value of all people, empowering the agency of each, and enhancing capacities for working collaboratively, and for holding in tension compassion and accountability. Flourishing values diversity and complexity and requires the inclusion that gives life—not the exclusion that creates suffering and often kills. And so, while flourishing surely has something to do with people being alive—an individual saying "yes" to her own aliveness—it also means saying "yes" to "God's" intention of flourishing for every other life and all creation.

Achieving this "yes"—both for oneself and for all else—also depends, then, on resisting what is destructive of the Good; flourishing also requires saying "no" to oppressive systems and actively dismantling them. In other words, humans' flourishing is part and parcel of becoming more maturely, complexly human, and it includes a profound solidarity with all of creation and the ability to care for selves, others, the environment, and institutions.[98] At its most basic material level, flourishing requires equal distribution of resources, the embrace of interdependence, and capacities for creating just social systems. Engaging in efforts toward just systems—in other words, actualizing the Sacred on earth—is the way human beings create meaning in their lives and in the world, effect Goodness, and enhance their own flourishing and that of others.

Practices That Cultivate Flourishing

Cultivating Strengths and Virtues

What can be said about the *ways* toward well-being, then? As noted, a life of well-being—or better, flourishing—is a collective endeavor that has unique, local, contextual, and deeply personal aspects. Flourishing necessitates the development of one's strengths and the possibilities for living out one's deepest values, as affirmed by wise others. Flourishing requires being clear and realistic about one's gifts *and* limitations and having opportunities for ongoing growth and development.[99] Flourishing depends on both opportunities and capacities for self-definition and self-expression through imagination, reflection, and creativity. To flourish, one must be able both to experience and to develop one's exquisite uniqueness even as one develops moral capacities for generous participation for the good of others.[100] Flourishing is enlivened by and enlivens one's sense of being a being animated by Goodness Beyond Being's Insistence in a world invited into existence by that life force—and loved by it. Experiences of flourishing increase as individual and group capacities for helping create and nurture such a world increase. "Whatever we think 'God' means it must mean life—more life," Caputo writes.[101]

Flourishing, then, is active and it is perspectival: both immediate and personal, and also whole thinking and future directed. A sense of flourishing holds together the now and the future. It attends to both the individual and the deeply personal while always keeping an eye on the world.[102] More than just self-actualization or loving and working better, the highest value in flourishing is the cultivation of what is required for the flourishing of all—and the meaning of life is found in this pursuit. Those who would cultivate flourishing must be able to account for the many paradoxes of human existence, including care and accountability, giving and receiving non-possessive love, and committing deeply while holding loosely. Flourishing includes awareness and ownership of finitude, faults, and brokenness—one's own and others'. It requires taking responsibility for and being accountable to the wounds each, in finite humanness, inevitably inflicts on others. Because of this, flourishing must incorporate coming to some terms with the losses and the inevitable griefs of life rather than their escape. The fullness of one's humanity—which necessarily includes finitude, pain, and grief—must be included in an understanding of flourishing. For this reason, flourishing will require that people are resilient, courageous, resolute, responsive, relational, dynamic, and responsible to one another, to themselves, and to the earth, both in periods of intense activity and also in quiet solitude.

The complex task of flourishing, then, requires the exercise, or practice, or the *discipline* of *wisdom*,[103] which the Greeks considered the most important virtue.[104] Wisdom, defined as the "ability to make theoretical as well as practical distinctions that allow one to see beyond appearances, below the surface" must be applied so that one develops an intuitive knowing in a way appropriate to the situation.[105] Wisdom both flows from and allows the capacities to see the connections in one's life experiences, between all people, and, indeed, in all of life. It also comes from intentionally reflecting on one's experiences, values, behaviors, and goals as life is being lived. Taking care to apply what one has learned in one's moment-to-moment responses and behaviors is the "alpha and omega" of wisdom.[106]

In order to realize flourishing, then, people will have to strive to be virtuous and wise, but this is a goal not without obstacles. Because human beings live between the Unconditional and the conditional, each must *intentionally develop* the ability to respond to the Sacred Insistence and cultivate capacities for love, justice, "interpathy," and nonviolence.[107] The wise person will be skilled at analyzing what is going on, diagnosing what is not working, and seeing clearly and correctly what the response should be.[108] But these capacities are significant achievements for those who accomplish them, and they are not guaranteed; growing into wise maturity is not an inevitable outcome of life or the passage of time. To be developed most fully, these capacities require conscious effort, focused awareness, and a willingness to be vulnerable to oneself and with others.

Becoming Wise

The ancient Greeks agreed that wisdom and the virtues must be learned and developed over time and that to be virtuous, people must cultivate the knowledge, perspectives, and skills (the *character*) that will guide them in perceiving, evaluating, understanding, planning, managing, and responding to the events in their lives. The best way to cultivate these understandings is through the exploration of emotions.[109]

Wise people (*phronimoi*) are able to understand deeply and with complex nuance the situations they are in.[110] They do not only experience their own emotions, moods, and feelings; they are also able to understand *why* they are feeling what they feel. They do not just react; they understand the motives and reasons for what is happening. They also understand, or at least consider, the social, economic, political, and cultural contexts of their circumstances and their experiences. And they use their emotions—of hopelessness, of love, of care, and of anger—to resist what goes against flourishing.[111]

Each human life begins for each person in a radically connected and utterly dependent state (that is, in the womb) and ends radically connected, when the energy of an individual's body rejoins the earth at death to become the dust, energy, nutrients, and features that nurture the next generation. Between the two, human life ideally also includes periods and processes of growth, change, differentiation, and deepening of capacities for intimacy and empathy, for non-possessive love, and for justice.[112] One might say that the more complex each one is as a person, the more fully one is able to contribute to creating the kin-dom of God. Indeed, only the fullest complexity allows the fullest response to the gift of the Sacred that is life.[113] Awareness and intentionality allow people to respond more fully to the Sacred Insistence that we create the kin-dom of "God" than can, say, a rock.[114] And no one is born with these capacities.[115] Each person must *learn* the virtues that support flourishing by engaging his or her own growth with intention.

The Insistent Urge toward what is loving and just presupposes growth and persistent change at the heart of the lifespan across a variety of factors. It requires that physical, cognitive, emotional, relational, and moral capacities develop and increase in complexity during processes of maturation. While the contours (or the raw materials) for the process are present at birth, it takes a lifetime to develop the capacity to hold oneself and all else in creative, interdependent tension.[116] Everything that exists is invited to live into its fullest capacities, but that requires individual intentionality and sociocultural support. It also takes courage.

Such a life depends on developing the strengths that have been shown to support the virtues, including the ability to take into perspective one's own most significant needs and desires, wisdom, the capacity to love non-possessively, and to be loved, an understanding of what is just and deep commitment to it, courage, self-control, gratitude, appreciation for beauty and excellence, willingness to allow oneself joy and zest, the capacities for faith and hope, the capacity for forgiveness,[117] a sense of humor, and capacity for serious reflection—all of which contribute to flourishing.[118] Thus, flourishing requires conscious and intentional exploration of one's emotions.

Implications for Emotions

Emotions play a critical role in cultivating flourishing—if understood and used rightly—and they are crucial for the growth and maturation of the virtues that support it. However, some emotions—at certain times—can prevent growth and constrain one's sense of creativity and freedom. For example, when emotions restrict increasing complexity (e.g., when fear or anxiety limits one's growth), and when they prevent meaningful engagement with other people and in groups and social organizations, then emotions limit flourishing. Emotions in relation to human flourishing, then, must be understood as part of a complex system that indicates, motivates, and allows peoples' growth, encourages their capacities for just and loving interpersonal relationships, deepens their awareness of being nested in an interdependent ecological system, and capacity and willingness to participate in common life that is just and caring. Those interested in the journey toward flourishing will need to go beneath the slick messaging of popular culture and politics—and the manipulations of marketing—to explore the complexities of their emotions.[119] The following diagram suggests the examination of emotions in multiple, contemporaneous systems; it is an examination that will need to be constant and ongoing. Emotions and the feelings that attend them are related to one's goals, values, motives, physiology, relationships, memories, experiences in the past, hopes for the future, level of self- and other-awareness, needs, beliefs, perceptions, and emotional and cognitive capacities. Emotions and feelings can be mixed and even competing. Emotions and feelings can be pleasant and unpleasant, positive and negative, adaptive and maladaptive, and they often lead to choices and behavior—both life-giving and life-limiting. Emotions are not conscious, but feelings can be. Intentional practices of critical discernment about emotions, feelings, their sources, and potential meanings must constantly be evaluated along several axes and within several concentric circles, the outermost (and most fundamental) being human flourishing as understood herein.

If genuine flourishing requires at its most fundamental level complexity, creative participation, and responsiveness, then lack of awareness of one's interconnections must be a root problem. *Not* flourishing, then, has something to do with believing and acting as if one is disconnected from oneself, others, and from the Goodness Beyond Being, or "God." When one inflicts pain on others intentionally or out of spite, when one serves only one's own interest, when people impoverish, exploit, or deny basic rights to anyone (including recognition, dignity, and justice), when they incite hatred or denigrate others, when groups resort to tribalism and define their identity by the exclusions fueled by mistrust and contempt, then they deny creation's radical interdependence; despite the fact that flourishing has to do with a sense of fulfillment, meaning, abundance, and joy, not all that feels pleasant or good supports flourishing. The work of flourishing includes coming to terms with the proper place of one's self within the great nest of being in which everything and everyone is understood to have ontological value. Emotions, in this view, then, are useful insofar as they communicate something about the realities of life in relation to oneself (intrapsychic dynamics informed by experiences over time) and others (interpersonal relationships, also informed by experiences over time) and tell people something true about their world. And we all need to pay attention.[120]

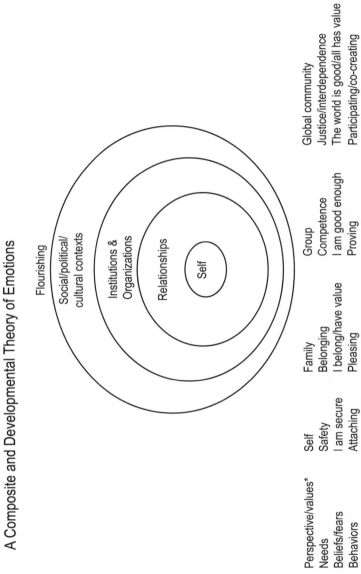

A Composite and Developmental Theory of Emotions

Flourishing

Social/political/
cultural contexts

Institutions &
Organizations

Relationships

Self

Perspective/values*	Self	Family	Group	Global community
Needs	Safety	Belonging	Competence	Justice/interdependence
Beliefs/fears	I am secure	I belong/have value	I am good enough	The world is good/all has value
Behaviors	Attaching	Pleasing	Proving	Participating/co-creating

*Labels for arrow diagram based on Brian Hall, *Values Shift* (Twin Light Publishers, 1995)
Arrow indicates a developmental trajectory from infancy to mature adulthood

Figure 3: Emotions and Complex Systems

Individuals' emotions are phenomena that arise within people in the interplay of physiology and between people in the experience of interpersonal relationships and sociopolitical contexts. Emotions are related to one's values and goals. Emotions lead to actions and behaviors, are often below conscious awareness, and are informed by past, present, and future. Emotions often emerge when people are unable to adapt to life situations or get their most significant needs met. Emotions point to the welcome and the unwelcome parts of themselves and help people recognize the ways their choices limit their own flourishing and that of others. Indeed, when individuals and groups forget the interdependence at the heart of all that is, their engagement with their emotions reflects this: they often resort to repression (blocking conscious perceptions of feelings and instincts), avoidance of emotions and feelings, passive-aggressive behavior (sublimated aggression expressed indirectly by passivity), projection (relieving unacknowledged pain by projecting those feelings onto others), intellectualization (denying the experience of feelings by rationalizing the situation away), or acting out (engaging in tantrums, substance abuse, or violence) to avoid dealing with tension and one's own feelings.

In addition, people often use emotions to evade personal accountability: one excuses one's inappropriate behavior by appealing to the emotions as "demons beyond control" that cloud one's judgment and result in aberrant behaviors. Persons often imagine themselves as victims not responsible for their deeds; however, a psychological constructionist understanding of emotion supports this view only so far: it does not allow for such a wholly passive assessment of one's relationship to his emotions.[121] Because people's emotions are constructed in the moment, individuals and sociocultural contexts can also influence emotions' generation, expression, and action tendencies. While there are some difficult emotions human beings must accept and live with, at least for a time (grief is to be expected, given the human condition), all emotions invite exploration at all levels—from personal to systemic—for their life-giving or -limiting aspects.[122] Emotions such as guilt among those in power can indicate an unjust hierarchy, and depression, rage, or helplessness among subordinates, the oppressed, or underrepresented groups can indicate the same.[123] Other emotions are significant to examine in light of unjust systems, too. Take fear, for example. Darwin was correct: the expression of fear is useful for physical survival. However, when fear is born of wrong belief or of inaccurate assumptions about others, it is not useful, for that is when it divides and oppresses and excludes, as in xenophobia.[124] One could make a similar argument about anger: while anger can provide useful information about what matters to someone ("I did not get the promotion I worked so hard for"), it is also a site of control and management ("You will not express your anger at sexual harassment in the workplace unless you want to lose your job"). The construction of what is socioculturally permissible in emotions' experience and expression can limit the life-giving potential of anger.[125] For example, individuals with brown and black skin tones are often dismissed as "always angry" as a way to minimize their concerns, when actually their rage is justified given the systems of white privilege and oppression that prevent their flourishing. It is useful to recognize that anger has often been deemed "maladaptive" and that societies have tried to control it.[126] However, the anger of Black Lives Matter activists and allies and other resistance groups can be understood as maladaptive only in relation to an expectation of maintaining a status quo. In the context of a deeply and tragically unjust system, however, it is adaptive.[127] In other words, anger in the face of systemic and oppressive racism and the resistance it would ideally engender is utterly appropriate and understandable, even life-giving.[128] If attended to carefully and with critical discernment, then, and used to guide behaviors, including resistance, emotions can be guides to human flourishing and its impediments and also part of its cultivation.

Because emotions are constructed moment to moment using multiple components, they are the embodiment of physiological, developmental, and material, social, or structural realities—all of which are related to one's past, present, and the imagined future. Because of the complexities of emotions, the sources and meanings of people's feelings are not always clear.[129] For this reason, careful and disciplined attention to emotions is critical to flourishing. This is especially true because people's avoidance or particular uses of emotions can be life-limiting. For example, emotions such as jealousy and hate—and the blame they can construct—are usually life-limiting (though they *feel* valuable) because they support one's personal desire to avoid humiliation, best a rival, or disassociate from someone or something one does not like. However, in the long run, these patterns do not lead to life-giving relationships, management of conflict (even if that means ending that particular relationship), or forgiveness. Although these emotions can be instructive about what matters to individuals and thus are valuable for that purpose, allowing certain emotions to perdure or acting on them is often life-limiting.[130]

A social constructionist model of emotions provides flexibility and nuance when exploring emotions because there are so many possible components and so many options to investigate. For example, one might ask why one's core affect is being activated. Why now? What beliefs have been or are being attached to similar changes in core affect? What values do those beliefs suggest? What needs are at stake? Where did one learn such a response? In what ways is one's emotional episode related to one's past experience, and in what ways is it related to one's current context? What does one's emotional episode say about one's relational context, organizational context, or both? What has one learned about these feelings from parents, teachers, friends, television? Are there other ways one might think about or interpret one's experience?[131] Are there more worthy things one might value? Are there behaviors that might need to change in order to change one's own emotions or the emotions of a group/system? This view also offers multiple ways of working with emotions, from changing one's core affect with lifestyle changes to altering one's beliefs, or from shifting one's values to accepting one's needs and seeking to meet them.[132] A more complex view of emotions, then, offers more avenues for exploration and engagement. Because emotions and feelings are not "inside us" waiting to be triggered, but rather are re-created moment to moment, people have more freedom in the face of them than perhaps previously thought.[133] Emotions, feelings, and behaviors are not automatic or given, even if they seem that way. Exploring their different components, the components' history, and the ways they relate to one another in the current moment can allow for more life-giving engagement with oneself, others, and the world.[134]

In order to understand and use emotions in the cultivation of flourishing, then, individuals and human collectives would be helped if they kept in mind the constructed nature of emotions, analyzing critically the context in which they arise and recognizing that people often have varied and competing emotions simultaneously. At the personal level, individuals ideally will become more aware of their own emotions and learn to explore, use, and sometimes manage them. Do emotions indicate the need for something to change (a person, a relationship, or institutional or social policies, for example)? Does one's own or one's group's emotions need to be changed or regulated? At the interpersonal level, flourishing requires these personal capacities as well as capacities for exploring, understanding, using, and sometimes managing others' emotions (that is, exercising their EQ[135])—always toward the goals of justice, compassion, care, love, and respect. Add to these the ideals of diversity and inclusion, transparency, and a commitment for flourishing of the entire polis. Using emotions in the pursuit of the flourishing of all will require that all people concern themselves with what really matters (that is, what we all ought to "set our hearts on") and develop the capacities and discipline to actualize it. Emotions are the tools that will enable such a vision. It takes courage to feel, but if we attend carefully to our own and others' emotions and let them guide us toward flourishing, they will, in the end, be the world's salvation.

Conclusion

Gaining some clarity about emotions, their origins, and their functions—both for good and for ill—will help us understand ourselves better. If we interpret them in light of the ideal of human flourishing and find practical ways of discerning their lessons for us, they will be the keys to our well-being.

The earliest thinkers about emotions were right: emotions do indicate something about what is good and how to achieve it. However, the early philosophers' and theologians' understanding of eudaimonia were fairly narrow. The view of flourishing presented in this book is, I hope, more developed and more nuanced. Examining the features of flourishing as both a deeply personal and a wholly communal endeavor depends on our careful attention to emotions to illumine what is life-limiting and what is and will be life-giving. Emotions, then, are crucial for human flourishing.

Conclusion

Almost three thousand years of emotions scholarship has yielded very different conclusions about emotions' rightful place in human life. This has left us (especially in the West) with mixed messages about the value of our emotions, and many of us are confused about how to feel about our emotions and what to do with them. From the Stoics to the earliest Christian theologians, from the Enlightenment thinkers to the existentialists, from twentieth-century scientists to contemporary philosophers, from cognitive psychologists to psychodynamic analysts, theories of and opinions about emotions have varied widely.

In part, our confusion comes from some uncertainty about what emotions are, where they come from, and how they function. Some of this confusion is also due to the variance in language used for what is being studied: for example, the *passions* studied by Plato have a very different meaning than the *emotions* that captured the interest of William James. And what James examined was very different from the *emotional expressions* that interested Charles Darwin. *Feelings* are not the same as *emotions*, and emotions are different from *moods, sentiments, affections, appetites*, and *affects*. But our confusion about emotions is not only a result of the variance of terms and semantics—or even the differences between research programs and their conclusions. It is also the result of differing beliefs about emotions and their value in human life.

Assessments of emotions' value have ranged from the assumption that emotions are dangerous and impede the Good Life to considering them the key to wisdom and the means to living well. Early Greek philosophers such as Plato argued that the passions represent the baser qualities of human being and should be put in their proper place in the order of things—that is, they should be controlled by reason. The Epicureans argued that pleasure is the highest good, but the Stoics found all passions to be at the heart of suffering and recommended their total elimination. Although Jesus of Nazareth understood love as the greatest virtue, Jewish and Christian theologians debated the passions' value: Philo considered them a result of the Fall, and Augustine wrestled mightily with his fleshly desires, extrapolating his mostly negative assessments of the passions from that experience. Later philosophers would continue these convictions. For instance, Rene Descartes put the passions/emotions in direct opposition to the rational self, mistrusted and unimportant, and although Immanuel Kant argued that nothing is done without the passions and valued them for that reason, the negative view of the passions'/emotions' place in the Good Life prevailed.

There were, of course, more positive evaluations of the passions. Early scientists such as Galen argued that the passions are an integral part of the human body and *cannot* be eliminated, and Aristotle argued that the passions are important elements of personhood and should be harnessed for the development of people's virtues and character, enabling individuals to be good citizens in the polis. David Hume asserted that the passions have value for guiding reason, arguing that reason can help people figure out how to *get* what they want but cannot *guide* them in *what* they want; he saw that as the passions' role and believed they should be valued for that reason. Friedrich Nietzsche found the passions/emotions to be dependable clues to the more chaotic elements of human beings' inner selves, and thus worthy of examination in order to better understand human character.

It was scientists such as Charles Darwin and William James who helped bridge earlier philosophical and religious interest in emotions and turned the investigations to the scientific and psychological. In Darwin's view, "emotional" expressions play important roles in the survival of organisms and species and as such should be valued for their evolutionary function. James found emotions to be useful for understanding human behavior and physiology. Cognitive theorists such as Jerome Schachter, Stanley Singer, and Magda Arnold extended James' work and explored the relationship of thoughts, beliefs, and evaluations to emotions' generation, and how those cognitions enabled (or inhibited) adaptation to one's environment.

Twentieth-century psychodynamic theorists and practitioners incorporated much of the thinking that had come before them—especially the science and psychology—though their evaluation, too, was mixed. Evolutionary psychologists continued Darwin's positive assessment, arguing that emotions function for the survival of individuals and species. Others who followed Darwin, such as Sigmund Freud, found emotions both the cause and the result of pathologies. Although Freud studied emotions—especially anxiety—in minute detail, behaviorists argued emotions cannot be meaningfully studied and thus largely ignored them. Following Freud closely, however, psychodynamic and relational psychologists found emotions to be both clues to the depths of what it means to be human and the means to people's healing. However, they also recognized that emotions can also the source of dis-ease and suffering. Emotions can prevent people from living the life they wish: emotions disrupt important relationships, they can lead to self-sabotage, and they can lead to violence. Emotions function in a variety of ways, then: they can be sources of suffering, indicators of pain, and the keys to healing.

Whereas psychologists were primarily interested in emotions' value for understanding and addressing intrapsychic and interpersonal experiences, social theorists accept that emotions function to help individuals survive in groups and are generated within social hierarchies in relation to power and status. Social theorists, too, recognize that emotions are not neutral: for example, Karl Marx demonstrated the ways emotions can be used as tools of manipulation that create violence and suffering, and institutions such as racism and homophobia depend on emotions to be maintained. As helpful as these theories have been, social theorists, like natural scientists, erred in assuming basic, universal, and structural understandings of emotions and their origins. These assumptions, foundational to the so-called classical theories of emotion, have created conundrums for anyone who might wish to develop an understanding of emotions that integrates the insights from across the various fields in which emotions are studied.

Here the relatively recent work of psychological constructionists of emotion is useful. Recent neuropsychology has shown that emotions constitute people and their environments in mutually influential ways. In this view, emotions are not passive inner disturbances to be conquered by the power of reason, but active, embodied forces central to relational life—the relation of self both to itself and to others, to one's sociocultural, political context, and to ultimate reality. Neuropsychology demonstrates the ways human beings are formed in and through their emotions: "feedback loops" among perception, memory, body, brain, mind, other persons, and sociocultural environments, etc., are more extensive and more sensitive than has previously been imagined. Thus, although early philosophical language of the "passions" communicated the ways in which the passions often feel out of one's control, prompting a view of the passions as dangerous to the "more controlled" capacities for reason, contemporary researchers who propose emotions' neuropsychological construction understand emotions as *expectable phenomena* that can indicate to those who pay attention as much about the social and cultural contexts of the person experiencing the emotion as they do about the individual. Emotions reveal much about people *and* the worlds they inhabit and are to be valued for it.

While psychological constructionist understandings of emotion resolve some of the conundrums classical models posed, they do not explicitly address emotions' relation to flourishing. Indeed, although in the final third of the twentieth century and the beginning of the twenty-first the study of emotions has exploded across many disciplines, too few have asked the questions that so consumed early philosophers and theologians: how are emotions related to the telos, or final aim, of life? How ought we engage emotions in the pursuit of flourishing? I have argued that what is needed is a well-articulated value system against which emotions can be assessed. I have made a proposal that I hope is up to the challenging task of promoting people's flourishing in the contexts of relationships, organizations, and social-cultural-political contexts—at least as a place to start. I have argued that only a clearly articulated set of values that emphasizes care, nonviolence, justice, mutuality, and other virtues can help us adjudicate whether an emotion is useful or not, or whether it is adaptive or maladaptive. In order to ascertain whether a particular emotion at a particular time in a particular context for a particular person is life-giving or life-limiting, it needs to be carefully explored in relation to a clearly articulated vision of a flourishing life.

Against the critiques of attention to emotions as emblematic of narcissistic self-preoccupation, as unworthy of study, or as too confusing to be engaged, then, I am convinced that emotions have much to teach us about ourselves and our life in the global community. In this I affirm the view that emotions are eudaimonistic; that is, they are fundamental to human flourishing. I recognize that emotions' function in any moment is not easily understood. However, confusion and ambivalence about emotions should not lead to their dismissal. Because emotions are a fundamental part of being human, deepening our understandings of them—their origins, their meanings, their functions in human life—is a worthwhile project. So is committing to practices that carefully attend to our emotional lives. Such has been the work of this book. Indeed, I have sought to attend to two primary challenges: to integrate an understanding of emotions from a wide variety of theories using psychological constructionism, and to propose a perspective on flourishing by which emotions and their effects can be evaluated. Because emotions scholars bifurcated *passions* from *emotions* over time, the focus on the perspective of the Divine—or what is Sacred and Good—has been lost in much contemporary work on emotions. Where the first philosophers and theologians were writing about passions and their relationship to ultimate reality, scientific perspectives on emotions short-circuited that relationship, focusing more on the physiological and intrapsychic dynamics. I have argued that the two must be integrated for a more meaningful and useful understanding of emotions: flourishing cannot be engaged without including careful attention to emotions, and an adequate understanding of flourishing cannot be separated from the desires of the Sacred for the world.

An implicit argument in this book is that by attending to individuals we attend to the whole, and when we attend to systems, institutions, and organizations, we attend to people. Attending to our (and others') emotions helps each of us grow, commit, respond (rather than react), change, be generative, be responsible to (rather than for), develop our tolerance for ambiguity, and increase awareness of self that can increase empathy for others. And empathy, I believe, can lead to a commitment to justice and care.

If flourishing involves becoming as human as one can be (as defined in chapter 7), then an important part of human flourishing is to embrace and develop each person's worth and value, uniqueness and gifts. It also requires that we each awaken to, own, accept, and address our own limitations, failures, inconsistencies, finitude, and wounds. This invites each of one us to reflect on our own lives and on the world in which we live. Each of us is emboldened to be grounded in the realities of our life together, to be awakened to our individual experiences, and to use our emotions to connect us to the truths of our own development and of our interdependence. Human life is and will always be composed of complex, ambiguous, and ambivalent emotions. Sorting them out with an eye toward flourishing is a vital task.

In order to cultivate flourishing, then, it will help if you remain open to the mystery of the world and your particular life, to allow life itself to be a meaningful gift, to relearn wonder and awe, and to participate joyously in a worthy vision that includes your individual needs and desires and also transcends them to care for our world and all its inhabitants. If we all pay attention to our emotions and the feelings that accompany them as I am suggesting, we just might increase the possibility of noticing brushes with the Sacred ultimate reality that is inviting us into something deeper and richer than we have now—urging us to say "yes" to flourishing for ourselves and for all.

Notes

Preface

1 See Barbara J. McClure, "Pastoral Theology as the Art of Paying Attention: Widening the Horizons," *International Journal of Practical Theology* 12, no. 2 (2008): 189–209.

Introduction

1 The term *emotion* will be defined below. It is worth noting here, however, that what the word refers to, the meaning of the word, is a matter of disagreement. Suffice it to say here that I do not believe that emotions are always conscious, nor do I believe they are only personal, or merely psychological, points of contention in various disciplines. See chapter 6 for a more thorough exploration of what emotions are.

2 The question of whether terms such as *love* (as well as other terms) would qualify as emotions will be taken up in chapter 6; these, too, are contested matters.

3 Lisa H. Albers, Dana E. Johnson, and Margaret K. Hostetter, "Health of Children Adopted from the Soviet Union and Eastern Europe: Comparison with Preadoptive Medical Records," *Journal of the American Medical Association* 278, no. 11 (1997): 922–24.

4 Emotions are distinct from feelings. Although there is debate about this (see the notes on the work of Robert Zajonc and Richard Lazarus in chapter 4), I side with those who argue that emotions can be unconscious, whereas feelings are consciously reflected on and interpreted emotions. Thus, I agree that some animals and children have and can communicate emotions, though they may not have feelings per se. Recent neuroscience supports this position. See chapter 6.

5 For an exploration of this, see Andrew D. Lester, *Hope in Pastoral Care and Counseling* (Louisville, Ky.: Westminster John Knox), 1995.

6 For moving memoirs, see Rachel Lloyd, *Girls Like Us: Fighting for a World Where Girls Are Not for Sale—An Activist Finds Her Calling and Heals Herself* (New York: HarperCollins,

2011), and Katariina Rosenblatt with Cecil Murphey, *Stolen: The True Story of a Sex Trafficking Survivor* (Grand Rapids: Revel/Baker, 2014).

7 The *Military Times* reports Department of Veterans Affairs estimates that twenty veterans kill themselves every day. See Leo Shane III and Patricia Kime, "New VA Study Finds 20 Veterans Commit Suicide Each Day," July 7, 2016, https://www.militarytimes.com/veterans/2016/07/07/new-va-study-finds-20-veterans-commit-suicide-each-day/. This can be the result of PTSD, but also of moral injury, or "the lasting psychological, biological, spiritual, behavioral, and social impact of perpetrating, failing to prevent, or bearing witness to acts that transgress deeply held moral beliefs and expectations." Blair E. Wisco et al., "Moral Injury in U.S. Combat Veterans: Results from the National Health and Resilience in Veterans Study," *Depression and Anxiety* 34, no. 4 (2017): 340–47.

8 Again, some might not include these affective phenomena among emotions, but I think the argument can be made. See chapter 6 for more on this.

9 I am grateful to editor Uli Guthrie who read an early draft and suggested I add more examples. These are hers.

10 These differences are, in part, likely related to one's earliest childhood experiences, one's socialization, and the values that result. See chapter 6 for more on the connections of early experience and what one values.

11 One of the thirteen principal Upanishads. See Robert E. Hume, *The Thirteen Principal Upanishads: Translated from the Sanskrit with an Outline of the Philosophy of the Upanishads* (Oxford: Oxford University Press, 1921; London: Forgotten Books, 2010).

12 Sigmund Freud, *Civilization and Its Discontents* (1930; repr., New York: W.W. Norton, 2010).

13 Phillip Tracy, "Study Relates Facebook Addiction to Snorting Cocaine," *The Daily Dot*, January 3, 2018, https://www.dailydot.com/debug/facebook-dopamine-addiction/.

14 With little critical analysis, the movie depicts emotions as discrete balls that are moved around, activated, junked in a trash heap, and so on. This commonly held understanding of emotions and our relationship to them is debunked in chapter 6.

15 See the interview with the director of *Inside Out*, Pete Docter, on National Public Radio, "It's All in Your Head: Pete Docter Gets Emotional in *Inside Out*," interview by Terry Gross on NPR's *Fresh Air*, June 10, 2015, https://www.npr.org/2015/06/10/413273007/its-all-in-your-head-director-pete-docter-gets-emotional-in-inside-out.

16 For-profit organizations are now assessing their employees' emotional intelligence and demoting or firing leaders lacking it. Lidia Young, "Uber CEO Ousted Due to Low Emotional Intelligence and Hostile Company Culture," *ReThink Leadership Now*, June 30, 2017, http://rethinkleadershipnow.com/uber-ceo-ousted-due-to-low-emotional-intelligence-and-hostile-company-culture/.

17 Protests (generally peaceful) against police brutality toward people with black and brown bodies are routinely monitored by the FBI and the Department of Homeland Security "based on the presumption of violence." See Sweta Vohra, "Documents Show Monitoring Black Lives Matter," *Al Jazeera News*, November 28, 2017, http://www.aljazeera.com/news/2017/11/documents-show-monitoring-black-lives-matter-171128110538134.html.

18 Emotions have even been divided against themselves in categories such as unpleasant vs. pleasant, adaptive vs. maladaptive, and positive vs. negative, and these categories even further confuse their rightful place in people's lives, not to mention obscure their meaning and usefulness. These terms will be explored throughout the text. Here I want to

say only that I do not believe any emotions are negative or positive, though they may feel unpleasant or pleasant and may have adaptive or maladaptive effects. Their effects, however, must be evaluated in light of an understanding of flourishing, which I offer in chapter 7.

19 Philip Rieff, *The Triumph of the Therapeutic: Uses of Faith after Freud* (New York: Harper & Row, 1966).

20 Sara Ahmed, *The Cultural Politics of Emotion* (Edinburgh, U.K.: Edinburgh University Press, 2014), 205.

21 "Emotion work" is a term coined by sociologist Arlie Hochschild by which she means "inducing or inhibiting feelings so as to render them 'appropriate' to a situation." Emotion work is usually understood as managing one's own feelings (and expression of them) or managing others' emotions. Emotion work is often performed to maintain important social relationships. Examples of emotion work include talking about emotions (as in therapy), being apologetic, or expressing guilt. See Arlie R. Hochschild, "Emotion Work, Feeling Rules, and Social Structure," *American Journal of Sociology* 85, no. 3 (1979): 551–75.

22 Whether something or someone can "make" you feel anything will be taken up in chapter 6.

23 See Sigal G. Barsade and Olivia A. O'Neill, "What's Love Got to Do with It? The Influence of a Culture of Companionate Love and Employee and Client Outcomes in a Long-Term Care Setting," *Administrative Science Quarterly* 59 (2014): 551–98. Priya Krishna, "There Is a Free Lunch, after All: It's at the Office," *New York Times*, January 7, 2019, https://www.nytimes.com/2019/01/07/dining/free-food-employees.html. Name badges that recognize length of service, or cloth patches such as those worn by home improvement store employees to show particular awards and accomplishments, have been shown to increase significantly the bottom line. Monica Torres, "4 Ways Elizabeth Holmes Manipulated Her Theranos Employees: And How Not to Get Fooled if Your Boss Tries This," *HuffPost Life*, March 2, 2019, https://www.huffpost.com/entry/elizabeth-holmes -office-employees_l_5c92abe3e4b01b140d351b6f?ncid=engmodushpmg00000004.

Of course, there are effective ways to build positive cultures that value their employees and where people can thrive in their work. While some of these tactics may effectively encourage people to play together and get to know one another, it is doubtful that they alone will solve the many challenges in toxic organizations. In fact, these kinds of organizations may be accused of what cultural critic and social theorist Sara Ahmed calls the "technology of happiness" since, Ahmed argues, "being happy is conditional to proper subjectivity of heteronormative societies and organizations." Sara Ahmed, *The Promise of Happiness* (Chapel Hill, N.C.: Duke University Press, 2010).

24 These examples are Uli Guthrie's.

25 For these reasons, leveraging emotions in the workplace has become an explicit goal for many leaders of Fortune 500 companies. This has given rise to the concept of "emotional intelligence," commonly referred to as "EQ." EQ advocates a form of self-awareness and social intelligence involving the ability to monitor one's own and others' emotions, to discriminate among emotions, and to use this information to guide one's thinking and action. Research shows that people who demonstrate higher EQ (capacities to perceive, understand, and evaluate their own emotions as well as others') are better able to adapt to their work environments, more able to build and sustain collaborative, productive relationships, and thus more successful at their jobs. In fact, much of the research on leadership and career

success argues that EQ is more important than IQ in today's workplace. See, for example, Daniel Goleman, *Emotional Intelligence: Why It Can Matter More Than IQ* (1995; repr., New York: Bantam/Random House, 2006), and Peter Salovey and J. D. Mayer, "Emotional Intelligence," *Imagination, Cognition, and Personality* 9, no. 3 (2004): 185–211.

26 Contemporary use of the term *snowflake* to describe people sensitive to race- or gender-based or sexualized microaggressions is evidence of this.

27 It could be argued that historian E. Brooks Holifield takes this tone in *A History of Pastoral Care in America: From Salvation to Self-Realization* (Nashville: Abingdon, 1983).

28 Eleven worshippers in a Jewish center in Pittsburgh were killed by a man who was reported to have shouted "All Jews must die!" before opening fire. Nicole Chavez, Emanuela Grinberg, and Eliot C. McLaughlan, "Pittsburgh Synagogue Active Shooter," *CNN*, October 31, 2018, https://www.cnn.com/2018/10/28/us/pittsburgh-synagogue -shooting/index.html.

29 Research from the Korn Ferry leadership research and development group suggests that arrogance is the primary reason leaders are fired or demoted (gleaned during personal training in Korn Ferry Leadership Development instruments, 2002).

30 Jones preached about the possibility of a nuclear apocalypse and moved hundreds of his followers to Jonestown, Guyana, a place he billed as a socialist paradise. There Jones promoted his belief in the "Translation," in which Jones and his followers would die together and move to another planet where they could escape the evils of this world and live more peacefully. Almost one thousand people died in 1978 when Jones instructed them to drink cyanide-laced Flavor-Aid in an act of what he called revolutionary suicide, protesting the conditions of an inhumane world and escaping the fear of more intense suffering.

31 Philosopher Martha Nussbaum's recent book *Fear: A Philosopher Looks at Our Political Crisis* (New York: Simon & Schuster, 2018) explores this well. I recognize that this list includes some experiences or qualities that some would not consider emotions per se. See chapter 6 for exploration of what is and is not an emotion.

32 Physical development and emotional development occur together. When the emotional health is stunted, even in cases where physical needs are met, people's bodies do not develop normally. Lisa F. Barrett, "Your Emotions Are a Social Construct," *Tonic/Vice*, July 21, 2017, https://tonic.vice.com/en_us/article/qvpae5/would-someone-born-and-raised-in -solitary-have-any-emotions. See also Jack J. Bauer and Dan P. McAdams, "Growth Goals, Maturity, and Well-Being," *Developmental Psychology* 40, no. 1 (2004): 114–27.

33 Theodore D. Kemper, "Power and Status and the Power-Status Theory of Emotions," in *Handbook of the Sociology of Emotions*, ed. Jan E. Stets and Jonathan H. Turner (New York: Springer, 2007), 87–113.

34 Stevi Jackson, "Even Sociologists Fall in Love: An Exploration in the Sociology of Emotions," *Sociology* 27, no. 2 (1993): 201–20.

35 Robert C. Solomon, *The Passions: The Myth and Nature of Human Emotions* (Notre Dame: University of Notre Dame Press, 1983), 4. This view has informed whether—and how—emotions were studied.

36 Kenneth S. Isaacs, *Uses of Emotion: Nature's Vital Gift* (New York: Praeger, 1998), xv.

37 Andrew D. Lester, *The Angry Christian: A Theology for Care and Counseling* (Louisville, Ky.: Westminster John Knox, 2003).

38 William M. Reddy, *The Navigation of Feeling: A Framework for the History of Emotions* (Cambridge: Cambridge University Press, 2001), x.

39 Solomon, *The Passions*, 4.

40 Kenneth J. Gergen, "Metaphor and Monophony in the 20th-Century Psychology of Emotions," *History of the Human Sciences* 8, no 2 (1995): 2.

41 Gergen, "Metaphor and Monophony," 3.

42 Craig A. Smith, "Emotion and Adaptation," in *Handbook of Personality: Theory and Research*, ed. Lawrence A. Pervin (New York: Guilford Press, 1990), 609–37. Now, of course, emotions scholarship is exploding, both among researchers and scholars and among lay and popular writers as well. People representing fields as disparate as psychology and sociology, leadership studies, anthropology, neuroscience, nutrition science, history, cultural and intellectual historians, literature specialists, wellness coaches, and parenting experts are weighing in, but this has emerged most significantly in the United States in the last forty years or so.

43 See chapters 1 and 2 for more.

44 Michel Foucault recognized the cultural tendency to spend a great deal of time on what people or a collective found troubling. See Michel Foucault, *The History of Sexuality*, vol. 1, *An Introduction* (New York: Random House, 1978), 123–24.

45 As recently as 2018, *Time* magazine issued a special edition on emotions, for sale on grocery shelves and in bookstores everywhere. "The Science of Emotions: Love, Laughter, Fear, Grief, Joy," *Time* magazine, special edition (January 2018). And in 2015 *The New York Times* ran an article investigating "What Emotions Are (and Aren't)," *New York Times*, August 2, 2015, SR10.

46 Pastoral theologians often study human experience directly, in clinical settings or through case studies. However, this project studies *others'* reflections on human experience. Thus, human experience is only indirectly examined. Still, extant research on emotions demonstrates deep engagement with what is most important in people's lives, what the good life is, and how to effect it—a key interest for pastoral theologians. For a nice exploration of the value of this kind of exercise, see Robert C. Solomon, *The Joy of Philosophy: Thinking Thin versus the Passionate Life* (Oxford: Oxford University Press, 1999a).

47 Questions about what makes for human flourishing continue to dominate our collective psyches. A course called "Happiness" offered at Yale University is currently the most popular course ever offered in the history of the university. See "Yale's Most Popular Course Ever: Happiness," David Shimer, *New York Times*, January 26, 2018, https://www.nytimes.com/2018/01/26/nyregion/at-yale-class-on-happiness-draws-huge-crowd-laurie-santos.html. Because of its popularity, Yale has started offering the course online and for free.

48 Klaus R. Scherer, "What Are Emotions? And How Can They Be Measured?" *Social Science Information* 44, no. 4 (2005): 695–729. One scholar of emotions presents twenty-one different definitions, indicating that they are only "some" of the extant definitions. Robert Plutchik, "Landscapes of Emotion," in *Emotions and Life: Perspectives from Psychology, Biology, and Evolution* (Washington, D.C.: American Psychological Association, 2003), 18–19.

49 Arthur S. Reber, *Penguin Dictionary of Psychology*, 3rd ed. (London: Penguin, 2001).

50 Beverley Fehr and James A. Russell, "Concept of Emotion Viewed from a Prototype Perspective," *Journal of Experimental Psychology: General* 113, no. 3 (1984): 464–86.

51 Solomon, *The Passions*, 4.

52 Theologian Wendy Farley argues that what the early philosophers meant by *passions* is not what we mean by *emotions* today. Farley argues that the words translated as passions are not normal feeling states that arise in the "normal flow of life because we

are psychic, spiritual, embodied persons." Rather, she suggests, the passions are part of the deep structures of consciousness that are "deeply rooted dispositions" which shape the way we orient ourselves to the world. Wendy Farley, *The Wounding and Healing of Desire: Weaving Heaven and Earth* (Louisville, Ky.: Westminster John Knox, 2005), 44–45. As the next chapter will show, this distinction may not have been as clear to the earliest users of the term.

53 Nico H. Frijda, "The Psychologists' Point of View," in *Handbook of Emotions*, ed. Michael Lewis and Jeannette M. Haviland-Jones, 2nd ed. (New York: Guilford Press, 2000), 59.

54 Frijda, "Psychologists' Point of View," 60.

55 Thomas Dixon, *From Passions to Emotions: The Creation of a Secular Psychological Category* (Cambridge: Cambridge University Press, 2003).

56 Dixon, *From Passions to Emotions*, 202.

57 Dixon, *From Passions to Emotions*, 194. A definition of *emotion* is offered in chapter 6, as is a distinction between *emotion* and *feeling*.

58 David Hume, *A Treatise of Human Nature*, ed. L.A. Selby-Bigge (1740; repr., Oxford: Clarendon, 1888). There is disagreement on the first use of the word in English. While some assert that David Hume introduced the term, others disagree. See Amy M. Schmitter, "Passions, Affections, Sentiments: Taxonomy and Terminology," in *The Oxford Handbook of British Philosophy in the Eighteenth Century*, ed. James A. Harris (Oxford: Oxford University Press, 2013), 197–225.

59 Robert C. Roberts, "What an Emotion Is: A Sketch," *The Philosophical Review* 97, no. 2 (1988): 183–209. This can be heard in the statement, "She is so emotional." What is really meant is that she is acting on her emotions and clearly expressing her feelings. A more thorough exploration of the differences is in chapter 6.

60 Paul Griffiths, *What Emotions Really Are: The Problem of Psychological Categories* (Chicago: University of Chicago Press, 1997).

61 The meanings of these terms as used by various researchers will be explored in subsequent chapters, but I think of emotions as neutral: neither positive or negative, though they may feel pleasant and unpleasant and their effects may be positive and negative (for example, "negative" emotions such as sadness can tell us something significant about what it means to be human, and "anger" can highlight systems of injustice). Similarly, when evaluating whether an emotion is adaptive or maladaptive, I would want to have a clear value system in mind that takes into account an adequately complex understanding of well-being so that a person's "maladaptive" emotions might be understood as "adaptive" in the right context. See chapter 7 for more on this.

62 This exploration of emotions is intended to be about emotions in a general population. I am not taking up the questions about emotions in "nontypical" people, since, though interesting and valuable, such a study is out of the scope of this project.

63 Flourishing, incidentally, is not the same as happiness, though it includes it. It is not the same as physical health, though flourishing may include that. And flourishing does not require wealth, though having basic needs met is a component. Flourishing is a more complex term closer to well-being than to happiness, the meaning of which will unfold chapter to chapter as I draw on particular theories and highlight what each offers to my own view, articulated most fully in chapter 7.

1 Emotions as Dangerous, Disruptive, and Symptoms of Dis-ease

1 This includes research on emotions in disciplines as diverse as the natural sciences and the social sciences, psychology, literature, cultural anthropology, contemporary philosophy, and Jewish and Christian theologies.

2 In its earliest usage, the good life referred to right conduct, or ethics. See Daniel Robinson, *An Intellectual History of Psychology* (New York: Macmillan, 1976), 71. I opt for the terms *flourishing* and *well-being* and describe qualities of life as life-giving or life-limiting (language I heard first from my colleague, pastoral theologian Carrie Doehring, though it may not have originated with her. For example, existentialist philosopher Friedrich Nietzsche uses the language of "life-enhancing" and "life-stultifying" about specific drives or passions). On language in Nietzsche, see Robert C. Solomon, "Nietzsche and the Emotions," in *Nietzsche and Depth Psychology*, ed. Jacob Golomb, Weaver Santaniello, and Ronald L. Lehrer (Albany: State University of New York, 1999b), 131. I will most often use the term *flourishing* for the effect of a life of virtuous character, meaning, and joy. While a life of flourishing, for example, does include making ethical choices, it expands to imagine a more holistic personal and social well-being, as I argue in chapter 7.

3 The passions were understood as movements of the soul generated by both internal and external forces or events. Differences in terms authors used contribute to current confusion about emotions; each term represents differences in what was being studied, hints at the conclusions arrived at, and highlights competing views and commitments. Various terms including *passion, perturbation*, and *affect* were selected by writers such as Augustine and Stoic philosophers including Cicero and Seneca as they translated the Greek word *pathos* to indicate passions and sometimes sickness. In contrast, *sentiment* came to be used with increasing frequency by eighteenth-century British and French authors and is distinctively modern. Disagreements about whether to classify emotions among appetites, judgments, or volitions originated in the writings of Aristotle and continued with the Stoics' work and into Augustine's. As one philosopher notes, "Early modern associations between emotions and the body owe a lot to ancient and medieval sources as well as do the connection between emotions and motives for action. Such connections underlay the long running debate inherited by early moderns about the epistemic, eudaimonistic, and ethical value of the emotions, a central issue of which is the degree to which we can govern our emotions." Amy M. Schmitter, "17th and 18th Century Theories of Emotion," *Stanford Encyclopedia of Philosophy*, https://plato.stanford.edu/entries/emotions -17th18th/.

4 The word *pathe* was also used for disease. Diseases were considered passions of the body. (Our contemporary words *pathology, pathogen*, and *patient* share this etymology.) See James Averill, "Inner Feelings, Works of the Flesh, the Beast Within, Diseases of the Mind, Driving Force, and Putting on a Show: Six Metaphors of Emotion and Their Theoretical Extensions," in *Metaphors in the History of Psychology*, ed. David E. Leary (Cambridge: Cambridge University Press, 1990), 108. Given that the same generic term was used to cover both emotion and disease, it is not surprising that an association was often made between the two conditions. The Stoics in particular considered emotions to be diseases of the mind. Because the passions connote interruptions of reason over which people struggle to exercise their will, the "myth of passions" is that they are irrational responses over which human beings have little control and must fight using whatever tools are at hand.

5 Even now some courts of law recognize crimes of passion, in which a crime committed during an intense emotional experience is mitigated by this "brief moment of insanity." Plutchik, "Landscapes of Emotion," 6.

6 Robinson, *Intellectual History of Psychology*, 45.

7 Robinson, *Intellectual History of Psychology*, 83.

8 Robinson, *Intellectual History of Psychology*, 47.

9 Socrates did not write down his understandings. He left it to his students Xenophon and Plato to record his teachings, and it is to Plato's work especially that we are indebted for the record of Socrates' philosophy. Socrates was Plato's teacher, and Socrates figures as a character in many of Plato's *Dialogues*; for this reason, I sometimes refer to Socrates/Plato to represent this perspective, although I also shorten it to Plato. Although there are some of Plato's works that do not include Socrates' voice, the material presented here reasonably refers to both philosophers' thinking.

10 Attributed to Socrates in Plato's *Dialogues*. In the *Dialogues of Plato*, 2 vols., trans. Benjamin Jowett (New York: Random House, 1937). Cited in Robinson, *Intellectual History of Psychology*, 55. Emphasis added.

11 At the center of center of Plato's cosmology is a god (or Demiurge) who is "unique and rational," and who is essentially a craftsman, a "producer of beauty," or the "final, intrinsic good," or the "world-mind." John M. Cooper, *Pursuits of Wisdom: Six Ways of Life in Ancient Philosophy from Socrates to Plotinus* (Princeton, N.J.: Princeton University Press, 2012), 321–31. Plato's Demiurge can only make the world as beautiful as the ideal model or Form of it. Richard D. Mohr, "Plato's Theology Reconsidered," in *Essays in Ancient Greek Philosophy*, vol. 3, *Plato*, ed. John P. Anton and Anthony Preus (Albany: State University of New York Press, 1989), 293–94.

12 V. J. McGill, *The Idea of Happiness* (New York: Praeger, 1967), 62. This is true at least of their concerns as represented by Plato in his dialogue *Republic*. Although this dialogue is often understood to be primarily about justice, it might better be understood as a treatise examining the virtues and the role of philosophy, community, and the state in helping to create the conditions that make living well possible. Socrates/Plato suggest that people *want* to do what is just, so doing what is just will make them happy. See Panos Dimas, "Wanting to Do What Is Just in the *Gorgias*," in *The Quest for the Good Life: Ancient Philosophers on Happiness*, ed. Oyvind Rabbas et al. (Oxford: Oxford University Press, 2015), 66–87.

13 Early Platonic dialogues suggest that Socrates thought human beings are psychological beings and that happiness and the good life are a matter of having the right psychology. This psychology, for Socrates, underlies the life of practical wisdom regarding ethical matters, and human beings become practically wise through the "love of wisdom." Thomas A. Blackson, *Ancient Greek Philosophy: From the PreSocratics to the Hellenistic Philosophers* (Malden, Mass.: Wiley-Blackwell, 2011), 39. Socrates/Plato go on to say that wisdom and truth are good for the soul and that the care of the soul is the most important thing to which one can devote oneself. Blackson, *Ancient Greek Philosophy*, 57. Contemporary thinkers may agree. See, for example, Solomon, *Joy of Philosophy*.

14 Most ancient Greek philosophers agreed that in order to be happy, one must be virtuous, which, they argued, requires philosophical contemplation and deliberation on what is good. For example, the Stoics found wisdom to be sufficient to happiness, while Christians theologians such as Augustine did not. See Katerina Ierodiakonou, "How

Feasible Is the Stoic Conception of *Eudaimonia?*" in Rabbas et al., *The Quest for the Good Life.*

15 Glaucon was one of Socrates' interlocutors who challenged Socrates to answer why it is not sufficient *to pretend to be just* in order to live a good life.

16 They do this through laws, policies, etc. McGill, *Idea of Happiness*, 17–21.

17 Plato argued that justice is something good in itself and requires temperance and courage, for "it is not possible for a just man to be licentious or cowardly." McGill, *Idea of Happiness*, 36. Injustice is associated with malfunctioning and failure. Thus, the happy man chooses justice, no matter what the consequences might be. McGill, *Idea of Happiness*, 37. However, Plato *was* open to telling the "just lie" that a just life is more pleasant than an unjust life. McGill, *Idea of Happiness*, 42. The issue of inclusive language will be addressed in n. 25 below (ch. 1).

18 See John M. Cooper, *Reason and Human Good in Aristotle* (Cambridge, Mass.: Harvard University Press, 1975) for a good discussion of terminology.

19 McGill, *Idea of Happiness*, 19.

20 Cooper, *Pursuits of Wisdom*, 35. Plato (and later, Aristotle) argued that operating this way allows a city to thrive; further, it is in everyone's best interest to be part of a well-functioning polis. When challenged about whether or not this arrangement would make people happy, the character Socrates responds that he is not as much interested in individuals' happiness but rather in the thriving of the city as a whole. For Socrates/Plato, a well-ordered society is more important than individual freedom.

21 See Plato, *Phaedrus* 246–254, http://www.gutenberg.org/files/1636/1636-h/1636-h .htm. His schema imagined the rational/immortal part of the soul in the head and the irrational/mortal part in the body. By making rational thought (in the head) the highest part of the soul and the irrational/mortal soul in lower parts of the body, Plato intentionally created a dichotomy between them. Because everything except reason takes place in the lower body, Plato de facto argued for a soul–body dichotomy: functions of the immortal rational soul are part of the divine realm of truth, while the mortal, irrational, emotive soul is the material part of human beings. This division, of course, would prevail in Western thinking, culminating, perhaps, in seventeenth-century philosopher Rene Descartes' dictum "I think, therefore I am." Descartes' view, and that of Platonists before him, has significantly informed Western understandings on emotions and flourishing. Many scholars argue that Descartes had a negative influence on our thinking about emotions, the body, and human experience.

22 Averill, "Inner Feelings," 109.

23 One scholar suggests there are three kinds of "disturbances": the bodily ones include itches and other physical pains, to be satisfied with a scratch or a bandage. The second kind also involves the bodily drives and requires replenishment: hunger, thirst, and so on. A third kind of disturbance involves the soul, independent of the body. These disturbances include anger, fear, envy, and love. It is the third kind of disturbance that Plato and his followers meant by *passions*. See William W. Fortenbaugh, "Aristotle and Theophrastus on the Emotions," in *Passions and Moral Progress in Greco-Roman Thought*, ed. John T. Fitzgerald (New York: Routledge, 2008), 30.

24 The Greek philosophers shared the idea that happiness as the final good of human beings consists in godlikeness. As one scholar notes, "Humans become godlike if they exercise in as unadulterated a form as possible their intellect because God is, for the philosophers,

intellect." Svavar H. Svavarsson, "On Happiness and Godlikeness before Socrates," in Rabbas et al., *The Quest for the Good Life*, 28–48.

25 It is worth noting here that Aristotle and his colleagues did not believe that all people can be truly happy: women and slaves, for example, lack the requisite rational capacities and the freedom, leisure time, and material well-being to achieve it. Raymond A. Belliotti, *Happiness Is Overrated* (Lanham, Md.: Rowman & Littlefield, 2004), 13. Children, too, are incapable of happiness because their lives are so incomplete and because their capacity for reason is not well enough developed to allow contemplation, careful deliberation, and rational choice. McGill, *Idea of Happiness*, 32. In Plato's view, women and children judge by appearances, not reasoned wisdom. McGill, *Idea of Happiness*, 44. In other words, the ways various philosophers understood the passions and the good life, of course, were inextricably connected to the social and political views of the time. The good life as they understood it was not universal or free of gender and class considerations. The "sage" discussed by everyone from Plato to the Stoics, and the Christian theologians' understanding of the saved or wise soul, was typically male, monied, and educated. The ways these philosophers viewed men and women were imbued with the assumptions born of a deeply patriarchal and class-oppressive political system. Plato even posited a kind of reverse evolution. A man who failed to live a life of reason could be punished by reincarnation as a woman or an animal. Plato, *Timaeus*, 92c, cited in Averill, "Inner Feelings," 109. More about this will be said in chapter 7 but suffice it to say that my understanding of flourishing is local, contextual, and particular, but also necessarily radically inclusive and just.

26 Plato's understanding of forms prefigured structural accounts of emotions, to be explored in chapters 3, 4, and 5.

27 Socrates/Plato argued that truth is nonphysical, ideational, and of ultimate reality, transcending human experience. Plato saw truth and reason as the same thing. Mohr, "Plato's Theology Reconsidered," 293–307. Plato's view was that the goodness of all things flows from and is caused by the transcendent form of the good and suggested that the vision of this highest form is the highest happiness, whereas Aristotle did not think there was such a thing as a transcendent, ideal form of the good. McGill, *Idea of Happiness*, 46.

28 Robinson, *Intellectual History of Psychology*, 53. Emphasis in the original.

29 The etymological root of *passion* (*pathe*) is added to other words to name a disease or condition. We also get such emotional terms as *pathetic, empathy*, and *antipathy*. Psychologist James Averill notes that in its original Greek and Latin forms, *passion* had a very broad connotation. *Passion* could refer to any object (animate or inanimate) that is undergoing suffering—defined as some kind of change through the action of an external agent. It could also be any psychic or internal agent of such change. Averill, "Inner Feelings," 108.

30 For this Plato is considered an early ascetic. There is some discussion among about just how much detachment was required, but most agree that full detachment was Plato's ideal approach to one's passions. Simo Knuuttila, *Emotions in Ancient and Medieval Philosophy* (Oxford: Oxford University Press, 2004), 7. For more on this, see also John M. Cooper, "Plato's Theory of Human Good in the Philebus," *Journal of Philosophy* 74, no. 11 (1977): 714–30. Reverence and gratitude are the two mechanisms for turning madness into virtue, Platonists thought. Martha Nussbaum, "Eros and the Wise: The Stoic Response to a Cultural Dilemma," in *The Emotions in Hellenistic Philosophy*, ed. Juha Sihvola and Troels Engberg-Pederson (Boston: Kluwer Academic Publishers, 1998), 271–304.

31 Plato, *Theaetetus* 176a5–e4. Cited in Svavarsson, "On Happiness," 28.

32 Knuuttila, *Emotions in Ancient and Medieval Philosophy*, 11–12.

33 This use of masculine language is both intentional—it is the pronoun used exclusively for much of Western history—and instructive: early philosophers and theologians contributed to the belief that the female sex is weak, irrational, and must be controlled, supporting centuries-long justifications for patriarchy and the abuse of women and "feminized" men.

34 In his later work, Plato suggested a two-part understanding of reason: (1) cognitive activity and (2) emotional response and reasoned reflection. Knuuttila, *Emotions in Ancient and Medieval Philosophy*, 17. Martha Nussbaum argues that in Plato's later work he revised his indictment of passions to understand that the appetites can also possibly involve complex and selective responses of the entire soul and thus can be positive. To argue this, Nussbaum points out that the unruly, spirited horse of passion requires constant control but also should be well fed, as it can play an important role in the pursuit of the good and in teaching the person about the Truth. In other words, the passions are not necessarily sources of distortion: their insight may provide necessary information for the well-being of the whole person. See Martha Nussbaum, *The Fragility of Goodness: Luck and Ethics in Greek Tragedy and Philosophy*, 2nd ed. (New York: Cambridge University Press, 2001). Most scholars agree, however, that the passions were understood by Socrates/Plato to be mostly negative.

35 Remember that the word *philosophy* is translated as "the love of wisdom," and contemplation was understood as the best means to the good life. Cooper, *Pursuits of Wisdom*, 92.

36 Although we have little direct access of Socrates' work, Hippocrates likely would have known of his ideas. See Ann Ellis Hanson, "Hippocrates: The Greek Miracle in Medicine," *Medicina Antiqua*, https://www.ucl.ac.uk/~ucgajpd/medicina%20antiqua/sa_hippint. html. Often called the father of modern medicine, Hippocrates was one of the most influential figures in the early history of philosophy and medicine, establishing medicine as a discrete discipline apart from philosophy or religion. See Michael Boylan, "Hippocrates," in *The Internet Encyclopedia of Philosophy*, http://www.iep.utm.edu/ hippocrates/, and Hanson, "Hippocrates." Galen, who followed Hippocrates' thinking several hundred years later, extended Hippocrates' work in important ways. Though they are not the same, they are reasonably aligned for the purposes of representing one of the five strands of thought about the passions, and are presented together.

37 Robinson, *Intellectual History of Psychology*, 71.

38 Hippocrates was first to call certain symptoms *hysterical* in reference to their presumed cause. *Hysteria* is derived from the Greek word for uterus. See Averill, "Inner Feelings," 118. Sigmund Freud, of course, would follow Hippocrates' lead centuries later and identify the female organ as the source of much pathology.

39 Because of the Greek prohibition against dissecting human bodies, Hippocrates had to focus on observable symptoms and prognoses rather than careful autopsies for the diagnoses of cause. Nevertheless, Hippocrates believed he had identified the "healing power of nature," arguing that the body is able, through its own capacities, to rebalance and thus heal itself and that the doctor's role was to support this natural process. Michael Boylan, "Hippocrates."

  According to Hippocrates, healing requires self-knowledge. He recommended examining the disturbances of the soul and body and taught his patients (and students) that in many cases, long-term training is needed: over time one can learn to control manifestations of the passions, and eventually their disturbances will subside. Hanson,

"Hippocrates." To diminish passions, Hippocrates had doctors attend to patients with kindness and with calm and gentle encouragement, keeping the patients immobile and resting, having them fast, and maintaining both patients' and doctors' own cleanliness; Hippocrates even went so far as to recommend the appropriate length of a doctor's fingernails.

40 Chronologically, Galen came after the Stoics, whose views we engage below, and he was heavily influenced by their physical, metaphysical, epistemological, and ethical views on the passions. However, as a scientist and medical doctor he was more closely aligned with Hippocrates' intense interest in and focus on the body. Galen claimed that in his youth—partly in response to the confusion caused by mutually contradictory philosophical sects, all claiming certainty on unprovable issues—he nearly succumbed to the lures of Skepticism. Galen, *Lib. Prop.* 14/11, 18, "Galen," *Encyclopaedia Britannica Biography*, https://www.britannica.com/biography/Galen. Galen claimed that the possibility of certainty, as provided by science and mathematics, is what saved him. But an understanding of the limits of human knowledge is as important as the project of acquiring it in those areas where that is possible, Galen argued. Galen was scathing about those who commit themselves rashly to ideas based on insufficient evidence and about philosophers who debate propositions on which demonstrative knowledge is impossible (such as the existence and nature of the void outside the cosmos). Galen, *Aff. Pecc. Dig.* 2.6–7, 308–13, "Galen," *Encyclopaedia Britannica Biography*.

41 Galen's dates are not certain and there is a fairly wide disparity between those proposed. Some put them at 129 CE through 199 CE. See M. A. Soupios, "Galen (A.D. 129–199): Physician, Scientist, Philosopher," in *The Greeks Who Made Us Who We Are: Eighteen Ancient Philosophers, Scientists, Poets and Others*, ed. M. A. Soupios (Jefferson, N.C.: McFarland & Company, 2013), 192–202.

42 Galen was not a Christian, but he was a monotheist. "Galen," *Greek Medicine*, http://www.greekmedicine.net/whos_who/Galen.html.

43 Indeed, he set forth a connection between the two in his great work *On the Doctrines of Hippocrates and Plato*.

44 This modification of the theory allowed doctors to make more-precise diagnoses and to prescribe specific remedies to restore the body's balance. As a continuation of earlier Hippocratic conceptions, Galenic physiology became a powerful influence in medicine for the next 1,400 years. Galen was both a genius and a prolific writer: about 300 of his works are known, of which about 150 survive wholly or in part. Susan P. Mattern, *The Prince of Medicine: Galen in the Roman Empire* (Oxford: Oxford University Press, 2013), 280. One historian notes that "while Galen did not have the kind of transcultural impact comparable to that of Plato or Aristotle, in the medical sciences his influence upon researchers and practitioners alike was without equal in Western history." Soupios, "Galen," 192. Hippocrates, Galen, Islamic physicians such as Avicenna, and others adopted this view until modern research disabused medical researchers of it in the nineteenth century.

45 The research of philosopher, psychologist, and empirical researcher William James, who lived almost two thousand years after Galen, demonstrated that Galen was correct in this.

46 Soupios, "Galen," 195–96. Galen provided a physiological basis for what became a commonplace distinction between angry (or irascible) emotions directed at overcoming obstacles, and simple desiring (or concupiscible) emotions that would significantly inform Christian philosophers' thinking about appetites vs. affections.

47 Peter Brain, *Galen on Bloodletting* (Cambridge: Cambridge University Press, 2010). Galen worried about the extremes of passions. He wrote, "Whenever a man becomes violently angry over little things and bites and kicks his servants, you may be sure this man is in a state of passion. The same is true in the case of those who spend their time in drinking to excess, with prostitutes, and in carousing." Galen, *Passions*, 1.2, 29–30. Cited in C. A. Alexander Loveday, "The Passions in Galen and the Novels of Chariton and Xenophon," in *Passions and Moral Progress in Greco-Roman Thought*, ed. John T. Fitzgerald (New York: Routledge, 2008), 176.

48 Galen's work had enormous and lasting effects. His physiological understanding of emotions had significant impact on scientific and medical views well into the seventeenth century, including those of many Christian theologians. For example, Nemesius, a fourth- and fifth-century philosopher, physiologist, and Christian theologian, was heavily informed by Galen and wrote *On Human Nature* while serving as Bishop of Emesia (present-day Syria). In that book, which was highly influential in later Greek, Arabic, and Christian thought, Nemesius sought to develop an anthropology based on the Hippocratic corpus, on Aristotle's, and on Galen's work, synthesizing them with Christian understandings of God and sin. Later, Nemesius' book was read by Juan Luis Vives (1493–1540 CE), who provided a seminal contribution to the study of emotions that combined Galenic medicine with observations of people's lived experience and demonstrated how "humor-laden temperaments" (that is, people whose passions—that is, humors—are out of balance) can be modified by things like age, health, climate, and circumstance as well as by thought, judgment, and will. Galen's work was largely ignored by philosophers, but his ideas have found resurgence since the Scientific Revolution. Brain, *Galen on Bloodletting*. See also R. J. Hankinson, "Body and Soul in Galen," in *Common to Body and Soul: Philosophical Approaches to Explaining Living Behavior in Greco-Roman Antiquity*, ed. Richard A. H. King, 232–58 (New York: de Gruyter, 2006), and Susan James, *Passion and Action: The Emotions in Seventeenth-Century Philosophy* (Oxford: Oxford University Press, 1997).

49 Mattern, *Prince of Medicine*, 284. Galen's thinking was also disseminated through an anthology of six medical texts (later known as *Articella*) compiled in the twelfth century that entered the university curriculum in the thirteenth century and was still being printed in the sixteenth. The *Articella* was a collection of works by writers including Hippocrates and Galen but also Constantine (272–337 CE) (who translated some Arabic scientists' contributions into Latin) and the Persian and Islamic philosopher Avicenna (980–1037 CE), another significant bridge figure between Platonic, Galenic, and Christian thinking. Avicenna developed a complex theory of the passions based on this taxonomy: animals make emotional judgments according to earlier experiences or instincts, which is why their behavior is instinctual and often stereotyped. Animals' desires serve the survival of the species, but there are few variations in their social activities. The more-sensitive emotions of human beings are based on a more conceptual, reasoned orientation to the world. Because of humans' unique abilities, they can feel fear and hope in relation to not-yet-actualized events or experiences. Because human beings are more complex than animals, their social life is based on learned attitudes and habits rather than on instincts, and the passions can play a part in this. For example, shame at wrong action (which Avicenna argued animals cannot experience) demands understanding of a system of rules. In other words, Avicenna imagined *consciousness* as a unique capacity that differentiates human beings from animal creatures, making humans more responsible for their emotions and their behaviors than less-conscious beings are. Knuuttila, *Emotions in*

Ancient and Medieval Philosophy, 224. Avicenna's tripartite model of the soul prefigured scientist Paul MacLean's tripartite model of the brain, in which he proposed a reptilian part from which instincts arise; a limbic part shared by all mammals where emotions, capacities to bond, and so on are located; and a strictly human or neocortical part, which holds consciousness and the capacities to reason. See chapter 3 for more on this.

50 Unfortunately, however, many of the most influential philosophers (such as Rene Descartes) and Christian theologians (including Augustine) followed Plato rather than Hippocrates and Galen, disavowing the body and embodied experience in their search for the means of salvation.

51 Aristotle is often considered the "canonical expression" of ancient ethics. Oyvind Rabbas, "*Eudaimonia*, Human Nature, and Normativity," in Rabbas et al., *The Quest for the Good Life*, 88.

52 One scholar argues that Aristotle was the "first great Platonist" and Plato's first great critic. Blackson, *Ancient Greek Philosophy*, 153.

53 Knuuttila, *Emotions in Ancient and Medieval Philosophy*, 5. William James would pick this up: despite his physiological bent, James gave a powerful prod to the phenomenology of emotion. Robert C. Solomon, "Emotions in Continental Philosophy," adapted from *Blackwell Companion to Phenomenology and Existentialism, Philosophy Compass* 1, no. 5, ed. Dreyfus and Wrathall (2006), 414.

54 Robinson, *Intellectual History of Psychology*, 77.

55 Robinson, *Intellectual History of Psychology*, 79. In this sense, Aristotle is often considered an early empiricist.

56 Nevertheless, eudaimonia, for Aristotle, is at least partially rationalistic. Rabbas, "*Eudaimonia*," 88. In his ethics, Aristotle did not discuss individual actions but rather certain kinds of structured activity or organized practice, often referred to as *techne*, or fields of expert knowledge, including practicing medicine or military training: what Aristotle regarded as the foundation of civil society because they are purportedly for the good of the whole. Rabbas, "*Eudaimonia*," 90.

57 "Reversals of fortune" can crush happiness if they are great enough, Aristotle noted, "for they bring pain with them and hinder many activities." Thus, the practice of virtues is not sufficient for happiness, though it enables us to bear the challenges of life with dignity. Aristotle, *Nicomachean Ethics*, 1100b29–33. Cited in McGill, *Idea of Happiness*, 30–31. In *Nicomachean Ethics* Aristotle laid out the premises and outline for his thinking on eudaimonia. While Aristotle did not believe in a "divine maker of the cosmos," he did accept that certain behaviors in "natural bodies" were for the sake of becoming like "some divine object whose existence is perfect," which Aristotle called the "unmovable first mover." Blackson, *Ancient Greek Philosophy*, 182. See also Cooper, *Pursuits of Wisdom* for a helpful discussion of Aristotle's understanding of the good life and the means to it. Aristotle was not interested in positing a transcendent good and instead focused on eudaimonia on earth. He challenged Plato on this: Plato argued that virtues or good things are good because they participate in and contribute to the transcendent good. Aristotle, on the other hand, argued that virtues and good things are good in themselves, though they are not final ends but rather means to the chief and final end of happiness. McGill, *Idea of Happiness*, 14. In other words, there is a higher good than virtue and pleasure: this highest good is happiness, or eudaimonia, not desired for any other reason but for itself. It is the "glow or radiance" that accompanies well-functioning of the senses and rational faculties. McGill, *Idea of Happiness*, 29.

58 There are discussions of this translation and whether it is appropriate. John M. Cooper proposes the alternate translation of "human flourishing." This is taken up more fully in chapter 7. See Cooper, *Reason and Human Good in Aristotle*.

59 Even so, for Aristotle contemplation was the most important activity for happiness: "complete" or "perfect" happiness is achieved by philosophical reflection, and a life of reflection is the most self-sufficient and leisurely—meaning there is time to devote to the "best" objects. McGill, *Idea of Happiness*, 19 and 31.

60 Rabbas, *"Eudaimonia,"* 93.

61 Aristotle's understanding of the good or the end of a thing was its functioning well according to its nature; thus eudaimonia is a capacity, something of a developmental achievement. McGill, *Idea of Happiness*, 22. Contemporary philosophers Martha Nussbaum and Amartya Sen develop Aristotle's ideas. See John M. Alexander, *Capabilities and Social Justice: The Political Philosophy of Amartya Sen and Martha Nussbaum* (New York: Ashgate, 2008).

62 This is an expression of Aristotle's hylomorphism, or the attention to both matter and form in objects.

63 Rabbas, *"Eudaimonia,"* 95.

64 Aristotle imagined two kinds of virtues: intellectual virtues, which are directly related to one's rational capacities (such as wisdom), and character virtues, which are "moral" virtues, having to do with courage and justice, for example. Moral virtues differentiate "good" people from "bad." Thus, a virtuous man is "a man of virtuous habits." McGill, *Idea of Happiness*, 24.

65 These virtues occupy a middle ground between the vices of excess and of deficiency that are relative to each individual; for example, the virtue of courage occupies the middle ground between being cowardly and being foolhardy.

66 For Aristotle, the happy man is the one who mobilizes all his resources and operates "at the top of his abilities." McGill, *Idea of Happiness*, 226. Whereas for the Stoics happiness could be accomplished in a moment of tranquility, Aristotle thought of it as continuous, cumulative, and developmental. Aristotle named at least twelve diverse moral virtues, including wittiness, courage, temperance, self-respect, gentleness, friendliness, and modesty. McGill, *Idea of Happiness*, 239.

67 More contemporary scholars sometimes translate it as "well-being," but I use "flourishing." Chapter 7 takes up the issue of terminology in more depth.

68 "What is exemplary" in Aristotle's thinking was his understanding that "morality comes in a sequence of stages with both cognitive and emotional dimensions." Myles F. Burnyeat, "Aristotle on Learning to Be Good," in *Explorations in Ancient and Modern Philosophy*, vol. 2 (Cambridge: Cambridge University Press, 2012), 260.

69 Rabbas, *"Eudaimonia,"* 103.

70 Aristotle proposed that the best form of government is one "in which every man, whoever he is, can act best and live happily" and that the best-governed cities are the ones in which citizens have the greatest opportunity for achieving happiness. Aristotle, *Nicomachean Ethics*, 1324a12–13 and 24.

71 On the difference between institutions and organizations, see chapter 7, note 12.

72 Cooper, *Pursuits of Wisdom*, 58.

73 Aristotle argued that legislators must possess the intellectual virtue of *phronesis*, or wisdom: knowing what is virtuous and helping people accomplish it.

74 Knuuttila, *Emotions in Ancient and Medieval Philosophy*, 5.

75 Robinson, *Intellectual History of Psychology*, 82.

76 Later (and long before Sigmund Freud), Aristotle asserted that there is a "pleasure principle" that informs people's interpretation of their experience, guiding their behaviors and the formation of their character; thus, understanding the passions and knowing when to follow them and when not to has everything to do with the good life in Aristotle's schema. Because Aristotle was convinced that understanding and training the passions was a fundamental tool for eudaimonia, he was one of the first philosophers to provide a detailed and systematic analysis of several individual passions. He was also among the first to write about the role of personal and social elements in a life properly lived. Aristotle wrote extensively on memory, learning, sleep and dreams, perceptions, behavior, emotion, and motivation, integrating both ideational and physical or sensate experience in his descriptions of them. Robinson, *Intellectual History of Psychology*, 84. Aristotle was also one of the earliest thinkers to argue that human eudaimonia is an evolving process. On this last point, he disagreed with the Socratic/Platonic school that posited only two psychological states (one in which the person is enlightened, the other in which he or she is ignorant or "mad"). Instead, Aristotle described the process of character formation and explored the role of practice, rewards, and punishment in such formation. In this way, he contributed to a dynamic theory of psychological development. Robinson, *Intellectual History of Psychology*, 89.

77 We discover what is right, in the end, by "perception." Aristotle, *Nicomachean Ethics*, 1106b20–23.

78 Nussbaum, *Fragility of Goodness*, 390–91.

79 Rabbas, "*Eudaimonia*," 91.

80 Aristotle, *Rhetoric*, 1.11. Cited in Knuuttila, *Emotions in Ancient and Medieval Philosophy*, 19.

81 Aristotle even went so far as to claim that even something as "ideational" as moral excellence "is concerned with bodily pleasures and pains" and is under the control of biological processes. Aristotle, *Physics*, 247a. Cited in Robinson, *Intellectual History of Psychology*, 84.

82 Remember Aristotle's understanding of the passions as composites of multiple factors, including perceptions and belief. This is a distinct mode of seeing things from the point of view of a sensitive being. Animals thus may experience fear and anger, which are simple passions, but not pity, since it presupposes certain evaluative beliefs. Perceptions are feelings (which animals have) but perceptions + feelings + evaluations = passion, where perception is awareness of having received information. Knuuttila, *Emotions in Ancient and Medieval Philosophy*, 30. Thus, animals do not have passions in Aristotle's view because real passions involve judgments, which animals cannot make. Rabbas, "*Eudaimonia*," 98–100. Contemporary scientists of emotion would likely say that animals have emotions but not feelings. See chapter 6 for why.

83 However, in Aristotle's schema, certain passions (e.g., spite and envy) are always bad. Note that not everyone would include these particular passions among emotions in contemporary usage. See chapter 6 for more on this.

84 The idea of catharsis or "discharge" of the unpleasant emotions of pity and fear "may be the most famous part of Aristotle's poetics." Joe Sachs, "Aristotle: Poetics," *Internet Encyclopedia of Philosophy*, https://www.iep.utm.edu/aris-poe/#H3.

85 Another example Aristotle provided of a passion that is neither always bad nor always good is courage, which he suggested is having the right amount of fear, aimed at the

right thing. Courage is not being either foolhardy or cowardly. Robert C. Solomon, "The Philosophy of Emotions" in Lewis and Haviland-Jones, *Handbook of Emotions*, 2nd ed., 5. Indeed, the practice of forgiveness is a complex one. See Joretta Marshall, *How Can I Forgive? A Study of Forgiveness* (Nashville: Abingdon, 2005) for a helpful exploration of forgiveness, the conditions for it, and its limits as a virtue.

86 Solomon, "Philosophy of Emotions," 3–16. Aristotle's composite view of emotions is affirmed by contemporary neuroscientific understandings. See chapter 6 for more on this.

87 Knuuttila, *Emotions in Ancient and Medieval Philosophy*, 46.

88 Aristotle believed that "all knowledge and every pursuit aims at some good" and that political science aims at "what is the highest of all goods achievable by action." Aristotle, *Nicomachean Ethics*, 1097a28–30. Cited in McGill, *Idea of Happiness*, 14. It is important, then, to cultivate one's gifts and skills, such as becoming an effective flute player, or a sculptor, or any technical expertise. Aristotle, *Nicomachean Ethics*, 1.7.1097b22–33. Cited in McGill, *Idea of Happiness*, 17. Because ignorance is the primary obstacle to right action, education and developing oneself toward the virtues are vital practices.

89 Aristotle understood the potential to develop wisdom as a fundamental quality of human being. He argued that "a stone hurled into the air a thousand times will not learn to ascend" (that is, wisdom is a part of humans' potential and cannot be learned by nonhuman entities). He also argued that there are differences between natural law and human nature: the latter can be changed through practice, reward, and punishment. Robinson, *Intellectual History of Psychology*, 204. Aristotle called the knowledge of what is noble and virtuous "the *that*," by which he meant the habituation of wisdom and right behaviors. Burnyeat, "Aristotle on Learning to Be Good," 265. Wisdom, then, is a "gift from the gods" that comes to people through "divine inspiration." Blackson, *Ancient Greek Philosophy*, 107.

90 However, because the soul guides the body but is also implicated by what happens in the body and, given that what arouses the passions generally lies outside the body, Aristotle wondered to what extent individuals can control their passions. The fact that the soul is a unified entity means it is aware of its movements, registering them as pleasant or unpleasant, and that it evaluates events on the basis of anticipated spiritual, bodily, and cognitive pleasures and pains. Like Socrates/Plato, Aristotle had to account for why people often do that which is against their own discerned wisdom. To this end, Aristotle posited *akratic* (or unpremeditated) and *enkratic* (controlled) responses to passions. Sometimes, unpremeditated or *akratic* actions are those that are against people's better judgment (such as vicious, vindictive acts that exact revenge but cause more violence in the end), and others are acted upon without any consideration, motivated by what seems pleasant. Fortenbaugh, "Aristotle and Theophrastus on the Emotions," 29–47. In contrast, *enkratic* people feel the same disruptive passions but *do not act* on them. The *enkratic* person is superior to the *akratic*, but neither is as virtuous as the person who feels only passions that are in line with the dictates of right thinking. In other words, the wise man (*sic*) or sage feels the right passions about the right things in the right degree and acts out of them in the appropriate ways. For this reason, Aristotle was deeply interested in how to train and instruct young people to join in the "emotional patterns of culture" in such a way that their habits of feelings and emotions contribute to the good life. Knuuttila, *Emotions in Ancient and Medieval Philosophy*, 25.

91 Most passions can be "trained" toward the good and are often good in moderation—in fact, Aristotle valued the median between extremes in most passions. However, things such as murder and spite are bad in themselves, and not only when they occur in excessive or deficient amounts. And for Aristotle, the love we confer on a few select people can never be too much: "the more of this kind of love the better." McGill, *Idea of Happiness*, 27.

92 Fortenbaugh, "Aristotle and Theophrastus on the Emotions," 44.

93 Panos Dimas, "Epicurus on Pleasure, Desire, and Friendship," in Rabbas et al., *The Quest for the Good Life*, 164.

94 Epicurus can be considered an ethical hedonist and a psychological hedonist. The first indicates that pleasure is the only good and pain the only bad. In the second, Epicurus argued that most people recognize what is pleasurable and what is painful. Thus, his is a description of human psychology. See Dimas, "Epicurus," 166.

95 Epicurus based his naturalistic view of pain and pleasure on his study of animals and infants, arguing that as soon as every creature is born, it seeks pleasure and enjoys its gratification; at the same time, creatures naturally reject pain as the greatest "bad" and avoid suffering the best they can. Freedom from suffering and the achievement of what one desires generate the static pleasure of tranquility, which, together with absence of bodily pain, forms the telos, or goal, of life in Epicurus' schema. Knuuttila, *Emotions in Ancient and Medieval Philosophy*, 81. This instinctual and natural dynamic of avoiding pain and seeking pleasures explains people's motivations to act at times against their own best interest (that is, what is good and right). Thus, one must consider what pleasures are natural and necessary and keep to them. Blackson, *Ancient Greek Philosophy*, 233–34.

96 Aristotle, "Letter to Menoeceus." See also David Konstan, *A Life Worthy of the Gods: The Materialist Psychology of Epicurus* (Las Vegas: Parmenides, 2008), and Whitney J. Oates, *The Stoic and Epicurean Philosophers: The Complete Extant Writings of Epicurus, Epictetus, Lucretius, Marcus Aurelius* (New York: Modern Library, 1957).

97 Epicurus, *De Fin.* 1.30. Cited in Dimas, "Epicurus," 168. For Epicurus, pleasure and pain were physiological sensations *and* psychological experiences.

98 Epicurus and the Epicureans argued that knowledge is important not in itself, but "only because it displaces the disturbing opinions to which human beings are naturally prone." Physics is important, for example, because it "dispels the fears based on mythology that undermine happiness." Blackson, *Ancient Greek Philosophy*, 232.

99 Pleasures, Epicurus argued, can come in many forms and include short-term pleasures, such as slaking one's thirst, which are "kinetic" (that is, related to the motions and needs of material bodies and "the forces and energy associated therewith"). Other pleasures, such as reflecting on one's life, are ongoing and long-term.

100 Epicurus approved of satisfying one's sexual appetites, but in order to avoid mental suffering, he argued, people should have promiscuous and indiscriminate sex so as not to get emotionally attached to one lover. Knuuttila, *Emotions in Ancient and Medieval Philosophy*, 82–83.

101 In contemporary psychology this is referred to as the "hedonic treadmill." See chapter 7 for more on this.

102 Epicurus suggested that two self-inflicted thoughts make people unhappy or create suffering: the belief that the gods will punish them for their bad actions and, second, the belief that death is something to be feared. Epicurus argued that both of these are unnecessary: they are based on fiction. As a strict materialist, Epicurus did not believe there are

gods who can punish people, nor did he believe the soul would outlive the body. Thus, Epicurus opined that death is meaningless for the living because they are living, and death is meaningless to the dead because . . . they are dead. Epicurus, *Ep. Men.* 128.1–11. Cited in Dimas, "Epicurus," 170–71.

103 Dimas, "Epicurus," 172–73.

104 With thanks to my colleague, historical theologian Bryce Rich, for his suggestion to include this term in reference to Epicurus. Personal conversation, March 5, 2018.

105 Early philosophers such as Epicurus encouraged their fellow citizens to understand that life's most difficult problems have a solution. In other words, there is an "easy-to-execute and effective plan for living in a way that is overwhelmingly likely to result in a life in which the pleasure taken in one's circumstances vastly outweighs the pain." Blackson, *Ancient Greek Philosophy*, 236.

106 Hippocrates and Galen, Aristotle, and Epicurus presaged later scholars such as psychoanalyst Sigmund Freud, evolutionary psychologists such as Sandor Rado, and developmental theorists such as Abraham Maslow, who would examine the role of pleasure and pain in social accommodations, learning, and the emergence of the *id*, individual and group survival, and human development. They also anticipated the importance of confession as developed by early Christian theologians, and free association, promoted by psychoanalysts. Nevertheless, none of the early thinkers imagined the complexity of intrapsychic realities as understood by Freud or the challenges of human development in the complexities of a late modern world. Still, their work laid the groundwork for these later scholars' careful explorations.

107 This includes the work of Zeno of Citium (334–262 BCE, founder of the Stoic school), Chrysippus (280–207 BCE, third leader of these Stoic school, who wrote more than 700 books), Porcia Catonis (c. 70–43 BCE, a female Stoic philosopher), Posidonius (135–51 BCE), Seneca (4 BCE–65 CE), and Marcus Aurelius (121–180 CE). Each of these represents a period in Stoic philosophy—early, middle, and late—and each period had distinctive qualities to it. Indeed, Stoicism is a philosophical school that extends from early thinkers such as Zeno of Citium in the third century (BCE) to Marcus Aurelius, who died in the third century (CE), wielding enormous influence in the philosophy of more than six centuries. Though it glosses over important nuances and differences between them, for my purposes it is reasonable to present a "Stoic" position on the passions. Tad Brennan, "The Old Stoic Theory of Emotions," in Sihvola and Engberg-Pedersen, *Emotions in Hellenistic Philosophy*, 21–70. See also Cooper, *Pursuits of Wisdom*, chapter 4 on this.

108 The Stoics "go much further than any schools of the West in reducing happiness to self-discipline and self-control." McGill, *Idea of Happiness*, 227.

109 McGill, *Idea of Happiness*, 49.

110 Seneca, *Moral Letters to Lucilius*, Letter 9.2. Aristotle rejected the idea of perfect tranquility, arguing that those who claim that a man can be happy while tortured on a rack do not know what they are saying.

111 Like Socrates/Plato, the Stoics thought that human reason is akin to divine reason. However, they often referred to it as "world-mind" or "world-soul." Cooper, *Pursuits of Wisdom*, 166–71.

112 In this view, a person's senses and the dynamics of the material world are only "matter in commerce." Robinson, *Intellectual History of Psychology*, 102.

113 In the Stoic system, even death and illness have no value in themselves, no meaning apart from the meaning we give them. Thus, a person who knows the good and "does not attribute to anything else a value it does not possess, is wise." Blackson, *Ancient Greek Philosophy*, 242.

114 Katerina Ierodiakonou, "How Feasible Is the Stoic Conception of *Eudaimonia?*" 182.

115 Robinson, *Intellectual History of Psychology*, 101.

116 The passions (*pathai*) in Stoic philosophy are merely "unruly" disruptions to one's material reality. They can be dealt with.

117 Richard Sorabji, *Emotion and Peace of Mind: From Stoic Agitation to Christian Temptation* (Oxford: Oxford University Press, 2000), especially chapter 13.

118 There is no perfect accomplishment of this. Rather, the Stoics, like Aristotle, allowed for a progressive achievement: that is, human development toward the maturity of a sage entailed progression from the "mediocre nonvirtuous" to the "horrendously vicious." Ierodiakonou, "How Feasible Is the Stoic Conception of *Eudaimonia?*" 195.

119 For the Stoics, the passions are not comprised of beliefs, values, or motivations, as Aristotle understood them. They are purely mistaken judgments and misguided evaluations. Indeed, all errors/mistakes are conceptual ones. Cooper, *Pursuits of Wisdom*, 159. The Stoic process of changing beliefs to effect change in one's experience of passions has analogs in modern cognitive therapies.

120 Sorabji, *Emotion and Peace of Mind*, 169.

121 Ierodiakonou, "How Feasible Is the Stoic Conception of *Eudaimonia?*" 194.

122 Solomon, "Philosophy of Emotions," 5.

123 Knuuttila, *Emotions in Ancient and Medieval Philosophy*, 6.

124 Knuuttila, *Emotions in Ancient and Medieval Philosophy*, 6.

125 Robert C. Roberts, "Emotions among the Virtues of the Christian Life," *The Journal of Religious Ethics* 20, no. 1 (1992): 42. First emphasis added, second and third in the original.

126 In the process of letting go of self-concern, other-concern will develop (at least ideally): people will grow out of an instinctual (and mistaken) attachment to family members and relatives into having concern for all people simply because they are human. Impartial concern for others is the part of moral consciousness that develops as one grows in the right ways, according to Stoic thinking. Blackson, *Ancient Greek Philosophy*, 240–41.

127 In fact, Stoic philosopher Chrysippus compared the passions to diseases. Chrysippus wrote, "Just as when the blood is in a bad state or there is too much of phlegm or bile . . . so the disturbing effect of corrupt beliefs and their fight against one another rob the soul of health and introduces the disorder of disease." Chrysippus went on to compare "diseases of soul" to "diseases of body," saying that false beliefs make the confused mind unstable and feverish and lead to infirmity. Chrysippus, *Tusculan Disputations* 4.23. Quoted in Knuuttila, *Emotions in Ancient and Medieval Philosophy*, 72.

128 Knuuttila, *Emotions in Ancient and Medieval Philosophy*, 53. Cicero considered translating the Greek word *pathos* into Latin *diseases* but found it did not always suit his subject of study. He eventually accepted *perturbations*, which also had a negative connotation. Seneca preferred *affectus* or *passion*, thus relating passions to suffering. All Stoics emphasized passivity of the passions and the sense in which they are out of our voluntary control and thus not a proper part of our selves.

129 Roman scholar Cicero called this state *tranquillitas*. Although it is possible to achieve the status of *apatheia*, they thought very few people (by whom the philosophers meant men)

are capable of it. For the Stoics, especially the late Stoics, freedom from the passions is something great and perfect, but moderation is at least a matter of progress. Ierodiakonou, "How Feasible Is the Stoic Conception of *Eudaimonia?*" 194. Others disagreed. For example, Plotinus, a Neoplatonist and late Stoic, was against moderation, arguing that likeness to God is the highest good for humans and the only acceptable goal. Cooper, *Pursuits of Wisdom*, 348–49. (In fact, Plotinus is considered the father of Western mysticism.) M. A. Soupios, "Plotinus [A.D. 205–270]: Mystic Philosopher," in Soupios, *The Greeks Who Made Us Who We Are*, 203. Because the late Stoics were committed to the view of an impassible God (one without any passions), they believed moderation can misdirect one from the highest goal of assimilating oneself to the apathetic part of the soul—that is, an ultimate and impassible state of reason. This metaphysic informed Plotinus' ethics as well: according to Plotinus, the phenomena of the visible world are only pale reflections of a "more real" and higher level of reality. It follows, then, that civic virtues are distorted versions of transcendent virtues. Knuuttila, *Emotions in Ancient and Medieval Philosophy*, 102. Despite their negative evaluation of the passions, Stoic philosophers allowed that the sage can experience *eupatheia* (the edification of reason and rational habits and the good feelings that result). These feelings are appropriate judgments about what is truly important to the good life, including kindness, generosity, warmth, and affection (the virtues) toward one's fellow creatures. Instead of feeling hedonistic pleasure, however, the sage experiences joy. Instead of suffering, the sage experiences the realities of life dispassionately and without response (unless he feels joy or generosity toward others for their shared humanity, or experiences pleasure at his own *apatheia*). As such, some philosophers suggest that the possibility of *eupatheia* indicates an expansion of the soul from beyond oneself to include others: for example, Martha Nussbaum wonders what kind of joy one can have without real attachment. She argues it is not a joy she would recognize. See Martha Nussbaum, "Emotions as Judgments of Value and Importance," in *Thinking about Feeling: Contemporary Philosophers on Emotions*, ed. Robert C. Solomon (Oxford: Oxford University Press, 2004), 183–99.

130 Stoic philosophers developed exercises for dealing with one's passions in an effort to achieve *apatheia*. These included *catharsis* (or "venting"); playing one passion against another as a way of controlling both (e.g., fear of the consequences of murder vs. desire for revenge); reminding oneself of the futility of life; and changing one's beliefs about a particular situation or experience.

131 Knuuttila, *Emotions in Ancient and Medieval Philosophy*, 57.

132 Stoic philosopher Chrysippus said these "infections" are generated through social interaction "through the persuasiveness of appearances." Knuuttila, *Emotions in Ancient and Medieval Philosophy*, 58.

133 This was Seneca's view. The doctrine of pre-passions or first movements became one of the most highly influential elements of Stoic philosophy on later thinking about the passions, especially for Christian theologians, as discussed in chapter 2.

134 This line of thought emphasized the role of the will, a quality of human experience that would be examined in great detail by Christian theologians. If the physical or mental pain is intolerable, the Stoic sage is permitted to commit death by suicide so as not to assent, or give in, to it. (The theory of assent was a "favorite whipping boy" in the schools of philosophy.) Augustine would later argue that this belief demonstrates they did not actually believe their teaching that *apatheia* was always the answer and that it could be achieved. McGill, *Idea of Happiness*, 74.

135 Chrysippus' analysis of emotion as judgment remained the orthodox view for later scholars of emotions. Knuuttila, *Emotions in Ancient and Medieval Philosophy*, 6.

136 Robinson, *Intellectual History of Psychology*, 105. This view has been used to oppress women, the differently abled, persons who identify as queer, and people of color because they do not conform to the "ideal Form" of human being (that is, male, white, educated, cisgendered, etc.). Natural theological arguments against homosexuality, or the "love the sinner, hate the sin" view that derives from this kind of thinking, are equally problematic. These uses of what is "natural" must be resisted.

137 Influential figures who agreed that emotions are bestial, including Italian philosopher and politician Niccolo Machiavelli (1469–1527 CE), also thought they could be useful: Machiavelli would suggest ways to leverage emotions for political gain. Machiavelli's advice to leaders included "a great deal of material" on how to manipulate the passions of subjects to keep public order. One technique, he suggested, was to adopt a public persona that can project emotions and character traits that may be very different from the ruler's true private feelings in order to control the perceptions of their subjects. Machiavelli also argued that fear provides a particularly reliable motivation for action and envy a "well-nigh universal" one. Rulers should aim for glory, indulge their ambition, seek recognition and honor, and use emotions to leverage their subjects to attain what they desire. Robinson, *Intellectual History of Psychology*, 175–76 and 204.

138 Cognitive behavioral psychologists would later agree with the Stoics that certain thoughts lead to suffering, though only the behavioral psychologists eschewed the value or uses of passions (emotions) as strongly as the Stoics had. This will be taken up in chapter 4. See, for example, Aaron Beck, *Cognitive Therapies and the Emotional Disorders* (Madison, Conn.: International Universities Press, 1976).

139 As subsequent chapters show, Aristotle's thinking is echoed by others (especially philosophers, theologians, and psychologists) who are interested in the person in sociocultural context, in human development, and in a nuanced understanding of the good life in relation to others in community. Scientific explanations for the passions in the manner of empirical methods promoted by Hippocrates and Galen motivated later scientists, including Charles Darwin and Paul MacLean, providing much of the basic vocabulary for the contemporary discussion of the physiology of emotions. Stoic understandings of misdirected attachments informed twentieth-century cognitive psychologists' work. Aristotle and the Stoics provided the first taxonomies of emotions that became popular in Renaissance discussions of specific emotions such as love and melancholy or glory. The Stoic view of the passions was transmitted through Latin authors and the neo-Stoic revival of the sixteenth century represented by Justus Lipsius and Montaigne. Nevertheless, Stoic philosophers' thinking, as transmitted through later writers, received a mixed reception. Even those heavily influenced by Stoicism (such as René Descartes and Baruch Spinoza) criticized certain Stoic doctrines, especially the idea that passions are erroneous judgments.

Earlier figures' work on the passions, such as that of Immanuel Kant, made many significant contributions to the history of psychology: for example, the concept of object permanence would figure prominently in later developmental theories, and general rationalist contributions include the stage-specific cognitive abilities of humans during development from infancy and a priori faculties, both of which have been carried forward into contemporary psychology. Robinson, *Intellectual History of Psychology*, 272. Furthermore, Kant argued that nothing great is ever done without passion before Hegel did. Solomon,

"Nietzsche and the Emotions." Nevertheless, in Kant, reason and desire are in "permanent conflict." Thus, one cannot have both virtue and happiness. McGill, *Idea of Happiness*, 107. Immanuel Kant conflated eudaimonia with the feeling of happiness, or the result of being virtuous. On this he was very critical of the Stoics' view, arguing that they subordinate practical reason to pleasure. This is likely a misunderstanding of the Stoic view of happiness. T. H. Irwin, "Kant's Criticism of Eudaemonism," in *Aristotle, Kant, and the Stoics: Rethinking Happiness and Duty* (Cambridge: Cambridge University Press, 1996), 63–101.

In Descartes, the soul becomes more private and personal, emerging as the only source of certain knowledge. The soul is the self, or *myself*, and is contrasted with my body, other selves, and with Society. The inner self is posed over against the alien society, whereas in Aristotle, the soul is integrated in the life of the state and is meaningless outside of it. McGill, *Idea of Happiness*, 163.

Giants in philosophy and their theories, including Descartes and his mind/body dualism (strongly influenced by Plato), Thomas Hobbes and materialism, and Baruch Spinoza and parallelism, all tried to figure out the passions'/emotions' relationship to soul and body. As part of their embrace of the new science, many seventeenth-century philosophers considered the passions to have a mechanical explanation. Descartes proposed a dualism of mind and body, privileging the mind while always, as a natural scientist, remaining interested in the relationship of human experience and material reality. It is a well-worn critique to say that his assumptions have plagued understanding of human beings throughout Western history. As one historian writes, "Cartesian dualism of this type is the most widespread Western model of the 'subject'—that is, of the subjective self that is a locus of unique experiences." Reddy, *Navigation of Feeling*, 66. It is just this notion of the self that has sustained the Western "common sense" about emotions, according to which they are viewed as a "naturally occurring composite of involuntary physiological arousal states and subjective 'feelings.'" Reddy, *Navigation of Feeling*, 66. The Cartesian dualisms between material and nonmaterial worlds was a distinction that would come to be applied in many and various ways since Descartes, informing psychology, theology, and the sciences still centuries later, though philosophical or practical commitment to keeping them distinct is weakening, as we shall see.

Historically and philosophically, then, the commitments and values of the Enlightenment/Age of Reason eventually gave way to those of the Romantic Era in the early nineteenth century. In the eighteenth, nineteenth, and early twentieth centuries, humanism, Romanticism, and existentialism would recast the views of personal subjectivity and, consequently, scholars' views on emotions and their origins and purposes. All were reactions against the Age of Reason and sought to reclaim the importance of the intuitive, emotional, and less rationalistic ways, rooted in the conviction that Enlightenment philosophies were too abstract and too removed from human experience. Humanism, with its roots in the Italian Renaissance, would focus on the individual, examining human values and meaning, rethinking human existence and purpose without benefit of a transcendent, Divine Being or the emphasis on a supraworldly hierarchy. A fundamental characteristic of the earliest humanists was a deep optimism: hope in progress and freedom and people as agents of change, and emotions were understood to be a part of that. The Romantic movement validated strong emotions (especially terror, awe, anxiety, and fear) as authentic sources of knowing and important experiences, and Romantic artists and writers including Edgar Allen Poe, Amadeus Mozart, and Friedrich

Schleiermacher are examples of those who prized the deep affective experience they could effect in their audiences. Existentialism as a philosophical position would emphasize not only the importance of human experience but also the importance of emotions (especially anxiety) for understanding that experience. Existentialist philosophers such as Friedrich Nietzsche, Soren Kierkegaard, Simone de Beauvoir, and Jean-Paul Sartre all explored the human condition through the examination of emotions, thoughts, behaviors—especially in relation to the purpose of life, individual freedom and responsibility, and despair.

Against the rationalistic and empirical scientific view that the world (and people) were predictable and knowable, existentialist writers in particular would emphasize the chaotic, the anxiety-producing, the threat of meaninglessness, and the struggle for meaning in one's life. Such a perspective, of course, would have a significant and lasting impact on how emotions were understood then and how we view them now. David M. Rosenthal, "Emotions and the Self," in *Emotions: Philosophical Studies*, vol. 2, ed. K. D. Irani and Gerald E. Myers (New York: Haven Publications, 1983), 179.

140 Solomon, *The Passions*.

141 Solomon, *The Passions*.

142 Historian Peter Goldie asserts that "there is [still] much still to be learned from a careful study of the history of philosophical work on the emotions," and I agree. Peter Goldie, "Introduction," in *Oxford Handbook of Philosophy of Emotion*, ed. Peter Goldie (Oxford: Oxford University Press, 2009), 5.

2 Emotions as Sinful, Signs of the Fall, and Impediments to Salvation

1 Scholars have long identified Stoicism as a significant foundation for Christianity or, as Augustine called it, the world's Christianity before the world knew Christ. M. A. Soupios, "Zeno (335–263 BCE): Stoic Sage," in Soupios, *The Greeks Who Made Us Who We Are*, 172–91.

2 Dixon, *Passions to Emotions*, 5.

3 Robinson, *Intellectual History of Psychology*, 173. Emphasis in the original. In the universe of the philosophers Plato, Aristotle, and Plotinus, the beings of the highest order are abstract and impersonal. This changes in the Christian cosmology, in which there is something above and beyond the good or reason: the personal God who created it. This shift makes a "profound difference" in the understanding of happiness: the historical revelation of a personal God (as revealed in Jesus Christ) now becomes the primary orientation, and happiness can be understood only as a relation to "Him" and to "His" infinite will, love, and goodness. McGill, *The Idea of Happiness*, 68. See chapter 7, note 86 of this text for a discussion of choices of terms for what one considers to be ultimate reality, such as Yahweh, God, "the Universe," or "God."

4 Upon hearing of the death of his young son, Anaxagoras is recorded as saying only, "I knew I had begotten a mortal." Sorabji, *Emotion and Peace of Mind*, 197. See chapter 1 of this volume for more.

5 In their theory of "indifferents," the Stoics specified "preferred and dis-preferred" indifferents. They recognized that life and health are naturally preferred, but they are nonetheless indifferents, as they, too, fade: human beings should remember always that even the universe does not last. Sorabji, *Emotion and Peace of Mind*, 242. See chapter 1 for more on the Stoic position.

6 The question of human beings' place in the "natural hierarchy of creation" was one that captured some philosophers' and Christian theologians' attention, but it was not until the thirteenth century that Thomas Aquinas developed natural theology; still, there was

interest early on in articulating the differences between humans and animals. Some argued that the passions and will represent a fundamental difference between animals and humans (the ability to control one's passions was a primary distinction), though this notion would be disrupted by the case of Phineas Gage, a figure who helped disabuse philosophers' and theologians' assumptions of human beings' unique experience of passions, as we shall see in chapter 3. Others argued that human beings alone have a conscience, implying a natural capacity to discern their moral duty to God and their fellow human beings. In this view, the passions, will, and conscience are God-given capacities that lead individuals directly to "reverence and awe, hope and fear—capacities unavailable to 'lower' creatures." Dixon, *Passions to Emotions*, 184–85. Many early Christian theologians argued that humans can grow in these God-given capacities, which is a departure from Stoic philosophy in which there is "no such thing, strictly speaking, as moral progress." See Ierodiakonou, "How Feasible Is the Stoic Conception of *Eudaimonia*?"

7 Sorabji, *Emotion and Peace of Mind*, 236.

8 Ierodiakonou, "How Feasible Is the Stoic Conception of *Eudaimonia*?" 187.

9 Stoics did allow that it is in accordance with nature to regard all human beings (even slaves) as part of the same household because they are rational, and that one should practice treating others with justice and appropriate (though still preferably indifferent) care. Nevertheless, Epictetus suggested we are always to remind ourselves that our wives and children are mortal and not get too attached to them (Sorabji, *Emotion and Peace of Mind*, 216–18) and that erotic love does harm. (For this reason some Stoics and Epicureans recommended indiscriminate sex so as not to create misguided attachments and inevitable pain at separation.) Sorabji, *Emotion and Peace of Mind*, 283. Martha Nussbaum has an interesting exploration of this in her essay, "Eros and the Wise."

10 Robinson, *Intellectual History of Psychology*, 122.

11 Robinson, *Intellectual History of Psychology*, 103 and 106.

12 With the Christian theologians, the previous Greek philosophers' language for the telos shifted from reason or the good life to the Divine life or God's will, salvation, redemption, and so on.

13 This is a reference to the *seelsorge*, or the cure/care of souls, tradition. This tradition is described as primarily having to do with care and includes the tasks in the care of a person or thing, or to the "mental experience of carefulness or solicitude concerning its object." John T. McNeill, *A History of the Cure of Souls* (New York: Harper Torchbooks, 1951), vii. Pastoral theologian Don Browning defines this tradition as the care of people within a moral community, a tradition that has developed a set of understandings to connect individual, personal suffering and larger social-ethical questions. Don S. Browning, *Moral Context of Pastoral Care* (Louisville, Ky.: Westminster John Knox, 1983), 17. Early philosophers and Christian theologians understood care of the soul to be the most important exercise in life.

14 Aristotle was largely lost to Jewish and Christian theologians until their contact with Islam. With thanks to historical theologian Bryce Rich, personal conversation, March 5, 2018. See also Mauro Zonta, "Influence of Arabic and Islamic Philosophy on Judaic Thought," *Stanford Encyclopedia of Philosophy*, https://plato.stanford.edu/entries/arabic -islamic-judaic/.

15 Knuuttila, *Emotions in Ancient and Medieval Philosophy*, 122. The process began with Philo, who harmonized Hebrew Scriptures with Platonism. The practice continued with the

Greek fathers, and their work (especially that of Origen) influenced Ambrose and then Augustine and others.

16 Luke 19:41-44.

17 John 11:35.

18 Matthew 26:39.

19 Their work was not made easier by the fact that the apostle Paul, too, was heavily informed by Platonic and Stoic philosophy, preaching that Christians are not to be sad "as those without hope are sad," that reward does not depend on the one who wills but on God's mercy, and that avarice is the root of all evil, as well as holding a derogatory view of the flesh. Sorabji, *Emotion and Peace*, 315.

20 Dixon, *Passions to Emotions*, 40. Though the word *emotions* does not appear in any of the major English translations of the Bible, many writers have continued to interpret the early term *passion* to mean emotion. It is noteworthy that one of the words in New Testament discussions of passions or desires is *epithumia*, which is variously translated as "lusts" in the King James Version and as "sinful desires" and "evil desires" in the Revised Standard Version. Dixon, *Passions to Emotions*, 39.

21 Dixon, *Passions to Emotions*, 39.

22 Sorabji, *Emotion and Peace*, especially chapter 2. The English word *passion* is etymologically related to *passive*, something over which individuals have no control; the closest classical term to *emotion* was the Latin word *motus*, which just meant movement, though it was sometimes used to indicate the movements of the soul that were expressions of humanity's sinful nature. See the introduction of this text for more on the term "emotions" and its historical definitions.

23 Philo's treatise *Legit. Alleg.* 3.143–144 was studied by Clement of Alexandria, Origen, and the Cappadocian Fathers who "paid close attention" to Philo, even as they added nuance to some of his views. In it Philo theorizes about the passions, the goal of life, and possible exercises to accomplish the goal. Sorabji, *Emotion and Peace*, 386.

24 Philo's acceptance of some passions as helpful became a common argument among later Christian advocates for *apatheia*. Themes in Philo and other early bridge thinkers (many of whom were converts to Christianity from Stoicism) were picked up by other early Christians, including Justin Martyr (100–165 CE), who wrote that the aim of the Christian life is to be similar to God, who is free from passions (as the saints will be in heaven, he thought), that one should keep the irrational movements under strict control in order to achieve godlikeness, and that uncontrolled passions are the sources of vices. And because the passions are partly physical, it would be unfair that only the soul was punished: the body must be too, Martyr thought. Another Christian theologian, the "Father of Latin Christianity" Tertullian (155–240 CE), would emphasize the power of choice in the process of controlling the passions, while others, such as Clement of Alexandria (150–215 CE), would emphasize that *apatheia* was the ideal but believed that because of the Fall it could not have been achieved before the resurrection of Christ. Sorabji, *Emotion and Peace*, 387.

25 Sorabji, *Emotion and Peace*, 387. Clement (and later Clement's student Origen) is a prime representative of early Alexandrian theology, which was then modified by the Cappadocian Fathers and Egyptian desert monks. Clement's teaching on the passions came to influence Western thought through the works of John Cassian. Sorabji, *Emotion and Peace*, 391–95.

26 Knuuttila, *Emotions in Ancient and Medieval Philosophy*, 113. Clement was an educated man intimately familiar with Greek philosophy and literature, especially Plato and the Stoics (perhaps more than other Christian scholars of his time; Knuuttila, *Emotions in Ancient and Medieval Philosophy*, 114) and was heavily influenced by Philo, whose work informed the foundational principles of Christianity. Clement's understanding of revelation had a significant influence on Christian perspectives that followed.

27 Clement and Origen write about cutting away the affective part of the soul. Knuuttila, *Emotions in Ancient and Medieval Philosophy*, 119.

28 Origen has been called the "greatest figure of Alexandrian theology and one of the most original Christian thinkers in ancient times." His work on the passions and their relation to salvation had a deep and lasting impact. Knuuttila, *Emotions in Ancient and Medieval Philosophy*, 114.

29 In so doing, Origen blurs the Stoic distinction of thoughts from bodily movements, or the Stoic understanding of pre-passions. It is a conflation Augustine would adopt. Sorabji, *Emotion and Peace*, 343–51.

30 Knuuttila, *Emotions in Ancient and Medieval Philosophy*, 113–27. Both Clement and Origen avoided the concern of satiety (a pleasure about which they and their contemporaries were concerned) by arguing for the ever-increasing desire for God that results from the process toward perfection: one can be sated in one's desire for God only after Christ's return, when the faithful are fully united again with God. Other examinations would provide a different, more nuanced perspective on the same question of first movements. For example, Persian and Islamic scholar Avicenna's (980–1037 CE) theory of emotion adopted much of what Clement and Origen had proposed, influencing medieval philosophical theology well past the thirteenth century. Avicenna parsed even more carefully the theory of first movements, arguing that the titillation of the flesh was unavoidable (even in Jesus, the apostle Paul, or the saints) but as long as one did not take pleasure in it, it was just a pre-passion. One of Avicenna's novel contributions was the argument that these pre-passions are sins because they highlight a defect in the self: the fact that they cannot be avoided does not mean they are not a kind of sin. He took this from the apostle Paul's seeming wrestling with himself and against his desires: "I do not what I will to do, and it is not me but the sin which dwells in me that does it." Romans 7:17. Avicenna's interpretation on Origen's first movements or pre-passions would inform Christian theology for centuries to come, invoking the theology of the Fall and condemning even pre-passions as signs of it. Knuuttila, *Emotions in Ancient and Medieval Philosophy*, 177–78.

31 Another significant Christian theologian, Nemesius, explored these themes. Nemesius (ca. 390 CE) emphasized the brokenness of this world and the perfection of heaven. Along with Philo, Clement, and Origen, Nemesius helped set the stage for much of Christian thinking about the passions, especially among both his relative contemporaries, such as Augustine, and those who came later, including Aquinas. Nemesius accepted Platonic understandings that viewed the soul as a substance distinct from the body, unaffected by the body though united with it. And like other Christian theologians, Nemesius divinized the telos of life in ways the philosophers had not. But Nemesius added something more: he imagined that humans originally held "lofty positions" as rulers of creation but that they have "deteriorated" because of the Fall. This, Nemesius thought, was obvious because the passions have become spontaneous and unruly and can be mastered only through "laborious" effort. Despite the fallen nature of human beings,

however, one can see in nature traces of God's plan: that humans were to be God's "viceroys on earth." Knuuttila, *Emotions in Ancient and Medieval Philosophy*, 104–6.

32 For example, Evagrius and Augustine would take this position.

33 Knuuttila, *Emotions in Ancient and Medieval Philosophy*, 140. Evagrius was an Eastern ascetic who lived out his ascetic life in Egypt. He was ordained by the Cappadocian Fathers and heavily influenced modern Christianity.

34 The phrase "thought of" is significant: it imagines the thing but is not the thing. Sorabji, *Emotion and Peace*, 359.

35 Evagrius describes a monk devoted to poverty who considers how useful it would be to do some fundraising to alleviate the lot of the poor. The monk knows some wealthy ladies who would help. The monk imagines how admired he would be if he succeeded in raising a significant amount, thinking that he would surely be given the ecclesiastical post whose incumbent is dying. Evagrius writes that the monk, sitting in his bare cell, has now succumbed at least to thoughts of avarice and vanity. Evagrius provides another example: a monk thinks it quite harmless to indulge in thoughts of home, and he does so. But soon he feels pleasure at the memory of his past life and realizes he can never have it again. What follow are the demons of distress, anger, the desire for sex, or depression; just by fondly remembering home the monk has committed egregious sins. Sorabji, *Emotion and Peace*, 362.

36 Sorabji, *Emotion and Peace*, 364.

37 I am indebted to my colleague, historical theologian Bryce Rich, for this information. Personal conversation, March 5, 2018.

38 On the question of *apatheia* as a goal, Jerome strongly objected to Evagrius, saying it was not possible on earth. Sorabji, *Emotion and Peace*, 396. Becoming more like God is a process to be undertaken over the course of a lifetime through strict practices proposed by Origen and later by the Cappadocian Fathers. Jerome's "unique contribution" related *degrees* of sin to *stages* of struggle: pre-passions are a kind of sin because they issue from humans' sinful nature after the Fall, but these sins are not as egregious as the sins of assent and acting on the pre-passions. Sorabji, *Emotion and Peace*, 355. Aquinas would develop Jerome's thoughts on the relevance of *degrees* of felt passions and acts of sin.

39 The Fathers were not of one mind on these matters. For example, Basil imagined that Christ had, indeed, experienced genuine passion (not just pre-passion), and both Gregorys allowed for grief because in it one could be consoled and put back on the righteous path. Sorabji, *Emotion and Peace*, 393–95. These understandings had previously shaped the thinking of Augustine, Bishop of North Africa, who is perhaps the most widely known Christian theologian on the subject of the passions. Augustine's understanding of the passions will be explored, but it is worth noting here Evagrius' impact on Pope Gregory the Great, whose thinking about the passions was also enormously influential.

Pope Gregory the Great (540–604 CE) followed very closely thinkers such as Evagrius and Augustine. Gregory the Great helped develop and widely disseminate suggested practices for their management, attending closely to cataloging and exploring various sins that prevented *apatheia* in ways that shaped theological thinking and practice for many centuries. He accepted Evagrius' notion that people's thoughts are a kind of passion (even if only a pre-passion), though Gregory's understanding of Stoic philosophy came through Augustine, which meant that he understood *all* first movements (even physiological ones) to be sins. Pope Gregory accepted the notion that pre-passions are not yet *mortal* sins, but he agreed with Clement, Origen, Nemesius, and Evagrius that the fact that people have them and are not free of all movements of the soul (except perhaps the pure and correct movement toward God) is a sign of the Fall and original sin. Once Pope Gregory accepted this, he took up the challenge to understand which sins were the most egregious. He adapted Evagrius' list of eight first movements, and by a "series of adjustments" he made them the seven cardinal sins. Sorabji, *Emotion and Peace*, 358. He conflated pride and vainglory, and his list of deadly sins became pride, envy, anger, distress/*akedia* (boredom with the life of prayer), avarice, gluttony, and fornication. Pope Gregory agreed that pride was the root of all sin because it convinced people that they had been perfected and did not need to practice the remedies of the Fall to save their evil souls. Followers of Christ should be free from anger and ungodly desire; they may be tempted by pre-passions, but as long as they do not assent to them and expel them as quickly as possible, they are not serious sins, only venial (that is, slight) ones. He argued that the only way to salvation was to control one's pre-passions and passions through fasting, manual labor, being alone in one's cell, singing psalms, reading Christian Scriptures, sitting vigil, and continuously praying. Gregory called these the "remedies of Christ, the doctor of the soul." Knuuttila, *Emotions in Ancient and Medieval Philosophy*, 142.

40 Ambrose (Augustine's mentor) also read Origen in Latin. Thank you to my colleague, historical theologian Bryce Rich, for this added detail. Personal conversation, March 5, 2018.

41 See, for example, Knuuttila, *Emotions in Ancient and Medieval Philosophy*.

42 Christian Tornau, "Happiness in This Life? Augustine on the Principle That Virtue Is Self-Sufficient for Happiness," in Rabbas et al., *The Quest for the Good Life*, 265. Augustine deviated from Aristotle and his followers, however, when he argued that eudaimonia is not achievable in this life but only after resurrection, thus giving eudaimonia a "decidedly eschatological" character and holding that human beings cannot achieve it outside of divine grace. Tornau, "Happiness in This Life," 266. See chapter 1, note 25 on the inclusion of women, children, and slaves in the good life.

43 McGill, *The Idea of Happiness*, 75.

44 Aquinas deferred most often to Aristotle and Augustine, especially on the passions. McGill, *The Idea of Happiness*, 75.

45 Throughout his work, Augustine would distinguish between the *passiones animae* (often translated as *passions, appetites,* or *emotions*) and the *motus animae* (or *movements of the soul,* or *affections*). Dixon, *Passions to Emotions*, 40. Augustine sometimes called the passions *perturbations,* but he also uses more positive terms, such as *affections.* Indeed, affections and virtues are related in Augustine's work, and he finds them compatible. In fact, Augustine redefines the Stoic understanding of virtue and emphasizes that virtue is "nothing other than the greatest love of God." Tornau, "Happiness in This Life," 272. Augustine's virtues include virtue in everyday life (especially politics) and virtue as love as commanded by the New Testament, and he includes virtues' role in contemplation of God in eternal bliss. Tornau, "Happiness in This Life," 275.

46 Sorabji, *Emotions and Peace*, 375–84.

47 Sorabji, *Emotions and Peace*, 382.

48 Philosopher Richard Sorabji argues that Augustine's conflation of the pre-passions and real passions can be read, in part, as the result of a mistake in a summary of Stoicism that changed one letter of the alphabet (the double *l* in *pallescere* ["to grow pale"] to a *v* to make the word *pavescere* ["to grow jittery"]). In other words, Augustine misunderstood the Stoic position of allowing initial shocks (by which they meant first movements—like the sage's first movements in the midst of a storm) to mean the sage had genuine fear,

which is the exact opposite of what Stoic philosophers meant. Stoic philosophers such as Seneca and Epictetus allowed that the sage could have first movements and argued that though one might have a first movement (they might mean an instinctive reaction), it did not necessarily lead to a genuine emotion such as fear. From this Augustine concluded that the Stoic philosophers were not indifferent about their own life but rather understood certain things as good or bad. The sage must then moderate his passions, Augustine concluded, though this is not what the Stoics believed. Augustine assumed, then, that sin (in the form of wrongly directed passions) is unavoidable because of the Fall but that there are degrees of sin: people can sin in their heart, in their actions, and in their habits. Sorabji, *Emotion and Peace*, 377–84. In this error, Sorabji writes, "we have an example of how important good philology can be to good philosophy." Sorabji, *Emotion and Peace*, 384. Philosopher Simo Knuuttila disagrees with Sorabji on this point, asserting that Augustine was not blind to the distinction; rather, he believes Augustine used it with qualifications. Knuuttila argues that what Augustine wanted was to challenge the Stoic thinking that first movements are innocent and not initial stages of emotion. See Knuuttila, *Emotions in Ancient and Medieval Philosophy*, 172.

49 Augustine, *City of God* 14.6. Cited in Tornau, "Happiness in This Life," 277. Augustine points out that people who set their hearts on riches will fear the loss of them, and those who are fearful do not have what they want. Only wisdom and knowledge, rooted in God, are steadfast, "rockproof against change and disaster." McGill, *The Idea of Happiness*, 68.

50 Augustine wrote, "Our heart is restless 'til it rests in thee." *Confessions* 1.6. Our desire for happiness (for Augustine, truth) is a kind of "instinct" given by God so that we will be drawn toward God. McGill, *The Idea of Happiness*, 70.

51 Augustine's view was that salvation is the only worthwhile aim of this life and that real happiness belongs in the next. McGill, *The Idea of Happiness*, 75.

52 Tornau, "Happiness in This Life," 278–80. Augustine agreed with Plato and Aristotle that happiness is a life of virtue, but he specified that virtue is a "perfection of the soul" attainable only by following God. Although Augustine differs from Aristotle in many ways, he does accept that the person seeking happiness (seeking God) is realizing his or her own true nature and destiny, fulfilling deepest yearnings. It can only be fully accomplished, however, after this life. McGill, *The Idea of Happiness*, 73.

53 Augustine adopted the Stoic philosopher Cicero's categorization of four "principal passions"—desire/love, fear, joy, and sorrow—but he Christianized them by relating them to God as revealed in the life and death of Jesus of Nazareth.

54 Robinson, *Intellectual History of Psychology*, 128. Emphasis in the original.

55 Augustine's view of the will is reminiscent of Plato's spirited part of the soul. It can be persuaded by God through grace to direct one to salvation. Augustine, *City of God* 14.6. Augustine found what he viewed as an examination of passions, will, and reason in the story of the Fall in the book of Genesis. Reading the story of Adam and Eve as an allegory (something he most likely got from his mentor, Ambrose, which he wrote about in *De Paradiso*—with thanks to my colleague, historical theologian Bryce Rich, from personal conversation March 5, 2018), Augustine equated the serpent with people's temptation to engage sinful pleasures (like Plato's appetitive soul). He equated Eve with the will that moves people in one direction or the other (like Plato's spirited soul), which, unless properly directed, tends to "overestimate mundane things" and to react receptively to evil suggestions. Adam, Augustine decided, was associated with the highest rational

level of the soul. When the serpent suggests eating the fruit and Eve imagines the pleasure of it (already in danger of being a sin for Augustine), she is in danger of accepting the suggestion. If that movement is not prevented by reason, she has consented to the pleasure of the thought of a desire. If an *intention* to act follows (as it did for Eve and then for Adam), there is *consent* to action. For Augustine the suggestion itself is not a sin, nor is the pleasure of thinking about it, as long as both are destroyed by the reasonable part of the soul "as soon as it becomes aware of it." Knuuttila, *Emotions in Ancient and Medieval Philosophy*, 170. The will, following reason, directs the mind back to divine thoughts. On a related note, treatments of gender in Augustine's reading are deeply problematic, and critiques of Augustine's patriarchal and misogynistic perspectives are trenchant. See, for example, *Feminist Interpretations of Augustine*, ed. Judith Chelius Stark (University Park: Pennsylvania State University Press, 2007).

56 Augustine, *City of God* 14.6.

57 Robinson, *Intellectual History of Psychology*, 121.

58 Robinson, *Intellectual History of Psychology*, 121. Emphasis added. Hear the influence of Socrates'/Plato's view here.

59 Indeed, Augustine's *Confessions* exposed the "genuinely personal and psychological dimensions of the conflict" between passion and reason and the weakness of human will to control the passions. Robinson, *Intellectual History of Psychology*, 123.

60 To sort out the sometimes minute differences between appetites and affections, Augustine theorized and theologized at length about why people do what they do, considered whether people have control over themselves (and if so, how much), and explored carefully the relationship of human beings and God. Augustine was especially interested in the differences between the irascible and concupiscible movements. Augustine carefully examined the *concupiscible* (lustful, desirous) and *irascible* (angry, having to do with temperament) passions. Philosopher Simo Knuuttila argues that Augustine understood the concupiscible movements as signs of original sin not counted as fresh additional sins if they are immediately defeated. They become sins only through consent. Knuuttila, *Emotions in Ancient and Medieval Philosophy*, 169. For Augustine, concupiscent and irascible passions are the primary differentiation between human beings and animals, though he understood human beings to be a mixture of animal and angel, body and soul. In Augustine's thinking, concupiscence is the permanent, inherited weakness human beings have that inclines them to evil desires. Humans' original sin, then, directs a person's attention to pleasurable things (such as sex) or to that which helps a person attain evil desires: for example, individuals become angry when their desires are thwarted. However, there can be positive uses to these: human beings depend on sex for their continuance as a species, and people's irascible movements such as anger can be used to defeat adversaries or to repel things considered harmful or destructive if one wills them thus. Knuuttila, *Emotions in Ancient and Medieval Philosophy*, 152–72.

61 Dixon, *Passions to Emotions*, 29–30. The nuances of Augustine's use of the term *soul* (he used two words: *anima* and *animus*) and their significance to Augustine's thought will not be reviewed here. Suffice it to say that Augustine was not always consistent in his use of the term, and *soul* both "covered all the functions of the person from the organic to the spiritual" and indicated, in a more divided sense, the distinction of the spirit from the body. See Dixon, *Passions to Emotions*, 30.

62 Eve was aligned with the senses and the passions, and thus Eve was considered untrustworthy. Feminist interpretations of this story in the book of Genesis read Eve's role very

differently. See, for example, Phyllis Trible, "Adam and Eve: Genesis 2–3 Reread," Andover Newton Theological School, 1973, https://www.law.csuohio.edu/sites/default/files/shared/eve_and_adam-text_analysis-2.pdf.

63 Appetites, the movements away from God and toward earthly things, are to be controlled and (if possible) properly directed by reason, will, and the strength of virtue. The affections, the passions that are willed toward God, are always directed toward goodness, truth, and the divine life. Passions such as love (if directed rightly) and joy (if generated as a result of being aligned with God) are to be prized and cultivated.

64 In fact, in *The City of God* Augustine said of the Stoic position that it would change the nature of people's humanity. He wrote, "As for those few who, with a vanity which is even more frightful than it is infrequent, pride themselves on being neither raised nor roused nor bent nor bowed by any emotion (*affectus*) whatsoever—well, they have rather lost all humanity than won true peace." Augustine, *City of God* 14.9.

65 Dixon, *Passions to Emotions*, 57. Human beings share the lower powers of the soul with animals, but they also have the rational soul and powers of intellect and will. The acts of animals are morally indifferent—they cannot take place contrary to reason, which animals do not possess.

66 Tornau, "Happiness in This Life," 279. See also book 8 of Augustine's *Confessions*.

67 Even still, certain bodily appetites such as lust are never good, even in moderation. Augustine decided that lust is always bad because it seems *never* to be under control of the will as it would have been before the Fall. Augustine himself famously struggled mightily with this in his own life: his lack of control over his male genitalia and his "sinful" thoughts caused him much consternation (or at least this is the rhetoric he employs in his *Confessions*). In the development of practices to encourage strength of will against the appetites and emotions, Augustine took counsel from the work of Antony the hermit, who encouraged Christians to recall their actions and all the "movements of their soul"—writing them down as if giving an account to another person. Antony imagined that the sheer shame at the thought of doing so would eliminate sinful thoughts. Following Antony's advice, Augustine wrote his *Confessions*, which marks a "turning point in philosophical inquiry that would significantly inform the Christian thinking about personal, affective experience for centuries." (Augustine's *Confessions* has been translated into "practically every Western language.") Knuuttila, *Emotions in Ancient and Medieval Philosophy*, 152. Unfortunately for Augustine, Antony's suggestion that shame would embolden the will did not work for him: Augustine found he could not control the movements of his penis with his thoughts or will. This led to Augustine's preoccupation with the nature of will and convinced Augustine that his original sin prevented his will from having complete control. In Augustine's understanding of prelapsarian (that is, before the Fall) Eden, Adam had complete control over his male organ. Even still, sex is not a sin for Augustine: concupiscence is. (With thanks to my colleague, historical theologian Bryce Rich, for this last note. Personal conversation, March 5, 2018.)

68 Dixon, *Passions to Emotions*, 60.

69 Later theologians such as Anselm (1033–1109 CE) and Thomas Aquinas (1225–1274 CE) continued in Augustine's tradition with a more nuanced view of the passions than Plato or the Stoics had offered. For example, Anselm accepted Augustine's views on sin, differentiating between *venial* sins (those that involve pleasure that is not willed and which one fights against as soon as possible, including pre-passions) and *mortal* sins (sins in which pleasure is allowed to grow into a sinful passion culminating in an evil action). Anselm's

thinking added something of a social justice dimension, parsing differences between the will toward justice and the will toward self-advantage in his discussion of right living. Anselm thought both are given by God and that people sin not by seeking their own happiness, but by seeking happiness without also seeking justice. In this Anselm informed later scholarship on happiness, its relationship to right living and the virtues, and the participation in a life-sustaining polis. Thomas Aquinas, too, was interested in the question of passions and the will. He added even more detail, focusing especially on the relationship between the passions and the physical body, thus returning to some of the thinking and methods of Hippocrates and Galen and integrating them with philosophy and with Christian theology. Knuuttila, *Emotions in Ancient and Medieval Philosophy*, 210. Like the Stoics and Augustine before him, Aquinas argued for the hierarchy of the superior, higher intellect over and against the lesser bodily passions or appetites. An interesting addition to earlier thinking, however, is Aquinas' conviction that passion is always of the body and affects a physical (and presumably detectable) change in the body, such as a dangerous change in the heart rate. Dixon, *Passions to Emotions*, 52. Aquinas added to his belief that the passions could be either positive or negative, differentiating between them based on their direction (as Augustine did) and also their *intensity*. Like Galen, then, Aquinas was interested in some kind of balance, or homeostasis. For example, Aquinas argued that passions always cause a change in heartbeat (either faster or slower) and warned that even love could cause serious harm to the body if it were excessive. Saint Thomas Aquinas, *Summa Theologica*, trans. Anton Pegis, in *Basic Writings of Thomas Aquinas* (New York: Random House, 1945), Ia.2ae.24, 22,3. It is possible, then, that any passion can be good if it is rationally controlled, experienced in the right degree, and directed toward God. Aquinas followed Augustine's teachings a long way, though he elaborated on them and differed from them as well. Aquinas accepted Augustine's views that the passions were negative forces that implied imperfections or "deficiencies." Margaret R. Miles, *Desire and Delight: A New Reading of Augustine's Confessions* (New York: Crossroad, 1992), 126–30.

70 For a contemporary example of this kind of thinking, see David Powlison, "What Do You Feel?" *Journal of Pastoral Practice* 10, no. 4 (1991): 50–53.

71 James D. Whitehead and Evelyn E. Whitehead, *Shadows of the Heart: A Spirituality of the Negative Emotions* (New York: Crossroad, 1994), 13–14. Not surprisingly, then, although the Christian Scriptures are replete with images of both God and Jesus Christ as emotional beings, a significant element of defending God's holiness in the history of theology was the denial that God had any emotional life at all. Rather, in early Christian theology (and in many contemporary churches), God is understood to be impassive and immutable, "unmoved by emotion either toward or from the world." If God has no passions, then God cannot sin, early Christians argued. Lester, *Angry Christian*, 41. Such a negative view of emotions has persisted into contemporary theological anthropologies. Pastoral theologian Andrew Lester, in his study of anger, writes that "good Christians" were taught not to express anger and the best Christians "did not even feel it." Lester, *Angry Christian*, 1. Indeed, negative emotions were considered part of our "carnal nature," and by the Middle Ages anger had become counted among the seven deadly sins. Historian Carol Z. Stearns notes that before the end of the seventeenth century, most religious diarists "had difficulty thinking of themselves as angry [or] . . . as having emotions which could be named at all." Carol Z. Stearns, "'Lord Help Me Walk Humbly': Anger and Sadness in England and America, 1570–1750," in *Emotions: A Cultural Studies Reader*, ed.

Jennifer Harding and E. Deidre Pribram (New York: Routledge, 2009), 170–90. Stearns goes on to note that the anger of others made early modern people uncomfortable (172).

72 Some prominent later theologies of the passions resisted the passions as God given and signs of faith. In general, Christian theologians from the seventeenth to the twentieth centuries resisted the Stoics' complete negation of the passions, accepting them (though in varying degrees and in various ways) as created by God and contributing to the good and virtuous life, even though they also had potential for harm. For example, reforming theologian Martin Luther (1483–1546 CE) held that "God did not create humans to be like stones . . . but purposively gave us five senses and a heart so that we can love, be angry and feel grief." Not to be moved by the affections, he argued, "would be altogether contrary to nature, which was created by God to have such inclinations." Martin Luther, compiled by Ewald M. Plass, *What Luther Says: An Anthology*, vol. 1 (St. Louis: Concordia, 1959), 510–11. Cited in Lester, *Angry Christian*, 45. However, central to Luther's understanding of the passions is the importance of people's wills: like Augustine and Aquinas, Luther understood the soul's purification to require renunciation of the flesh. (It is important to note that renunciation of the flesh is read more broadly than sexual relations; Augustine understood sex in marriage as good. Nevertheless, "consecrated virginity" is preferred over marriage. Historical theologian Bryce Rich, personal conversation, March 5, 2018.) See also Elizabeth A. Clark, *Reading Renunciation: Asceticism and Scripture in Early Christianity* (Princeton, N.J.: Princeton University Press, 1999). Thus, one's spiritual status can be assessed only in terms of one's intentions, which Luther understood to be capable of being inspired both by God and by Satan. Accepting the passions as God given did not temper Luther's emphasis on the importance of the will and the need for purification, and Luther advocated practices that cultivated both. Lester, *Angry Christian*, 130–31. Reforming Christian theologian John Calvin understood anger as a sin. Lester, *Angry Christian*, 131–32.

73 Indeed, despite the nuances in Augustine's and Aquinas' work, "negative" passions—especially the appetites that appear in Aquinas' list—have long been maligned in the Western Christian tradition. For a relatively recent example, see contemporary evangelical counselor David Powlison's essay, "What Do You Feel?" where he argues that emotions are usually selfish and idolatrous. There are exceptions to this, of course, as noted above. Scottish philosopher David Hume was more sanguine about the benefits of the passions, as was John Wesley. Hume (1711–1776 CE) afforded the passions a central place in his epistemology and argued that our emotions are natural, elicited by sensations and impressions, and directed by an interior (and also natural) sense of sympathy. Robinson, *Intellectual History of Psychology*, 227. According to Hume, the passions are a core element of universal human capacities for "moral sentiments" such as sympathy, and they inform our ethics. Thus, for Hume, the passions "deserve central respect and consideration." Solomon, "Philosophy of Emotions," 7. Indeed, Hume argued that some passions move us toward others, allowing us to "feel with" others and share, at least at some level, their suffering. For this reason, he argued, our emotional capacities should not be an embarrassment or seen as unnecessary, but rather as "the very essence of human social existence and morality." Solomon, "Philosophy of Emotions," 8. Despite the fact that Hume "ultimately fell back on the old models and metaphors" (Solomon, "Philosophy of Emotions," 3), the "two pillars" of a classically conceived Christian soul—will and reason—"vanished" in Humean psychology, replaced by a "multitude of passions, sentiments, affections, desires or emotions, each the product of the learned association of

certain impressions with other impressions of pleasure or pain in past experience." Dixon, *Passions to Emotions*, 106.

74 Knuuttila, *Emotions in Ancient and Medieval Philosophy*, 195.

75 This is true, in part, because this position was defended by Peter Lombard, whose book *Sententiae* (c. 1155 CE) was used widely as a university textbook and the text that students of theology had to lecture and comment on "as the last requirement for obtaining the highest academic degree." Knuuttila, *Emotions in Ancient and Medieval Philosophy*, 181. Influential ("though not very original") theologians Duns Scotus (1266–1308 CE) and William of Ockham (1288–1347 CE) extended the voluntarist theory of emotions, increasing scholars' interest in human psychology and motivation, human development, and processes of change. Knuuttila, *Emotions in Ancient and Medieval Philosophy*, 265 and 268. French philosopher Rene Descartes (1596–1650 CE) argued for the value of introspective methods in the last part of his study on emotions, and in his *New Essays on Human Understanding*, German philosopher Gottfried Leibniz (1646–1716 CE) dealt with the question of how people can "learn to master their spontaneous appetites." Even now "their influence perdures in philosophical works on ethics and psychology." Knuuttila, *Emotions in Ancient and Medieval Philosophy*, 195.

76 The views of Origen and Evagrius informed the thinking of John Cassian (360–435 CE), the Cappadocian Fathers (ca. 330–389 CE), and Gregory the Great (540–604 CE), who established practices designed to control the passions in monastic life that were intended to be a model for lay people as well. These figures especially shaped the views and practices of Christian communities for many centuries. For them, moderating or extirpating the passions and properly directing the will were the primary ways one's soul could prepare to ascend to heaven and godlikeness. The achievement of a mature spiritual life was described in some terms that sounded like passions (for example, love and pity), though it was made clear that these were not ordinary passions, but God-given graces. Knuuttila, *Emotions in Ancient and Medieval Philosophy*, 172–73. Monastic culture considered all wrongly directed movements of the soul especially harmful because they hindered or prevented the aspired-to ascent toward God. In this context monks analyzed the spontaneous first movements, thoughts, and other passions in order to diagnose the sickness of the soul, and they used ascetic practices to lessen the power of sinful passions and strengthen efforts to defeat them. Theologians wrote rules for monasteries that promoted *apatheia* as the ideal for monks because it restored the monks to God. Recommended practices include a regular and honest review of the day's conduct, along with fasting, staying awake to pray, and singing the Holy Scriptures (as many early converts to Christianity were illiterate).

77 Management of one's passions through reason and will and the ongoing examinations of one's motives are still popular devices for self-control, for the formation of one's character, and for the exercise of the mechanisms of change in one's desires, the direction of one's will, and one's actions.

78 This is particularly true because writers such as Evagrius and John Cassian are again attracting interest and have increasing numbers of readers and aspiring followers among certain Christian traditions today. Historical theologian Bryce Rich, personal conversation, March 5, 2018.

79 This history of mixed messages about the passions and their role in the good or saved life continued through the fifteenth to the twenty-first centuries. Some Christian theologians—for example, Martin Luther, William Fenner, Jonathan Edwards, Friedrich

Schleiermacher, Soren Kierkegaard, and Paul Tillich—considered certain emotions as fundamental to understanding and pursuing a life of faith. However, central to Luther's psychology is the will: similar to Augustine and Aquinas, he understood the soul's purification to require renunciation of the flesh. He believed that the spiritual status of people can be assessed only in terms of their intentions and that intentions will either be inspired by God or be against God. William Fenner (1600–1640 CE), an English Puritan clergyman, wrote prolifically about the role of the affections in the moral life. See, for example, William Fenner, *A Treatise of the Affections* (London: Rothwell, 1642). In the eighteenth century, influential Christian theologian Jonathan Edwards (1703–1758 CE) was one of the strongest and best-known proponents of the importance of the affections and other emotions in the life of faith, especially valuing their role in conversion. Edwards proposed a balance of reason and passion ("light and love")—essentially a creative tension between will and understanding, feelings and intellect. See J. R. Fulcher, "Puritans and the Passions: Faculty Psychology in American Puritanism," *Journal of the History of the Behavioral Sciences* 9, no. 2 (1973): 123–29. Quoted in Dixon, *Passions to Emotions*, 75.

Other spiritualities have focused on "befriending" rather than "mastering" the emotions and hold the body and soul not as opposed to one another but as "potential partners that can connect us with the creator." However, these views and accompanying practices have not been emphasized in the Christian tradition until, perhaps, more recently. See Whitehead and Whitehead, *Shadows of the Heart*, 14–15. Perspectives such as those of philosopher Rene Descartes became the dominant views. Descartes extended the Platonic understanding of the dualism of mind and body. Descartes privileged the mind while always remaining a natural scientist, interested in the relationship of human experience and material reality. It is a well-worn critique to say that his assumptions have plagued understanding of human beings throughout Western history. As one historian writes, "Cartesian dualism of this type is the most widespread Western model of the 'subject'—that is, of the subjective self that is a locus of unique experiences." Reddy, *Navigation of Feeling*, 66.

The Cartesian dualism between material and nonmaterial worlds was a distinction that would come to be applied in many and various ways since Descartes, informing psychology, theology, and the sciences still centuries later, though the commitment to keeping them distinct is weakening, as we shall see. There is an interesting discussion about the relationship of the self and society among the sociologists Robert Bellah and Richard Madsen, coauthors of *Habits of the Heart: Individualism and Commitment in American Life* (Berkeley: University of California Press, 1986), pastoral theologian Donald Capps, and sociologist of religion Richard Fenn in which they debate the challenges and merits of individualism and individuality. See Donald Capps and Richard K. Fenn, *Individualism Reconsidered: Readings Bearing on the Endangered Self in Modern America*, series 1 (Princeton, N.J.: Princeton Theological Seminary, Center for Religion, Self, and Society, 1993).

Although Friedrich Schleiermacher (1768–1834 CE) wrote extensively about feeling (*Gefuhl*), he surely did not mean what we do by the word. Rather, for him, *feeling* (as opposed to *feelings*) meant the feeling of absolute dependence on God, or the God-consciousness that is the human capacity for God, and his was not a systematic examination of emotions per se. For an extensive discussion of this, see Friedrich Schleiermacher, *The Christian Faith*, 2 vols., trans. and ed. H. R. Mackintosh and J. S. Steward (1821; repr., New York: Harper & Row, 1963). See also Marcia Mount Shoop, *Let the Bones Dance: Embodiment and the Body of Christ* (Louisville, Ky.: Westminster John Knox, 2010), for a discussion of Schleiermacher's understanding of *feeling* and implications for contemporary faith and practice. Though he did not take up the passions or emotions in a full treatment, Christian philosopher and theologian Soren Kierkegaard (1813–1855 CE) did give love a "subtle and complex" role in religious faith. See Rick Furtak, *Wisdom in Love: Kierkegaard and the Ancient Quest for Emotional Integrity* (Notre Dame: University of Notre Dame Press, 2005). Christian theologian Paul Tillich (1886–1965 CE) touches on the emotions as a category of human experience in only a tangential way; his study of anxiety, especially in books such as *The Courage to Be*, is a deeply existential treatise of what, to him, is one of the most significant qualities of human life. Paul Tillich, *The Courage to Be*, 3rd ed. (New Haven: Yale University Press, 1963). Other theologians such as Karl Barth (1866–1968 CE) and Reinhold Niebuhr (1892–1971 CE) thought emotions unimportant. Barth "did not believe that theology should attend to the affections as significant vehicles for knowing God or discerning humans' relationship with the Divine," and the word *emotion* is not included in Reinhold Niebuhr's index of *The Nature and Destiny of Man: A Christian Interpretation* (New York: Charles Scribner's Sons, 1941; repr., Louisville, Ky.: Westminster John Knox, 1996). Lester, *Angry Christian*, 48. There are other, more contemporary theological positions on the emotions, especially in reference to biblical exegesis, and they vary, too, in their positions. On the one hand, there is a theological tradition of asserting God's unemotionality (that is, God, the "unmoved mover"). In this tradition, "the contrivance of an impassible, unemotional God" is the result of a pejorative view of emotions—that they are inherently unruly and capricious. Sam Williams, "Toward a Theology of Emotion," *The Southern Baptist Journal of Theology* 7, no. 4 (2003): 63. In this view, emotions are "irrational and intemperate," a sign of weakness, dependence, and contingency. This is a legacy of the Stoic ideal of impassiveness, which became the ideal and was eventually imposed on God. (For example, the Thirty-Nine Articles of the Church of England and the Westminster Confession of Faith describe God as "without body, parts, or passions"). Scriptural verses asserting the contrary were evaluated as anthropomorphic. See Williams, "Toward a Theology of Emotion," 63. Theologians on this side of the argument are committed to God's unchanging nature, utter stability, and dependability. As noted, others did not even engage the question of God and the passions or emotions.

In contrast, the empiricists thought of personal experience, including the senses and perceptions, as most real, even as experiences changed from moment to moment. Among these thinkers, it is perhaps the rationalist Rene Descartes and the empiricist David Hume who have had the most influence on contemporary perspectives on emotions, and the differences represented by Hume's *Treatise of Human Nature* (1738–1749) and Descartes' *Discourse on Method* (1637) and *The Passions of the Soul* (1649) are worth noting. Hume contributed to a relatively new understanding of the emotions, diverging from those who came before him. Some consider his use of the term *emotions* in his *Treatise of Human Nature* as the first use in the English language that is close to our use of it today. Dixon, *Passions to Emotions*, 104, n34. However, there is disagreement on this. See Schmitter, "Passions, Affections, Sentiments: Taxonomy and Terminology," 197–225. In his treatise, Hume (one of the strongest defenders of the empirical science developed by Francis Bacon) challenged the legacies of Augustine and Aquinas. While he shared their commitment to reason, he also argued that science was the more intellectually truthful lens to apply to the world, putting religion on the defensive. Solomon, *The Passions*, 7.

80 Whitehead and Whitehead, *Shadows of the Heart*,14–15.

81 Knuuttila, *Emotions in Ancient and Medieval Philosophy*, 282.

82 The Age of Reason, also called the Enlightenment, was, in part, a cultural and intellectual period oriented toward ideas of progress and faith in what is "natural."

3 Emotions as Functional for Physiological Survival

1 The language of what is being studied shifts around this time from *passions* to *emotions*. A key turning point in the separation from the Christian understanding of the affections to the introduction of a category of emotions into psychological and scientific literature was the publication of Thomas Brown's collection of essays entitled *Lectures on the Philosophy of the Human Mind*, 2 vols. (1828; repr., Miami: HardPress, 2017). Brown (1778–1820 CE), a doctor of medicine and a professor of moral philosophy at the University of Edinburgh, wrote the "single most important work" that integrated several features of affective psychologies that had become "detached from Christian psychology." Dixon, *Passions to Emotions*, 109. Brown developed an influential "secular psychological system" in which he introduced the term *emotions* in the first systematic way to an academic community, replacing the words *affections* and *passions* with it. Dixon, *Passions to Emotions*, 109. In so doing, Brown subsumed all the other terms under the single category of emotions, and because his work was one of the most highly regarded and most successful books at the time, eventually going through twenty editions, the usage stuck. Dixon, *Passions to Emotions*, 109–11. Following Brown's lead was philosopher, psychologist, and empiricist Alexander Bain (1818–1903 CE), who wrote the first major text on the emotions that could be considered psychological in the sense that Bain emphasized study of the nerves, animals, infants, outward observation, and physiology in his work. Under the influence of Brown and Bain, the emotions became an increasingly de-Christianized category discussed by moral philosophers and mentalists, and the emotions became passive products of the mind, subject to the laws of physics and chemistry. Dixon, *Passions to Emotions*, 133–134. Charles Darwin and other scientists would continue this trajectory.

2 This story can be found in many references, including Keith Oatley, *Emotions: A Brief History* (Malden, Mass.: Blackwell, 2004), and Joseph LeDoux, *Synaptic Self: How Our Brains Become Who We Are* (New York: Penguin, 2002).

3 Both artifacts are now in the museum of Harvard Medical School.

4 This assertion has been challenged forcefully by ecologists and others who argue it is a dangerous view that has contributed to much of the environmental degradation currently underway. See, for example, the work of religious studies scholar Whitney Bauman, who writes, "The processes of genetic manipulation of animals and plants all over the globe, among other things, all make it impossible to 'return' to some pre-modern nature, and impossible to maintain the false distinctions between human-Earth, culture-nature, and history-biology. In other words, we exist in an evolving world always, already as natural-cultural beings. Rather than thinking human projects such as 'culture' and 'technology' outside the rest of the natural world, perhaps they are better seen (as are humans in general) as emerging out of the process of planetary evolution. Rather than maintaining some sort of human exceptionalism from the rest of the natural world, we might begin to re-narrate ourselves back into the planetary community as meaning-making creatures." Whitney Bauman, "Meaning-Making Practices and Environmental History: Toward an Ecotonal Theology," in *Routledge Companion to Religion and Science*, ed. James Haag,

Gregory Peterson, and Michael Spezio (Malden, Mass.: Routledge, 2014), 370–71. My thanks to scholar of ecology and spirituality, Timothy H. Robinson, for this reference.

5 Darwin called these "idiots."

6 Reverend Henslow introduced Darwin to a number of scientific fields of study and recommended him to the captain of the *Beagle* as a researcher. Darwin's notoriety was largely due to Henslow's efforts: Henslow had, unbeknownst to Darwin, published many of his materials in respected scientific journals. See Francis Darwin, ed., *The Life and Letters of Charles Darwin* (New York: Appleton, 1896).

7 Darwin's interest in the study of emotional expressions coincided with the birth of his first child, William ("Willy"), in 1839 and his reading of Sir Charles Bell's *The Anatomy and Philosophy of Expression* in 1840 (repr., London: George Bell, 1877). Bell was a neurologist and a "natural theologian." Dixon, *Passions to Emotions*, 10. When Willy was born, Darwin began to observe and take careful notes on his development (especially Willy's emotional expressions), which eventually led Darwin to review the extant research on the scientific studies of passions/emotion. He undertook a thorough study of the available material on natural expressions and through his observations made careful descriptions and drawings of facial and bodily expressions that accompany the most familiar emotions in humans as well as other animals. It is worth noting that the idea of evolution was not new in Darwin's time; rather, it was the development of his theory of natural selection that remains one of his most important scientific contributions. Over the next twenty years Darwin would publish five more books, including his last major book, a classic 1872 text on emotion: Charles Darwin, *The Expression of the Emotions in Man and Animals*, ed. Francis Darwin, 2nd ed. (1890), in *The Works of Charles Darwin*, ed. Paul H. Barrett and R. B. Freeman, vol. 23 (New York: New York University Press, 1987–1989). Darwin would focus the questions about the functions of emotional expressions on physical survival and little more.

8 Charles Darwin, *Expression of the Emotions*, 1. The exception he notes is the work of Sir Charles Bell, who provided "graphic description of the various emotions," illustrating facial differences he found significant. In the end, however, Darwin found Bell's assertion that certain muscles have been specially adapted for the specific purpose of expressing emotions unsatisfactory. See F. Darwin, *Life and Letters*, 2 and 13.

9 Before Darwin's theory from *On the Origin of Species* became popular in the nineteenth century, essentialism ruled the study of the animal kingdom. Following the Platonic tradition, essentialists assumed each species had an ideal form, created by God, with defining properties (essences) that distinguished it from all other species (each with its own essences). Deviations from the ideal were said to be due to error or accident. Darwin's belief in emotion essences, as revealed in *Expression*, helped to launch the modern classical view of emotion to prominence. Darwin's most famous book, *On the Origin of Species*, triggered a paradigm shift that transformed biology into a modern science. Neuroscientist Lisa Barrett argues that Darwin's "greatest scientific achievement . . . was freeing biology from 'the paralyzing grip of essentialism.'" In a view incompatible with essentialism, Darwin argued in *Origins* that "variations within a species, such as length of stride, are not errors. Instead, variations are expected and are meaningfully related to the species' environment." Barrett argues that to Darwin, each species was a conceptual category—a population of unique individuals who vary from one another, with no essence at their core. The ideal dog does not exist: it is a statistical summary of many diverse dogs. In fact, no features are necessary, sufficient, or even typical of every individual in a population.

This observation, known as population thinking, is central to Darwin's theory of evolution. Regarding emotion, however, Darwin made an "inexplicable about-face" thirteen years later by writing *Expression*, a book "riddled" with essentialism. In doing so, Barrett argues, he "abandoned his remarkable innovations and returned to essentialism's paralyzing grip, at least where emotions are concerned." Barrett, *How Emotions Are Made: The Secret Life of the Brain* (New York: Houghton Mifflin Harcourt, 2017), 158, quoting Ernst Mayr. Barrett argues that *Origins* is a profoundly antiessentialist book, and thus she finds it "baffling" that where emotion is concerned, Darwin reversed his greatest achievement by writing *Expressions*. Barrett, *How Emotions Are Made*, 159. Barrett goes on to write that it is "equally baffling, not to mention ironic" that the classical view of emotion (presented in this chapter and the next) is based on the very essentialism that Darwin is famous for vanquishing in biology. The classical view explicitly labels itself as "evolutionary" and assumes that emotions and their expressions are products of natural selection, yet natural selection is absent from Darwin's thinking on emotion. However, Barrett argues, "Any essentialist view that wraps itself in the cloak of Darwin is demonstrating a profound misunderstanding of Darwin's central ideas about evolution." Barrett, *How Emotions Are Made*, 159. The idea of "conceptual categories" will become more meaningful in chapter 6, as will the assertion that emotions are psychological constructs rather than essentialized entities.

Barrett also notes that scientist Herbert Spencer coined the term "survival of the fittest" in 1864 after reading Darwin's *Origin*. Barrett, *How Emotions Are Made*, 386n10. Darwin shifted the focus of the function of passions/emotions from the good life or salvation to survival by arguing that the goal of any species or phylum is successful reproduction. A variety of mechanisms can be used to anchor this concept. See, for example, Ernst Mayr, *What Makes Biology Unique? Considerations on the Autonomy of a Scientific Discipline* (New York: Cambridge University Press, 2007), chapter 10. Cited in Barrett, *How Emotions Are Made*, 159.

10 It is important to note that Darwin is focusing on something quite different than were the philosophers and theologians who had preceded him, and his language reflects it. Darwin's interest was in the *expression* of emotions rather than a person's *experience* of them; the significance of this will become clear when we review William James' theory, as James was more interested in people's *experience* of emotion rather than their expression of them. This difference led to distinct questions and lines of research: some who followed Darwin and some who followed James.

11 One of the scholars whose work Darwin used was Duchenne de Boulogne, a French physician who studied "the laws that govern the expressions of the human face." His book, the *Mechanism of Human Facial Expression* (ed. and trans. R. Andrew Cuthbertson [1862; repr., Cambridge: Cambridge University Press, 1990]), consists of a series of photographs by Duchenne of facial expressions of emotions that he created in a group of human models by means of electrical stimulation. Darwin drew heavily on Duchenne's work, including borrowing his photos and not returning them. (Some of Duchenne's pictures appeared in Darwin's book but were missing in Duchenne's.) Duchenne, unlike Darwin, believed that the patterns of facial muscular activity had been created specifically for the purpose of emotional expression, and the "Duchenne smile," as the wide toothy smile with crinkled eyes came to be known, was named for him. It is interesting to note that the word *smile* does not exist in Latin or Ancient Greek and that the Duchenne smile was neither

common nor expected before the eighteenth century when dentistry became more accessible. Barrett, *How Emotions Are Made*, 51.

12 Robert Plutchik, *Emotions in the Practice of Psychotherapy: Clinical Implications of Affect Theories* (Washington, D.C.: American Psychological Association, 2000), 41.

13 Plutchik, *Emotions in Practice*, 42. Self-sacrifice can have a place in survival, Darwin argued, because it serves the larger good of the survival of offspring.

14 Charles Darwin, *The Descent of Man* (1871; repr., London: Penguin, 2004). Cited in McGill, *Idea of Happiness*, 155. In this text Darwin argues that what develops out of emotional expressions—that is, emotions themselves—are magnified in human beings and are the foundation for civilization. McGill, *Idea of Happiness*, 154.

15 The inaccurate claim that Darwin argued that emotions originally evolved to serve a survival function is in manuscripts of an early twentieth century American psychologist, Floyd Allport (1890–1979 CE), who wrote extensively on Darwin's ideas. In 1924 Allport made a "sweeping inference" from Darwin's writing that significantly changed its original meaning. Allport wrote that expressions begin as vestigial in newborns but quickly assume function: "Instead of the biologically useful reaction being present in the ancestor and the expressive vestige in the descendant, we regard both these functions as present in the descendant, the former serving as a basis from which the latter develops." Floyd Allport, *Social Psychology* (Boston: Houghton Mifflin, 1924), 215. Cited in Barrett, *How Emotions Are Made*, 387n23.

16 C. Darwin, *Expression of the Emotions*, 10.

17 C. Darwin, *Expression of the Emotions*, 28. One scholar suggests that part of Darwin's concern in developing this theory was to counteract "any trace of creationism," the view that prevailed in his time. Thus, his theory had to offer a view outside of the possibility of intention, imitation, recent habit, or adaptive instinct, as these could have been bestowed by a creator. Sue Campbell, *Interpreting the Personal: Expression and the Formation of Feelings* (Ithaca, N.Y.: Cornell University Press, 1997), 18–19.

18 Disserviceable habits are those that are habitual but serve no function for a person or species, and which can sometimes even cause the organism harm, as we will see later in this chapter.

19 The origin of weeping continues to baffle scientists. See Mandy Oaklander, "Why Do We Cry? Science Is Close to Solving the Mystery of Tears (and Why Some People Don't Shed Them)," in *Time* magazine's special edition "The Science of Emotions," 28–33. Laughter is also a challenge for scientists. See Michael J. Owren and Jo-Anne Bachorowski, "Reconsidering the Evolution of Nonlinguistic Communication: The Case of Laughter," *Journal of Nonverbal Behavior* 27, no. 3 (2003): 183–200.

20 C. Darwin, *Expression of the Emotions*, 168.

21 C. Darwin, *Expression of the Emotions*, 173–77.

22 C. Darwin, *Expression of the Emotions*, 28.

23 John Black, "Darwin in the World of Emotions," *Journal of The Royal Society of Medicine* 95, no. 6 (2002): 311–13.

24 C. Darwin, *Expression of the Emotions*, 350.

25 C. Darwin, *Expression of the Emotions*, 66. Darwin also wrote that emotional imbalance could cause wiry, curly hair as a disserviceable byproduct, or an example of what happens when energy or tension overflows. C. Darwin, *Expression of the Emotions*, 297.

26 C. Darwin, *Expression of the Emotions*, 66. Emphasis added.

27 Randolph R. Cornelius, *The Science of Emotion: Research and Tradition in the Psychology of Emotions* (Upper Saddle River, N.J.: Prentice Hall, 1996), 25.

28 Cornelius, *Science of Emotion*, 25. Sigmund Freud's thinking about psychic discharge, which is explored in the next chapter, was significantly influenced by this principle in Darwin's work. See, for example, Lucille B. Ritvo, *Darwin's Influence on Freud: A Tale of Two Sciences* (New Haven: Yale University Press, 1990).

29 C. Darwin, *Expression of the Emotions*, 71. In this hear the echoes of Epicurus' and the Stoics' commitment to the idea that animals and humans are primarily driven to obtain what is pleasant and avoid what is unpleasant.

30 C. Darwin, *Expression of the Emotions*, 72.

31 C. Darwin, *Expression of the Emotions*, 72.

32 Recent research has corroborated this view regarding swearing and pain. Catharine Paddock, "Cursing Relieves Pain, But Not if Overused," *Medical News Today*, December 2, 2011, https://www.medicalnewstoday.com/articles/238525.php.

33 C. Darwin, *Expression of the Emotions*, 177.

34 C. Darwin, *Expression of the Emotions*, 82.

35 Subsequent researchers such as Paul Ekman would call these the "basic" emotions. Ekman would significantly develop this idea, though his work has been challenged, as we see in chapter 4. Paul Ekman, "Are There Basic Emotions?" *Psychological Review* 99, no. 3 (1992): 550–53. Ekman followed Darwin's work closely. See *Darwin and Facial Expression: A Century of Research in Review* (New York: Academic Press, 1973).

36 C. Darwin, *Expression of the Emotions*, 38.

37 The force of will has been shown to be largely ineffective in controlling one's emotions. Changing one's beliefs, however, can be a useful tool in managing emotions, though this, too, has limits in controlling emotions. See chapter 4 for a more thorough exploration of this.

38 Cornelius, *Science of Emotion*, 21–22.

39 James established a place for himself in emotions research in 1884 when he published an article in the newly established journal *Mind*, edited by Alexander Bain. William James, "What Is an Emotion?" *Mind* 9, no. 34 (1884): 188–205. Bain was a Scottish philosopher and "mentalist," or early psychologist, who was a significant figure in the shift from philosophical to scientific study of emotions. His journal *Mind* was the first journal of psychology and philosophy. James' famous essay "What Is an Emotion?" articulated the ideas James would develop more fully in his book *The Principles of Psychology*, published in 1890 (New York: Dover). Historian Thomas Dixon notes that most philosophers and psychologists have, over the last twenty years, related their work to James'. He argues, too, that James and Darwin are the two nineteenth-century theorists whose work continues to be engaged today. Dixon, *Passions to Emotions*, 231. He notes that over the past one hundred years or so, many psychologists have attempted to prove or disprove James' hypotheses. Thus, the development of James' theory stimulated researchers to study autonomic changes in relation to emotion and led to important advances in the understanding of autonomic physiology, lie detection, and physiological arousal's role in the generation of emotions. Plutchik, *Emotions in Practice*, 42.

　　Around the time James was publishing his ideas, Danish psychologist Carl Lange was also presenting the results of his research, which mirrored James' theories in many ways. Like James, Carl Lange was curious about "what bodily manifestations accompany each of the affections." Carl G. Lange, "The Emotions: A Psychophysiological Study," in Carl G. Lange and William James, *The Emotions* (Baltimore: Williams and Wilkins, 1922), 66. The connection between physiological changes and the experience of emotion is so strong that Lange wrote, "Take away the bodily symptoms from a frightened individual; let his pulse beat calmly, his look be firm, his color normal, his movements quick and sure, his speech strong and his thoughts clear; and what remains of his fear?"—a conclusion almost identical to James'. Lange, "The Emotions: A Psychophysiological Study," 66. However, there were some subtle differences between them. For example, James thought Lange overemphasized the vasomotor (that is, relating to the dilation or constriction of blood vessels) account. Cornelius, *Science of Emotion*, 67. Because of the similarities in their research and conclusions, the understanding of *emotions as the result of physical reactions to a stimulus*, and the argument that the *physiological reaction to an event in the environment precedes the subjective experience of an emotion* is commonly called the James-Lange theory. This definition or some version of it is still found in many textbooks, and it has influenced the thinking of many generations of psychologists. However, since Lange made some essentialist assumptions that James did not, I prefer to keep their names separate as a way to indicate the differences in their work. See Plutchik, "Landscapes of Emotion," 19; see also Barrett, *How Emotions Are Made*, 161. Chapter 6 will explore this antiessentialist view in more detail.

40 Although their work diverged in significant ways, James' insistence that an emotion is felt only to the extent to which it is expressed in some way can be seen as a critical connection between his theory and Darwin's.

41 This line of exploration is taken up more fully in chapter 6.

42 This definition or some version of it is still found in many textbooks, and it has influenced the thinking of many generations of psychologists. See, for example, Plutchik, "Landscapes of Emotion," 19. James presented a new way of looking at emotion and at the same time founded a second major tradition in the psychology of emotion. Plutchik, *Emotions in the Practice of Psychotherapy*, 42.

43 This assertion was supported by neuroscience more than one hundred years after James' writing of his seminal article, though with deeper understanding of the mechanisms of how emotions are created, and with more scientific nuance. See chapter 6 of this volume for a closer examination.

44 James, "What Is an Emotion?" 193.

45 Cornelius, *Science of Emotion*, 60.

46 James, "What Is an Emotion?" 189–90.

47 James, "What Is an Emotion?" 194.

48 Howard M. Feinstein, "William James on the Emotions," *Journal of the History of Ideas* 31, no. 1 (1970): 133–42.

49 James focused on changes in the heart and circulatory system but left the way open for almost any physiological response to be included in the list of bodily changes associated with emotion, an idea that has borne out in contemporary neurophysiological research. See chapter 6 for more.

50 James, "What Is an Emotion?" 194.

51 Differences in these terminologies are explored further in chapter 6.

52 Dixon, *Passions to Emotions*, 204. What is striking, Dixon notes, is the importance James gave to the viscera rather than the brain.

53 Feinstein, "William James on the Emotions," 133–34. James' 1,200-page tome *Principles of Psychology* contains most of Western psychology's most important ideas and remains,

after more than a century, the foundation of the field. Barrett, *How Emotions Are Made*, 160. His name graces the highest honor that can be bestowed on a scientist from the Association for Psychological Science, the William James Fellow Award, and Harvard's psychology building is named William James Hall.

54 Feelings, then, are the phenomenological awareness of an emotion. Sociologist Norman Denzin argues that conscious awareness of emotions (the term he uses rather than "feelings") requires stream of consciousness, experience, situation, time, person, associates, reality, and world because it has a "double structure": an inner phenomenological dimension and an outer interactional dimension. These two elements, he argues, are "united in the stream of emotional experience, or the stream of emotional consciousness." Norman K. Denzin, *On Understanding Emotion: With a New Introduction by the Author* (New Brunswick: Transaction Publishers, 2007), 67.

55 James was likely familiar with Galen's work, and was interested in the physiological activities that resulted in emotion. James, however, did not equate the passions/emotions with the flow and balance of humors but understood instead that nerves are responsible.

56 James, *Principles*, 2:454. James is widely understood to mean that each category of emotion (for example, fear or anger) has a distinct physiological fingerprint. But James never made this claim. Instead, James argued that each *instance* of emotion comes from a unique bodily state, not each *category* of emotion. See Barrett, *How Emotions Are Made*, 160. This concept has been borne out in recent neuroscience and is revisited with more detail in chapter 6 of this volume, where concepts and categories are defined and explained.

57 James, "What Is an Emotion?" 190.

58 James, *Principles*, 2:450. Contemporary neuroscientists Lisa Barrett and James Russell argue that their sophisticated brain studies show that James was more right than wrong. See chapter 6 for the ways contemporary neuroscience is confirming James' understandings.

59 William James, *Talks to Teachers on Psychology: And to Students on Some of Life's Ideals* (1899; repr., New York: Henry Holt, 1912), 201. Cited in Cornelius, *Science of Emotion*, 63. James was so committed to his ideas about how to generate or manage one's emotions that he made this one of the topics of in one of his lectures called "Talks to Students on Some of Life's Ideals," a series on what "could be considered lectures on moral and mental hygiene." James, *Talks to Teachers*. Cited in Cornelius, *Science of Emotion*, 63. While the notion that in order to feel a feeling one must practice its expression may sound counterintuitive, other research and subsequent practice theories corroborate this concept. Chapter 6 will explore this further. The popular saying "Fake it 'til you make it," for example, in relation to confidence, evokes James' thinking.

60 Remember that early philosophers and theologians puzzled about the fact that an individual could not will away or reliably control certain emotions and reactions to them. Scientists (including, as noted, Darwin) were publishing similar findings based on empirical studies. Other scientists wondered about the relationship of different physiological responses to different emotions. For example, physiologist Walter Cannon's research suggested that the body's responses were not distinct enough to evoke different emotions. Cannon asked, does a racing heart signal fear, anger, or love? David Myers and C. Nathan Dewall, "Theories of Emotion," in *Psychology*, 7th ed. (New York: Worth Publishers, 2004), 500–505. James' work tangentially addressed this. Although James did not explicitly say so, his theory was read to suggest that different emotions are associated with different types of physiological arousal, that there was "autonomic specificity" in the bodily

responses that produced various emotions. Cannon, however, could not find evidence of this connection. His experiments clearly demonstrated that contributions from the sympathetic nervous system (that is, the "viscera") were not necessary for the experience of emotions. Walter Cannon, "The James-Lange Theory of Emotions: A Critical Examination and an Alternative Theory," *The American Journal of Psychology* 100, nos. 3–4, Special Centennial Issue (1987): 567–86. This theory is often called the Cannon-Bard theory because another physiologist, Philip Bard, conducted similar research and made similar conclusions. Some reports suggest that Bard was Cannon's collaborator, while others indicate that they were two independent researchers working on similar studies simultaneously. See, for example, Gretchen M. Reevy, Yvette Malamud Ozer, and Yuri Ito, *Encyclopedia of Emotion* (Santa Barbara, Calif.: Greenwood, 2010), 31. One emotions scholar notes that in the many decades that followed Cannon's critiques, emotion researchers spent vast amounts of time and energy trying to obtain evidence that different emotions were characterized by different patterns of autonomic response, but that such research was inconclusive. Researchers on emotion following Cannon's research trajectory followed two distinct and opposing lines of work. First, some sought to vindicate James and assumed that the visceral changes that accompany emotions were essentially undifferentiated. These researchers sought other factors (such as beliefs and appraisals, as we see in the next chapter) that might account for the variety of emotions humans typically experience. In fact, until the end of the 1970s the assumption that emotions were autonomically undifferentiated directed most of the research. Second were those who proposed that the visceral changes that accompany different emotions are themselves differentiated. However, much of the Cannon-Bard theory has been challenged, largely because the theory is too vague. Reevy, Ozer, and Ito, *Encyclopedia of Emotion*, 31. It would take neuroscience in the late twentieth and early twenty-first centuries to clear up some of the confusion. See chapter 6 for more.

In 1938 neurologist James Papez proposed the existence of certain brain pathways that mediate emotional experience. He argued that the word *emotion* refers to both a way of acting (emotional expression) and a way of feeling (subjective experience) and that different parts of the brain were involved in these two aspects of emotion. Further, Papez argued, information coming into the thalamus (considered early on the center of conscious thought) was split into three "streams": a "stream of thought," "a stream of movement," and "a stream of feeling." In what came to be called the *Papez Loop*, nerve fibers from the *feeling stream* were found to connect to the hypothalamus, which in turn connects to the front of the thalamus. From there, Papez suggested, the circuit connects to the cingulated cortex and the hippocampus, which completes the loop in its connections to the hypothalamus. The importance of the Papez Loop was that it provided a possible circuit by which emotional meaning gets added to the analysis of incoming stimulus information. As Papez understood it, the cortex first receives emotional information from the "lower," subcortical areas of the brain, "tagging" it with emotion. "Higher" areas of the brain such as the hypothalamus and the hippocampus influence the expression of emotion when they connect to the autonomic nervous system (ANS). Emotions are "triggered," Papez argued, when an external stimulus activates certain parts of the brain, exciting both the faster and slower neural processes that generate emotions. Still, Cannon could not find such evidence of this pathway. See Walter B. Cannon, "The Interrelations of Emotions as Suggested by Recent Physiological Researchers," *American Journal of Psychology* 25, no. 2 (1914): 252–82.

While Papez assumed that the hypothalamus was the integrating center for the emotions, he attempted to identify some of the other brain structures that were involved in generating and processing emotions as well. Papez pointed out that nerve impulses that come from the receptor organs of the body such as the ears, eyes, skin, and muscles all go first to various parts of the thalamus. One pathway, he suggested, goes to various structures (such as the corpus striatum) and coordinates movement patterns. A second pathway, Papez suggested, goes to lateral parts of the cerebral cortex and handles the stream of thought. The third pathway, Papez claimed, goes through the hypothalamus to the mammillary body to the medial wall of the cerebral hemispheres and handles the stream of feeling. Following Papez's line of research, the search for emotions' "seat" in the brain continued, and many researchers followed and developed Papez's thinking. For example, arguably one of the best-known (and popularized) American neuroscientists, Joseph LeDoux's early scientific contribution was his research on the amygdala and its role in emotions. However, these ideas were "partly based on fact and partly speculative," limited as research was by the relatively unsophisticated tools that were then available. LeDoux's theory about the amygdala's role in the emotions generated a good deal of excitement; perhaps this was the answer for how the brain functioned in an emotional episode. Indeed, it had the potential to answer many questions. However, despite the fact that earlier research had located emotions in a particular place in the brain, subsequent research was less successful in finding emotions' central location, suggesting that in fact many parts of the brain share the responsibility for emotions and that it is "tightly inter-woven with structures of cognition, memory." Subsequent research has shown that the amygdala *is* associated with emotions, though not to the exclusion of other parts of the brain, and it is not involved in all emotions. In addition, human beings actually have two amygdalae, one each in the left and right temporal lobes. See Barrett, *How Emotions Are Made*, 17, subscript, and David Franks, "The Neuroscience of Emotions," in Stets and Turner, *Handbook of the Sociology of Emotions*, 51. Chapter 6 takes this up in more detail.

61 James, "What Is an Emotion?" 21–22.

62 James' view, of course, does not fully grasp the neurophysiological factors in, say, depression. Nor does he give account to systems that oppress—for example, patriarchy, sexism, and homophobia—and their influence on people's emotional lives. Nevertheless, he was onto something about the physiology of emotions and the feelings that attend them. These issues are addressed more fully in chapters 5, 6, and 7.

63 Reddy, *Navigation of Feeling*, 60.

64 This idea was a blow to Western philosophers and Christian theologians who had empha-sized the differences between animals and humans, arguing that the ability to control one's passions was a primary distinction. These early ideas began to give way under the burden of science. For example, LeDoux continued the evolutionary-focused trajectories begun by Darwin, James, and others, although he benefited from advanced technologies unavailable to early scientists. Like James, LeDoux proposed that each emotion devel-oped from particular physiological changes, though his theory differs significantly from Darwin's. As LeDoux describes it, *emotion* is a word that human beings apply to different experiences that have some characteristics in common. Thus, a different type of bodily and subjective experience is associated with the activity of different activities in different parts of the brain and accompanies each emotion (such as fear, anger, sadness, or happi-ness). Individuals, he argued, each have a physiological system intended to defend them against danger, and they use the word *fear* as a label for this reaction and experience.

Likewise, LeDoux argued, human beings have a physiological system for expelling toxic substances (usually rotten food) and use the word *disgust* for this. LeDoux agreed with Darwin that physiological systems developed for the purpose of survival, and claimed that his research demonstrated that each of these systems has some separate brain and body physiology involved (although he believed there is also overlap). LeDoux's contemporary, Antonio Damasio, agreed that humans and "lower" animals have nervous systems that are "prewired" to respond to significant features of the environment (especially those that are related to threats to survival). However, Damasio argued that an individual does not need to recognize the threat consciously; rather, the "key features" of a source of danger are received by the amygdala, which produces an almost immediate reaction, which may later be followed by a "rational" response. At least in mammals with large neocortices (such as primates), emotional feelings are a cortical response to a subcortical reaction, according to Damasio. Antonio R. Damasio, *Descartes' Error: Emotion, Reason, and the Human Brain* (New York: G. P. Putnam, 1994). These ideas are developed by evolutionary psychologists such as Robert Plutchik. See, for example, Robert Plutchik, "Emotions and the Brain," in *Emotions and Life*, 285. See also Robert Plutchik, *Emotion: A Psychoevolutionary Synthesis* (New York: Harper & Row, 1980). These ideas are challenged in chapter 6 of this volume.

65 Joseph LeDoux, *The Emotional Brain: The Mysterious Underpinnings of Emotional Life* (New York: Simon and Schuster, 1996); Joseph LeDoux, "Emotional Memory Systems in the Brain," *Behavioural Brain Research* 58, no. 1 (1993): 69–79; and Joseph LeDoux, "In Search of an Emotional System in the Brain: Leaping from Fear to Emotion and Consciousness," in *The Cognitive Neurosciences*, ed. Michael S. Gazzaniga and George R. Mangun (Cambridge, Mass.: MIT Press, 1995), 1049–61.

66 Dixon, *Passions to Emotions*, 211.

67 Dixon, *Passions to Emotions*, 212. Emphasis added.

68 Stephanie van Goozen, Nanne Van de Poll, Joseph Sergeant, eds., *Emotions: Essays on Emotion Theory* (Hillsdale, N.J.: Lawrence Erlbaum Associates, 1994), viii.

69 James' work straddled two fields: he was hired by Harvard to teach a course in the relationship between psychology and physiology. In 1875 he established a psychology lab there, which became a central place for research in the field of psychology, and in 1876 James was appointed assistant professor of psychology at Harvard. In 1885 he was promoted to full professor of philosophy, and four years later became full professor of psychology. Because of the significance of his work in the physiology of psychology—particularly emotions—James is often considered the father of modern psychology. See Reevy, Ozer, and Ito, *Encyclopedia of Emotion*, 380. Reevy, Ozer, and Ito also note that (the misunderstanding of) James' idea that sensorimotor activations constitute the experience of emotion "drives one of the most compelling ideas in the psychology of emotion: that emotional states have specific and unique patterns of somatovisceral changes, and the perception of these bodily events constitutes the experience of emotion." Reevy, Ozer, and Ito, *Encyclopedia of Emotion*, 381. However, although James is credited with the idea that invariant autonomic nervous system patterns and behaviors correspond to anger, sadness, fear, and so on, he did not appear to hypothesize invariant autonomic nervous system patterns for each category of emotion. See Barrett, *How Emotions Are Made*, 160. In fact, Barrett argues that James explicitly rejected the idea that there is a single set of bodily symptoms to describe instances of a given emotion category across individuals: "Surely there is no definite affection of 'anger' in an 'entitative' sense," he wrote. William

James, "The Physical Basis of Emotion," *Psychological Review* 101, no. 2, Special Centennial Issue (1994): 206. See also Reevy, Ozer, and Ito, *Encyclopedia of Emotion*, 381.

In fact, James argued *against* essentialism in emotions' generation. However, his work was misconstrued. In fact, notes Barrett, although James' writings are full of detailed descriptions of the bodily symptoms that characterize anger, grief, fear, and the like, he explicitly stated in several places that variability within each emotion category is the norm. More importantly, Barrett writes, James "argued for the heterogeneity of instances within each emotion category. According to James, there can be variable sets of bodily symptoms associated with a single category of emotion, making each a distinct feeling state and therefore a distinct emotion." Lisa Feldman Barrett, "Solving the Emotion Paradox: Categorization and the Experience of Emotion," *Personality and Social Psychology Review* 10, no. 1 (2006): 41. By the term *emotion*, James is referring to particular instances of feeling, not to discrete emotion categories, she writes. Different instances of an emotion, even if within the same category, will feel different if the somatovisceral activations are different.

Thus, although James is widely cited for saying that each type of emotion—happiness, fear, and so on—is generated by a particular physiology, with a distinct fingerprint, he never said such a thing. Barrett argues that this is the result of an essentialist idea that is a key fact of the classical view of emotions, and generations of James-influenced researchers have searched for those "fingerprints" in heartbeats, respiration, blood pressure, and other bodily markers (and have written some best-selling books on emotion asserting their locations in the brain). However, these physiological "fingerprints" for emotions or "emotional locations" in the brain have not been found, and as noted, even James did not claim they existed. In other words, Barrett asserts, the widely believed claim that James believed in a physiological fingerprint comes from a hundred-year-old misinterpretation of his words through the lens of essentialism. She notes that James actually wrote that each *instance* of emotion, not each *category* of emotion, comes from a unique bodily state. This is a wildly different statement: "It means you can tremble in fear, jump in fear, freeze in fear, scream in fear, gasp in fear, hide in fear, attack in fear, and even laugh in the face of fear. Each occurrence of fear is associated with a different set of internal changes and sensations. The classical misinterpretation of James represents a 180-degree inversion of his meaning, as if he were claiming for the existence of emotion essences, when ironically, he was arguing against them." Barrett, *How Emotions Are Made*, 160. See James, "The Physical Basis of Emotion." For more on this see also Barrett, *How Emotions Are Made*, chapter 8, 386n13. See also Kristen A. Lindquist, Tor D. Wager, Hedy Kober, Eliza Bliss-Moreau, and Lisa Feldman Barrett, "The Brain Basis of Emotion: A Meta-Analytic Review," *Behavioral and Brain Sciences* 35, no. 3 (2012): 121–43.

Barrett explores how this widespread misunderstanding of James arose and blames it on one of James' contemporaries, philosopher John Dewey. See Barrett, *How Emotions Are Made*, 161, subscript. Today, Dewey's role in this, "one of the great mistakes" in modern psychology, is forgotten, and countless publications attribute his theory to James. A prominent example is the writings of neurologist Antonio Damasio in his *Descartes' Error* and other popular books on emotion. To Damasio, an emotion's unique physical fingerprint, which he calls a "somatic marker," is a source of information used by the brain to make good decisions. These markers are like little bits of wisdom. Emotional experience, according to Damasio, occurs when somatic markers are transformed into conscious feelings. However, Barrett argues, Damasio's theory is actually a "child of the James-Lange merger," not of James' actual views on emotion. Nevertheless, Damasio's hypotheses have been promoted in three best-selling books: *The Feeling of What Happens: Body and Emotion in the Making of Consciousness* (New York: Harcourt Brace, 1999); *Descartes' Error*, and *The Self Comes to Mind: The Construction of the Conscious Brain* (New York: First Vintage Books/Random House, 2010).

70 Psychologist Floyd Allport (1890–1979 CE), who was convinced by what he understood to be the James-Lange theory of emotions, also wondered what made the difference between the experience of *different* emotions. Aware of Cannon's and others' challenges to the James-Lange theory that physiological responses are too slow and undifferentiated to produce different emotions, he suggested the face was the "ideal candidate" for a source of bodily feedback. Later researchers would build on Allport's work and propose that feedback from facial muscles in emotional expression was a "major factor" in distinguishing between emotions. Allport, *Social Psychology*, 92. See also Dacher Keltner and Paul Ekman, "Facial Expression of Emotion," in Lewis and Haviland-Jones, *Handbook of Emotions*, 2nd ed., 236–49. (Allport's theories were supported by the work of Silvan Tomkins, Carroll Izard, and others.) In this view (called the "facial feedback hypothesis"), awareness of one's facial expressions *is* the emotion, and different patterns of expressive activity of the face precede and cause in some qualitatively different way a variety of subjective experiences. The possibilities the face held as a significant physical and expressive source for emotions seemed to mitigate concerns that the viscera of the body are too slow in responding to stimuli: the face is a very fast responder and could account for the reactive speed of many emotions, and, they argued, facial feedback plays a significant part in certain basic and "simple" emotions such as happiness and anger. Cornelius, *Science of Emotion*, 103 and 108. However, there are various critiques of this theory. For example, while it has been demonstrated that facial expressions of emotion *do* generate some particular emotions, especially relatively simple emotions, not everyone is as susceptible to facial feedback as others are. See Barrett for a critique of Allport's interpretation: Barrett argues that Allport too, misunderstood James' work. Barrett, *How Emotions Are Made*, 166.

71 Dixon, *Passions to Emotions*, 133–34.

72 Plutchik, "Landscapes of Emotion," 20. This line of questioning is marked by the early twentieth century's transition away from "speculative, descriptive" and philosophical approaches to psychology and toward "experimental and reductionistic" approaches through which basic psychological processes could be deduced through self-report, observation, and technological assessment. John M. Watson, "From Interpretation to Identification: A History of Facial Images in the Sciences of Emotion," *History of the Human Sciences* 17, no. 1 (2004): 39.

73 In his search for where the passions were located in the brain, Broca argued that there is an "ancient" section deep within the human brain. Broca called it "the limbic lobe," and over the next one hundred years it came to be understood as a unified "limbic system"—in Broca's and others' minds, the seat of language. Current textbooks in psychology and neurology still point to Broca's area as the "clearest example" of localized brain function, even as neuroscience has shown that the region is neither necessary nor sufficient for language. In fact, Broca had "scant" evidence for his claims, and other scientists had "plenty of evidence" that he was wrong, but that has not stopped them from adopting Broca's model. Neuroscientist Barrett notes that "scientists continue to debate the function of Broca's area (better referred to as lateral prefrontal cortex), but few continue to believe that it is

specific to language production, grammatical abilities, or even general language process-ing." Barrett, *How Emotions Are Made*, 167. This is discussed in more detail in chapter 6. However, Paul MacLean accepted Broca's schema and popularized it, convinced as he was that the "great limbic lobe" is a common denominator of all mammals. Paul MacLean, "Cerebral Evolution of Emotion," in *Handbook of Emotions*, ed. Michael Lewis and Jeannette Haviland (New York: Guilford Press, 1993), 74. This idea has since been debunked. See Lennart Heimer, Gary W. Van Hoesen, Michael Trimble, and Daniel S. Zahm, "The Eroding Relevance of the Limbic System," in *Anatomy of Neuropsychiatry: The New Anatomy of the Basal Forebrain and Its Implications for Neuropsychiatric Illness* (Burlington, Mass.: Academic Press, 2008), 15–26.

74 MacLean's theory of the triune brain became a highly popular view, significantly influ-encing brain science for many decades. His theory has since been disproved, however. See chapter 6.

75 The cerebral cortex is now understood to be made up of two parts, the allocortex and the cerebral cortex, and these parts do not function in quite the way MacLean imag-ined they did. Suzanne Oosterwijk, Alexandra Touroutoglou, and Kristen A. Lindquist, "The Neuroscience of Construction: What Neuroimaging Approaches Can Tell Us about How the Brain Creates the Mind," in *The Psychological Construction of Emotion*, ed. Lisa F. Barrett and James A. Russell (New York: Guilford Press, 2015), 110 and 116, and Tor D. Wager, Lisa Feldman Barrett, Eliza Bliss-Moreau, Kristen A. Lindquist, et al., "The Neuroimaging of Emotion," in *Handbook of Emotions*, ed. Michael Lewis, Jean-nette M. Haviland-Jones, and Lisa Feldman Barrett, 3rd ed. (New York: Guilford Press, 2008), 249–67.

76 MacLean, "Cerebral Evolution," 74–76.

77 There is debate about whether such a thing as a "limbic system" is a relevant designation, what parts of the brain it would contain, and whether its functions are as distinct as some scientists, such as MacLean, suggest. See, for example, Joseph E. LeDoux and Elizabeth A. Phelps, "Emotional Networks in the Brain," in Lewis and Haviland-Jones, *Handbook of Emotions*, 1st and 2nd ed., 157. For example, limbic areas have been shown to have more to do with thinking and memory than emotions. Nevertheless, the idea of a tripartite brain is commonly used and seems to have heuristic value. See, for example, Thomas Lewis, Fari Amini, and Richard Lannon, *A General Theory of Love* (New York: Vintage Books/Random House, 2001).

78 For example, evolutionary psychologists such as Robert Plutchik and neuroscientists including Antonio Damasio and psychologists such as Keith Oatley. However, more recent neuroscience has challenged this view. See chapter 6.

79 This illusory hierarchy embodied Darwin's ideas about human evolution—base appe-tites having evolved first, followed by wild emotional passions, with rationality as our crowning glory, which Darwin had gotten from Plato. Barrett, *How Emotions Are Made*, chapter 8, 387n27.

80 Or "new cortex," often referred to simply as the cortex.

81 MacLean's proposal was simple enough, straightforward enough, and familiar enough to become highly popular; indeed, its influence continues today, though, like the primacy of reason in general for thinking and making decisions, it is increasingly being discredited, though it is sometimes still assumed. See, for example, John Tooby and Leda Cosmides, "The Past Explains the Present: Emotional Adaptations and the Structure of Ancestral Environments," *Ethology and Sociobiology* 11, nos. 4–5 (1990): 375–424. See also Leda

Cosmides and John Tooby, "Evolutionary Psychology and the Emotions," in Lewis and Haviland-Jones, *Handbook of Emotions*, 2nd ed., 91–115. Despite its popular acceptance, the thinking on this has shifted, as we see in chapter 6.

82 Jaak Panksepp, "Emotions as Natural Kinds within the Mammalian Brain," in Lewis and Haviland-Jones, *The Handbook of Emotions*, 2nd ed., 137–56. Early brain scientists believed that environmental events triggered messages in the brain that were communicated to the muscles for action via "special fluids" that flowed through tiny tubes that were the nerves. Oatley, *Emotions*, 70. Philosopher Rene Descartes was one who promoted such a theory. A blow to this thinking came at the end of the eighteenth century when researchers determined that electricity, not fluid, was the medium by which nerves communicated with each other and other parts of the body. In the twentieth century came the discovery that it is not only electricity that regulates the brain's activities, but that chemicals play a significant role too.

83 Oatley, *Emotions*, 67.

84 Joseph LeDoux, "The Neurobiology of Emotion," in *Mind and Brain: Dialogues in Cognitive Neuroscience*, ed. Joseph LeDoux and William Hirst (Cambridge: Cambridge University Press, 1986), 301–54.

85 Keep in mind that Darwin did not argue that emotional expressions *developed* for this purpose, but that evolutionary processes such as natural selection *led* to our interpretation of expressions and our naming of them as "emotional." Based on Darwin's theory of the survival of the fittest, the argument went that those who could read and interpret expressions and anticipate behaviors were those most likely to survive.

86 Darwin's work began a contentious debate about emotions' universality in contemporary emotionology: social theorists and contemporary neuroscientists vehemently disagree with his position. See chapters 5 and 6 for a more detailed exploration of this.

87 For example, Sigmund Freud's debt to Darwin's theories of emotion has been well documented. See Ritvo, *Darwin's Influence on Freud*.

88 Feleky was one of the first women to enter the field of emotions research. Interestingly, as important as Feleky is to emotionology, it is very difficult to find biographical information about her. In fact, I have scoured the library for accurate dates of her birth and (presumed) death and have even contacted the Hungarian Historical Society in Massachusetts for the information, to no avail.

89 Antoinette M. Feleky, "The Expression of the Emotions," *Psychological Review* 21, no. 1 (1914): 33.

90 Feleky, "Expression of the Emotions," 35.

91 Feleky's research became the basis for one of the first standardized psychological assessments and continues to influence contemporary study of the facial expressions of emotion and to point to the face as a primary site for the generation and interpretation of emotions. Watson, "Interpretation to Identification," 31–33. Though French neurologist Guillaume Duchenne had pioneered the use of photography to record and study emotions in response to electromuscular stimuli, Feleky's work was directly responsible for psychologists' interest in using photographs to classify and standardize emotional expression. Elspeth H. Brown, *The Corporate Eye: Photography and the Rationalization of American Commercial Culture, 1884–1929* (Baltimore: Johns Hopkins University Press, 2005), 57. Cited in Watson, "Interpretation to Identification," 33. Feleky's research generated a collection of twenty-four photographs known as the Feleky photographs that became the basis for one of the first standardized psychological tests. Her photographs were sold

by the C. H. Stoelting company for just this purpose well into the 1930s and used widely. Feleky's method of photographing particular emotional expressions was repeated by many emotion researchers; for example, a group of researchers made their own series of photographs of Dartmouth students' emotional expression following different stimuli including classical music, religious paintings, pornography, and electric shock. See Brown, *Corporate Eye*, 57–58. Other researchers have followed Feleky's argument and methods, suggesting that the face has more to do with emotions than does any other part of the body. For example, Polish-born social psychologist Robert Zajonc (1923–2008) argued, like Darwin, that emotions are not for the purpose of anything but to manage the organism's survival; in his case, he was most interested in them as functioning to regulate the volume of blood to the brain. Zajonc's research convinced him that "muscles of the face, when contracted, act as ligatures on various blood vessels, increasing or decreasing cerebral blood flow. These changes in cerebral blood flow . . . bring about direct changes in subjective experience," Zajonc argued. Robert Zajonc, "Emotion and Facial Efference: A Theory Reclaimed," *Science* 228, no. 4695 (1985): 15–21. The implication is that one can regulate emotions and moods by changing facial expressions, a suggestion that echoed James' idea, but Zajonc provided an explanation. As Zajonc argued, if you smile and breathe deeply when you are down you will feel better because you are getting more air over the hypothalamus, cooling it down and returning the body to a state of homeostasis.

92 Ekman is virtually a household name in the science of emotions, and his work has influenced contemporary psychology, perhaps more than any other living psychologist. He worked at the University of California, San Francisco, from 1960 to 2004, often as a research professor at the Langley Porter Neuropsychiatric Institute. Ekman conducted groundbreaking research early in his career, during which time his work was funded by numerous federal grants. Beginning in the 1960s and continuing through the 1970s and 1980s, Ekman and his colleagues studied facial expressions in humans across cultures. Since his retirement from the University of California, San Francisco, in 2004, Ekman has been manager of the Paul Ekman Group, a small company that conducts research on emotional expression for security and law enforcement applications and which produces training devices to enhance emotional skills. He has received numerous awards and honors: he was named one of the world's top one hundred psychologists of the twentieth century by the American Psychological Association, was among *Time* magazine's top one hundred most influential people of 2009, and was awarded both the Distinguished Scientific Contribution Award by the American Psychological Association in 1991 and the William James Fellow Award by the Association for Psychological Science in 1998, among others. He has appeared on or been featured on numerous television shows, including the *News Hour with Jim Lehrer, 48 Hours, Dateline, Good Morning America, Larry King, Oprah, Johnny Carson*, and others. Articles describing or reporting on his work have appeared in the *New York Times, Washington Post, Time* magazine, *Smithsonian, Psychology Today*, and other newspapers and magazines, both American and international. However, many of his conclusions about emotions and their expressions have been undermined by social theorists' work on emotions (see chapter 5) and by psychological constructionists working at the level of neuroscience (see chapter 6).

93 Cornelius, *Science of Emotion*, 31.

94 Carroll Izard, a well-known and frequent collaborator of Ekman's, differs theoretically from Ekman, but they share similar interests, foci, and research methods. See, for example,

Carroll E. Izard, "Innate and Universal Facial Expressions: Evidence from Developmental and Cross-Cultural Research," *Psychological Bulletin* 115, no. 2 (1994): 288–99. See also Carroll Izard, *Human Emotions* (New York: Plenum, 1977). There are many instances in which Ekman's research could not be consistently repeated. See chapters 5 and 6 for more.

95 The one exception was the emotion of fear. Subjects confused fear and surprise: among the *Fore*, events that are likely to elicit fear also tend to be events that are surprising or unexpected. Paul Ekman and Wallace V. Friesen, "Constants across Cultures in the Face and Emotion," *Journal of Personality and Social Psychology* 17, no. 2 (1971): 124–29.

96 Ekman and his primary research partner, Wallace Friesen, published their findings in 1975 in their book *Unmasking the Face*, in which they provided photographs and described in detail the movements of facial muscles that are associated with specific emotions. Paul Ekman and Wallace Friesen, *Unmasking the Face: A Guide to Recognizing Emotions from Facial Clues* (Englewood Cliffs, N.J.: Prentice Hall, 1975).

97 Despite the fact that these findings have been challenged (see chapters 5 and 6), Ekman and his collaborators' conclusions continue to be accepted as fact, especially in popular culture.

98 Hochschild called these "feeling rules." Hochschild, "Emotion Work, Feeling Rules, and Social Structure." For a discussion of how emotion rules function in organizations, see, for example, Sigal G. Barsade, Lakshmi Ramarajan, and Drew Westen, "Implicit Affect in Organizations," *ScienceDirect: Research in Organizational Behavior* 19 (2009): 135–62. Emotions among groups and in organizations are often contagious. See, for example, Sigal Barsade, "The Ripple Effect: Emotional Contagion and Its Influence on Group Behavior." *Administrative Quarterly* 47, no. 4 (2002): 644–75.

99 Paul Ekman, Wallace Friesen, and Phoebe Ellsworth, *Emotion in the Human Face* (New York: Pergamon Press, 1972).

100 Ekman, Friesen, and Ellsworth, *Emotion in the Human Face*, 119.

101 Paul Ekman, "Expression and the Nature of Emotion," in *Approaches to Emotion*, ed. Klaus Scherer and Paul Ekman (Hillsdale, N.J.: Erlbaum, 1984), 319–43. Others, such as evolutionary psychologist Robert Plutchik, would add granularity to Ekman's basic emotions, posing a "multidimensional model" that differentiated between subtle emotions such as surprise, fear, rage, terror, boredom, and pensiveness. Plutchik, *Emotions in Practice*, 63.

102 Barrett, *How Emotions Are Made*, 53.

103 Paul Ekman et al., "Universals and Cultural Differences in the Judgments of Facial Expressions of Emotion," *Journal of Personality and Social Psychology* 53, no. 4 (1987): 717. See also Paul Ekman, "Universal Facial Expressions in Emotion," *Studia Psychologica* 15, no. 2 (1973):140–47.

4 Emotions as Pathological, Signs of Dysfunction, and Indicators of Need

1 In the Romantic Era in the early nineteenth century, the context within which Friedrich Nietzsche (1844–1900 CE) wrote, the intuitive, emotional, and less rationalistic ways of thinking about the passions and the emotions were emphasized. The *Romantic movement* validated strong emotions (especially terror, awe, anxiety, and fear) as authentic sources of knowing, and Romantic artists such as Wolfgang Amadeus Mozart (1756–1791 CE), and Edgar Allen Poe (1809–1849 CE) prized the deep affective experience they could effect in their audiences. Christian theologians such as Soren Kierkegaard (1813–1855 CE) and Paul Tillich (1886–1965 CE) were heavily influenced by these perspectives, and

the commitment to attending to feelings as sources of wisdom has continued among psychologists. For example, pastoral theologian Bonnie Miller-McLemore has argued for attention to feeling (what she defines as "the recognition and enactment of diverse emotions" that are often seen as "more directly body-located than emotion"), or "tactile knowledge" as a source and site for knowledge, insight, exploring the relationships between feelings, bodies, and knowledge. Bonnie Miller-McLemore, "Coming to Our Senses: Feeling and Knowledge in Theology and Ministry," *Pastoral Psychology* 63, no. 5/6 (2014): 690.

2 Martha Nussbaum, *Upheavals of Thought: The Intelligence of Emotions* (New York: Cambridge University Press, 2001), 93.

3 It should be remembered that Darwin's understanding of emotional expression is not that emotional expressions developed *in order to* communicate, but that as certain expressions became associated with certain actions, they *evolved* a communicative function. See chapter 3 for more on this.

4 Plutchik, *Emotions in the Practice of Psychotherapy*, 41.

5 As discussed in the introduction and chapters 1 and 2 of this text, philosophers, theologians, and "mental philosophers" (precursors to modern-day psychologists) used the words *passions, desires, appetites, affections* and *moral sentiments* as basic categories of affective psychology and in effect, the history of the modern emotions, as they are now commonly called, is rooted in philosophical and religious perspectives. Dixon, *Passions to Emotions*, 104.

6 James Hillman, *Emotions: A Comprehensive Phenomenology of Theories and Their Meanings for Therapy* (Evanston, Ill.: Northwestern University Press, 1961). The objections are reasonable. The hazards of trying to access what is "really" happening in people's subjective experience through verbal reports are widely recognized. A number of factors make studying the subjective experience of emotions difficult: people deliberately attempt to deceive others, especially those in authority such as a researcher; people distort the truth for conscious and unconscious reasons; studying emotions depends on people's particular facility with self-awareness and ability to articulate their inner state; awareness of emotions is often retrospective (depending on memory), which is subject to misrepresentation; the process of observation distorts what is being observed; language is ambiguous (that is, what means one thing to one person may mean something else to another); defenses such as repression create distortions (that is, no emotions are reported because the person is defended from them); and emotions are rarely in a pure state but rather are mixed, ambiguous, and ambivalent, which makes them difficult to identify and describe clearly. Plutchik, "Landscapes of Emotion," 17.

7 Plutchik, "Landscapes of Emotion," 15.

8 Barrett, *How Emotions Are Made*, 171.

9 Russian physiologist Ivan Pavlov's work on classical conditioning (often called the Pavlovian response) is a good example of this. For an overview, see Robert A. Rescorla and Allan R. Wagner, "A Theory of Pavlovian Conditioning: Variations in the Effectiveness of Reinforcement and Nonreinforcement," in *Classical Conditioning II: Current Theory and Research*, ed. Abraham Black and William F. Prokasy (New York: Appleton-Century, 1972), 64–99.

10 This is what early psychologists were called.

11 For example, Walter Cannon argued that the body constantly monitors factors such as water content, sugar and salt levels, fat, protein, calcium, oxygen, and the temperature of

the blood, and that changes in these can affect one's emotional state. Cannon, "The Interrelations of Emotions as Suggested by Recent Physiological Researchers." Appetite, then, arises from the lack of nutrients in the body, and the impulse to breathe from a low level of oxygen. The same is true of other physiological needs such as sleep, thirst, sex, and excretion. The body ingests or expels material to reestablish physiological homeostasis. Cannon presaged evolutionary psychologists' thinking as well as findings in recent neuroscience about the ways core affect influences emotions' generation. See chapter 6 for more.

12 Although existentialist philosopher Friedrich Nietzsche did not have a theory of emotions (Solomon, "Nietzsche and the Emotions," 131), he celebrated the "irrational, darker and instinctual qualities" of human being. And while he was often critical of the passions (they can "drag us down with their stupidity"), he also held that sometimes the passions contain more reason than does reason itself does. Friedrich Nietzsche, *On the Genealogy of Morals* (1887; repr., New York: Random House, 1967). Cited in Solomon, "Philosophy of Emotions," 8. Freud, of course, was an astute scholar of the nonrational and nonconscious elements of human motivation and experience and agreed with Nietzsche that the nonrational side of human being was worth analysis, acceptance, and guidance. Freud would be influenced by Nietzsche's anthropology, although he claimed that he had not opened the books by Nietzsche that he owned. At the same time he claimed he found nothing of interest in Nietzsche's work. Peter Gay, *Freud: A Life for Our Time* (New York: Norton, 1988), 45.

13 Nietzsche's work influenced others, too, as they developed ethics on the basis of emotions; as noted above, Martin Heidegger (1889–1976 CE), Ricoeur, and Jean-Paul Sartre—who wrote a short book called *Sketch for a Theory of the Emotions* (1962; repr., New York: Routledge, 1994)—also developed philosophies that took seriously the emotional life as central to human existence and engaged Nietzsche's thinking.

14 Leslie Greenberg and Jeremy D. Safran, "Emotion in Psychotherapy," *American Psychologist* 44, no. 1 (1989): 19–29. Later, Freud would postulate that negative affect was a primary mechanism in repression: to avoid unpleasant experience of affect or traumatic memory, one would repress the experience and thus avoid the affect.

15 Sigmund Freud, *Inhibitions, Symptoms and Anxiety* (1926; repr., New York: W. W. Norton, 1959). Psychologist James Hillman writes that Freud developed the idea that the buildup of "energetic tension" causes pain, and therefore, all stimulation that leads to this buildup causes pain. "Pleasure," in Freud's view, is the affect that results in the conscious animal as a result of discharge, or neutralization of tension. Hillman, "Emotion as Energy," 66n3.

16 Freud's debt to Darwin's theories of emotion has been well documented. See, for example, Ritvo, *Darwin's Influence on Freud*.

17 Freud's interest in the subjective aspects of emotion did not arise until the mid-1920s. James Hillman, "Emotion as Energy," in Hillman, *Emotions*, 76n3.

18 Freud's "genius" theory of *libido* contained the complex understanding of various energies in one concept and term. Hillman, *Emotions*, 76.

19 Freud, *Inhibitions, Symptoms and Anxiety*.

20 Sigmund Freud, *New Introductory Lectures on Psychoanalysis*, trans. and ed. James Strachey (1933; repr., New York: W. W. Norton, 1965), 104.

21 In this Freud accepted that certain affects indicated certain experiences. That is, anxiety signals particular experiences in one's past, most commonly painful experiences such as birth or repressed memories of sexual activity.

22 Plutchik, *Emotions in Practice*, 45. Freud was correct that some patients were more prone to anxiety than others: this is borne out in contemporary scholarship—although the differences have little to do with birth or sexual trauma. For example, Harvard psychologist Jerome Kagan argues that one's *tendency* to feel anxious (and how anxious one gets) is primarily genetic, though social context also plays a role. Jerome Kagan, *The Temperamental Thread: How Genes, Culture, Time and Luck Make Us Who We Are* (New York: Dana Press, 2010).

23 In a 1924 publication psychologist Otto Rank developed Freud's initial theory of primary anxiety, calling the physical event of birth the "ultimate biological basis of the psychical," and the "nucleus of the unconscious." Otto Rank, *The Trauma of Birth* (Eastford, Conn.: Martino Fine Books, 2010), xxiii.

24 Freud, *New Introductory Lectures*, 104–5.

25 Toward the end of his life, Freud would posit an opposite drive from the pleasure principle: the Thanatos principle. Sigmund Freud, *Beyond the Pleasure Principle*, trans. and ed. James Strachey (1961; repr., New York: W. W. Norton, 1990).

26 Greenberg and Safran, "Emotion in Psychotherapy." The development of catharsis can be attributed in large part to Bertha Pappenheim ("Anna O."), who would describe to Breuer her symptoms of the day, memories, thoughts, and feelings. She liked to refer to the process as "chimney sweeping," suggesting that she saw the process as one of "getting out" her feelings, which she understood to be a curative process. Breuer later told Freud about his work with Anna O., and this became the model for the "talking cure." Isaacs, *Uses of Emotion*, 45. Psychologist Kenneth Isaacs suggests that it is akin to other systems of getting out "bad" contents from the body. For example, he notes that from the first through the sixteenth centuries in Europe, bloodletting had been prescribed for a variety of human ills. Isaacs, *Uses of Emotion*, 46. This practice was within the bounds of other common cultural practices made popular in the eighteenth century by Franz Mesmer, who treated patients in emotional crises based on theories of universal energy and the need to balance the personal energy with the energy of the universe. Hillman, *Emotions*, 73. Pappenheim applied the concept of the "high colonic" to the work of the mind. This understanding made sense to Freud and his colleagues, who lived in a society that shared the same common wisdom that accumulations cause illness and removal of accumulations rids the body of various noxious substances and thereby enhances health. In the nineteenth century, the common use of high colonics assured that "bowel irrigation" was often used in order to feel better. Despite the probable harm of the practice, many accepted that their physical troubles were due to the buildup of waste in their bodies: "The idea of being clean inside, as an approach to Godliness, was very attractive." Isaacs, *Uses of Emotion*, 45. Free association to purge "toxic" memories and their affect is also reminiscent of Galen's bloodletting. However, Freud eventually changed his mind about the need for catharsis after he found that cures obtained with the use of hypnosis were unreliable, but he continued to believe in his theory of the origin of symptoms.

27 This understanding of emotions and how they are triggered has had long-lasting effect. It was portrayed in the animated Disney/Pixar movie *Inside Out* and continues to prevail in everyday language in the west. However, contemporary neuroscience disabuses us of this view. See chapter 6 for more.

28 It has been argued that Freud's practice of encouraging his analysands' free association is directly informed by the religious practice of confession. See Rieff, *Triumph of the Therapeutic*. To facilitate this link between emotions and the recall of repressed information,

Freud often encouraged *abreaction* in his patients. Abreaction entails recalling a painful experience that had been repressed, working through that painful experience and the conflicts it created by reliving in memory the experience and its associated emotions, analyzing that experience, and finally achieving an emotional release. Later Freud argued for the ego to control the passions: "Where there is id, there shall ego be."

29 Roth, *Psychotherapy*, 67.

30 In Freudian psychoanalysis, accessing the emotions through the process of transference is the primary means of leading the therapist and client "back to the scene of the crime" where the pain and frustrations of development were experienced and where "unhelpful" adaptive patterns were used to cope. Freud, *New Introductory Lectures*, 131–38.

31 Josef Breuer and Sigmund Freud, "Studies on Hysteria," *Standard Edition* 2 (1893–1895): 305.

32 Developmental psychologist Erik Erikson claimed Freud had said this, though there appears to be no written record of it.

33 As we explore in this chapter, relational psychologists such as Heinz Kohut, for example, pay attention to the relationships in one's past as well as the relationship between clinician and client as a way to understand deficiencies in care and the subsequent development of one's self. See Heinz Kohut, *The Restoration of the Self* (Madison, Conn.: International Universities Press, 1977).

34 As noted in the previous chapter, at about the same time William James was conducting his research, Danish scientist Carl Lange was also conducting very similar studies. Their research questions, protocol, and conclusions were very similar, and for that reason theirs is often called the James-Lange theory of emotions. However, because of significant and important differences between them (though, perhaps, not in the ways they were interpreted and used), I will continue to refer to James' theories and not Lange's.

35 Cannon, "The James-Lange Theory of Emotions," 568.

36 Ira Roseman and Craig A. Smith, "Appraisal Theory: Overview, Assumptions, Varieties, Controversies," in *Series in Affective Science: Appraisal Processes in Emotion: Theory, Methods, Research*, ed. Klaus R. Scherer, Angela Schorr, and Tom Johnstone (Oxford: Oxford University Press, 2001), 3–19.

37 The physiological responses associated with emotions were understood to be "a kind of bubbling physiological soup, which is stirred up and given its distinctive taste by the subject's cognitive appraisal." Peter J. Lang, "A Bio-informational Theory of Emotional Imagery," *Psychophysiology* 16, no. 6 (1979): 507. Cited in Cornelius, *Science of Emotion*, 78. Spanish researcher Gregorio Maranon was the primary scholar in establishing this challenge to Lang's work. Maranon found that the physiological differences were slight or nonexistent between different emotions: something else had to be responsible for differences in the variety of emotions people experienced. Rainer Reisenzein, "The Schachter Theory of Emotion: Two Decades Later," *Psychological Bulletin* 94, no. 2 (1983): 239–64. Maranon's work "launched a thousand studies and helped determine the shape of social psychology in the last quarter of the twentieth century." Cornelius, *Science of Emotion*, 73.

38 Roseman and Smith, "Appraisal Theory," 3. It would later be shown that these beliefs and perceptions are often formed in the context of earlier experiences. Contemporary neuroscience helps explain how these earlier experiences generate beliefs that create emotions in the moment. See chapter 6 for more.

39 Schachter himself saw his theory as being a direct descendant of James' theory, albeit one that corrected James' faults. In fact, Schachter understood his theory as "modified Jamesianism." Stanley Schachter, "The Interaction of Cognitive and Physiological Determinants of Emotional State," in *Advances in Experimental Social Psychology*, ed. Leonard Berkowitz (New York: Academic Press, 1964), 70.

40 Stanley Schachter and Jerome Singer, "Cognitive, Social, and Physiological Determinants of Emotional State," *Psychological Review* 69, no. 5 (1962): 379–99.

41 For example, in one experiment, a group of subjects was randomly divided and separated. The subjects then watched a film clip of adolescent boys in a ritual in which the foreskin of their penises was cut in preparation for manhood. One group was told the experience was very painful and traumatic. Another group of observers was told it was a joyful occasion (a rite of passage into adulthood) about which the boys were excited. The first group of observers was very distressed as they watched the film. Members of the other group—who had been informed that this was a positive experience for the boys—displayed none of the emotions the first group did. Evidence for the role that cognitive functions play in the experience and intensity of emotions is exemplified by cases such as the experiments noted here in which different subjects were told different narratives about what was happening in a film about ritual cutting. The subjects who were told before watching the film that the ritual was neither painful nor harmful showed the lowest levels of skin conductance, indicating low stress. The researchers who performed these studies concluded that subjects' experience of a particular event is strongly influenced by their expectations or beliefs about the event—even before it happens. These studies set the research on emotions in a new direction, focusing it on the relationships between cognitions (one's beliefs about what is happening), appraisals (one's assessments of what it means), and physiological events, all of which are informed by past and current emotional experiences. Schachter and Singer, "Cognitive, Social, and Physiological Determinants," 380.

42 Theodore Kemper, *A Social Interactional Theory of Emotions* (New York: Wiley, 1978), 328. See also Theodore Kemper, "How Many Emotions Are There? Wedding the Social and the Autonomic Components," *American Journal of Sociology* 93, no. 2 (1987): 263–89.

43 Schachter and Singer, "Cognitive, Social, and Physiological Determinants," 380.

44 Schachter and Singer, "Cognitive, Social, and Physiological Determinants," 380–81.

45 Schachter and Singer, "Cognitive, Social, and Physiological Determinants," 381.

46 Schachter and Singer did not closely examine the characteristics of the "perception-cognition" they identified, and so *beliefs* rather than *appraisals* play the most significant role in their theory. Magda Arnold would focus on the role of appraisals in the generation of emotions.

47 Arnold is one of the few prominent women researching psychology in the early and mid-twentieth century, and she was the first on record who developed a theory of value (in her word, appraisals) and their relation to beliefs and to emotions.

48 The theory that combines beliefs and appraisals is often referred to as a cognitive theory. It is interesting to remember that Aristotle had argued something similar, and in fact, Arnold quotes Aristotle in her work.

49 Arnold's work is responsible for the modern cognitive approach, one that came into its own at the height of behaviorism in the mid-1960s and reached its largest audience at the

end of the behavioristic era in the late 1970s and early 1980s. The "cognitive" approach brings together both beliefs and appraisals.

50 Magda Arnold, "Neural Mediation of the Emotional Components of Action," in *The Nature of Emotions* (London: Penguin, 1968), 330.

51 Arnold, "Neural Mediation of the Emotional Components of Action," 318.

52 This is implicit in Darwin's work, though he did not develop the idea. Contemporary neuroscience eschews this idea of *any* predictable sequence in emotions' generation. See chapter 6 for more.

53 James had argued that "bodily changes follow directly the *perception* of the exciting fact." James, "What Is an Emotion?" 189. However, James did not define what he meant by the term or explain how such a perception sets in motion the bodily process that ultimately results in the experience of emotion. See the update of James' theory in chapter 6. James was not as wrong as Magda Arnold took him to be.

54 Arnold wrote that "James . . . explains the choice of attack or flight [say, from a bear] as a mechanical association of ideas based on past experience and insists that this association of present situation with past danger produces the visceral changes felt as emotion. But mechanical association cannot account for the connection of this situation with a past dangerous one. We may have seen bears in zoos or pictures of bears innumerable times, may always have liked them and never thought of danger from them. . . . Sheer association would bring back only the many earlier perceptions in which there was no hint of either fight or flight. . . . In this explanation James really presupposes an appraisal that the bear is harmful. It is this realization that this bear means danger for us that makes this particular idea of 'bear' overpowering by driving everything else from our mind." Magda Arnold, *Emotion and Personality*, vol.1, *Psychological Aspects* (New York: Columbia University Press, 1960), 108.

55 Arnold's two-volume *Emotion and Personality*, published in 1960, offered a thorough review of the extant research in the psychological (volume 1) and physiological (volume 2) contributions to the experience of a particular emotion. Judging from the many references to her work in the literature, Arnold made a significant impact on commonly accepted understandings of emotion.

56 Arnold, *Emotion and Personality*, 1:182.

57 Arnold, *Emotion and Personality*, 1:182.

58 Arnold, *Emotion and Personality*, 1:178. According to Arnold, appraising one's situation in a particular manner sets in motion physiological responses that are experienced as a kind of "unpleasant tension." When the action implied by the appraisal, be it fleeing in fear or removing an obstacle in anger, has been completed, the physiological responses abate, and one experiences a relief from the tension. Thus, she wrote, "'to flee as fear prompts us means not only escape from danger but relief from internal discomfort.'" Arnold, *Emotion and Personality*, 1:179. This is an idea that was common in many "drive reduction" models of behavior at the time Arnold was writing. See also Nico H. Frijda, Peter Kuipers, and Ter Schure, "Relations among Emotion, Appraisal, and Emotional Action Readiness," *Journal of Personality and Social Psychology* 57, no. 2 (1989): 212–28.

59 Arnold, *Emotion and Personality*, 1:179.

60 Arnold, *Emotion and Personality*, 1:107. Emphasis added.

61 Arnold, *Emotion and Personality*, 1:171.

62 Arnold, *Emotion and Personality*, 1:171.

63 Arnold, *Emotion and Personality*, 1:175.

64 Arnold, *Emotion and Personality*, 1:171.

65 Arnold, *Emotion and Personality*, 1:171.

66 A green apple might arouse a pleasant emotion if, say, one has memories of her mother putting green apples—her favorite as a child—in her lunch box.

67 Arnold recognized that a person's past experience and his or her goals are important aspects of the way that person appraises a situation, something that neither Darwin nor James had adequately accounted for.

68 Arnold, *Emotion and Personality*, 1:174. Arnold's components of emotion are supported by contemporary neuroscientific research, though she argued that each emotion had its own physiological pattern, an idea that was later shown to be false. See chapters 5 and 6.

69 Others argue something similar. For example, American psychoanalytic theorist Christopher Bollas argues that *moods* are the vague emotional responses to "unthought" memories (often expressed in dreams) of one's earliest life experiences. See Christopher Bollas, *The Shadow of the Object: Psychoanalysis of the Unthought Known* (New York: Columbia University Press, 1987), 115.

70 In addition to apples, another example is the American flag: for a middle-class white American, the flag may elicit feelings of pride and enthusiasm, but for members of an ethnic group that has been targeted or colonized, it may arouse feelings of hate, distrust, and vengeance. This example is in Plutchik, *Emotions in Practice*, 67.

71 For example, individuals sometimes take an instant dislike to someone they have just met. The reason may not be obvious either to an observer or even to the individual. In such a case, one may assume that an unconscious interpretation or a cognition has occurred, and so one makes an inference about the cognition on the basis of the behavior shown. This is clearly what happens in cases of transference, where the therapist makes inferences about the patient's thoughts on the basis of certain behaviors shown by the patient. See Matthias Siemer, Iris Mauss, and James J. Gross, "Same Situation—Different Emotions: How Appraisals Shape Our Emotions," *Emotion* 7, no. 3 (2007): 592–600.

72 Years after Arnold's work, motivations theorists continued to explore the goals and values and motivators that led people to evaluate whether a situation supported or inhibited their goals, and they imagined other motives beyond the physical. Richard Lazarus is one well-known example. The foundation of Lazarus' theory is the concept of *appraisal*, which refers to a decision-making process through which an individual evaluates the personal harms and benefits existing in each interaction with the environment. *Primary appraisals* concern the relevance of the interaction for one's goals, the extent to which the situation is goal congruent (that is, thwarting or facilitating personal goals), and the extent of one's own ego involvement (or degree of commitment). *Secondary appraisals* are those in which the individual makes decisions about blame or credit, one's own coping potential, and future expectations. In this view, emotions are discrete categories, each of which can be placed on a weak-to-strong continuum. Several emotions can occur at the same time because of the multiple motivations and goals involved in any particular encounter, and each emotion involves a specific action tendency (e.g., anger with attack, fear with escape, shame with hiding).

　　A key ingredient of Lazarus' concept of secondary appraisal is the idea of coping, which refers to ways of managing and interpreting conflicts and emotions. According to Lazarus, there are two general types of coping processes. The first is *problem-focused coping*, which deals with conflicts by direct action designed to change the relationship (e.g., fighting if threatened). The second is *emotion-focused (or cognitive) coping*, which deals with conflicts by reinterpreting the situation (e.g., denial in the face of threat). The concept of appraisal implies nothing about rationality, deliberateness, or consciousness.

Another important aspect of Lazarus' theory is the concept of core relational themes. A *core relational theme* is defined as the central harm or benefit that occurs in each emotional encounter. For example, the core relational theme for anger is "a demeaning offense against me and mine"; for guilt it is "having transgressed a moral imperative"; and for hope it is "fearing the worst but yearning for better." Richard Lazarus, *Emotion and Adaptation* (Oxford: Oxford University Press, 1991), 122. One implication of these ideas is that emotions and the cognitions that attend them are developmental. In fact, Lazarus argued that beliefs and appraisals are a necessary and sufficient cause of the emotions and that the emergence of different emotions in infants and young children at different ages reflects the growth of understanding about self and world. In a trenchant academic argument, researcher Robert Zajonc levied a strong objection to Lazarus' theory, arguing that cognition and emotion are independent psychological systems and that it is possible to generate emotions without the participation of any cognitive processes. Robert Zajonc, "Feeling and Thinking: Preferences Need No Inferences," *American Psychologist* 35, no. 2 (1980): 151–74. See also Robert Zajonc, "Evidence for Nonconscious Emotions," in *The Nature of Emotion: Fundamental Questions*, ed. Paul Ekman and Richard Davidson, (Oxford: Oxford University Press, 1994), 293–97. This went against Lazarus' claim that cognition is both a necessary and sufficient condition for emotion. See Richard Lazarus, "Thoughts on the Relations Between Emotion and Cognition," *American Psychologist* 37, no. 9 (1982): 1019–24. Other academics took sides. For example, Gerald L. Clore argued forcefully that emotions require cognition. See Gerald L. Clore, "Why Emotions Require Cognition," in Ekman and Davidson, *The Nature of Emotion*, 181–91, and Kent Berridge and Piotr Wikielman, "What Is an Unconscious Emotion? (The Case for Unconscious 'Liking')," *Cognition & Emotion* 17, no. 2 (2003): 181–211.

Although it is out of the purview of this project to discuss, there is much written about emotions' relationship to motivation. See, for example, Abraham Maslow, "A Preface to Motivation Theory," *Psychosomatic Medicine* 5, no. 1 (1943): 85–92; Abraham Maslow, "A Theory of Human Motivation," *Psychological Review* 50, no. 4 (1943): 370–96; and Paul Thomas Young, *Motivation and Emotion: A Survey of the Determinants of Human and Animal Activity* (New York: John Wiley & Sons, 1961).

73 Arnold is challenged on the basis of her research methods, her interpretations of the data she observed in her subjects, and the fact that her studies were difficult to replicate. In addition, the limits to the power of cognitive, reasoning assessment and control have been well established. See, for example, Gary D. Marshall and Philip G. Zimbardo, "Affective Consequences of Inadequately Explained Physiological Arousal," *Journal of Personality and Social Psychology* 37, no. 6 (1979): 970–88.

74 Christina Maslach, "Negative Emotional Biasing of Unexplained Arousal," *Journal of Personality and Social Psychology* 37, no. 6 (1979): 965. Cited in Cornelius, *Science of Emotion*, 89. These additional sources of emotion are explored in chapter 6.

75 See, for example, Lazarus, *Emotion and Adaptation*, 87. Cognitive psychologist Keith Oatley and his research collaborators developed Lazarus' assertion that goals were a significant element of the generation of emotions, though they took a slightly different direction than Lazarus had. Like Lazarus, Oatley and his group proposed that it is not the appraisals themselves that generate emotions, but a person's appraisals of the relationship of the affect-eliciting event to his or her goals or plans. What are sometimes called *affect*

program emotions (surprise, fear, anger, disgust, joy, and sadness) are considered basic to most sentient creatures, while other emotions (including higher-cognitive emotions and socially constructed emotions) are peculiar to humans. Keith Oatley and Jennifer M. Jenkins, *Understanding Emotions* (Malden, Mass.: Blackwell, 2006). Closely related to goals, values, too, are implicated in emotions. What one considers important, what one prioritizes, what we consistently act on are the values that structure our lives, and we often feel emotions when our values are at stake, being acted against, or being thwarted. A person's values signify his or her priorities and provide information about needs and individual development. They have an epistemological role in evaluative thought and experience. Sabine Roeser and Cain Todd, "Emotion and Value: Introduction," in *Emotion & Value*, ed. Sabine Roeser and Cain Todd (Oxford: Oxford University Press, 2014), 1–14. Indeed, emotions and value define the way each of us perceives the world. Values and emotions also underlie the way each of us behaves in the external world: they "mediate a human being's inner and outer worlds and enable us to express our inner selves outwardly in our daily activities." See Brian P. Hall, *Values Shift: A Guide to Personal and Organizational Transformation* (Rockport, Mass.: Twin Lights Publishers, 1995), 21. Practical theologian Brian Hall defines values as "the ideals that give significance to our lives, that are reflected through the priorities that we choose, and that we act on consistently and repeatedly." Hall, *Values Shift*, 35. Hall, drawing on the work of developmental psychologists such as Erik Erikson, Milton Rokeach, Abraham Maslow, and others, argues that people's dominant values are related to their developmental level of maturity. Hall identifies "foundational" values of special concern to the very young—such as safety and survival—as distinct from "vision" values—such as ecological harmony and sustainability—ideally of special concern to the mature and wise. Each person has foundational and vision values, but they are emphasized depending on life experience. See chapter 7 for more, especially figure 3, which depicts the developmental nature of values, and emotions' relationship to multiple levels of reality. In addition, the development of values and emotional development must be put in the context of culture. See Carolyn Saarni, "The Social Context of Emotional Development," in Lewis, Haviland-Jones, and Barrett, *Handbook of Emotions*, 3rd ed., 307–22. There are updates to the life course's role in human emotions. See Carol Magai, "Long-Lived Emotions: A Life Course Perspective on Emotional Development," in Lewis, Haviland-Jones, and Barrett, *Handbook of Emotions*, 3rd ed., 378–91.

76 One psychoevolutionary theorist goes so far as to argue that "neither humans nor animals teach their infants and children how to express emotion, although it is possible for individuals to learn not to inhibit the expression of emotions. Considerable evidence now indicates that genetic predispositions underlie emotional expressions." Plutchik, *Emotions in Practice*, 78. We learn in chapter 6 that Plutchik is not wholly correct about this.

77 Paul MacLean, *The Triune Brain in Evolution: Role in Paleocerebral Functions* (New York: Plenum Press, 1990), 425. Cited in MacLean, "Cerebral Evolution of Emotion," 68.

78 While physical survival is not an ultimate goal (all organisms die), survival is important—at least for a period of time—in order for the individual's genetic material to be passed on. Darwin was interested in the survival of the species through the survival of the individual until mating; consequently, his theory of emotion was focused on the communicative function of emotional expression ("I intend to attack you" or "Do not attack; I am withdrawing"), which had evolved because it enhanced an organism's ability to mature and reproduce. While natural scientists tend not to speculate on philosophical,

ethical, or religious matters, MacLean ends an essay with the hopeful note that the value of survival will extend to all creatures. He writes, "For the first time in the known history of biology, we are witnessing the evolution of a spirit with a concern for the future of suffering and dying of all living things." MacLean, "Cerebral Evolution of Emotion," 82. I argue in chapter 7 that this is a necessary part of an adequate understanding of flourishing.

79 See Plutchik, "Emotions and the Brain," 262, for a good discussion of this. Ecologists, environmentalists, etc., resist the notion that humans are the "highest point of evolution" for many reasons, including the impact such thinking has had on environmental degradation. See, for example, the work of historian of consciousness Donna Haraway; she writes,

> I am a creature of the mud, not the sky. I am a biologist who has always found edification in the amazing abilities of slime to hold things in touch and to lubricate passages for living beings and their parts. I love the fact that human genomes can be found in only about 10 percent of all the cells that occupy the mundane space I call my body; the other 90 percent of the cells are filled with the genomes of bacteria, fungi, protists, and such, some of which play in a symphony necessary to my being alive at all, and some of which are hitching a ride and doing the rest of me, of us, no harm. I am vastly outnumbered by my tiny companions; better put, I become an adult human being in company with these tiny messmates. To be one is always to become with many. Some of these personal microscopic biota are dangerous to the me who is writing this sentence; they are held in check for now by the measures of the coordinated symphony of all the others, human cells and not, that make the conscious me possible. I love that when 'I' die, all these benign and dangerous symbionts will take over and use whatever is left of 'my' body, if only for a while, since 'we' are necessary to one another in real time. As a little girl, I loved to inhabit miniature worlds brimming with even more tiny real and imagined entities. I loved the play of scales in time and space that children's toys and stories made patent for me. I did not know then that this love prepared me for meeting my companion species, who are my maker.

Donna J. Haraway, *When Species Meet* (Minneapolis: University of Minnesota Press, 2007), 3–4. With thanks to scholar of ecology and spirituality, Timothy H. Robinson, for this reference.

80 "Nonconceptive," or prosocial, sexual behavior is also well documented among the bonobos, for example. Bonobos are primates who frequently use sexual behaviors to create social bonds and communal loyalties, thus increasing the likelihood of their survival. Joseph H. Manson, Susan Perry, and Amy R. Parish, "Nonconceptive Sexual Behavior in Bonobos and Capuchins," *International Journal of Primatology* 18, no. 5 (1997): 767–86. One might note here the emotional differences represented by the words *mating* and *making love* for humans.

81 Their research also showed that play is a fundamental means of learning and development. For more on this see Tina Bruce, *Learning Through Play: For Babies, Toddlers and Young Children*, 2nd ed. (London: Hodder Education, 2011). In addition, research shows how important emotions are for learning social cues, for bonding, and for learning socially and culturally appropriate behaviors. Agneta H. Fischer and Antony S. R. Manstead, "Social Functions of Emotion and Emotion Regulation," in *Handbook of Emotions*,

ed. Lisa Feldman Barrett, Michael Lewis, and Jeannette Haviland-Jones, 4th ed. (New York: Guilford Press, 2016), 424–39. On the importance of play for adults, see Jaco J. Hamman, *A Play-Full Life: Slowing Down and Seeking Peace* (Cleveland: Pilgrim Press, 2011), and Jaak Panksepp, "The Quest for Long-Term Health and Happiness: To Play or Not to Play, That Is the Question," *Psychological Inquiry* 9, no. 1 (1998): 56–66.

82 The quality of one's social environment is especially important for higher mammals, including humans. This is explored more fully in chapter 5.

83 This understanding emphasizes the view of an emotion as a change from a normal, baseline, homeostatic level of activity in the body to something new. This definition does not say what brings this change about, though it does suggest that the changes are extensive and involve most of the systems of the body. In addition, this definition of emotion suggests that an emotion could be expressed in the form of overt action but is not always. It could be simply a state of mind or state of preparation for action. More complex emotional systems include the ability to assess pain and pleasure, but also weigh factors beyond pain and pleasure, determining what is most beneficial to be sought or avoided, even when a mix of emotions is at work. Finally, then, the "crown jewel" of life regulation is highly nuanced emotions, helping more-complex organisms get their increasingly complex set of needs for survival met. Larry I. Jacoby, Andrew P. Yonellinas, and Janine M. Jennings, "The Relation between Conscious and Unconscious (Automatic) Influences: A Declaration of Independence," in *Scientific Approaches to Consciousness*, ed. Jonathan D. Cohen and Jonathan W. Schooner (Hillsdale, N.J.: Erlbaum, 1997), 13–48. Cited in Franks, "Neuroscience of Emotions," 53. These include highly complex social and cultural contexts, as we see in chapter 5. In this view, "states of mind" are likely the exclusive capacities of more-complex organisms, such as humans. This definition is frequently seen in textbooks stating that emotions have three components (subjective feelings, overt behavior, and physiological changes). This understanding of emotions is revisited and expanded in chapter 6.

84 Consciousness is believed to be a very late evolutionary development that comes long after emotion; thus, while emotional systems and conscious feelings both exist in the brain and are interrelated, processes of emotions and processes of feelings are distinct processes. Franks, "Neuroscience of Emotions," 53. Some argue that the fear system, for example, is available to consciousness but operates independently of it, making fear a prototypical unconscious emotional system. Leslie Brothers, *Mistaken Identity* (New York: State University of New York Press, 2001). Cited in Franks, "Neuroscience of Emotions," 53. This idea of prototypical emotions is explored more fully in chapter 6. Note here the distinction between emotions and feelings (usually understood to be the consciousness of emotions). As evolutionary psychologist Robert Pluchik writes, "The evolutionary perspective suggests that these [physiological] patterns are the prototype of what are called emotions in higher animals and in humans. These interactional patterns of adaptation may be thought of as the prototypes of fear and anger, acceptance and disgust, and joy and sadness. The subjective feelings *usually* identified as emotions are relatively late evolutionary development and should not be used as the only or major criterion of the presence of an emotional state. Emotions are complex, interactional adaptations and must therefore have a variety of expressive forms, each of which can be used to infer properties of the underlying state." Robert Plutchik, *Emotions in Practice of Psychotherapy*, 79. Emphasis added.

85 For example, psychologist Nicola Ricci pointed out that every protozoan is a functional unit and that single-celled organisms carry out a whole series of important activities—that is, feeding, reproduction, sexually related behavior, avoidance of danger, search for safety, colonization of new habitats, and predatory behavior. Ricci concludes, "Protozoon [emotional] behavior . . . is the complex and variable adaptive response of protozoa to the problem of reconciling their necessities and activities with varied and constantly changing external conditions, by means of which response the organism equilibrates its relationship with the environment." Nicola Ricci, "The Behavior of Ciliated Protozoa," *Animal Behavior* 40 (1990): 1048–69. Cited in Plutchik, "Emotions and the Brain," 262.

86 For example, to achieve safety and survival, individuals are born with the capacity to feel anxiety and fear in the face of threat and with ways to respond to or communicate their need to caregiving adults in the face of that. While some very young mammals are capable of running within minutes of birth (e.g., an equine foal), and in other organisms, such as humans, the very young communicate those emotions and the needs they indicate by crying. Some higher mammals (this list often includes whales, dolphins, elephants, dogs, and cats) may communicate their emotions by acting depressed when a member of their group dies. This is explored more fully in chapters 6 and 7.

87 Sandor Rado, *Adaptational Psychodynamics: Motivation and Control* (New York: Science House, 1969). Rado was a student of Freud's. Historian of Sigmund Freud and psychoanalysis Peter Gay argued that Rado was one of the "most conspicuous talents" in psychoanalysis. Gay, *Freud*, 460.

88 Rado, *Adaptational Psychodynamics*, 27.

89 Silvan Tomkins reversed this order: following James, Tomkins argued that motives are primarily signals of bodily need and that emotions then amplify these signals. As an illustration, he pointed out that oxygen deprivation creates a need for oxygen, but the affect "fear" creates the sense of urgency or panic. World War II pilots who neglected to wear oxygen masks at thirty thousand feet suffered gradual oxygen deprivation. Although the need was present, the slow process of deprivation did not produce an awareness of the need, and no panic occurred. Without the emotion being present, Tomkins argued, the pilots took no action and lost their lives. Silvan Tomkins, *Cognition*, vol. 4 of *Affect, Imagery, and Consciousness* (New York: Springer, 1992).

90 The challenge, of course, comes when pleasurable behaviors (such as eating candy) do not have positive outcomes. This is further addressed in chapters 6 and 7.

91 A. J. Willingham, "A Mourning Orca Mom Carried Her Baby for Days Through the Ocean," *CNN*, July 27, 2018, https://www.cnn.com/2018/07/27/us/killer-whale -mother-dead-baby-trnd/index.html.

92 For an accessible but sophisticated and helpful exploration of the psychological defensive mechanism of splitting, see Elinor Greenberg, *Borderline, Narcissistic, and Schizoid Adaptations: The Pursuit of Love, Admiration, and Safety* (New York: Greenbrooke Press, 2016).

93 On this see also Michael Lewis, *The Rise of Consciousness and the Development of Emotional Life* (New York: Guilford Press, 2014), and Michael Lewis, and Carolyn Saarni, "Culture and Emotions," in *The Socialization of Emotions*, ed. Michael Lewis and Carolyn Saarni (New York: Plenum, 1985), 1–17.

94 Emotional eating, drug abuse, and forms of addiction are challenging behaviors to change, in large part because they affect both the psychological element in emotions and the physiological.

95   At this level, Rado championed the power of reason and will. However, because he recognized reason's and will's limits to control emotions as they arise, he proposed that reason can create coping mechanisms, or defenses, such as repression of emotions, which then lead to what he called neurotic habits. Indeed, Rado was a psychoanalyst who agreed with Freud that repression of emotions can create psychopathologies (in fact, Rado was Freud's student and mentee). See Rado, *Adaptational Psychodynamics*. Psychologist Leigh M. Vaillant, too, has elaborated on the role of emotions in psychopathology. Leigh M. Vaillant, *Changing Character: Short-Term Anxiety-Regulating Psychotherapy for Restructuring Defenses, Affects, and Attachments* (New York: Basic Books, 1997).

96   These "emotional" capacities led to single-celled organisms becoming multicellular and increasingly complex. Evolutionary scientists suggest that larger organisms can develop new methods for taking in food and new methods of movement, and they may enter new environments not easily available to smaller ones, which also fuels their development and organisms' increased complexity. There are difficulties that come with an increase in size, however; it creates challenges, for example, for the organism to support the body and to move. Plutchik, "Emotions and the Brain," 263.

97   Because emotions are believed to apply to all living things, they are considered to be a functional adaptation for dealing with life's challenges to survival. This view, then, emphasizes emotions rather than subjective reports or *feelings*, arguing, in part, that feelings are accessible only in certain organisms (such as humans) because they require consciousness and self-awareness.

98   Psychological constructionism is explored in chapter 6.

99   Psychoevolutionary theorists often argue that there is a small number of basic, primary, or prototype emotions, and all others are mixtures, compounds, or blends of the primary emotions. They understand this as the foundation for understanding basic interrelations between emotions and personality traits. Personality traits are seen as compromise formations based on conflicts and the repeated mixing of basic emotions. Robert Plutchik and H. R. Conte, "The Circumplex Structure of Personality Disorders: An Empirical Study," paper presented at the annual meeting of the Society for Psychotherapy Research, York, England, 1994.

100   Plutchik, *Emotions in Practice*, xii.

101   Plutchik, *Emotions in Practice*, 74–75. See also Randolph Nesse, "Evolutionary Explanations of Emotions," *Human Nature* 1, no. 3 (1990): 268–69.

102   For example, a baby might use the feeling of fear to connect with a parent: "I need soothing, so I will cry as a way to call my mother, whose relationship I need and desire." British psychiatrist John Bowlby, often considered the father of attachment theory, argued against the prevailing view among the upper classes that love and attention from parents led to children's "spoiling." He pressed the needs of infants and young children to be held, talked to and connected with emotionally in order to develop fully and well. John Bowlby, *A Secure Base: Parent-Child Attachment and Healthy Human Development* (New York: Basic Books, 1988). Others built on this idea. See, for example, L. Alan Sroufe, "The Coherence of Individual Development: Early Care, Attachment, and Subsequent Developmental Issues," *American Psychologist* 34, no. 10 (1979): 834–41.

103   Vernon C. Kelly, "Affect and the Redefinition of Intimacy," in *Knowing Feeling: Affect, Script, and Psychotherapy*, ed. Donald L. Nathanson (New York: W. W. Norton, 1996), 84. Cited in Plutchik, *Emotions in Practice*, 66.

104 Randolph Nesse, "Psychiatry," in *The Sociobiological Imagination*, ed. Mary Maxwell (New York: State University of New York Press, 1991), 33.

105 Radu J. Bogdan, *Interpreting Minds* (Cambridge, Mass.: Bradford Books, 1997). Cited in Plutchik, *Emotions in Practice*, 67.

106 As we see in chapter 5, this is a challenge. Those who study the social, cultural, and political functions of emotions argue that while certain emotions may be founded on an evolutionarily based emotional repertoire, they are far from universal in their expression, their feeling-state, their function, or even their existence. Cultural anthropologists and sociologists, for example, have tested some of the most significant assumptions that natural scientists developed, leading to an emphasis on the social and cultural etiologies and functions of emotions. As the philosopher Claire Armon-Jones put it in an outline of the constructivist position, according to constructivists, "'emotions are characterized by attitudes such as beliefs, judgments and desires, the contents of which are not natural, but are determined by the systems of cultural belief, value and moral value of particular communities.'" Claire Armon-Jones, "The Thesis of Constructionism," in *The Social Construction of Emotions*, ed. Rom Harre (New York: Blackwell, 1986), 32–56. This is explored more fully in chapters 5 and 6.

107 Wounds of trauma from war, racism, sexism, homophobia, transphobia, etc., never fully go away, even when one attends the emotions related to them. See Shelly Rambo, *Resurrecting Wounds: Living in the Afterlife of Trauma* (Waco: Baylor University Press, 2017).

108 See Joseph Sandler, *From Safety to the Superego: Selected Papers of Joseph Sandler* (New York: Guilford Press, 1987); Carl Rogers, *Client-Centered Therapy, Its Current Practice, Implications, and Theory* (Boston: Houghton Mifflin, 1951); and Carl Rogers, "The Necessary and Sufficient Conditions of Therapeutic Personality Change," *Journal of Consulting and Clinical Psychology* 60, no. 6 (1992): 827–32. Contemporary Western cultures, then, assume that emotions have in them the seeds of healing, even salvation. See Eva Illouz, *Saving the Modern Soul: Therapy, Emotions, and the Culture of Self-Help* (Berkeley: University of California Press, 2008).

109 Heinz Kohut, *The Restoration of the Self*, and Heinz Kohut, *How Does Analysis Cure?* (Chicago: University of Chicago Press, 1984).

110 Peter Fonagy, *Attachment Theory and Psychoanalysis* (New York: Other Press, 2001).

111 Rosenthal, "Emotions and the Self," 179.

112 Psychologists and psychotherapeutic practitioners are not always as explicit or clear about their understanding of what "health" means or the goals in their clinical work as we might wish. I make a proposal in chapter 7.

113 Carl Rogers, *On Becoming a Person: A Therapist's View of Psychotherapy* (Boston: Houghton Mifflin, 1961), 23–24. Other clinicians would build on this idea. See, for example, Crayton E. Rowe, Jr., and David S. MacIsaac, *Empathic Attunement: The "Technique" of Psychoanalytic Self Psychology* (Northvale, N.J.: Jason Aronson, 1995).

114 Rogers, "The Necessary and Sufficient Conditions," 829.

115 Rogers, *Client-Centered Therapy*, 162–72. The degree to which any of us can be fully free of defenses is an interesting question. In addition, I have challenged the idea of a "real" or "true" self. See Barbara J. McClure, *Moving Beyond Individualism in Pastoral Care and Counseling: Reflections on Theory, Theology, and Practice* (Eugene, Ore.: Cascade Books, 2010).

116 The humanistic influence of Rogers is in the idea that the power of healing is in acceptance of feelings (that is, they are neither good nor bad but are instead neutral sources of

information). For relational theorists and practitioners such as Heinz Kohut and D. W. Winnicott, it is the relationship that is key: empathic attunement of the caregiver to the person in need allows the client to internalize the relational and emotional template provided by the counselor or caregiver. Sheldon Roth, *Psychotherapy: The Art of Wooing Nature* (Northvale, N.J.: Jason Aronson, 1990), 125. From this perspective, then, emotions are the aspects of the self that join the physical and social world of individuals, and in psychotherapeutic work, "rational capabilities" of "knowing and judging are put aside in the interests of being and sharing." Roth, *Psychotherapy*, 43. Here it is important to emphasize that with the possible exception of psychologist Leslie Greenberg, no psychological theorist or practitioner has offered a comprehensive study of emotions per se; however, "affect theory" is implicit in their work. See, for example, Leslie Greenberg, "Emotion and Change Processes in Psychotherapy," in Lewis and Haviland-Jones, *Handbook of Emotions*, 1st ed., 499–508; Leslie Greenberg, "Emotion and Cognition in Psychotherapy: The Transforming Power of Affect," *Canadian Psychology* 49, no. 1 (2008): 49–59; and Leslie Greenberg, "On the Nature and Development of Affects: A Unified Theory," *Psychoanalytic Quarterly* 43 (1974): 532–56. See also Charles Brenner, "A Psychoanalytic Theory of Affects," in *Emotion: Theory, Research, and Experience*, vol. 1, ed. Robert Plutchik and Henry Kellerman (New York: Academic Press, 1980), 341–48. In addition, there are myriad nuances, for example, between models of diagnosis, of understandings of the unconscious and conscious, views of intrapsychic dynamics vs. interpersonal relationships, and so on. For this reason, the resources are so vast, varied, and complex that it would be foolish to claim to be presenting an exhaustive overview of a clinical or psychotherapeutic perspective. It is reasonable, however, to say that in general, psychodynamic psychotherapists accept the view that emotions tell us something important about people's lives and that attending to them will bring us to a clearer and deeper understanding of a person's core concerns and conflicts. Some of the theories presented here are well known, others less so, though they are all found in overviews and textbooks of psychodynamic psychotherapeutic theory and practice and thus, I suggest, are representative of common beliefs and approaches to emotions in contemporary psychodynamic therapeutic clinical work. It is fair to say that relational psychotherapists and existential philosophers believe that feelings are people's "most unique way of directly participating in the world." Lester, *Angry Christian*, 26.

117 Leslie S. Greenberg, *Emotion-Focused Therapy: Coaching Clients to Work Through Their Feelings* (Washington, D.C.: American Psychological Association, 2002), 6.

118 Kohut examined the differences between what he called "tragic man" and "guilty man." The guilty man suffers from internal conflicts, and the tragic man suffers from developmental deficits caused by parental empathic failure. See Kohut, *Restoration of the Self*. American psychoanalytic theorist Christopher Bollas explored this too, arguing that nightmares and unpleasant moods are primarily related to one's earliest painful childhood relational experiences. See Bollas, *The Shadow of the Object*, 115.

119 Analysis of the transference of these dynamics from patient to therapist is a focus of the healing process. Jules Glenn, "Empathy, Countertransference, and Other Emotional Reactions of the Therapist," in *Psychotherapy: The Analytic Approach*, ed. Morton J. Aronson and Melvin A. Scharfman (Northvale, N.J.: Jason Aronson, 1992), 73–83.

120 Greenberg and Safran, "Emotion in Psychotherapy," 20.

121 Kohut in particular wished to focus on the present in an approach that emphasizes empathy. In fact, Kohut differentiated himself from classical ego psychologists and other

psychoanalytic theorists by positing that empathy was the "most important source of information about the patient, a form of data gathered through vicarious introspection." Pamela Cooper-White, *Shared Wisdom: Use of the Self in Pastoral Care and Counseling* (Minneapolis: Fortress, 2004), 22. This is often done through the use of transference (the redirection of a relational template and the emotions that attend it from client to therapist) and countertransference (the therapist's response to transference. It is often emotional as well). In both transference and countertransference, intense emotional reactions are not pathological or dangerous; rather, they are merely information provided to both the client and the therapist for inspection and understanding. In addition, it is inevitable that empathy will fail, that the therapist and client will experience "ruptures" in their connection and relationship. These ruptures, both inevitable and useful, encourage the empathic exploration and interpretation of the patient's earliest experiences and the emotions that accompanied them. This kind of alignment with the patient and experience ideally results in a process Kohut called "transmuting internalizations," by which he meant the process by which the client internalizes the therapist's willingness and ability to understand the world of the patient and allows the client to "take in" that new relational and emotional experience and build new self-structures in the process. For Kohut, the observable self (rather than Freud's understanding of the unconscious) was the focus of analysis, and the experience and identification of feelings was the best way in. Kohut, *Restoration of the Self*, and Kohut, *How Does Analysis Cure?*

122 Greenberg and Safran, "Emotion in Psychotherapy," 20. By *objects*, object-relations theorists such as Winnicott mean the template of relationships formed in one's earliest experiences.

123 Transference is also very important in relational psychologists' work, and it is empathy that allows clinicians to contain and rebuild the early "self-object" reflected in the transference relationship. See, for example, Kohut, *Restoration of the Self*, and Bollas, *Shadow of the Object*.

124 Greenberg and Safran, "Emotion in Psychotherapy," 21.

125 Isaacs, *Uses of Emotion*, 94.

5 Emotions as Relational and Sociocultural Artifacts

1 Reddy, *Navigation of Feeling*.

2 Historian and cultural anthropologist William Reddy suggests that an emotional regime is "a set of normative emotions and the official rituals, practices, and emotives that express and inculcate them; a necessary underpinning of any stable political regime." *Navigation of Feeling*, 128–30. See, for example, Norbert Elias, *The Civilizing Process: Sociogenetic and Psychogenetic Investigations*, rev. ed., trans. Edmund Jephcott, ed. Eric Dunning, Johan Goudsblom, and Stephen Mennell (Malden, Mass.: Blackwell, 2000). For a more thorough treatment of diverse emotions in various settings, see *Civilizing Emotions: Concepts in Nineteenth-Century Asia and Europe*, ed. Margrit Pernau, Helge Jordheim, Emmanuelle Saada, Christian Bailey, et al. (Oxford: Oxford University Press, 2015). For historical expressions or constructions of different emotions, see, for example, Peter N. Stearns, *Jealousy* (New York: New York University Press, 1989); Peter N. Stearns, "History of Emotions: Issues of Change and Impact," in Lewis and Haviland-Jones, *Handbook of Emotions*, 2nd ed., 17–31; Gordon Clanton, "Jealousy and Envy," in Stets and Turner, *Handbook of the Sociology of Emotions*, 410–42; and Kathy Charmaz and Melinda J. Milligan, "Grief," in Stets and Turner, *Handbook of the Sociology of Emotions*, 516–43.

3 Reddy, *Navigation of Feeling*, x.

4 Note the gendered nature of this comment: how different would your response to reading those words be if I had written "*he* is so emotional!"?

5 This admonition is common in Western, often hypermasculine cultures where views of masculinity do not include vulnerability. This is a contemporary issue, and some men are beginning to recognize it as a problem. See, for example, Hannah Seligson, "These Men Are Waiting to Share Some Feelings with You," *New York Times*, December 8, 2018, https://www.nytimes.com/2018/12/08/style/men-emotions-mankind-project.html. For a poignant treatment of the effects of this kind of culture on boys, see Robert C. Dykstra, "Losers and the Struggle for Self-Awareness," in *Losers, Loners and Rebels: The Spiritual Struggles of Boys*, ed. Robert C. Dykstra, Allan Hugh Cole Jr., and Donald Capps (Louisville, Ky.: Westminster John Knox, 2007), in which he argues that cultures of toxic masculinity that do not allow a full emotional life for boys oversimplify boys' inner experience, pressuring them to draw rigid distinctions between themselves and others that can lead to intense loneliness or rebellion. Dykstra, "Losers and the Struggle for Self-Awareness," 45.

6 William H. McNeill, *Keeping Together in Time: Dance and Drill in Human History* (Cambridge, Mass.: Harvard University Press, 1995).

7 McNeill, *Keeping Together in Time*, 10–11.

8 McNeill, *Keeping Together in Time*, 8.

9 Lewis, Amini, and Lannon, *A General Theory of Love*.

10 Attachment and human development theorists have suggested a new explanation for Sudden Infant Death Syndrome (SIDS): that a sleeping mother and infant share physiologic rhythms exhibiting "mutual concordances and synchronicities" that are life-sustaining for the child, "protecting them from the possibility of respiratory arrest." James J. McKenna, Sarah Mosko, Claibourne Dungy, and Jan McAninch, "Sleep and Arousal Patterns of Co-Sleeping Human Mother/Infant Pairs: A Preliminary Physiological Study with Implications for the Study of Sudden Infant Death Syndrome," *American Journal of Physical Anthropology* 83, no. 3 (1990): 331–47. Cited in Lewis, Amini, and Lannon, *A General Theory of Love*, 195. To underscore their point, the authors cite research that demonstrates that cultures that are more communally oriented and where parents and children routinely co-sleep have much lower incidents of SIDS than cultures that are more individual oriented and which tend to remove infants to a separate room, an isolated crib, often connected only by a blinking light on a plastic monitor. Babies will often cry in distress at the separation.

11 For example, see this NPR interview on how ants survive floods: Scott Simon and Jessica Purcell, "How Do Ants Survive Floods? Rafts of Course," April 23, 2016, http://www.npr.org/2016/04/23/475388734/how-do-ants-survive-floods-rafts-of-course.

12 Emil Durkheim, *The Elementary Forms of Religious Life*, trans. Joseph W. Swain (London: Allen and Unwin, 1915).

13 Ole Riis and Linda Woodhead, *Sociology of Religious Emotion* (Oxford: Oxford University Press, 2010), 31. As Durkheim himself put it, "individual sentiments 'present the noteworthy property of existing outside individual consciousness' and 'we are the victims of the illusion of having ourselves created that which has actually forced itself [on us] from without.'" Emil Durkheim, *The Rules of Sociological Method* (1895; repr., London: Macmillan, 1982), 5. Cited in Riis and Woodhead, *Sociology of Religious Emotion*, 32.

14 Durkheim, *Elementary Forms of Religious Life*. As cited in Riis and Woodhead, *Sociology of Religious Emotion*, 32.

15 Neoliberalism is the name for the resurgence of nineteenth-century economic liberalism that values free markets, privatization, deregulation, free trade, and limited government control of what "should" be private. Pastoral theologian Bruce Rogers-Vaughn argues that it is a "re-institution of white supremacy." Bruce Rogers-Vaughn, *Caring for Souls in a Neoliberal Age* (New York: Palgrave Macmillan, 2016), 139.

16 It may not need to be said that eating disorders and alcohol abuse often develop as a way to manage and negotiate one's feelings about one's self and the expectations or disapproval of others, and to feel like one either belongs or can hide in social situations. This is also true of the collection of material goods far beyond what one needs. For example, think of the term "conspicuous consumption," or the use of material goods (cars, homes, clothes, expensive jewelry) to signal to others that one has wealth. Those who practice conspicuous consumption do not always have the means, but want to suggest they do. In these cases, shoppers would rather go into debt to cultivate the desired regard of their peers than live within their means and risk going without that admiration. See, for example, Marilyn Clark and Kirsten Calleja, "Shopping Addiction: A Preliminary Investigation among Maltese Students," *Addiction Research & Theory* 16, no. 6 (2008): 633–49.

17 Employee satisfaction has been shown to increase customer satisfaction. See Joelle F. Majdalani and Bassem Maamari, "Emotional Intelligence: A Tool for Customer Satisfaction," *Journal for Global Business Advancement* 9, no. 3 (2016): 275–83.

18 Sociologist Arlie Hochschild explored this phenomenon in her classic book *The Managed Heart: The Commercialization of Human Feeling*, 3rd ed. (Berkeley: University of California Press, 1983). In it she documents the ways flight attendants' emotions are used by the airline to leverage positive "fellow feeling" among passengers and increase sales. See also Arlie Hochschild, *The Commercialization of Intimate Life: Notes from Home and Work* (Berkeley: University of California Press, 2003).

19 As noted in the previous chapter, Paul Ekman and his associates developed an elaborate schema of facial expression and its relation to emotion in the latter part of the twentieth century that became a very popular theory. They allowed for "display rules" while maintaining their commitment to five or six basic emotions they contend are universal. While the idea of display rules makes sense to social theorists of emotion, Darwin's and Ekman's assumption that there are "basic, universal" emotions that are or are not displayed depending on social context, or whose means of expression vary by context, is challenged by constructionist theorists of emotion, presented in this chapter and in chapter 6.

20 As we see in chapter 6, recent neuroscientific studies on emotion support this idea.

21 Weston LaBarre, "The Cultural Basis of Emotions and Gestures," *Journal of Personality* 16, no. 1 (1947): 55. Emphasis added.

22 Ray L. Birdwhistell, *Kinesics and Context: Essays on Body Motion Communication* (Philadelphia: University of Philadelphia Press, 1970), 34. Cited in Cornelius, *Science of Emotion*, 39.

23 Birdwhistell, *Kinesics and Context*, 34. Birdwhistell founded *kinesis* (the study of body language) as a legitimate field of scientific research. In response to these criticisms, however, Ekman argued that the many cultural differences in emotional expressions "do not indicate that there are no universal expressions of emotion but that cultures differ in the extent to which they modify those expressions by means of display rules." Birdwhistell, *Kinesics and Context*, 34. Cited in Cornelius, *Science of Emotion*, 39.

24 Members of neuroscientist Lisa Feldman Barrett's team traveled to West and East Africa to see if test subjects from the isolated groups sorted facial expressions and vocalizations into the same emotion categories we have in the United States. Barrett's team found they did not: Barrett's research collaborators found that people in these groups not "contaminated" by U.S. cultures sorted emotions differently than we do in North America and labeled photos of posed facial expressions differently, often naming them, instead, as behaviors. In another experiment in the United States, Barrett's team showed photos of famous actors displaying realistic emotional facial expressions (such as fear) to volunteers. Certain volunteers saw only faces, some saw faces set in context, and some received only verbal description of the situation. The researchers found that for all emotions, the context mattered significantly. For example, only 38 percent of those who saw a fear face alone perceived it as "fear" (56 percent perceived it as "surprise"), while 66 percent who saw the face in context read it as expressing fear. Knowing the situation changed viewers' interpretation of which emotion was being expressed in the face. Barrett, *How Emotions Are Made*, 10. Even more significantly, perhaps, Barrett's team also performed a meta-analysis of 220 neuroimaging studies on anger, disgust, happiness, fear, and sadness. Barrett, *How Emotions Are Made*, 14. The meta-analysis covered 22,000 test subjects over a span of twenty years. What they found supported their hypotheses: there was no brain region that consistently held a "fingerprint" for any emotion. Even the amygdala, which we are often told is associated with fear, was shown to increase in fear-experience studies, but only in a quarter of them. *And*, contrary to almost one hundred years of previous research, they found that the amygdala also showed increases during episodes of anger, happiness, disgust, and sadness and when the subject was experiencing pain, learning something new, meeting new people, or making decisions. Barrett, *How Emotions Are Made*, 21–22. See chapter 6 for more on this.

25 Critics also argued that while Ekman's data may be clear, their meaning is not. One group of scholars demonstrated that Ekman's studies demonstrate only that people in different cultures are capable of matching simple emotions to a relatively small number of facial expressions; even so, they pointed out, Ekman could not do this with 100 percent accuracy even considering the small number of emotion labels that have been studied. James A. Russell, "Is There Universal Recognition of Emotion from Facial Expression? A Review of the Cross-Cultural Studies," *Psychological Bulletin* 115, no.1 (January 1994): 102–41. These critics contend that the brief words or phrases that Ekman and his associates used in their matching assessments are not good representations of the emotions of those whom they were studying: they argue that *knowledge about* or *awareness of* emotions differs, *experiences* of emotions differ, and *terms used for emotions* differ by context, both historical and cultural. In order for any study of commonalities between emotions, terminologies for them, and expressions of them to be meaningful, Ekman's critics argue, one must first compare the emotional lexicons, what emotions are experienced, and which are valued or devalued in a particular context. In other words, these critics contend that emotions and one's language about them are informed by culture and history, and simply comparing emotional experiences across cultures to find what is universal renders any findings meaningless because they cannot recognize the differences in experience, interpretation, terminology, and expression. Rom Harre, "An Outline of the Social Constructionist Viewpoint," in Rom Harre, *The Social Construction of Emotions* (Oxford: Basil Blackwell, 1986), 10. The implication is that Darwin, Ekman, and those who follow them fail to appreciate sufficiently the fundamentally social nature, origin, and function

of human and animal expressive displays. Alan Fridlund, "The Behavioral Ecology and Sociality of Human Faces," in *Review of Personality and Social Psychology*, vol. 13, *Emotions*, ed. Margaret S. Clark, 90–121 (Thousand Oaks, Calif.: SAGE, 1992). See also Alan Fridlund, *Human Facial Expression: An Evolutionary View* (San Diego: Academic Press, 1994); Robert A. Thamm, "The Classification of Emotions," in Stets and Turner, *Handbook of the Sociology of Emotions*, 16; and Harre, "An Outline of the Social Constructionist Viewpoint," 10.

26 Ekman's model is a structural one, meaning that in his schema, certain circumstances and social arrangements will likely give rise to predictable emotions. There are other structural models, including those of Richard Lazarus, Theodore Kemper, and others, as we shall see later in the next chapter. See, for example, Andrew Ortony, Gerald Clore, and Allan Collins, *The Cognitive Structure of Emotion* (New York: Cambridge University Press, 1988); Ira Roseman, "Cognitive Determinants of Emotion," in *Review of Personality and Social Psychology*, vol. 5, *Emotions, Relationships and Health*, ed. Phillip Shaver (Thousand Oaks, Calif.: SAGE, 1984), 11–36; and Craig A. Smith and Richard S. Lazarus, "Appraisal Components, Core Relational Themes, and the Emotions," *Cognition and Emotion* 7, no. 3–4 (1993): 233–69. Recent neuroscience challenges cognitive and social structural models, showing that emotions are constructed in the moment given what is happening physiologically and what one has learned socioculturally as well as how emotions vary across historical epochs. See chapter 6 for more.

27 Jeffrey T. Ulmner, Casey T. Harris, and Darrell Steffensmeier, "Racial and Ethnic Disparities in Structural Disadvantage and Crime: White, Black and Hispanic Comparisons," *Social Science Quarterly* 93, no. 3 (2012): 799–819.

28 David L. Scruton, "The Anthropology of an Emotion," in *Sociophobics: The Anthropology of Fear*, ed. David L. Scruton (Boulder, Colo.: Westview Press, 1986), 41–42.

29 Cornelius, *Science of Emotion*, 176 and 179.

30 See, for example, the discussion in Ahmed, *Cultural Politics of Emotion*.

31 Larry Burd, "Language and Speech in Tourette Syndrome: Phenotype and Phenomenology," *Current Developmental Disorders Reports* 1, no. 4 (2014): 229–35.

32 Burd, "Language and Speech in Tourette Syndrome."

33 How this happens is outlined in chapter 6.

34 Riis and Woodhead, *Sociology of Religious Emotion*, 33.

35 James R. Averill, "A Constructivist View of Emotion," in *Emotion: Theory, Research and Experience*, ed. Robert Plutchik and Henry Kellerman (New York: Academic Press, 1980), 305–39.

36 Russell, "Is There Universal Recognition of Emotion?" Ekman responded to the critiques of his research, challenged the most strident criticisms, and, at least one scholar suggests, "effectively defused what would have been the most damaging" critiques of his work. Ekman, "Expression and the Nature of Emotion." Recent neuroscience may offer a way to reconcile the previously opposed perspectives. See chapter 6 for more.

37 Craig A. Smith and Paul C. Ellsworth, "Patterns of Cognitive Appraisal in Emotion," *Journal of Personality and Social Psychology* 48, no. 5 (1985): 813–38.

38 Thamm, "The Classification of Emotions," 17.

39 Neuroscientist Lisa Feldman Barrett calls these theories part of the "classical" models of emotions. In contrast, a neuroscientific constructivist model is presented in chapter 6.

40 Klaus Scherer, "Studying the Emotion-Antecedent Appraisal Process: An Expert System Approach," *Cognition and Emotion* 7, nos. 3–4 (1993): 325–55. Emphasis in the original.

41 Scherer, "Emotion-Antecedent Appraisal," 330. Contemporary neuroscientists argue something similar, though they disagree with Scherer's structural approach. See chapter 6.

42 Recent psychological constructionist approaches argue that beliefs and appraisals are only *some* of the components that go into emotions' generation. Roseman and Smith, "Appraisal Theory." See chapter 6 for more.

43 Robert A. Thamm, "The Classification of Emotions," 16. An alternative analysis of the function of anxiety (a focus of Sigmund Freud's work) as a trait is given in Peter Trower and Paul Gilbert, "New Theoretical Conceptions of Social Anxiety and Social Phobia," *Clinical Psychology Review* 9, no. 1 (1989): 9–35.

    Social theorists point out that most mammals and especially primates live in social groups that are organized and stabilized by means of dominance hierarchies. The fact that each individual in a group enacts a role that defines his or her position within the hierarchy functions to maintain cohesiveness of the group. If someone else of higher dominance status threatens another group member, escape from the group is rarely possible because survival generally depends on the group's support. The result is usually some form of submissive ritual or gesture that allows the threatened individual to remain in the group. Social anxiety may have evolved as a method for maintaining group cohesion. According to this hypothesis, the socially anxious person has an appraisal and coping style that is particularly sensitive to threats and loss of status in a hostile and competitive world. Cited in Robert Plutchik, *Emotions in the Practice of Psychotherapy*, 7.

44 Pastoral theologian Robert C. Dykstra provides a useful exploration of repression, language, and the care of people through stories and the emotions they convey in Robert C. Dykstra, *Finding Ourselves Lost: Ministry in the Age of Overwhelm* (Eugene, Ore.: Cascade Books, 2018), especially chapter 3.

45 Harre, "An Outline of the Social Constructionist Viewpoint," 10. Emphasis added.

46 Zoltan Kovesces, *Emotion Concepts* (New York: Springer-Verlag, 1990), 3. See also James A. Russell and Ghyslaine Lemay, "Emotion Concepts," in Lewis and Haviland-Jones, *Handbook of Emotions*, 2nd ed., 491–503.

47 Kovesces, *Emotion Concepts*, 52–58.

48 Kovesces, *Emotion Concepts*, 52–58. It is my assertion that this view of anger is informed by early philosophers such as the Stoics and early theologians such as Clement. That is, we have inherited these "concepts" about anger from the earliest Greco-Roman philosophers and Jewish and Christian theologians. See chapters 1 and 2 for more.

49 Kovesces, *Emotion Concepts*, 52–58. This appears to be a particularly Western understanding of emotions, which leads to how those in the West *experience* these emotions.

50 James R. Averill, "The Emotions," in *Personality: Basic Aspects and Current Research*, ed. Ervin Staub (Englewood Cliffs, N.J.: Prentice-Hall, 1980), 151. For example, much emotion talk imagines a passive relationship to emotions, as if emotions are something human beings are at the mercy of. Even the word *passions*, the preferred term in early Greek philosophy, is derived from the Latin *passe*, or "passive," and early philosophers such as Plato and the Stoics considered emotions unruly and disruptive. See chapter 1 for more on this.

51 Averill, "Emotions in Relation to Systems of Behavior," 385–404.

52 Lisa Feldman Barrett, "Emotions Are Real," *Emotion* 12, no. 3 (2012): 413–29.

53 Elinor Ochs and Bambi Schieffelin, "Language Has a Heart," *Text* 9, no. 1 (1989): 7–25. Cited in Cornelius, *Science of Emotion*, 166.

54 Catherine Lutz, "The Domain of Emotion Words on Ifaluk," in Harre, *The Social Construction of Emotions*, 267–88.

55 Rom Harre and Grant Gillett, *The Discursive Mind* (Thousand Oaks, Calif.: SAGE, 1994). Cited in Cornelius, *Science of Emotion*, 168.

56 Paul Heelas, "Emotion Talk across Cultures," in Harre, *The Social Construction of Emotions*, 36.

57 Lila Abu-Lughod and Catherine Lutz, "Introduction: Emotion, Discourse, and the Politics of Everyday Life," in *Language and Politics of Emotion*, ed. Catherine Lutz and Lila Abu-Lughod (Cambridge University Press, 1990), 1–23. This is also why it is also difficult to come up with a definition of emotion that can be applied to all cultures at all times, much less a list of what is and is not an emotion that is universally relevant.

58 Heelas, "Emotion Talk across Cultures," 237.

59 Anna Wierzbicka, "Human Emotions: Universal or Culture-Specific?" *American Anthropologist* 88, no. 3 (1986): 584–594. Wierzbicka argues that Ekman and his colleagues were assuming that language was a simple and uncomplicated transmission of meaning for emotion terms across culture.

60 Maria Gendron, Kristen A. Lindquist, Lawrence Barsalou, and Lisa Feldman Barrett, "Emotion Words Shape Emotion Precepts," *Emotion* 12, no. 2 (2012): 314–25.

61 Lutz, "Domain of Emotion Words on Ifaluk," 273.

62 Takeo Doi, *Anatomy of Dependence*, 1st ed. (Tokyo: Kodansha International, 1973), 15. See also H. Morsbach and W. Tyler, "A Japanese Emotion: *Amae*," in Harre, *The Social Construction of Emotions*, 289–307. This is compounded by the fact that emotions vary by culture: in Russia, there are two cultural concepts for anger, in Germany there are three, and in Mandarin China there are five. If one were an English speaker learning the language in those cultures, she might feel incapable of understanding and communicating as she tries to grasp what situations and feelings correlate with each word, for example, "anger." When she finally does understand, it would will still take a while before she can "feel" that emotion automatically, the way she feels "anger" in her own context. See Barrett, "Your Emotions Are a Social Construct."

63 Jan Plamper, *The History of Emotions: An Introduction*, trans. Keith Tribe (Oxford: Oxford University Press, 2012), 251. There is resistance to the idea that emotions are constructed. Using the example of *gham*, for example, historian and cultural anthropologist William Reddy argues that the view that emotions are constructed (as cultural theorists Catherine Lutz, Lila Abu-Lughod, and others argue—and I will agree in chapter 6) does not account adequately for the ways emotions *do* something to the world. William Reddy, "Against Constructionism," *Current Anthropology* 38, no. 3 (1997): 327–51. In his critique, I believe Reddy misunderstands the fact that what is constructed is also real, with real implications and effects.

64 Riis and Woodhead, *Sociology of Religious Emotion*, 24.

65 Averill, "A Constructivist View of Emotion," 326.

66 A helpful recent book exploring (at least implicitly) the role of emotions in creating and maintaining a neoliberal capitalist society is Ryan LaMothe's *Care of Souls, Care of Polis: Toward a Political Pastoral Theology* (Eugene, Ore.: Cascade Books, 2017).

67 Karl Marx, *Selected Writings in Sociology and Social Philosophy*, trans. T. B. Bottomore, ed. T. B. Bottomore and Maximillian Rubel (New York: McGraw-Hill, 1964).

68 Kemper, *Social Interactional Theory of Emotions*, 21, and Theodore D. Kemper, "Social Models in the Explanation of Emotions," in Lewis and Haviland-Jones, *Handbook of Emotions*, 2nd. ed., 45–58.

69 Max Weber, *From Max Weber: Essays in Sociology*, trans. and ed. Hans H. Gerth and C. Wright Mills (Oxford: Oxford University Press, 1946).

70 Riis and Woodhead, *Sociology of Religious Emotion*, 62–63 and 189.

71 It is interesting to note that Sigmund Freud's cousin, Edward Bernays, is the founder of public relations and marketing—a highly manipulative use of emotions—to sell products.

72 There are a number of interesting treatments of psychology, emotions, and capitalism. See, for example, Philip Cushman, *Constructing the Self, Constructing America: A Cultural History of Psychotherapy* (Cambridge, Mass.: Perseus, 1995); Eva Illouz, *Cold Intimacies: The Making of Emotional Capitalism* (Cambridge, U.K.: Polity Press, 2007); Illouz, *Saving the Modern Soul*; Rogers-Vaughn, *Caring for Souls in a Neoliberal Age*; Bruce Rogers-Vaughn, "Powers and Principalities: Initial Reflections toward a Post-Capitalist Pastoral Theology," *Journal of Pastoral Theology* 25, no. 2 (2015): 71–92; Bruce Rogers-Vaughn, "Class Power and Human Suffering," in *Pastoral Theology and Care: Critical Trajectories in Theory and Practice*, ed. Nancy J. Ramsay (Hoboken, N.J.: Wiley-Blackwell, 2018), 55–77; and Hochschild, *Managed Heart*. See also Ryan LaMothe, *Pastoral Reflections on Global Citizenship* (New York: Lexington Books, 2018), and William Davies, *The Happiness Industry: How the Government and Big Business Sold Us Well-Being* (New York: Verso, 2015). Davies argues that the pursuit of happiness has become the preoccupation of global elite business because "the future of capitalism depends on our ability to combat stress, misery and illness, and put relaxation, happiness and wellness in their place." Davies, *Happiness Industry*, 7.

73 G. J. Barker-Benfield, *The Culture of Sensibility: Sex and Society in Eighteenth-Century Britain* (Chicago: University of Chicago Press, 1992). Cited in Adela Pinch, "Emotion and History: A Review Article," *Comparative Studies in Society and History* 37, no. 1 (1995): 100–109. The study of the emotional phenomenon of "sentimentalism" is instructive here, as it challenges the understanding of emotions as strictly personal or interpersonal and instead demonstrates that emotions are personal, relational, *and* cultural phenomena, set in the context of a particular sociocultural context and a history. Sentimentalism arose as a cultural phenomenon at the end of the Victorian age in which emotions had been carefully managed so as to appear "appropriate." Defined as the "capacity of all people to be invaded and divided by excesses of pathos, pity, and sympathy," and the capacity of both men and women "to tremble and weep" in personal displays of deep and dramatic emotion, sentimentalism became common experiences of affect and forms of expression that were both taught and encouraged by eighteenth-century novels. Pinch, "Emotion and History," 101. Germaine de Stael, writing in 1800, argued that "reading novels allowed people to have new, more nuanced, feelings." As quoted in Reddy, *Navigation of Feeling*, xii. It is important to note the *taught* nature of both the *experiences* of emotion people were encouraged to have as well as the *forms of their expression*. Such affective phenomena were relatively new among Europeans and Americans, though they were accepted as the "true" expression of personal experience. On further examination, however, such personal displays were shown to be "deeply enmeshed" with eighteenth-century social theory, moral philosophy, gender roles, and economic shifts. Pinch, "Emotion and History," 101.

74 For more on this, see, for example, Abu-Lughod and Lutz, "Introduction: Emotion, Discourse, and the Politics of Everyday Life," 1–23; Joseph J. Campos et al., "A Functionalist Perspective on the Nature of Emotion," *Monographs of the Society for Research in Child Development* 59, nos. 2–3 (1994): 284–303; and Dacher Keltner and Jonathan Haidt, "Social Functions of Emotions at Four Levels of Analysis," *Cognition and Emotion* 13, no. 5 (1999): 505–21. Keltner and Haidt propose functioning at the individual level (primarily related to regulating physiology); "dyadic level," or the regulation of interactions of people in "meaningful relationships" (510); group level, where emotions function to help groups meet their shared goals; and finally a cultural level, in which emotions are shaped by historical and economic factors, are embedded in cultural institutions and practices, and are shaped by cultural scripts for the "proper expression and experience of emotions" (513). See also Scott Rick and George Lowenstein, "The Role of Emotion in Economic Behavior," in Lewis, Haviland-Jones, and Barrett, *Handbook of Emotions*, 3rd ed., 138–56. This exposes some limitations of adaptive vs. maladaptive criteria in the evaluation of emotions, an idea explored further in chapter 7.

75 This school of thought came into its own in the 1980s with the publication of two important texts: Rom Harre, ed., *The Social Construction of Emotions* (Oxford: Basil Blackwell, 1986), and Kenneth Gergen and Keith Davis, *The Social Construction of the Person* (New York: Springer-Verlag, 1985).

76 Indeed, social constructionism is part of a larger movement that prevails in sociology, anthropology, literary criticism, and sociocultural criticism, to name just a few fields.

77 Kemper, "Power and Status and the Power-Status Theory of Emotions," in Stets and Turner, *Handbook of the Sociology of Emotions*, 110. See also Jan E. Stets and Jonathan H. Turner, "The Sociology of Emotions," in Lewis, Haviland-Jones, and Barrett, *Handbook of Emotions*, 3rd ed., 32–46.

78 For example, women and men consistently report being afraid of different things and express fear in ways different from one another. Inconsistencies between genders could be explained by social or cultural differences in display rules and also by social constructionists' opinions that men and women likely *feel* different emotions, not just express the same emotions differently. See examples of this in chapter 4. See chapter 6 for more on why this might be.

79 Lutz, "Domain of Emotion Words on Ifaluk," 114.

80 In fact, Lutz argues that among the Ifaluk, *ker* (happiness/excitement) is often viewed as "dangerous" because it usually means the person is getting food or other goods he wants, and is at risk of unequally tilting the distribution of sparse resources in his own favor. Lutz, "Domain of Emotion Words on Ifaluk," 121 and 123.

81 John B. Pryor, Glenn D. Reeder, and Julie A. McManus, "Fear and Loathing in the Workplace: Reactions to AIDS-infected Co-workers," *Personality and Social Psychology Bulletin* 17, no. 2 (1991): 133–39.

82 Claire Armon-Jones, "The Social Functions of Emotion," in Harre, *The Social Construction of Emotions*, 57–82.

83 Armon-Jones, "Social Functions of Emotion," 63.

84 Keltner and Haidt, "Social Functions of Emotions at Four Levels of Analysis," 505–21.

85 Like each of the theories explored in this text thus far, this one offers some useful insights but is flawed in its assertion that *any* emotions are universally predictable, given certain structural realities. Chapter 6 offers a way to understand the ways certain sociopolitical

structures predict certain emotions, but also account for personal and sociocultural flexibility.

86 Thamm, "Classification of Emotions," 14.

87 Kemper, *Social Interactional Theory of Emotions*, 50–71.

88 Kemper, *Social Interactional Theory of Emotions*, 50–71.

89 Kemper, *Social Interactional Theory of Emotions*, 50–71. See also pastoral theologian Nancy Ramsay's essay on white privilege and the mental anguish of the privileged and the dominated that current unjust systems engender. She writes of the "painful evidence of a faltering social network." Nancy J. Ramsay, "Where Race and Gender Collude: Deconstructing Racial Privilege," in *Women Out of Order*, ed. Jeanne S. Moessner and Theresa Snorton (Minneapolis: Fortress, 2010), 343. In this she implies that the pain is shared by those across status positions, though Ramsay surely would not claim the pain is equal (and the dominated experience more of it than the privileged and are likely more aware of inequalities and the suffering associated with them as well). Social constructionists would argue that people do feel emotional pain in unjust situations, not necessarily because of something inherent in us but because we have been taught that privilege and oppression are morally wrong. Psychologist Christopher Bollas would assert that we learn the lessons of dominance and submission in the context of our earliest caregiving relationships. Bollas, *Shadow of the Object*.

90 Theodore D. Kemper, "Sociological Models in the Explanation of Emotions," in Lewis and Haviland-Jones, *Handbook of Emotions*, 1st ed., 41–51.

91 Kemper, *Social Interactional Theory of Emotions*, 72–79, and Kemper, "Sociological Models," 43. Kemper also asserts that an imaginative projection of future interaction is as capable of evoking emotion as the actual interaction itself. Kemper, *Social Interactional Theory of Emotions*, 49.

92 Kemper, *Social Interactional Theory of Emotions*, 350.

93 This further enhances the (false) sense that emotions are merely personal, outside the realm of social context. Imagining emotions in this way limits our understanding of emotions' flexibility and our ability to use them to cultivate flourishing. Chapter 6 will suggest a way to bring together personal and social perspectives of emotion in a theory supported by contemporary neuroscience.

94 There have been many others who followed in the line of Lutz's research. See, for example, Robert I. Levy, "Emotion, Knowing, and Culture," in *Culture Theory: Essays on Mind, Self, and Emotion*, ed. Richard A. Shweder and Robert A. LeVine (Cambridge: Cambridge University Press, 1984), 214–37.

95 The question of how emotional cultures have changed in modern societies is taken up by a number of social commentators and critics, including David Riesman in his well-known *The Lonely Crowd* (1950; repr., New Haven: Yale University Press, 1965). Paying close attention to emotional characteristics, Riesman identifies three social types in late modern societies: the traditional, the inner directed, and the other directed. In Riesman's schema, the traditional type conforms to emotion norms from the past, the inner-directed type is emotionally self-controlled and directed by an inner moral compass, and the other-directed type seeks signals of approval from far and near. According to Riesman, the other-directed type has become dominant in modern life. All three types seek recognition and approval, but for the other-directed type this becomes the chief area of sensitivity: life revolves around receiving recognition and social approval or being curdled with resentment when it is not forthcoming. It is possible that regardless of the realities of

social structures and relationships, an individual will respond emotionally to *perceptions of* or *felt sense* of the social relations, which may, at times, violate the conventional relational conditions associated with social position. (This means that people whose social position involves giving orders may not feel the "predictable" emotions of confidence, assurance, and energy if they perceive that the order-receiver is indifferent or resistant to their authority.) On this, see Kemper, *Social Interactional Theory of Emotions*, 348. This demonstrates that emotions' emergence in the social-structural model depends on all parties in that hierarchy to accept that particular social structure. (This may be a reason women and other underrepresented groups often struggle to live into high-level positions as fully as they might: those around them are often unwilling to accept their position, credibility, or authority.) It also requires persons in excluded groups to *believe* that they belong and have a right to that authority, a belief that can be difficult if one has inherited centuries (or millennia) of oppression.

96 The social-structural model of emotions has been used to analyze the ways particular contexts generate particular feelings by nations, organizations, and small groups. What have been called emotion regimes are responsible for bellicose nations, depressive and unproductive work environments, or even the increase in diagnoses of disorders such as Attention Deficit/Hyperactivity Disorder (ADHD) in children. Sociologist Theodore Kemper, for example, argues that even mental illnesses such as schizophrenia are the result of particular structures of power relations. Kemper, *Social Interactional Theory*, 200–214.

The term "emotion regimes" captures the ways emotions are integrated into the structured social and material relations that constitute a particular social unit or setting. For example, "adult male coal miners, women garment workers in a sweatshop, or flight attendants, all have different social relationships and live in very different emotional atmospheres." Reddy, *Navigation of Feeling*, 128. Historian William Reddy suggests that emotional regimes are "a set of normative emotions and the official rituals, practices, and emotives that express and inculcate them; a necessary underpinning of any stable political regime," *Navigation of Feeling*, 128–30. Emotions and their expression, then, can be a tool for diagnosing social, cultural, and political structures. As is the case for other social structural contexts, emotional regimes have "internal coherence and boundedness," making the emotions within them predictable and difficult to resist. Sociologists argue that emotion regimes tend to be stable: they persist over time and transcend individuals, "shaping what [people] can feel, how they can feel it, the way they can express their feelings, and hence the forms of social relationship and courses of action that are open to them." Riis and Woodhead, *Sociology of Religious Emotion*, 10. This does not mean that social and political structures cannot or should not be resisted and changed, however. Because emotions play important roles in shaping and reproducing structures of power, understanding the ways emotional regimes function—and the emotions they both generate and discourage—provides a useful tool for relating deeply personal experiences such as emotions to the larger structural contexts in which people find themselves. Language for, expressions of, and understandings of emotions vary by culture, by social context, and by an individual's relationship to those cultures and contexts. This model counters the widespread assumption that emotions are of little public or political significance. For more on this see Barbara J. McClure, "The Social Construction of Emotions: A New Direction for the Pastoral Work of Healing," *Pastoral Psychology* 59, no. 6 (2010): 799–812.

An example of the kind of critical analytical work I am thinking of here is that of Sara Ahmed, whose work combines the study of emotions and the study of sociocultural and political structures. Ahmed is critical of a certain kind of happiness and its use, arguing that emotions (such as the promise and expectation of happiness) are often used to oppress. For Ahmed, "happiness" functions as a "technology of the individual" (in Foucauldian terms) in that it is offered as a promise of the future if one only orients oneself to the proper object (that is, a feeling, an identity, a history, etc.). Ahmed suggests that bad feelings must be converted to good feelings to maintain the status quo. Ahmed, *Promise of Happiness*, 44–45. Another example of this kind of work is that of cultural critic Ann Cvetkovich. Cvetkovich argues that depression is a historical category that should be an entry point into analysis of contemporary culture and experience in everyday life. For Cvetkovich, embodied and felt experiences can play important roles in resistance, political activism, and social transformation. Ann Cvetkovich, *Depression: A Public Feeling* (Durham, N.C.: Duke University Press, 2012).

97 Stearns, "History of Emotions," 27.

98 Resistance to the emotions of targeted and dominated groups is a powerful way to maintain unjust status quo with negative consequences. However, emotions can be used to increase well-being of the oppressed as well. For example, in a powerful display of emotions as political tools, in protests against injustice such as the Black Lives Matter movement, the #MeToo movement, and the women's marches on Washington, activists have used anger to resist current structural situations. (Not surprisingly, those protests have been dismissed as incendiary, selfish, and overdrawn by those in power: these words are used to invoke shame and guilt and passivity in activists and shut down their resistance to oppression.) On the importance of emotions in targeted groups such as women, see Chiara Fiorentini, "Gender and Emotion Expression, Experience, Physiology and Well-Being: A Psychological Perspective," in *Gender and Emotion: An Interdisciplinary Approach*, ed. Ioana Latu, Marianne Scmid Mast, and Susanne Kaiser (Bern.: Peter Lang, 2013), 15–40.

99 Psychologists Heinz Kohut and Harry Stack Sullivan are exceptions to this generalization. Kohut argued that culture provides idealized objects that people admire and internalize, and Sullivan proposed, for example, that mothers mediate the wider sociocultural world to their infants. Harry Stack Sullivan, *Interpersonal Theory of Psychiatry* (New York: W.W. Norton, 1968). There are, of course, others who mediate social ideologies and norms to the young, including other care providers such as fathers and members of extended families, siblings, daycare workers, teachers, pastors and youth group leaders, and multiple forms of media.

100 There are exceptions to this, of course. American biologist E. O. Wilson is one. A world-renowned expert on the biological and social worlds of ants, Wilson has won Pulitzer prizes for his work on the moral imperative to save the planet (and thus promote the flourishing—or at least survival—of all living creatures), the genetic inheritances of cooperation and altruism (sacrifices to save the whole over oneself), and his exploration of human nature and existence. Of his many books, see especially *Genesis: The Deep Origin of Societies* (New York: Liveright/W.W. Norton, 2019), and *The Meaning of Human Existence* (New York: W.W. Norton, 2014). A social-constructionist view of emotions' value for human flourishing is something neuroscientist Lisa Feldman Barrett hints at, although she does not fully develop the implications of her work along these lines. See chapters 6 and 7 for more.

6 Emotions as Psychological Constructions in Context

1 The ways we experience and think about emotions are reinforced by popular representations of them, for example, in Disney's relatively recent movie *Inside Out*.

2 Physiological, neuroscientific theories like Paul MacLean's are often called a "faculty psychology" and "natural kinds" approaches to emotions to indicate that there are certain "natural, basic" emotions that are universal, and that there are specific causal mechanisms in the brain that hold certain emotional functions and generate specific emotions. See Oosterwijk, Touroutoglou, and Lindquist, et al., "The Neuroscience of Construction," 111 and 116. By the 1960s, basic emotions theory had solidified into the belief that emotions are innate programs in the brain, providing an understanding of emotions that linked Darwin and human psychology in the brain. See Joseph LeDoux, "Afterword: Emotion Construction in the Brain," in Barrett and Russell, *The Psychological Construction of Emotion*, 459–63. However, the idea of "emotional faculties" was tested and rejected beginning in the mid-twentieth century. In particular, the newer evidence in human brain imaging and in brain evolution (reviewed, for example, in Lisa Feldman Barrett, "Are Emotions Natural Kinds?" *Perspectives on Psychological Science* 1, no. 1 [2006]: 28–58; and Lisa F. Barrett, Batja Mesquita, Kevin N. Ochsner, and James J. Gross, "The Experience of Emotion," *Annual Review of Psychology* 58, no. 1 [2007]: 373–403) does not support the idea of emotions as faculties or entities per se. Nevertheless, scientific articles, textbooks, and even newspaper articles, television documentaries, and science shows on television continue to claim that universal, "basic" emotions exist, "as if this is an air-tight empirical fact." Lisa Feldman Barrett, "Construction as an Integrative Framework for the Science of the Emotion," in Barrett and Russell, *The Psychological Construction of Emotion*, 448.

3 For much of the last century, emotion-related research, guided by the faculty psychology/ natural kind research programs, has sought classifications and origins of emotions by identifying the autonomic nervous system (ANS) patterns, brain circuitry, and predictable—even universal—social functions for phenomena corresponding to a small group of emotion words using a variety of methods in a range of contexts. See Oosterwijk, Touroutoglou, and Lindquist, et al., "The Neuroscience of Construction," 111 and 116.

4 Well-known psychologists such as Richard Lazarus and Robert Plutchik have proposed a schema for the emergence of more-complex, nuanced emotions than these "basic" emotions. See the endnotes of chapters 4 and 5 for more detail.

5 See, for example, Barrett, "Are Emotions Natural Kinds?" and Mitchell Herschbach and William Bechtel, "Mental Mechanisms and Psychological Construction," in Barrett and Russell, *The Psychological Construction of Emotion*, 21–44.

6 Walter B. Cannon, *Bodily Changes in Pain, Hunger, Fear, and Rage*, 2nd ed. (New York: Appleton, 1929).

7 The *allocortex* is one of two parts of the cerebral cortex; the other is the neocortex. Oosterwijk, Touroutoglou, and Lindquist, et al., "The Neuroscience of Construction," 111 and 116. See chapter 3 for more on this.

8 See, for example, Barrett, "Are Emotions Natural Kinds?" and Herschbach and Bechtel, "Mental Mechanisms and Psychological Construction," 31.

9 See, for example, Barrett, *How Emotions Are Made*; Barrett, "Are Emotions Natural Kinds?"; Lisa Feldman Barrett and Ajay B. Satpute, "Large-Scale Brain Networks in Affective and Social Neuroscience: Towards an Integrative Functional Architecture of the

Brain," *Current Opinion in Neurobiology* 23, no. 3 (2013): 361–72; Oosterwick, Tourou-toglou, and Lindquist et al., "The Neuroscience of Construction"; and James A. Coan and Marlen Z. Gonzalez, "Emotions as Emergent Variables," in Barrett and Russell, *The Psychological Construction of Emotion*, 209–28.

10 Oosterwijk, Touroutoglou, and Lindquist, et al., "The Neuroscience of Construction," 116.

11 See chapter 5 for more.

12 William James may have been more correct than he knew, or at least more correct than others' interpretation of his work would suggest. Barrett, "Solving the Emotion Paradox."

13 That is, domains of the brain that service multiple functions. In fact, it has been demon-strated that this is how the brain works: many areas have multiple purposes, and none are specifically designated to be "emotional." See for example, Barrett and Satpute, "Large-Scale Brain Networks."

14 Gendron, Lindquist, Barsalou, and Barrett, "Emotion Words Shape Emotion Precepts." See also Lisa Feldman Barrett, "Construction as an Integrative Framework of the Science of the Emotion," 453. What is becoming increasingly clear, for example, is that reason and emotions/passions are not as discrete as earlier scholars thought.

15 Many contemporary research psychologists are "no longer searching" for the *engram* (the place in the brain where a memory resides), for example, because a memory as an entity cannot be found. Oosterwijk, Touroutoglou, and Lindquist, et al., "The Neuroscience of Construction," 132–34. Neuroscientist Suzanne Oosterwijk and her team note that if a person recalled an event that happened last week (or even yesterday), the content of that memory will likely differ (sometimes greatly) from what happened in the actual event or from how someone else remembers the event. And both sets of memories for this event may differ from what they are today and how it will be remembered tomorrow. In con-trast to classical understandings of mental processes in which each was once assumed to be a fixed entity with an identifiable causal mechanism or essence, each is now accounted for by distinct but interacting systems. A given instance of a memory, personality, or concept is constructed in the moment and is sensitive to context (both immediate and past), and so it may be somewhat different from what occurs at some other instance. This variability, rather than being viewed as a source of error or bias, is a valid reflection of a person's psychological state that must be modeled and explained as part of the way the brain and mind work. Oosterwijk, Touroutoglou, and Lindquist, et al., "The Neurosci-ence of Construction." See also Barrett, "Solving the Paradox," 21.

16 Oosterwijk, Touroutoglou, and Lindquist, et al., "The Neuroscience of Construction," 115.

17 While in principle appraisal models do acknowledge the enormous variety in emotional responding and do not assume that particular emotions are basic in any biological way, as we have noted, they continue to organize emotional response into the familiar set of discrete categories such as anger, sadness, and fear. Barrett, "Solving the Emotion Paradox," 21.

18 This model suggests that animals have emotions, which are complex physiological events, but not feelings, which require the ability to be self-aware and reflect on those physiologi-cal events. There is a long debate about whether emotions are conscious or not (see, for example, the discussion of Robert Zajonc and Richard Lazarus in chapter 4).

19 Barrett, "Solving the Emotion Paradox," 21. Figure 1 distills the assumptions that are common to many models of emotion, regardless of how those models differ in their

surface features. Substitute the terms "affect program," "internal signals," or a literal neural circuit defined by a specific brain area or a neurotransmitter system for "emotion" and
Figure 1 summarizes the "basic" emotion approach. Barrett notes that natural and social-
scientific models have not adequately understood that distinct kinds of emotions are
generated from specific contexts and that each "emotion episode" can differ physiologically from other episodes of the same emotion. Barrett, "Solving the Emotion Paradox,"
22. Furthermore, psychological constructionist James Russell argues, Figure 1 does not
portray all of the complexity in emotions' origins (e.g., facial movements and peripheral
physiology). Nor does it acknowledge the epigenetic influences (such as context and
learning history) that are generally assumed to play a role in emotional responding. Nevertheless, neuroscientist Barrett writes, "it is not uncommon for emotion researchers to
discuss specific kinds of emotions as if they were invariant responses to particular kinds
of antecedents." See Barrett, "Solving the Emotion Paradox," 22.

20 Barrett, "Solving the Emotion Paradox," 21–22. Neuroscientist James Russell allows for
some "prototypical" emotions such as fear but argues that they are more like reflexes than
they are actual emotions. James A. Russell, "Core Affect and the Psychological Construction of Emotion," *Psychological Review* 110, no. 1 (2003): 145–72. Russell notes that
there are some neurological responses often present in "prototypical" emotions (defined
as a cognitive structure that specifies the typical ingredients, causal connections, and
temporal order for the emotion concepts), but these are not present in all instances of
that particular "emotion." See Russell, "Core Affect and the Psychological Construction
of Emotion," 147. See also Christine D. Wilson-Mendenhall, Lisa F. Barrett, W. Kyle
Simmons, and Lawrence W. Barsalou, "Grounding Emotion in Situated Conceptualization," *Neuropsychologia* 49, no. 5 (2011): 1105–27.

21 Emotions are difficult to get a "hold" of. For example, disparities between verbal self-
reports and body language suggest that observers of emotions are often exceptionally
tuned to expressions of their nuances, even when the person they are observing denies
they are feeling a particular emotion. If a person says he is angry but moves his head in
a way that suggests sadness, observers will likely believe him to be sad. People tend to
believe that behavior trumps self-reporting; however, empirical research shows that it is
difficult "if not impossible" to find an objective way of measuring a person's emotional
experience. See Barrett, "Solving the Emotion Paradox," 22.

22 Barrett, "Solving the Emotion Paradox," 23.

23 Karen S. Quigley, Lisa Feldman Barrett, and Suzanne Weinstein, "Cardiovascular Patterns Associated with Threat and Challenge Appraisals: A Within-Subjects Analysis,"
Psychophysiology 39, no. 3 (2002): 1–11; Joe Tomaka, Jim Blascovich, Robert M. Kelsey,
and Christopher L. Leitten, "Subjective, Physiological, and Behavioral Effects of Threat
and Challenge Appraisal," *Journal of Personality and Social Psychology* 65, no. 2 (1993):
248–60; and Joe Tomaka, Jim Blascovich, Jeffrey Kibler, and John M. Ernst, "Cognitive
and Physiological Antecedents of Threat and Challenge Appraisal," *Journal of Personality
and Social Psychology* 73 (1997): 63–72. Cited in Barrett, "Solving the Emotion Paradox," 23.

24 Russell, "Core Affect and the Psychological Construction of Emotion," 148. See also,
for example, John T. Cacioppo et al., "The Psychophysiology of Emotion," in Lewis and
Haviland-Jones, *Handbook of Emotions*, 2nd ed., 173–91.

25 Barrett, "Solving the Emotion Paradox," 23.

26 Oosterwijk, Touroutoglou, and Lindquist, et al., "The Neuroscience of Construction." This can be shown at multiple levels of analysis by examining the varying functions that different instances of the same emotion category can play (rather than assuming that each emotion category reflects only one function, or that the function varies primarily by culture, not by moment). See, for example, Coan and Gonzalez, "Emotions as Emergent Variables."

27 Neuropsychologist James Russell defines a *component* of emotion as "an event that, by itself, an observer (the self, a witness, a scientist) would take to be a sign of emotion." Russell, "My Psychological Constructionist Perspective, with a Focus on Conscious Affective Experience," in Barrett and Russell, *The Psychological Construction of Emotion*, 194. Components, of course, depend on many processes, are difficult to observe, and are sometimes fast, automatic, and nonconscious. Each component is just the "tip of the iceberg" in a set of processes that are often unconscious. Russell, "My Psychological Constructionist Perspective," 200. It turns out that Aristotle was correct: emotions (for him the "passions") are the result of composite factors that include beliefs, expectations and hopes, values, goals, motivations, and so on. See chapter 1 for more on Aristotle's view. However, "Aristotle's commitment to essentialism runs deep," even where he denied essentialism when others emphasized it. See Christopher Shields, "Aristotle," *Stanford Encyclopedia of Philosophy*, https://plato.stanford.edu/entries/aristotle/. Aristotle was also committed to categories (see Paul Studtmann, "Aristotle's Categories," *Stanford Encyclopedia of Philosophy*, https://plato.stanford.edu/entries/aristotle-categories/), an idea revisited in this chapter, though contemporary neuroscientists imagine them somewhat differently than did Aristotle.

28 Lisa Feldman Barrett, "The Future of Psychology: Connecting Mind to Brain," *Perspectives in Psychological Science* 4, no. 4 (1990): 326–39. Barrett reminds us that the idea of emotion as a perception of physiological changes began with William James. She writes, "In the most general terms, James . . . suggested that the experience of emotion (which he merely called *emotion*) results from the self-perception of information in the body. He focused primarily on the ways that the peripheral nervous system reacts to the external environment, producing somatovisceral and voluntary muscle activation that is sensed via interoceptive mechanisms, constituting the experience of emotion." Barrett, "Solving the Emotion Paradox," 38. The view Barrett proposes is similar to what James wrote, though it differs from the way his ideas have been characterized by others. See chapter 3 for more on James' theory and misinterpretations of it.

29 Other researchers argue that the recipe model is too mechanistic: entries in a recipe book are "static entities." For this reason, they argue, the recipe model is not flexible enough. It is only when the ingredients and processes that make up recipes are engaged by a skilled chef that they come together to make delicious foods. Their understanding assumes that it is the chef (rather than the recipe) that is critical in the process of making something meaningful out of a variety of ingredients, and a "chef" (or some executive function of the brain) does so as an "endogenously" active system—that is, from deep tissue or from systems deep within an organism—engaged in ongoing variable interactions with the environment. There may be some mechanistic perspectives that create emotions (and other mental functions such as memory, cognition, and so on), they allow, but they emphasize that mechanisms involved in the brain are nonlinear operations organized in complex ways that researchers are only beginning to identify and understand. See, for example, Oosterwijk, Touroutoglou, and Lindquist, et al., "The Neuroscience of

Construction," 113–14. Neuropsychology researcher James Russell vehemently disagrees with the idea that there is an "executive function" in the brain directing emotions' generation. See Russell, "My Psychological Constructionist Perspective," 202–3.

30 Barrett, "Construction as an Integrative Framework for the Science of the Emotion," 453–54.

31 Lisa Feldman Barrett, "Ten Common Misconceptions about Psychological Construction Theories of Emotion," in *The Psychological Construction of Emotion*, ed. Lisa F. Barrett and James A. Russell (New York: Guilford Press, 2015), 45–82.

32 Barrett, "Solving the Emotion Paradox," 41.

33 Barrett, "Solving the Emotion Paradox," 27.

34 Barrett, "Solving the Emotion Paradox," 27.

35 Barrett, "Solving the Emotion Paradox," 27. This process has significant implications for the dynamics of prejudice, as implicit bias studies have shown.

36 Barrett, "Construction as an Integrative Framework for the Science of the Emotion," 448–58.

37 Barrett, "Ten Common Misconceptions," 47.

38 Barrett, "Ten Common Misconceptions," 49. Russell notes that "As occurrent events, emotional episodes are indeed constructed at the time of occurrence from simpler ingredients that are general ingredients of the mind (and body)." In Russell's view, any ingredient could play a role, but what he names as "components"—peripheral physiological changes, attributions and appraisals, subjective experiences, plans and goals and behaviors—are especially important and "usually play a role." Russell, "My Psychological Constructionist Perspective," 184. The experience of a *feeling* comes later, upon conscious reflection on an emotional event. A *feeling* (that is, the conscious reflection on an emotion) is an assessment of one's current internal physiological and mental condition on a spectrum between ecstasy and agony on the hedonic (pleasure/pain) scale, and from sleepy to frenetic excitement on the arousal scale. However, not all organisms have *feelings*, although they may experience emotions as Russell defines them.

39 See Russell, "Core Affect and the Psychological Construction of Emotion," 147, for a more detailed discussion of these processes.

40 Core affect is the register of the pleasant or unpleasant and the energized or enervated experience to an emotion episode, but core affect is always present, including times when no emotional episode is occurring. Russell writes, "I doubt that any of these processes are unique to humans, although perhaps emotional meta-experience [meaning the awareness of conscious feeling] is." Russell, "Core Affect and the Psychological Construction of Emotion," 184.

41 All organisms have core affect, even the most rudimentary such as amoebae. Russell gives the example of body temperature to explain core affect: one can become aware of it whenever one wants, but unless it is outside a particular range, set by and for the individual (and often by one's genetic profile), one's bodily temperature will go unnoticed. Russell argues that the same is true of core affect. Neuropsychologist Lisa Feldman Barrett argues, "In a sense, core affect is a neurophysiological barometer of the individual's relation to an environment at a given point in time. A person's momentary core affect is multiply determined and is an accounting of how events and objects influence his or her homeostatic state." Barrett, "Solving the Emotion Paradox," 31. She suggests that core affect may be a basic kind of "core" knowledge (as defined by Elizabeth S. Spelke, "Core Knowledge," *American Psychologist* 55, no. 11 [2000]: 1233–43). Cited in Barrett, "Solving the Emotion Paradox,"

31. The hardwiring to register core affect is present at birth (Katherine M. Bridges, "Emotional Development in Early Infancy," *Child Development* 3 [1932]: 324–34; Rene A. Spitz and W. Godfrey Cobliner, *The First Year of Life: A Psychoanalytic Study of Normal and Deviant Development of Object Relations* [Madison, Conn.: International Universities Press, 1965]), suggesting that all humans are endowed with the ability to be aware of core affective states. It functions in humans as it does in other mammalian species and likely nonmammals as well, as Sandor Rado recognized (see chapter 4). Rudolph N. Cardinal, John A. Parkinson, Jeremy Hall, and Barry J. Everitt, "Emotion and Motivation: The Role of the Amygdala, Ventral Striatum, and Prefrontal Cortex," *Neuroscience and Behavior Reviews* 26, no. 3 (2002): 321–52. Cited in Barrett, "Solving the Emotion Paradox," 31.

42 Russell, "Core Affect and the Psychological Construction of Emotion," 148.

43 Russell, "Core Affect and the Psychological Construction of Emotion," 148. This form of affective responding is "core" because it is influenced by a very simple form of meaning analysis—whether stimuli or events are helpful or harmful, or rewarding or threatening, for a given organism or person at a given point in time, and whether an active behavioral response is required. This basic type of meaning is "pancultural" (James A. Russell, "Culture and the Categorization of Emotion," *Psychological Bulletin* 110, no. 3 [1991]: 426–50), meaning that research demonstrates that all human languages have words or concepts to communicate pleasure and pain, reward and threat. Anna Wierzbicka, *Emotions across Languages and Cultures: Diversity and Universals* (Cambridge: Cambridge University Press, 1999.) Although it can be communicated with words, core affect is not an artifact of verbal labeling. It can exist and influence behavior without being noticed, labeled or interpreted and can therefore function unconsciously. Barrett, "Solving the Emotion Paradox," 31.

44 "Like-valenced" experiences are those that are similar to one another on the spectra of pleasantness and arousal.

45 Barrett notes that in graduate school, she went on a date with someone she was not particularly attracted to. But when she felt her face flush and her stomach flutter and she had trouble concentrating, she experienced a strong attraction to him after all and agreed to another date. It was not until she went home, threw up, and spent the next seven days in bed that she realized she had the flu, not love at first sight. Her brain had taken the sensations of her heart racing, stomach fluttering, and face flushing and constructed a feeling of attraction during the date rather than the sensations of being sick. The bodily sensations in attraction and the beginnings of illness can feel the same, and her brain had used the context (being on a date) to interpret them as attraction. Another example comes from a 2011 study that showed that judges are harsher before their lunch breaks than after. They interpret the gnawing in their stomach as a bad feeling about the suspect because of the categories of "criminal" or "young black man" they have learned. See Barrett, *How Emotions Are Made*, 234.

46 Russell calls this "mood-congruent priming." Core affect, then, is implicated in the *acquisition of preferences* and *attitudes* toward Objects (defined below). When people interact with an Object and the core affect is experienced as unpleasant, they associate the Object with a negative assessment. When they interact with an Object and the core affect experience is pleasant, they associate the Object with a positive assessment. Russell, "Core Affect and the Psychological Construction of Emotion," 149. The capital *O* is explained just ahead in the main text.

47 In other words, core affect is also involved in motivation, reward, and reinforcement. Russell, "Core Affect and the Psychological Construction of Emotion," 149. If we remember feeling warm and comforted by the fact that our mother made us chicken soup when we had the flu as children, it is likely that the just the *idea* of chicken soup brings us pleasure, and we are likely to choose that over minestrone soup when we feel ill. This is directly related to the idea of comfort food or emotional eating. Of course, these experiences get connected to the endocrine system as well, so that eating comfort food actually releases endorphins and opioid responses in the brain. This is part of what makes changing habitual or addictive patterns so difficult.

48 We can draw on memories of affect quality to relate to others' experience as well. Recall your chuckles of recognition when you read A. A. Milne's character Pooh Bear saying, "It must be time for a little smackerel of something." See A. A. Milne, *The Complete Tales of Winnie the Pooh* (New York: Dutton Children's Books/Penguin, 2016).

49 This is not to ignore the daily realities of chronic hunger many living in the United States and around the globe experience, but to point out that core affect often gets misinterpreted.

50 Hence the terms "retail therapy" and "emotional eating."

51 Homeostasis does not indicate a state of well-being but rather one of familiarity. Studies have shown that people who grew up in abusive homes feel "at home" (that is, a sense of homeostasis) in abusive situations. Obviously, we would not want to suggest that these situations are those of well-being.

52 "The process of changing core affect is not fully understood. Changes can be short lived (as in turning up the heat in a room) or long lasting (as in clinical depression). There are genetically based and socialized individual differences in average levels of core affect, its volatility, and its responsiveness to particular types of stimuli. There are also internal, more temporary causes for change, including the activity of immune cells, diurnal rhythms, and hormone changes. External causes work on this floating baseline." Russell, "Core Affect and the Psychological Construction of Emotion," 148–66. In addition, core affect can be changed with drugs, including stimulants (e.g., caffeine, alcohol) and depressants (e.g., marijuana). Occasionally, an obvious external cause overwhelms all others. For example, seeing a bear while hiking can cause one's core affect to change quickly from calm to extremely agitated.

53 That is, objects that have affective qualities *attached* to them become Objects (capital "O"). Russell, "Core Affect and the Psychological Construction of Emotion," 147. This model of emotion generation is similar in some respects to the level-of-processing views put forth by some appraisal theorists. What differentiates this conceptual act model from most appraisal perspectives is the emphasis on categorization processes as a core mechanism driving emotion experience. Separate cognitive mechanisms for computing a situation's meaning (as found in some appraisal models, such as Richard Lazarus' or Klaus Scherer's) are not necessary to account for the experience of emotion. Appraisals are not literal cognitive mechanisms but instead represent "dimensions of meaning" that are associated with particular emotions. Barrett, "Solving the Emotion Paradox," 25–26.

54 Russell capitalizes *Objects* to indicate that they rarely have intrinsic value or meaning (that is, they "rarely act directly on the nervous systems without involving prior learning"). That is, while certain Objects are important to individuals—and even, perhaps, to groups of individuals who share a social group or a culture—they are not objectively valuable. Their attributed affect is learned either through people's own

experience or learning from others'. Russell, "Core Affect and the Psychological Construction of Emotion," 147. The meaning of an Object is determined by a particular person in a particular context at a particular point in time. This is the basic point made by appraisal models of emotion such as Magda Arnold's (see chapter 4 of this volume). Barrett notes that "people are continually assessing situations for personal relevance, beginning with an evaluation of whether or not the stimulus is good for me/bad for me. The result of this constant evaluative processing at each moment in time is some change in a person's core affective state." Barrett, "Solving the Emotion Paradox," 31.

55 People often eat high-sugar and high-fat foods ("junk food") after a hard day at work or are tempted to buy a coveted pair of suede boots—in vogue this season—after seeing an ad for them on a billboard. Both of these experiences shift a person's core affect and are engaged with the hope of making one feel better (comforted in the first case, admired or "worthy" in the second). Advertising and marketing are attempts to make Objects out of objects, thus manipulating people's emotions and to induce material objects' (or a particular services') purchase. On the role of one's social and cultural context for the appraisal of value, see Antony S. R. Manstead and Agneta H. Fischer, "Social Appraisal: The Social World as Object of and Influence on Appraisal Processes," in Scherer, Schorr, and Johnstone, *Appraisal Processes in Emotion*, 221–32, and Batja Mesquita and Phoebe Ellsworth, "The Role of Culture in Appraisal," in Scherer, Schorr, and Johnstone, *Appraisal Processes in Emotion*, 233–48.

56 Russell, "Core Affect and the Psychological Construction of Emotion," 149.

57 This may play an initial role in addictive behaviors. One's body can become addicted to the substance after the mind does. Changing addictive behaviors requires addressing both the emotional and the physical aspects related to the addictive substance.

58 A *mood* is a prolonged core affect without a specific Object, and *affect regulation* is action intended to alter or maintain one's core affect without reference to an Object. Russell, "Core Affect and the Psychological Construction of Emotion," 149. American psychoanalyst Christopher Bollas argues that affective Objects (though he does not use that term) originate as the "unthought known," or what feels like *home* to someone. Bollas means to highlight the importance of the earliest caregivers in creating what feels like home and what does not, or what feels familiar, pleasant, and valued or not. Bollas argues that people's sense of home begins in preverbal experience. Because parenting figures sustain and facilitate an infant's survival, they define the infant's world and teach the preverbal infant their own particular "logic" of life. Bollas, *Shadow of the Object*, 13–14. Again, the unthought known is familiar—homeostatic—but that does not mean it is life-giving.

59 While core affect can change without reference to any external stimulus, a stimulus can be perceived as having affective quality with no change in core affect. The example Russell gives is that of a depressed patient who can recognize that a sunset is beautiful but is still not able to alter a persistently depressed mood. Russell, "Core Affect and the Psychological Construction of Emotion," 149.

60 Perhaps this is not the best example. There is actually research that shows that eating sugar can reduce experiences of pain, and sugar drops are sometimes given to infants just before they are given a shot. Nicholas Bakalar, "Childhood: A Little Sugar Does Seem to Ease the Pain," *New York Times*, December 17, 2012, https://well.blogs.nytimes.com/2012/12/17/childhood-a-little-sugar-does-seem-to-ease-the-pain/. In general, however, consumerism has been shown to be a very poor affect regulator. Nevertheless, North Americans live

in a culture saturated with the belief that retail shopping is "therapeutic." In fact, North Americans have been told they have a "responsibility" to buy, as president George W. Bush suggested in order to provide economic and patriotic support for the Iraq war. Certainly, buying things does have an influence on mood, though the pleasant feelings are often short-lived and followed by remorse. Consuming is not a particularly effective way to deal with one's emotions.

61 Although the attribution seems correct to the attributor, research has shown many attributions to be incorrect. See Russell, "Core Affect and the Psychological Construction of Emotion," 149, and Barrett, *How Emotions Are Made*, 77 and 195.

62 This is not necessarily true for a feeling. Feelings are conscious interpretations of emotional episodes that are learned and are socially attributed to a particular change in core affect. Awareness of feelings can also change core affect in an open-loop system.

63 Barrett, *How Emotions Are Made*, 29.

64 Sometimes attributed affect is the result of the capacities for imagination: a woman feels sad for her friend because her friend's husband has died, and she can imagine losing her own husband. This is the dynamic that happens in the process of empathy.

65 While there are what Russell calls "prototypical" cases of "emotional episodes," such as fear and anger, it is because most human beings are taught to fear snakes and to be angry when they feel slighted. Prototypical episodes usually include a stimulus that is perceived in terms of affective quality (that is, pleasant or unpleasant, and arousing or not), and the alteration of the core affect enough to be registered at some level, though not always consciously. Russell argues that prototypical cases of emotion are not a random sample of all the cases of a particular emotion. Rather, "they are selected after the fact to resemble most closely the mental script of [for example] fear." Russell, "Core Affect and the Psychological Construction of Emotion," 166. Core affect is *attributed to the stimulus* (say, a snake, a piece of cake, or a green apple), which then becomes the affective Object. These attributes can be learned through past experiences, socialization, or are the result of reflexes or startle responses (which people often do at sudden surprise). A person then comes to believe that the Object is responsible for the way he or she feels in the moment. Beyond the immediate affect attribution (pleasant/not or arousing/not arousing), the perceptual-cognitive-evaluative processing of the Object (snakes, green apple) continues, drawing on memory and context and assessing such qualities as its relevance to one's desires, most significant needs or goals, and imagined future in relation to the affective Object. To add complexity to why certain emotions arise in a particular moment and not others, judgments and information congruent with the core affect are more accessible—the principle of mood congruency—than those that are incongruent. Russell, "Core Affect and the Psychological Construction of Emotion," 149–50.

66 Russell, "Core Affect and the Psychological Construction of Emotion," 150. The intensity of a core affective response (the degree of sympathetic and parasympathetic activation at a given moment) results in a perceived urgency to act that is independent of the specific action taken (the specific action being tailored to the particular situation at hand). Barrett, "Solving the Emotion Paradox," 31.

67 Remember that there is no expressive signal or pattern of autonomic nervous system (ANS) activity unique to each emotion.

68 Russell, "Core Affect and the Psychological Construction of Emotion."

69 There is good evidence that stress causes people to overeat fatty and sugary foods. See "Why Stress Causes People to Overeat," *Harvard Medical School Mental Health Letter*,

https://www.health.harvard.edu/staying-healthy/why-stress-causes-people-to-overeat. "Metacognitive judgments," or feelings about comfort foods, are made "hot" or "arousing" by the accompanying affective quality. Russell, "Core Affect and the Psychological Construction of Emotion," 150. Augustine intuitively knew this when he found he could not *will* himself to want or not want a particular thing—in his case, God—and avoid certain behaviors that he felt directed him away from God (see chapter 1 of this text for more on this).

70 Russell, "Core Affect and the Psychological Construction of Emotion," 150. Russell's term "emotional meta-experience" can be understood as one's "feelings" and the experience of them. Russell uses it technically to replace what he calls the "folk terms" for emotion used among lay people in a particular sociocultural context.

71 Russell, "Core Affect and the Psychological Construction of Emotion," 150.

72 Barrett, *How Emotions Are Made*, 145–51. Just as there are levels of description in which most or all human activity is universal, other levels bring out cultural and individual variability: for example, although eating is a universal human activity, eating sushi, insects, arugula, or fried pork rinds often varies by group membership. Russell, "My Psychological Constructionist Perspective," 185. Intercultural difference and intra-group norming can lead to emotional regulation, which is the deliberate attempt at self-control and other-control based on social and cultural expectations. Russell, "Core Affect and the Psychological Construction of Emotion," 150.

73 Russell, "My Psychological Constructionist Perspective," 188.

74 Russell, "My Psychological Constructionist Perspective," 200–201. See Figure 2 for a visual schematic depiction of these components.

75 Psychoanalytic theorist Christopher Bollas' work implies that we learn our worth and value in the attention (or lack thereof) our earliest caregivers provide and in the ways they provide it. See Bollas, *The Shadow of the Object*. The Ifaluk had to be "taught" to feel a lack of worth and shame when in the presence of a superior without a gift. Furthermore, not everyone will feel "put down" in a social hierarchy: some were taught by their caregivers to find clear power structures a relief. This helps explain, for example, why some women are "content" to be "subservient" to their husbands: it is their "place," and one they "gladly" accept. I argue in chapter 7 that the "anger" one might feel about a hierarchy has more to do with significant needs that are dismissed by that power structure than it does with the hierarchy itself. Supporting a similar idea, pastoral theologian Christie Neuger argues that value and truth claims must be carefully evaluated in light of love and justice because they have often been based on criteria "grounded in the order of power in culture." Christie Neuger, "Power and Difference in Pastoral Theology," in *Pastoral Care and Counseling: Redefining the Paradigms*, ed. Nancy J. Ramsay (Nashville: Abingdon, 2004), 66.

76 Russell, "My Psychological Constructionist Perspective," 202.

77 For every neural connection that brings sensory input from the thalamus to the cortex, there are ten feedback connections from the cortex to the thalamus, and this is true of other parts of the brain as well. The amount of data coming in is far outweighed by the amount that already exists in the brain, predicting what is coming. This is one of the ways the brain can filter and organize data input into "meaningful" and interpretable experience. Barrett, "Ten Misconceptions," 49.

78 It seems the brain is wired to pay attention to the unexpected and the novel. Emory University Health Sciences Center, "Human Brain Loves Surprises, Research Reveals,"

ScienceDaily 16 (2001), https://www.sciencedaily.com/releases/2001/04/010415224316.htm.

79 Barrett, *How Emotions Are Made*, 26–30, 60–66.

80 Barrett notes that much of what we hear, see, taste, smell, and touch is a *simulation* of the world based on the brain's prediction of what is happening. Thus, our perceptions are not reactions to some objective reality, but to what we expect given past experiences in similar situations. While this is a relatively new theory, Barrett asserts it is an important one for understanding how the brain functions and claims that "forward-looking thinkers speculate that simulation is a common mechanism not only for perception but for understanding language, feeling empathy, remembering, imagining, dreaming, and many other psychological phenomena." Barrett, *How Emotions Are Made*, 27. These predictive processes of the brain are likely at least part of the reason for implicit bias and may help explain the phenomena of racism, sexism, homophobia, and transphobia, for example.

81 Barrett, *How Emotions Are Made*, 29.

82 Research shows that judges in courtrooms often (mis)interpret their core affect as a "gut feeling" that the defendant cannot be trusted and might be tempted to make a ruling based on that. Barrett, *How Emotions Are Made*, 30. These processes have other unjust consequences as well, such as an implicit bias each person internalizes that might lead to the assumptions that young black men wearing hoodies in the streets at night are dangerous. This is something people are taught; it is not categorically true.

83 Barrett, *How Emotions Are Made*, 29.

84 Barrett, "Ten Misconceptions," 50. Barrett writes that "recent evidence demonstrates that even instances of the same 'superordinate category' (e.g., emotion) involve relatively different combinations of the same set of distributed brain networks." See also Oosterwijk, Touroutoglou, and Lindquist, et al., "The Neuroscience of Construction," 131.

85 Barrett, *How Emotions Are Made*, 30.

86 Remember that affective Objects are people, things, events/experiences, memories, and so on that have some meaning to the person for whom they are Objects. Not everyone has the same Objects: these are determined by past experiences and one's sociocultural environment. Indeed, psychological construction models understand all the data in the world like a sheet of pastry: composed of uncountable numbers of molecules that are in constant movement. A person's *concepts* and *perceptions* of affective Objects are like cookie cutters that carve boundaries, not because those boundaries (or categories and concepts) are natural, but because they are *useful and efficient in a particular social and cultural context*. Barrett, *How Emotions Are Made*, 29. Changing what one predicts and simulates by having new experiences can be an effective way to deal with trauma. See also, for example, pastoral theologian Christy Sim, *Survivor Care: What Religious Professionals Need to Know about Healing Trauma* (Nashville, Tenn.: Wesley's Foundery Books, 2019).

87 The differences in concepts or categories depend on differences in culture and the myriad varieties of personal experiences.

88 Barrett, *How Emotions Are Made*, 102–7. Angela R. Laird et al., "Behavioral Interpretations of Intrinsic Connectivity Networks," *Journal of Cognitive Neuroscience* 23, no. 12 (2011): 4022–37, found that the intrinsic connectivity between AI (anterior insula) and ACC (anterior cingulate cortex), two major nodes of the salience network (an intrinsically connected large-scale network in the brain anchored in the AI that detects and filters salient stimuli and recruits relevant neural networks), is linked to a variety of general psychological

processes such as language, executive function, and affective and interoceptive processes. See V. Menon, "Salience Network," in *Brain Mapping: An Encyclopedic Reference*, vol. 2, ed. Arthur W. Toga (New York: Elsevier, 2015), 597–611. This calls into question the traditional distinction between emotion and cognition. Cited in Oosterwijk, Touroutoglou, and Lindquist, et al., "The Neuroscience of Construction," 126–27. Similarly, William W. Seeley et al., "Dissociable Intrinsic Connectivity Networks for Salience Processing and Executive Control," *Journal of Neuroscience* 27, no. 9 (2007): 2349–56, found that parts of the AI and ACC overlapped with both the executive function and salience network, creating clusters, networks between clusters, and clusters of networks in the brain. Cited in Oosterwijk, Touroutoglou, and Lindquist, et al., "The Neuroscience of Construction," 128. These form neighborhood clusters with short connection lengths that allow for specializations in specific types of information processing as appropriate, while longer-length connectors coordinate the activities of various clusters, allowing the person as a holistic organism to coordinate the operation of clusters as they engage their environment. Herschbach and Bechtel, "Mental Mechanisms and Psychological Construction," 26.

89 If a reader is interested in the technical brain science of this model, see a summary in Oosterwijk, Touroutoglou, and Lindquist, et al., "The Neuroscience of Construction," 122–23. For a good overview that includes interesting meta-analysis of memory, perceptions and imagination, see Oosterwijk, Touroutoglou, and Lindquist, et al., "The Neuroscience of Construction," 113–14, where they suggest that there may be an executive function that directs the creation of an emotion. Others disagree. As James Russell puts it, the rejection of essentialism in a theory of emotion means that "no emotion, affect program, neural module, appraisal, act of labeling, conceptual acts, bolt of lightning, or the like, brings the ingredients together in all and only emotional episodes (of fear episodes, anger episodes, etc.)." Russell, "My Psychological Constructionist Perspective," 202. Well-known psychologist and emotions researcher Joseph LeDoux has weighed in on this debate. He maintains his position that there are some primitive neural networks that allow for basic or reflexive emotions/actions, but he avers that they are not separate from those that generate other emotions. He writes, "I am a constructionist when it comes to conscious emotional experiences (feelings), but more of a faculty psychology kind of guy when talking about survival circuits. In other words, I do think there are innate systems that are relevant to emotions, even if they do not directly make feelings." LeDoux, "Afterword," 461. Again, Russell disagrees, arguing that only a pure construction model can disrupt the essentializations that pertain in LeDoux's account. In Russell's model, then, the source of information that is prioritized is at the forefront of attention in any given moment and is made meaningful by using the other sources of information such as memory, perception, and cognition. Russell, "My Psychological Constructionist Perspective." Emotional episodes are events that *emerge* from the interplay of more basic processes. In this model, the mind is understood as a "conglomeration of these internal forces, many of which battle with each other for control or behavior." Barrett, "Construction as an Integrative Framework," 449–50. For example, when core affect is at the forefront of attention and is made meaningful using exteroceptive sensations and conceptualization, a person is said to be experiencing an emotion such as fear or anger. On the other hand, when exteroceptive sensations are at the forefront of attention and made meaningful using core affect and conceptualization, a person is said to be experiencing a perception. Finally, when representations of prior experiences are at the

forefront of attention and comprise representations of exteroceptive sensations and core affect, "a person is said to be having a memory about past core affective and exteroceptive sensations, or a thought about future core affective and exteroceptive sensations." Oosterwijk, Touroutoglou, and Lindquist, et al., "The Neuroscience of Construction," 116. All three sources are present in every moment; it is the "relative" weight given to the processes depending on contextual and situational factors that gives rise to unique subjective experiences. Oosterwijk, Touroutoglou, and Lindquist, et al., "The Neuroscience of Construction," 117.

90 A large number of these have recently been found in the gastrointestinal system, which may explain why we say "I have a gut feeling." Emily Underwood, "Your Gut Is Directly Connected to Your Brain, By a Newly Discovered Neuron Circuit," *Science*, September 20, 2018, https://www.sciencemag.org/news/2018/09/your-gut-directly-connected -your-brain-newly-discovered-neuron-circuit.

91 Barrett, "Solving the Emotion Paradox," 28–29.

92 Barrett, "Solving the Emotion Paradox," 33–34.

93 Widen, "The Development of Children's Concepts of Emotions."

94 Barrett, "Solving the Emotion Paradox," 34–35.

95 Barrett, "Solving the Emotion Paradox," 20–21.

96 Barrett, "Solving the Emotion Paradox," 27. Emphasis added.

97 A.D. ("Bud") Craig, "Interoception and Emotion: A Neuroanatomical Perspective," in Lewis, Haviland-Jones, and Barrett, *Handbook of Emotions*, 3rd ed., 272–92.

98 For example, the visual information about a man with whom a woman is interacting—such as what he looks like or the sound of his voice—comes to her attention and mingles with the memory of her past experiences of him ("He is a person I do not like much; seeing him makes me feel anxious"). It is immediately put in conjunction with somatovisceral information about her core affective state—that is, the current homeostatic state of systems in her body—in that moment. In addition, motor programs for interacting with that person ("I usually frown and walk away when I see him") combine in a pattern in the brain with systems for regulating one's own core affective behavior that become associated with unpleasant, high-arousal states—for example, facial movements, body movements, the edge in her voice, or her urge to eat green apples when encountering that man. To this pattern is given the label *fear*—which is the category and concept provided by her caregivers in the process of learning—and all of these components are bound together to form an instance of fear in the woman and inform her response to it.

99 Remember that the word *anger* is a commonly used folk term for a category that has been socially and culturally created and learned.

100 The resulting conceptual system of "fear," then, is a distributed collection of category-specific memories captured across all instances of that category. These establish the conceptual content for the basic-level category "anger" and can be retrieved for later simulations of "fear." Barrett, "Solving the Emotion Paradox," 34.

101 See note 86 of this chapter.

102 When conceptual knowledge about anger is primed by an aspect of sensory environment, by a motor action, or by a deliberate need to explain core affect, the simulator becomes active and generates a representation of anger that is tailored to the particular context or situation. For example, the anger simulator might simulate a state of core affect with yelling on one occasion, the core affect that leads to running on another, and the core affect associated with crying on yet another. All the experienced content for an anger episode

resides within the simulator for anger, so different combinations can be simulated as the situation requires. Barrett, "Solving the Emotion Paradox," 34. In the situation of a child throwing a toy, a parent or teacher might explicitly "train" the simulator to adjust for more-appropriate behaviors, such as "using one's words." This is very different from the way emotions were displayed in Disney/Pixar's popular movie *Inside Out*.

103 Barrett, "Solving the Emotion Paradox," 33.

104 Barrett, *How Emotions Are Made*, 35.

105 Barrett, "Solving the Emotion Paradox," 34.

106 Dedre Gentner and Susan Goldin-Meadow, eds., *Language in Mind* (Cambridge, Mass.: MIT Press, 2003). Cited in Barrett, "Solving the Emotion Paradox," 34–35.

107 Widen, "The Development of Children's Concepts of Emotions."

108 Barrett, "Solving the Emotion Paradox," 34. Emphasis in the original. Barrett notes that the same process occurs as people learn colors as children. For example, the information hitting the retina is the same (light at 450 nm) and the detection of that wavelength is dictated by what the visual system produces in its early stages of processing. The experience of color that corresponds to this wavelength depends on the conceptualization of the sensory information. Depending on what a person has learned about color, he or she may see blue, navy blue, or even green. Barrett, "Solving the Emotion Paradox," 28.

109 Barrett, "Solving the Emotion Paradox," 35. In Barrett's work, the word *perception* refers to the process of assigning someone (or his or her behavior) to a meaningful category so that a perceiver "sees" an instance of that category and can infer something about the person's internal state or enduring disposition or both. In essence, perception refers to the process of conceptualization, akin to Russell's Objects. In the process of perceiving someone, then, their actions are categorized into discrete and meaningful behaviors, and the person is categorized as to what kind of person he or she is (the "concept" of that person). The general idea is that our knowledge of people and situations automatically and effortlessly shapes what we "see" people doing and gives rise to our explanations for that behavior as well as our feelings about them. In a sense, the study of perception is the study of theory of mind: understanding how the categorization process allows people to attribute mental states to identify, explain, and predict behavior. Barrett, "Solving the Emotion Paradox," 28. See also Eleanor Rosch, "Cognitive Representations of Semantic Categories," *Journal of Experimental Psychology: General*, 104, no. 3 (1975): 192–233. Cited in Russell, "My Psychological Constructionist Perspective," 204. Remember that Russell does not consider reflexes emotions. Russell, "My Psychological Constructionist Perspective," 202. Others agree (though, perhaps, for different reasons). Roberts, "What an Emotion Is," 184. Even in contemporary parlance these general terms' meanings are debated, and arguments for a particular emotion's inclusion or exclusion in a list of widely agreed-upon emotions sometimes defy clear logic. For example, Rene Descartes named forty-one passions, Thomas Hobbes forty-six, Baruch Spinoza forty-eight, and David Hume roughly twenty. Nineteenth- and twentieth-century philosophical lists of emotions are even longer: James McCosh listed over one hundred. Dixon, *Passions to Emotions*, 18. The debate continues with little agreement on how many passions/emotions should be included, and which ones: contemporary philosopher Amelie Rorty's list of emotions includes fear, religious awe, exuberant delight, pity, loving emotion, panic, pride, remorse, and indignation. Contemporary philosopher Robert Solomon includes on his list duty, indifference, faith, friendship, and innocence. Twentieth-century philosopher Gilbert Ryle allows avarice, patriotism, and loyalty, and still another offers

embarrassment, anger, shame, envy, gratitude, hope, anxiety, jealousy, grief, despair, remorse, joy, and resentment. Cited in Robert C. Roberts, *Emotions: An Essay in Aid of Moral Psychology* (Cambridge: Cambridge University Press, 2003), 64–68. Much of this confusion is the result of philosophy, theory, and research on emotions that began in early Greek philosophy that people now hold as intuition and common sense: indeed, these ideas have "gravitational pull." Russell, "My Psychological Constructionist Perspective," 203. A more helpful designation for what is an "emotion," then, is whatever one's sociocultural context says it is. Russell, "My Psychological Constructionist Perspective," 183.

110 Barrett, "Are Emotions Natural Kinds?"
111 Lisa A. Feldman, "Valence as a Basic Building Block of Emotional Life," *Journal of Research in Personality* 40, no. 1 (2006): 35–55. She is now known as Lisa Feldman Barrett.
112 For helpful treatments of the relationship of culture to emotions, see, for example, Batja Mesquita, "Emotions as Dynamic Cultural Phenomena," in *Handbook of Affective Sciences*, ed. Richard J. Davidson, Klaus R. Scherer, and H. Hill Goldsmith (Oxford: Oxford University Press, 2003), 871–90, and also Batja Mesquita and Robert Walker, "Cultural Differences in Emotions: A Context for Interpreting Emotional Experiences," *Behaviour Research and Therapy* 41, no. 7 (2003): 777–93.
113 Feldman reports that all people, without exception, are able to distinguish feeling good from feeling bad, but the same is not true of feeling aroused or sleepy; most, but not all, individuals can characterize themselves as energized or enervated. Lisa A. Feldman, "Valence Focus and Arousal Focus: Individual Differences in the Structure of Affective Experience," *Journal of Personality and Social Psychology* 69, no. 1 (1995).
114 Barrett notes that contrary to popular belief, it is "far from clear" that everyone (or every culture) experiences anger, sadness, fear, and so on, as necessarily or qualitatively different emotional states. Barrett, "Solving the Emotion Paradox," 24. See also Russell, "My Psychological Constructionist Perspective," 189, for a chart summarizing the critiques of basic-emotions theories.
115 Psychologist David Leary argues that understanding the sociohistorical context of "emotional terms" is essential if we are to know "not just *that* [language and] metaphors play an important role in [emotions], but why *this* or *that* particular metaphor plays *this* or *that* role at *this* or *that* time and in *this* or *that* place." David E. Leary, "Metaphor, Theory, and Practice in the History of Psychology," in *Metaphors in the History of Psychology*, ed. David E. Leary, (Cambridge: Cambridge University Press, 1990), 357–67. Emphasis added in first instance, in original in all others.
116 This does not mean that the person undergoing the emotional episode necessarily calls it emotional—just that someone else would. Russell, "My Psychological Constructionist Perspective," 201.
117 Russell argues that because the word *emotion* covers so many kinds of things, the term *emotional episode* is more accurate. He notes that because an emotional episode is any short-term episode that we call *emotional* and *emotion* is a folk term that includes dispositions, attitudes, occurrent events, and so on, the category of *emotional episode* is narrower and more tractable than the category of *emotion*. Russell, "My Psychological Constructionist Perspective," 200. Russell writes, "Emotional episodes are simply an especially interesting and important subset of human [mental] episodes, such as houses are an

interesting and important subset of physical systems." Russell, "My Psychological Constructionist Perspective," 205.

118 Lisa Feldman Barrett, "Psychological Construction: A Darwinian Approach to the Science of Emotions," *Emotion Review* 5, no. 4 (2013): 379–89.

119 Barrett, "Emotions Are Real."

120 As I argue in chapter 7, I understand well-being and flourishing to indicate something more complex than mere survival.

121 This is Nussbaum's primary reason for valuing emotions. See Nussbaum, *Upheavals of Thought*, 43. See also Michael Stocker, "How Emotions Reveal Value," in *Valuing Emotions*, ed. Michael Stocker with Elizabeth Hegeman (Cambridge: Cambridge University Press, 1996), 56–87. However, as I argue in the next chapter, what individuals or groups consider "well-being" must be critically examined in order for emotions and the feelings and behaviors that often accompany them to be used toward flourishing.

122 Russell, "Core Affect and the Psychological Construction of Emotion," 148.

123 Michael Davis and Paul Whalen, "The Amygdala: Vigilance and Emotion," *Molecular Psychiatry* 6, no. 1 (2001): 13–34. Cited in Barrett, "Solving the Emotion Paradox," 31.

124 John A. Bargh and Melissa J. Ferguson, "Beyond Behaviorism: On the Automaticity of Higher Mental Processes," *Psychological Bulletin* 126, no. 6 (2000): 925–45. Cited in Barrett, "Solving the Emotion Paradox," 31.

125 Carl Rogers, "A Theory of Therapy, Personality, and Interpersonal Relationships, as Developed from the Client-Centered Framework," in *Psychology: A Study of Science*, vol. 3, ed. S. Koch (New York: McGraw-Hill, 1959), 184–256.

126 Bargh and Ferguson, "Beyond Behaviorism."

127 Paula M. Niedenthal et al., "Embodiment in Attitudes, Social Perception, and Emotion," *Personality and Social Psychology Review* 9, no. 3 (2005): 184–211. Cited in Barrett, "Solving the Emotion Paradox."

7 Emotions as Crucial

1 Here I want to make clear that I am not referring to "keeping together" as only white, middle-class, educated folk. Or as United States citizens. Or as North Americans. Or as the globalized "monied" class. I mean that only keeping together as all humans—indeed, as all living things in the world, from trees and amoebae to all mammals, including humans—can ensure our collective well-being. We are *all* in this together, and we *all* need to recognize that and behave as such, as I argue in this final chapter.

2 In fact, recent books including those by pastoral theologians Bruce Rogers-Vaughn and Ryan LaMothe highlight the destructive elements of capitalism and neoliberalism to social well-being and the "muting and mutating" of suffering. Rogers-Vaughn, *Caring for Souls in a Neoliberal Age*, 139. Rogers-Vaughn refers to "third order suffering," by which he means the suffering that derives from "neoliberalization"—a highly efficient regime for the global production of suffering and the subsequent privatization of death and violence. Rogers-Vaughn contends that contemporary neoliberalism and its primary tool, capitalism, exacerbates the sufferings of entire populations of people and that it shapes the ways we attend to, ignore, or legitimate suffering. "Neoliberalization" is creating a new third order of suffering that both coexists with and transforms first-order or "existential" suffering (related to the universals of death, loss, grief, pain, and anxiety, especially regarding separation and limits of people's control) and second-order suffering, or the suffering produced by human evil, "whether individual or collective, direct or indirect" (that is, the outcome of social oppression and the abuse of our human vulnerabilities), making their

present forms more difficult to recognize. Rogers-Vaughn, *Caring for Souls in a Neoliberal Age*, 182–84 and 126. Third-order suffering is difficult and "perhaps impossible" to identify (126). It is the result of the marginalization and corruption of already-existing forms of suffering. It is a "corruption of a corruption." His example is racism, whose "older" practices and ideologies (creating second-order suffering), are not gone but rather "have been transformed, mutated, and recycled and have taken on new and in many instances more covert modes of expression." Henry Giroux, *America on the Edge: Henry Giroux on Politics, Culture, and Education* (New York: Palgrave Macmillan, 2006), 60. Cited in Rogers-Vaughn, *Caring for Souls in a Neoliberal Age*, 140. In third-order suffering, the enemy that used to be understood as outside (the government, people who are racist, etc.) is either so amorphous that it is nowhere (out in the "fog") or assumed to be inside those who are suffering. Rogers-Vaughn, *Caring for Souls in a Neoliberal Age, 127*. For this reason, Rogers-Vaughn argues, it is difficult to care for those experiencing third-order suffering. This is, in part, because those who seek to support people's flourishing do not take into sufficient account the ways capitalism and other forms of neoliberalism are "principal source(s)" of human (third-order) suffering but also those who *are* suffering cannot identify its source. Rogers-Vaughn, "Powers and Principalities," 71.

3 Turkish psychoanalytic theorist Vamik Volkan argues that early in their development, children identify with the individuals closest to them. Initially, a child's "group" is small, composed of immediate caregivers, which begins the bias toward their own kind. Vamik Volkan, *Immigrants and Refugees: Trauma, Perennial Mourning, Prejudice, and Border Psychology* (London: Karnac Books, 2017), 85. The sense of belonging to a larger group identity develops later in childhood, after children slowly stop being "generalists." That is, very young children do not understand that there are differentiators between people in regard to gender, class, race, and so on, or what meaning those differentiators have been socioculturally given. To very young children we are all indistinguishable outside of the sense of familiarity to caregivers. Children learn to identify with the cultural markers of their personal transformational objects as they accumulate years. Indeed, as one's sense of *home* develops in the context of a caregiver's idiom, so does the increasingly exclusive sense of it: it is when the sense of "us vs. them" begins. Although having "enemies" is a typical part of human experience—it is a way of creating boundaries and place between oneself and another—"enemies" are often the repositories of unwanted idioms of being and doing and are projections of unclaimed parts of oneself (Volkan, *Immigrants and Refugees*, 99). Thus, what people "have their hearts set on" as Augustine put it—what I have also called one's sense of "home"—must be critically examined in light of a flourishing life.

4 See chapter 6 for a discussion of the terms *emotion* and *feeling*.

5 Augustine, *Confessions* 1.1. There is a long and rich religious tradition of reflecting on what is salvific (for example, Christian theologians refer to the "fruits of the spirit of salvation" such as our love of the other, of the world, and of God) and what is death dealing (or, to use Christian language, sin). Jewish and Christian theologians argue that death-dealing ways of life include idolatry—or allowing the mundane to stand in for the eternal—and anything that disrupts our sense of interdependence and mutual responsibility. Drawing on these (usually religious) traditions can be useful, though one must be wary of them as well, examining critically their understandings of flourishing and its impediments. Not all elements of all traditions are life-giving.

6 For discussion of the considerations in different translations, see Cooper, *Reason and Human Good in Aristotle*.

7 I have explored this, at least implicitly, in almost everything I have written or taught, but I want to be more explicit here. For example, see McClure, "Pastoral Theology as the Art of Paying Attention."

8 While the "good life" was the goal of early philosophers and theologians, I will argue for the higher value of "well-being" or "flourishing" for a number of reasons. Not least of these is that the "good life" primarily indicated the ethical or moral life, and I seek to propose an understanding of emotions that contributes certainly to an ethical and moral life, but also to a personally, interpersonally, organizationally, and socially, culturally, and politically meaningful one. I also prefer the term *flourishing* because I think it encompasses feelings and expressions of zest and joyfulness that *well-being* may not convey as effectively.

9 MacLean, *Triune Brain in Evolution*, 82.

10 As noted earlier, Erik Erikson claimed Freud said this, but there seems to be no written record of it.

11 There is a distinction between "institutions" and "organizations," though organizations are kinds of institutions. Institutions include transpersonal systems that embody beliefs, values, habits, and practices, including the institutions of racism, sexism, or transphobia. Obviously, institutions have effects on individuals and groups. Organizations are institutions that also indicate a particular material, physical history, or group identity, such as "the Anglican Church," "Wells Fargo Bank," or "Facebook."

   In some cases, scientists have proposed ways emotions function at each of these levels, but they too have generally left implicit their assumptions about what is a flourishing life. There are exceptions, as recognized in a previous note. E. O. Wilson has used science to argue for an environmental and social ethic. See Wilson, *Genesis*, and Wilson, *The Meaning of Human Existence*. Likewise, neuroscientist Lisa Feldman Barrett seems to have an interest in the implications of emotions for contemporary life. Two chapters toward the end of her book are entitled "Emotion and Illness," and "Emotion and Law," the latter being especially concerned with issues of justice. See Barrett, *How Emotions Are Made*. Aristotle also argued that judges should be put into an "emotional condition" because feelings cause changes in judgment. See Fortenbaugh, "Aristotle and Theophrastus on the Emotions," 35.

12 Pastoral theologians' primary endeavor is to reflect critically and analytically about the human condition and people's experiences—especially those of pain and suffering—and to make normative proposals for the betterment of people and their worlds. As pastoral theologian Larry K. Graham writes, the goal of pastoral theology and its practices is to attend to people's souls, their psyches, their relationships, and their sociocultural contexts as well in order to care in ways that alleviate what is life-limiting. Larry K. Graham, *Care of Persons, Care of Worlds: A Psychosystems Approach to Pastoral Care and Counseling* (Nashville: Abingdon, 1992).

13 Pastoral theologians' operative understandings of happiness, the good life, and well-being are at least implicitly informed by the concept of eudaimonia, *whether or not they have read early philosophers on the topic*.

14 Belliotti, *Happiness Is Overrated*, 6.

15 Belliotti, *Happiness Is Overrated*, 14.

16 For example, if someone were to assert that she is healthy because she feels good but was found to have an as-yet-undetected serious tumor, she would objectively not be healthy.

One's community must affirm that she is well, defining what they mean by the term. (For example, she might be deemed physically ill because of the tumor, but spiritually and emotionally healthy by other measures.) In addition, historically developed understanding of what well-being entails must also be included in the assessment.

17 Nicholas White, *A Brief History of Happiness* (Malden, Mass.: Blackwell, 2006), 83–84.

18 Princeton University philosopher John M. Cooper argues that articulating the nature and means toward eudaimonia as a way of life was early Greco-Roman philosophers' primary goal. Cooper, *Pursuits of Wisdom*.

19 Belliotti, *Happiness Is Overrated*, 19.

20 John M. Cooper, "Eudaimonism, The Appeal to Nature, and 'Moral Duty' in Stoicism," in *Aristotle, Kant, and the Stoics: Rethinking Happiness and Duty*, ed. Stephen Engstrom and Jennifer Whiting (New York: Cambridge University Press, 1996), 275–78. Immanuel Kant would diverge from the understanding of happiness as the telos of life and focus on the importance of duty, although he did argue that it is everyone's duty to promote the happiness of other people. McGill, *Idea of Happiness*, 91 and 183.

21 Luc Ferry, *What Is the Good Life?* trans. Lydia G. Cochrane (Chicago: University of Chicago Press, 2005), 201–6.

22 The Stoics invented the happiness quotient: divide what you have by what you want. The higher the number that results, the happier you will be.

23 Belliotti, *Happiness Is Overrated*, 22. Clearly, many contemporary appropriations of Epicurus' work misunderstand his philosophy.

24 In this, elements of the Epicureans and Stoics resemble certain aspects of Buddhism. Ferry, *What Is the Good Life?* 171. Indeed, one of the "noble Truths" of Buddhism declares that life is suffering and suffering comes from passion (desire), which is eliminable.

25 White, *A Brief History of Happiness*, 144–47.

26 Belliotti, *Happiness Is Overrated*, 24.

27 White, *A Brief History of Happiness*, 62–65.

28 Aristotle is considered the father of modern ethics. The virtues are those mature capacities that seem to be ubiquitous across cultures, that generally do not hurt others, that are pursued for their own sake (rather than being a means to an end), and that are witnessed to or argued for in sacred texts. See, for example, Miroslav Volf's *Flourishing*, especially chapter 4, for a discussion of the important contributions of world religions to articulations of flourishing. Miroslav Volf, *Flourishing: Why We Need Religion in a Globalized World* (New Haven: Yale University Press, 2015). Volf is not as critical as I would wish about the view of flourishing world religions (and their followers) promote.

29 Belliotti, *Happiness Is Overrated*, 12.

30 Belliotti, *Happiness Is Overrated*, 12.

31 Remember that Aristotle did not believe that all people could accomplish genuine well-being. For example, he thought that women and enslaved people lack the rational capacities—as well as the freedom, leisure time, and material well-being—to achieve it. Rather than accept Aristotle's essentialist and negative assumptions about these groups of people, however, we might investigate in what ways systemic oppressions *prevent* the freedom, leisure, and material security (the living well and faring well) that are important to flourishing.

32 Belliotti, *Happiness Is Overrated*, 34.

33 Or rather "salvation" in Christian language—usually understood as believing in and following God as revealed through the life of Jesus Christ as found in the Christian Scriptures.

34 Plotinus merges a Platonic base—the celebration of immateriality, perfection, immutability, firm foundations, a higher reality, and complete fulfillment—with the One understood as a personal God as Christian theology developed. In this view, human beings achieve happiness only in relation to this highest being, as modeled in the life of Jesus Christ. Plotinus imagined that Christians find only imperfect happiness on earth but have the hope of happiness in the life beyond. Plotinus also believed that people are largely responsible for happiness through their own efforts: by "cutting away" from the body and turning to the One, or God. McGill, *The Idea of Happiness*, 58.

35 McGill, *The Idea of Happiness*.

36 Psychologists call this cycle the "hedonic treadmill": comparing many kinds of human pleasure seeking to the activity of a hamster on its wheel, running hard but getting nowhere. That is, as soon as a person satisfies one desire, another arises to take its place, creating an unending cycle. Joel J. Kupperman, *Six Myths about the Good Life: Thinking about What Has Value* (Indianapolis: Hackett, 2006), 11.

37 I want to make clear a distinction between pain and suffering. The first may support well-being if engaged in certain ways. The latter likely impedes it, a claim also made by Aristotle.

38 This does not adequately account for those people in the world who have lived or continue to live with unbearable amounts and forms of suffering. Surely one's personal experience of suffering and one's sense of what is bearable ought to be decided, at least in part, by each individual.

39 This is the title of philosopher Raymond Belliotti's book on ancient philosophies of eudaimonia. Indeed, much has been written in the last thirty years about "happiness" and its limits. See the following notes for some of the discussion.

40 Some more recent scholars such as the nineteenth-century English philosopher John Stuart Mill reiterated the importance of avoiding suffering for the happy life in his book *Utilitarianism* (1863; repr., Indianapolis: Hackett, 2001). Utilitarianism is a "continuation" of ancient hedonism, with some innovations: the good, or happiness, is still a favorable balance of pleasure over pain, but the ultimate goal of utilitarianism is not the greatest amount of pleasure for the individual but maximum pleasure for the greatest number. McGill, *The Idea of Happiness*, 119.

41 This is a thought experiment popular among some early philosophers including Socrates. McGill, *The Idea of Happiness*.

42 This exercise challenges the felicity of the hedonic treadmill.

43 Indeed, the idea of "happiness" has been severely critiqued of late. For example, the ideologies of capitalism and prosperity theologies that promote consumerism as fundamental to happiness and signs of being "blessed" have been challenged. One example of this is Lauren Berlant's book, *Cruel Optimism*, which calls the hopes for socioeconomic success among those struggling on the underside of neoliberalism and capitalism a kind of "cruel optimism." She worries that "cruel attachments" to ideals such as "happiness" and "success" (defined in emotional and economic terms that value optimism, good behavior, and hard work) set the stage for deep disappointment and lead to hopelessness given the current socioeconomic and political structures that prevail in the developed world—unjust political and economic systems that prevent the well-being of the oppressed, no matter

how hard they work to succeed. (Hence the term "the working poor" to describe people who work very hard but never get ahead). Lauren Berlant, *Cruel Optimism* (Durham, N.C.: Duke University Press, 2011), 24. Similarly, philosopher and cultural critic Sara Ahmed challenges the assumptions that we will be made happy by participating in the good life or by living our lives the right way, or that certain lifestyles make us "worthy" of happiness while others render us ineligible. By exploring the plight of the "feminist killjoy," the "unhappy queer," the "angry black woman," and the "melancholic migrant," Ahmed makes clear the ways the ideal of "happiness" is used to oppress minority groups and dismiss their real needs. Ahmed, *Promise of Happiness*. Ahmed argues for the right to be unhappy as a sign of political will and freedom, given that "happiness," as she reads it, is conditional to "proper subjectivity" and behavior within heteronormative and multicultural societies. (I agree.) Further, in her essay "Multiculturalism and the Promise of Happiness," Ahmed argues that "we need to think more critically about how cultural differences are associated with different affects" and how certain affective expectations serve to maintain unjust systems. Sara Ahmed, "Multiculturalism and the Promise of Happiness," *New Formations* 63, no. 63 (2007/2008): 129. She goes on to suggest that "unhappy effects" give an "alternative set of imaginings of what might count as a good or at least better life. If injustice does have unhappy effects, then the story does not end there. Unhappiness is not our end point. . . . We might want to reread the melancholic subject, the one who refuses to let go of suffering, and who is even prepared to kill some forms of joy, as offering an alternative social promise." Ahmed, "Multiculturalism," 135. I wholeheartedly agree with both Berlant and Ahmed, and argue this in the following pages. While these critiques are salient, however, they may not recognize the nuances in the differences between happiness and flourishing as carefully as I would hope.

44 Self-assessment can be inaccurate: imagine, for example, a middle-aged, deeply delusional man who is convinced he is Napoleon and derives great joy from contemplating his past victories in war. See Belliotti, *Happiness Is Overrated*, 71, for these and other examples.

45 See Martin Seligman, *Flourish: A Visionary New Understanding of Happiness and Well-Being* (New York: Free Press, 2011), 13. Seligman's work has been criticized for over-emphasizing the subjective experience of "happiness" in the past. In my view, it is a fair critique of his early work, especially *Learned Optimism: How to Change Your Mind and Your Life* (1990; repr., New York: Vintage Books/Random House, 2006) and *Authentic Happiness: Using the New Positive Psychology to Realize Your Potential for Lasting Fulfillment* (New York: Atria/Simon & Schuster, 2002). For example, sociologist Barbara Ehrenreich suggests that "negative" feelings can have a positive function and that "happiness" is a tyranny. Barbara Ehrenreich, *Smile or Die: How Positive Thinking Fooled America and the World* (London: Granta Books, 2010). Another social critic, William Davies, argues that happiness science (in which he includes positive psychology) presents itself as "radically new, ushering in a fresh start, through which the pains, politics and contradictions of the past can be overcome." Davies, *Happiness Industry*. Davies writes that he does not wish to denigrate the "ethical value" of happiness or trivialize the pain of those who suffer from "chronic unhappiness"; rather, Davies seeks to examine the "entangling of hope and joy within infrastructures of measurement, surveillance and government" and the strongly materialist, competitive values of capitalism that promote happiness and other emotions as the product of consumerism. Davies, *Happiness Industry*, 6. With these cautions in mind, however, it has also been shown that "positive" or pleasant emotions improve

problem solving and increase people's abilities to be flexible, creative, and efficient. See, for example, Barbara L. Fredrickson, "The Role of Positive Emotions in Positive Psychology: The Broaden-and-Build Theory of Positive Emotions," *American Psychologist* 56, no. 3 (2001): 218–26. Frederickson suggests that the "playful creativity associated with emotions like joy and interest motivate people to learn and achieve more than they otherwise would, which helps them to accrue future personal and social resources." Cited in Leslie S. Greenberg, "Emotion-Focused Therapy," *Clinical Psychology and Psychotherapy* 11, no. 1 (2004): 4.

46 Ed Diener, Shigehiro Oishi, and Richard E. Lucas, "Personality, Culture, and Subjective Well-Being: Emotional and Cognitive Evaluations of Life," *Annual Review of Psychology* 54, no. 1 (2003): 403–25.

47 Seligman, *Flourish*, 30.

48 Most people would prefer to be feeling creatures, even if it is unpleasant at times. Maya Tamir, "What Do People Want to Feel and Why? Pleasure and Utility in Emotion Regulation," *Current Directions in Psychological Science* 18, no. 2 (2009): 101–5. Cited in Russell, "My Psychological Constructionist Perspective," 200.

49 Empirical research suggests this. Seligman, *Flourish*, 30.

50 German philosopher Martin Heidegger argued that engaging caring is a mark of being human and emotions (moods) are aspects of what it means to be alive and in the world. See "Care," 2.2.7, in "Martin Heidegger," *Stanford Encyclopedia of Philosophy*, https://plato .stanford.edu/entries/heidegger/. I have argued elsewhere that participation in the Good, or the Life of God (broadly defined), is an important part of a well-developed theological anthropology (that is, what it means to be human). See Barbara J. McClure, *Moving beyond Individualism*. Participation in the life of "God" (understood as what is ultimately beautiful, good, just, and loving; see note 86, this chapter, for an explanation of this nomenclature) need not be grand: there are myriad ways to participate in it, from genuinely caring for oneself, to caring for others, ultimately to caring about and for the whole.

51 Seligman, *Flourish*, 60. This understanding requires a polis that encourages and allows all people agency, for example, toward exploration, expression, and creativity. However, current sociocultural, political, and economic structures constrain certain people and groups, preventing the pursuit of their most significant needs and desires.

52 The existentialist philosopher Friedrich Nietzsche understood a goal of happiness based on pleasure or the avoidance of suffering to be misguided thinking. He advocated for a highly creative, constantly changing life, which necessitates loss and anticipates emotions such as grief, frustration, and anger. Nietzsche argued that only fools and hypocrites want to eliminate the emotions, though much of what he says about particular emotions is "sharply critical and negative." Solomon, "Nietzsche and the Emotions," 134 and 136.

53 There are some interesting recent theological reflections on the importance of joy. See, for example, Mary Clark Moschella, *Caring for Joy: Narrative, Theology, and Practice* (Boston: Brill Academic Publishers, 2016).

54 Some of these examples are found in Seligman, *Flourish*, 53. It is possible that high achievers such as these (who are known not to have been "strikingly happy") demanded too much of themselves, saw reality too clearly, were unable to harbor self-flattering illusions, could not savor their feelings of pleasure, lacked the necessary biochemistry, or were "too heroic" to be happy. Meaningful lives, then, are not necessarily happy lives and are perhaps not what we want to claim as the ideal. Belliotti, *Happiness Is Overrated*, 49.

55 This begs the question about the relationship between melancholy and creativity, but that is a discussion for another project.

56 While "negative" or "unpleasant" feelings can have a positive function, and pressure to exhibit "happiness" can be a tyranny, as noted in earlier notes, I agree with those who count the *experience* of well-being and joy as important for the full understanding of flourishing. The idea of well-being may be contentment and a sense of meaning, but flourishing surely invokes the idea of joy.

57 Psychologist John Gottman argues that contempt is the surest indicator that an intimate relationship will likely end in divorce. John Gottman, *Why Marriages Succeed or Fail: And How You Can Make Yours Last* (New York: Simon & Schuster, 1994). It is important to note that these feelings may be motivations to activate change, and if they are, they are positive emotions, even if they are "unpleasant." See, for example, the work of Miguel De La Torre, whose book *Embracing Hopelessness* is an examination of the ways that hoping in the promise for something better in an unceasingly unjust system has been an illusion that has functioned to keep the oppressed in their place and maintain the unjust status quo. Hopelessness should be valued, De La Torre argues, because it may lead to radically liberative praxis and activate resistance to the system, quite literally overturning it so that opportunities might arise that can lead to a more just situation. De La Torre warns, however, that such acts of defiance usually lead to crucifixion (in reference to Jesus of Nazareth's murder). Nevertheless, feelings of hopelessness and the radical resistance they engender may be the only thing that can save us all, De La Torre suggests. See Miguel De La Torre, *Embracing Hopelessness* (Minneapolis: Fortress, 2017). Still, though De La Torre argues for the value of hopelessness, his work argues for the importance of a just system and at least *implies* that well-being should be available to all. I agree and dare suggest that more hope might emerge in such a world. Chronic hopelessness, then, seems to be what De La Torre is arguing against.

58 Here I am reminded of the classic essay by feminist theologian Valerie Saiving Goldstein, who challenged the thinking of prominent twentieth-century theologians such as Anders Nygren and Reinhold Niebuhr who suggested that *hubris*, or pride, is the gravest sin. Saiving Goldstein suggested that while this may be the case for white men and other privileged, dominant groups, it is not the case for those at the underside of history and representation, such as women (and other oppressed groups). For them, Saiving Goldstein noted, self-abnegation or the denial of the ontological value of one's self and one's life may be the gravest sin. Valerie Saiving Goldstein, "The Human Situation: A Feminine View," *The Journal of Religion* 40, no. 2 (1960): 100–112.

59 This is Aristotle's thinking. Seligman likens well-being to the idea of weather in meteorology: Weather is not in and of itself a thing. Rather, several elements contribute to weather, including temperature, level of humidity, wind speed, barometric pressure, and so on. Seligman, *Flourish*, 15. As noted in chapter 6, this is consistent with psychological constructionist understandings of emotions.

60 This echoes Aristotle's view of the importance of finding eudaimonia in the median of virtues; the extremes of anything, Aristotle argued, diminish the good life. Seligman, too, argues for the goal that people integrate the qualities of the good life in their own contexts. Flourishing people are not so much heroic as they are well suited for their environments, he suggests. They are typically sociable and vigorous but enjoy solitude as well. They are assertive but not aggressive, open to experience but not mercurial, have dreams and fantasies and illusions but also have a helpful perspective on reality. See

Seligman, *Flourish,* chapter 1. Seligman's view does not critique the nature of "their own contexts" as well as I would hope. Human flourishing cannot be divorced from just legal, economic, and political systems.

61 In the endnotes, see brief summaries the work of Sara Ahmed, Ann Cvetkovich, Barbara Ehrenreich, or Miguel De La Torre for examples of this line of thinking.

62 The particular shape of these components will vary by circumstance. For example, the opportunity to partner with the person of one's choosing might be a particular value in the United States, while being partnered well with a person of one's family's choosing might be the goal in other countries (as in parts of India).

63 Laura L. Carstensen, Monisha Pasupathi, Ulrich Mayr, and John R. Nesselroade, "Emotional Experience in Everyday Life Across the Adult Life Span," *Journal of Personality and Social Psychology* 79, no. 4 (2000): 644–55. This could include work, as in one's vocation. However, not all people have the opportunities for vocation as meaningful work. Still, there are many ways each of us can contribute to the good of the whole and thus live out the highest values of love, justice, and care. See practical theologian Brian Hall's treatment of a developmental schema of values, including one's "high-order values" ("vision values" such as global ecological harmony) vs. "lower-order" foundation values such as one's safety and security. See Hall, *Values Shift* for more.

64 Although I cannot explore it in depth here, my understanding of what is required for human flourishing includes healthy families (broadly defined), groups, teams, organizations, and global systems. For more of my perspective on this, see McClure, *Moving beyond Individualism,* 218–22. Emotions can aid in that endeavor, though the way forward will have to be more critically analytical of emotions and of the organizations we are in than the popular invocation of "emotional intelligence" recommends. There are some hopeful treatments of more life-giving organizations that "do well by doing good." See, for example, John Mackey and Rajendra Sisodia, *Conscious Capitalism: Liberating the Heroic Side of Business* (Cambridge, Mass.: Harvard Business School Publishing Corp., 2013); Rajendra Sisodia, Jagdish N. Seth, and David Wolfe, *Firms of Endearment: How World-Class Companies Profit from Passion and Purpose* (Upper Saddle River, N.J.: Pearson Education, 2014); and Rajendra Sisodia and Michael J. Gelb, *The Healing Organization: Awakening the Conscience of Business to Help Save the World* (New York: HarperCollins Leadership, 2019). As with all claims of "doing good," I would want the perspectives in these books to be held against the standard of flourishing I am proposing here. I leave to another time reflection on whether I think capitalism is the most life-giving and sustainable economic system; suffice it to say here that I am agnostic on the question.

65 I have argued that participation in something positive, that matters, and which benefits the whole is a significant part of what it means to be human. When we are not so engaged, it detracts from our humanness and, thus, our sense of flourishing. See McClure, *Moving beyond Individualism,* 231–34.

66 Pastoral theologian Mary Clark Moschella suggests joy as an important outcome of caring work, for both the caregiver and the care receiver. See Moschella, *Caring for Joy.*

67 Faith, it has been argued, is forged in the earliest life experiences: being loved, held securely, and cared for by guardians and communities. The idea of "faith" as explored here does not have prescribed content, but rather is a *capacity.* Faith assists people in their search for meaning and in their pursuit of "abundant life." See *Human Development and Faith: Life-Cycle Stages of Body, Mind, and Soul,* ed. Felicity B. Kelcourse (St. Louis: Chalice Press, 2004), 27, and Roy H. Steinhoffsmith, "Infancy: Faith before Language,"

in *Human Development and Faith*, ed. Felicity B. Kelcourse (St. Louis: Chalice Press, 2004), 129–46. On faith, see Kelcourse, *Human Development and Faith*, 1. Pastoral theologian Howard Clinebell understood one's positive relationship with the earth as a sign of faith and an important goal of care and counseling. See Howard Clinebell, *Ecotherapy: Healing Ourselves, Healing the Earth* (Minneapolis: Fortress, 1996). We might consider this an expanded list of the "fruits of the spirit." Galatians 5:22-23. See also the essays in Miroslav Volf's and Justin E. Crisp's edited volume, *Joy and Human Flourishing: Essays on Theology, Culture, and the Good Life* (Minneapolis: Fortress, 2015), for more exploration of biblical and theological themes and their contributions to an understanding of flourishing. There are secular explorations, too. Seligman notes five elements that empirically have been found to contribute to human flourishing according to his criteria that each is pursued for its own sake, and each is defined and measured independently of the other elements. First are positive emotions: the experience of happiness or at least a pleasant life that a person reports feeling and which is confirmed by the observations of those around him or her. Second is engagement, an experience of applying one's well-honed skills to a task that matters deeply and immersing oneself in that (psychologist Mihaly Csikszentmihalyi calls this "flow"; see his book *Flow* [New York: Harper & Row Publishers, 1990]). Third is meaning making, defined as being engaged in something that has genuine value, both subjectively—"I'm glad I did that"—as well as in the objective judgment of history, logic, and coherence—which of course can contradict a subjective judgment. Fourth is positive relationships, or the opposite of loneliness: the capacity to love and be loved (capacities to give and to receive love and care are both significant forms of participation). Last is a sense of accomplishment, the achievement of something one has set one's sights on, even when it brings none of the other elements with it. In other words, accomplishment is celebrated for its own sake—the satisfaction of meeting a goal. Flourishing, in this view, is some amalgam of one's experience of the subjective *feelings* of happiness and the *conviction* that one has engaged in meaningful, valuable activities (with confirmation by one's historical and immediate communities). By "historical communities" I mean philosophers, theologians (Christian and not, including leaders in nontheistic wisdom traditions), ethicists, pastoral theologians, etc.

68 Magda Arnold was correct: assessing the value of something is part of being human (see chapter 4). However, Arnold did not weigh in explicitly on what should/should not be valued. On this, Epicurus and Aristotle were correct: *what* one values, and how one (individually and as part of a collective) pursues it, matters. Emotions can both enhance and impede creative engagement in what is truly worthy. Much has been written about this recently. For example, Stjepan Mestrovic argues that we are now in a period he defines as a "postemotional society," a "new kind of bondage" in which any policy or event, no matter how it might be assessed by old-fashioned inner-directed standards, will be acceptable as long as it is packaged properly. Stjepan G. Mestrovic, *Postemotional Society* (Thousand Oaks, Calif.: SAGE Publications, 1997), xv. Mestrovic worries that the degree of manipulation of emotions and habits of the heart has resulted in the "McDonaldization" of emotions and human relationships so that we now experience only shallow, recycled emotions from the past or find that our emotional capacities have been deadened altogether. For Mestrovic this means we do not get outraged at what should outrage us, and instead we live through "sentimental representations" of emotions learned primarily through media depictions. In a similar vein, psychologist Sherry Turkle's book *Alone Together* argues that technology has come to determine what matters and how to

achieve it. For example, in our understanding of intimacy and with whom we seek it, we fall prey to the illusion of community and companionship by collecting Facebook friends and confusing Tweets with genuine communication. Turkle worries about what this will mean for our capacities for compassion, empathy, and relationship in a technological society. Sherry Turkle, *Alone Together: Why We Expect More from Technology and Less from Each Other* (New York: Basic Books, 2011).

69 Even infants are said to grieve loss. As one grief specialist puts it, if children are able to love, they are able to grieve. Linda Goldman, *Love & Loss: A Guide to Help Grieving Children*, 3rd ed. (New York: Routledge, 2014).

70 Sadness, anger, and joy tell us something about what it means to be human. To be human is, in some sense, to risk suffering, to endure pain, and to choose consciously to fully experience one's own or another's distress. I have come to believe that grief is a fundamental and pervasive experience of human life and that learning to do the work of grieving well can help us live well—or at least better. See also Miriam Greenspan, *Healing through the Dark Emotions: The Wisdom of Grief, Fear, and Despair* (Boston: Shambhala Publications, 2003).

71 In fact, to seek to eliminate all tension or pain from our lives is to seek to escape from life: as one psychologist writes, "One of the worst things to do is relieve people of [their pain] before they have learned its lessons." David G. Benner, *Human Being and Becoming: Living the Adventure of Life and Love* (Grand Rapids: Brazos, 2016), 53.

72 Benner, *Human Being and Becoming*, 38–42.

73 Subjective feelings of happiness are important, of course, but sometimes the immediate feelings of happiness must be sacrificed for higher moral values or enriched meaningfulness. But subjective feelings of happiness cannot be sacrificed indefinitely if one is in pursuit of flourishing. "Negative" or "unpleasant" feelings are to be expected, but people who are chronically unhappy cannot be said to be flourishing.

74 Belliotti, *Happiness Is Overrated*, 93.

75 Kupperman, *Six Myths about the Good Life*, 130–43. This is also what Aristotle seemed to imply about the criteria for what is valuable. See Nussbaum, *Upheavals of Thought*, 40–49, for a discussion.

76 That is, eudaimonia. Again, I want to be clear that I distinguish between pain and suffering. Pain (physical and emotional) can be used for growth, but chronic suffering limits the possibilities for flourishing.

77 See, for example, Miraslov Volf, "The Crown of the Good Life: A Hypothesis," in *Joy and Human Flourishing*, Volf and Crisp, ed., 127–36. It is important to note that flourishing is graded on a scale and is never fully accomplished. In other words, all lives are valuable, some are pleasant, and some are flourishing more robustly than others. Belliotti, *Happiness Is Overrated*, 85, and Seligman, *Flourish*, 242. Seligman distinguishes *the pleasant life* (in which one has most of what one needs and is free of chronic suffering), the *good life* (in which one has developed one's own gifts and talents and employs them in ways one finds satisfying), and the *flourishing life* (which includes the elements of the pleasant life and the good life but adds creative engagement, in which one applies one's gifts and talents in ways that are personally satisfying and also help others). See Seligman, *Flourish*, 9–26.

Seligman argues that the capacities for wisdom, courage, humanity, love, justice, temperance, and transcendence (what he considers the seven most important virtues for a flourishing life) are cultivated by developing twenty-four strengths, which he arranges from the most developmentally basic to the "most mature." Seligman, *Flourish*, 243.

These strengths include (though not necessarily in this order) open curiosity about and interest in the world; a love of learning and the capacity for critical thinking; emotional intelligence (about oneself and others); perspective (that is, seeing oneself and others as well as situations with a kind of "third eye" or objectivity); kindness and generosity; loving and allowing oneself to be loved; a commitment to justice; capacity for self-control; a sense of humility and modesty; capacities for gratitude and hope, optimism and future-mindedness; faith and a sense of purpose or spirituality; capacities for forgiveness and mercy; a sense of humor and playfulness; and passion, zest, enthusiasm for life. Seligman, *Flourish*, 243–65.

However, while these strengths support flourishing, no individual will hold all strengths at all times. Rather, Seligman's research has shown that all three "core features" (positive emotions, engagement/interest, and meaning/purpose) and at least three of six possible "additional features" (self-esteem, optimism, resilience, vitality, self-determination, and positive relationships) are necessary and sufficient for flourishing at any given time. Seligman, *Flourish*, 26–27.

Seligman's research also demonstrates that pessimism is a risk factor for cancer and heart attacks. On the other hand, optimism and a sense of well-being protect people from death from cardiovascular disease, renal failure, and HIV, though for some reason not significantly from cancer. See Seligman, *Flourish*, 190–204. See also Ken Pargament, *Spiritually Integrated Psychotherapy: Understanding and Addressing the Sacred* (New York: Guilford Press, 2007), and Ken Pargament, *The Psychology of Religion and Coping: Theory, Research, Practice* (New York: Guilford Press, 1997), for the importance of spirituality for a flourishing life. Pastoral theologian Carrie Doehring draws on Pargament's work for its implications for pastoral care in *The Practice of Pastoral Care: A Postmodern Approach*, rev. and expanded ed. (Louisville, Ky.: Westminster John Knox, 2015).

78 Robert Kegan argues that developmental growth involves increased ability to see oneself with some objectivity, to take perspective on oneself, and observe oneself as if from a distance. See Robert Kegan, *The Evolving Self: Problem and Process in Human Development* (Cambridge, Mass.: Harvard University Press, 1982). Seligman's research suggests that the ability to be somewhat objective about oneself and one's life is an important capacity for flourishing. Seligman, *Flourish*.

79 Martha C. Nussbaum and Amartya Sen have argued this in their edited volume, *The Quality of Life* (Oxford: Oxford University Press, 1993).

80 Deuteronomy 30:15-20.

81 See LaMothe, *Care of Souls, Care of Polis*, especially chapters 6 and 7 of this book for a helpful discussion that takes neoliberalism into account.

82 McNeill, *Keeping Together in Time*. See chapter 5 of this book for more on this.

83 This evokes, of course, the language of early philosophers. John D. Caputo, *Hope against Hope: Confessions of a Postmodern Pilgrim* (Minneapolis: Fortress, 2015). This is philosophical theologian John Caputo's language for the tension of living in what Karl Barth called the "now and not yet." Karl Barth, *Epistle to the Romans*, trans. from the 6th ed. by Edwin C. Hoskyns (1933; repr., Oxford: Oxford University Press, 1968). Although Caputo does not capitalize "Unconditional," I choose to do so, as the word can be understood as a theological concept indicating "God." My own understanding of human flourishing is different from early philosophers' and theologians'. My view requires a deep commitment to radical inclusion, justice, love, and nonviolence. Some people call the urging toward these goods "God," others a "Divine Creativity," the "Holy Other," and so

on. I prefer language that is less likely to be anthropomorphized, so when I use the word "God" I will put it in quotes to remind the reader that I am not imagining a human-like being in the sky per se. For this reason, I also opt to use nontraditional terms.

Indeed, not all Jewish and Christian theologians use the words *Yahweh* or *God* to refer to the Ultimate Reality. For example, one of the best-known Christian theologians of the twentieth century, Paul Tillich, describes God as the Ultimate Concern, Ground of Being, Being-Itself, the Power of Being, and occasionally as the Abyss, referring to God's Abysmal (or depth of) Being. Tillich's ontological view of God imagines that God is the foundation or ultimate reality that "precedes" all beings. God is the ground upon which all beings exist. Humans cannot perceive God as an object related to a subject because God *precedes* the subject–object dichotomy: God as Being Itself exists before humans' rational ability to think about God. Tillich, *Systematic Theology*, 1:271. Others, such as process thinkers, use language such as Beauty, Goodness, and Love (in Christian traditions Jesus Christ is the incarnation of these). Wendy Farley, a Christian theologian who also draws on Buddhist and Jewish imaginings, suggests that the deepest longing humans have is that for "Goodness Beyond Being." She suggests "more or less" Christian names for this power, including Divine Eros, Goodness Beyond Being, the Beloved, the Holy Spirit. Farley, *Wounding and Healing of Desire*, xiii. It is worth noting, too, that not all process thinkers are theists. (Process thought, by which my own thinking is informed, integrates both philosophical speculation and empirical verification that seeks to integrate all aspects of human experience—including human development, ecology, economics, physics, biology, social theory, and so on—into an explanatory scheme. See the description provided on the website of the Center for Process Studies, https://ctr4process.org/about/.) See also C. Robert Mesle, *Process Theology: A Basic Introduction* (St. Louis: Chalice Press, 1993), especially part 4. I have heard the principle captured in Caputo's language of the "Unconditional" referred to as the "Universe," although I would argue this offers less definition and clarity about the character of Ultimate Reality than, say, "God" or "Yahweh" does, as those terms invoke the traditions that have shaped our understanding of them. What I am trying to convey with all these terms is a variety of understandings of Ultimate Reality on which one might depend (explicitly and not) when faced with life's challenges and mysteries. One's Ultimate Reality is whatever it is that one trusts and turns to as she makes meaning of her life as it unfolds. Whatever language one uses represents a set of values and beliefs, images, and commitments that help transcend and make meaning of the present moment. The Unconditional is, one might say, the Good, Allah, Goodness Beyond Being, "God," or Yahweh, among many other terms. I do not mean to suggest that all religions point to the same single reality. I affirm the idea that various wisdom traditions "describe different (and sometimes related) realities." Duane Bidwell, *When One Religion Isn't Enough: The Lives of Spiritually Fluid People* (Boston: Beacon Press, 2018), 7. I am merely hoping to point to a variety of understandings of ultimate reality and the names used for it.

When I use "God" I am referring to the Ultimate Reality as understood in the Christian Scriptures, the Holy Other incarnate in the life and death of Jesus Christ, though I do not understand God as white, male, or even necessarily a personal being. Process theologian C. Robert Mesle suggests that "God is love. That is, God is the unique subject whose love is the foundation of all reality. It is through God's love that all things live and move and have their being. God is the supremely related One, sharing the experience of every creature, and being experienced by every creature." Mesle, *Process Theology*, 25.

Wisdom traditions of both the West and the East (Judaism, Christianity, Islam, Buddhism, Confucianism, and Taoism, for example, as well as the Platonic, Stoic, Epicurean, Aristotelian, and Galenic traditions, among others) have always had therapeutic—that is, healing—methods. These methods differed, but they all had the final goal of "profound transformation of the individual's mode of seeing and being, and the overcoming of anguish." Richard White, *The Heart of Wisdom: The Philosophy of Spiritual Life* (New York: Rowman & Littlefield, 2013), 9.

84 Benner, *Human Being and Becoming*, 54.

85 Thus, the Insistence of God is an insistence for life and love and forgiveness and mercy and justice, which remain nonexistent in the world until we bring them into being. Caputo, *Hope against Hope*, 108. Our living together in nonviolence, love, hospitality, justice, and so on is the "way God acquires mass and body"; such is the making of a meaningful life. Caputo, *Hope against Hope*, 90.

86 The language of "urging" and "invitation" is often used by process thinkers such as Catherine Keller, Charles Hartshorne, and others. Process theology integrates the idea of "God" with material and ecological realities on earth. See, for example, Catherine Keller, *On the Mystery: Discerning God in Process* (Minneapolis: Fortress, 2008), and *Political Theology of the Earth: Our Planetary Emergency and the Struggle for a New Public* (New York: Columbia University Press, 2018).

87 I am not making the mistake of accepting the Enlightenment or neoliberal assertions that all of life has improved for everyone over the course of history. Indeed, some may be worse off than they would have been seven centuries ago (people enslaved in the histories of colonialism might be one example). To be sure, life *is* better for some than it would have been five hundred years ago, and surely it would be more in line with the preferred future of the Goodness Beyond Being that this was true for all. As I have said earlier, theologies and their religious expressions must be evaluated for the contribution toward or impediments to flourishing as defined here.

88 Modern science's highly interconnected view of the physical universe confirms what scientists are learning about the human realm: this same force pulls everything that exists toward increasing wholeness and completeness, (which should not be confused with uniformity or sameness). This theory suggests that every atom, every cell, every plant and animal, every planet and star—*everything*—is pulled by the same primal force, the allurement toward the larger whole within which it is a part, growing in interconnected and interdependent complexity; everything within the universe is evolving into ever-deepening patterns of interdependence. See, for example, Charlene Spretnak, *Relational Reality: New Discoveries of Interrelatedness That Are Transforming the Modern World* (Topsham, Maine: Green Horizons, 2011). The work of string theorists, physicist Albert Einstein, and philosopher Alfred North Whitehead (who developed process thought), make these points as well. See Spretnak, *Relational Reality*, chapter 1, for a useful overview of the scientific perspectives. Scientists, psychologists, and theologians have sometimes intuited this and argued for deeper understandings of the patterns of increasing wholeness, which implies complexity. The movement of energy, they suggest, is the incorporation of smaller wholes (which are wholes in themselves) into larger wholes. One physicist argues that this is the movement of a self-organizing universe. Paul Davies, *The Cosmic Blueprint: New Discoveries in Nature's Ability to Order the Universe* (West Conshohocken,

Pa.: Templeton, 2004). If it is true that everything is radically interconnected and inter-dependent, then human beings must have perspective on their proper place in the universe. It may be helpful, then, to imagine all life as existing in an infinite series of nesting Russian dolls—from infinitesimally small subatomic ones that no existing technology allows scientists to see to the most expansive ones that exist at the cosmic level and that are beyond scientists' present ability to observe. Everything that is exists within this nesting of life, from the smallest particle to the system of billions of galaxies into uncountable universes. This organization has been described as the goal of evolution: a persistent pull toward increasing wholeness, complexity, and consciousness. (See, for example, Benner, *Human Being and Becoming*, 29.) This is not to deny the reality of entropy and constant processes of deconstruction. Rather, it imagines a stronger force of reimagination and re-creation, as Nietzsche proposed. The same could be said about human beings: humans are collections of cells that have learned to become viable and independent in their functioning in their particular frame of existence that then learned how to bond with each other to form group structures called organs, which learned how to cooperate with each other to form a higher entity than the body. The existence of the whole depends on this. (Indeed, when cells decide to pursue their own self-interest, doctors call it cancer and try eliminate it.) This understanding suggests a particular view of flourishing. Flourishing at the individual level presupposes connection and meaningful attachment, getting individual, personal needs met—from basic needs such as physical safety to "higher-order" needs such as engaging in creative activities—as well as caring for oneself, others, and the earth on which all life utterly depends. Flourishing in this understanding is an individual achievement, but it cannot be accomplished fully without the flourishing of all.

89 Especially the flourishing of underrepresented people and groups (e.g., those with black and brown skin, women, self-identified queer people, and so on) who historically have been left out of the hope for flourishing in colonial late-modernity. The understanding of eudaimonia being presented here is more inclusive and expansive than the early philosophers and theologians imagined. While we still live in a deeply patriarchal system, begun thousands of years ago and still perpetuated, my understanding of flourishing resists its exclusionary and oppressive practices.

90 See Martha Nussbaum's exploration of the virtues required for flourishing in her chapter "Non-Relative Virtues: An Aristotelian Approach," in *Quality of Life*, ed. Martha C. Nussbaum and Amartya Sen (Oxford: Oxford University Press, 1993), 242–67.

91 Having and practicing a religious faith has been shown to contribute to the flourishing life: all religious traditions propose systems of meaning, which, at least broadly, have been shown to contribute to the flourishing life. However, as previously noted, religious traditions have also been interpreted and practiced in ways that have promoted great violence. Thus, religious traditions, their teachings, and their followers must be judged on the basis of whether they promote flourishing as defined here. My understanding of *faith* is not as particular content (though particular faiths have content), but I am arguing here for a faith in what is in sacred, just, and loving ground. I believe faith in what is *on the side of all is the only faith that will cultivate genuine flourishing*. It is faith in this Goodness on which we rely as we face life's challenges and mysteries. Thus, flourishing requires the ability to trust in the reality and goodness of things not seen. It requires an attitude of trust and a way of finding meaning in life as it unfolds. The subject of faith is organized around a set of value principles and commitments as proposed here. Faith becomes concretized in practice and structures. Indeed, the *structure* of faith is a religion, and there

are many structures: the various ways beliefs, rituals, sacred texts, and faith communities have developed over time both locally and globally. In fact, religions are some of the most important resources for articulating a vision of flourishing and the meanings of life and the behaviors consonant with living in accordance with meaning. On "local" vs. "world" religions, see, for example, Volf, *Flourishing*. Volf argues that religions (containers for the content of faith) at their best "foster a connection to the ultimate reality, and sketch a moral vision embedded in an account of the self, social relations, and the good." Volf, *Flourishing*, 189.

92 Of course, entropy is also a powerful force, embodied in injustice, fragmentation of families and communities, the destruction of neighborhoods in "white flight," and death by suicide. But I have a deep hope (impossible as it seems) that the Insistence toward wholeness has a stronger pull.

93 "Love" is the word some cosmologists are bold enough to use to describe the attractional force that holds planets in orbit and provides the glue that holds atoms together. Thomas J. Oord, "Love and Cosmology," in *Defining Love: A Philosophical, Scientific, and Theological Engagement* (Grand Rapids: Brazos, 2010), 137–72. Christian theologians would likely agree. For example, scientist and theologian Teilhard de Chardin called the attraction at the heart of the universe "Love," or more frequently, "God-Omega." In de Chardin's understanding, all of creation is oriented toward the integral wholeness that is achieved through unity in love. See also Brian P. Hall, *The Genesis Effect: Human and Organizational Transformation* (repr., Eugene, Ore.: Resource Publishing/ Wipf and Stock, 2000), for a description of the values that express and work toward such wholeness.

94 Theologians have suggested that the meaning of human life is the participation in a "kin-dom" of God. But this kin-dom is not something to be held out for the future; we are called to live into it now. As we find ways to love our neighbors as ourselves, to live justly, and to be faithful stewards of the earth, we are creating together the kin-dom of God—we bring the kin-dom into existence. Ada María Isasi-Díaz, *Mujerista Theology: A Theology for the Twenty-First Century* (Maryknoll, N.Y.: Orbis Books, 1996), 30. As Caputo argues, the kin-dom of God "is not a reward for works—it *is* those works." Caputo, *Hope against Hope*, 62.

95 Paul Bloomfield, *The Virtues of Happiness: A Theory of the Good Life* (Oxford: Oxford University Press, 2014), vii. Bloomfield argues that morality is necessary for self-respect and that self-respect is necessary for happiness. Bloomfield, *Virtues of Happiness*, 6.

96 These values can be found in the work and lives of "paragons of virtue and character" (which is not the same as saying they are perfect people) that have commonly been seen as models (such as the Hebrew prophetess Miriam, Jesus of Nazareth and the Buddha, Mother Teresa, Gandhi, Desmond Tutu, and Martin Luther King, Jr.). The virtues that these models offer are historically and socially recognized checks and balances on hubris.

97 Inherent to the virtues is the recognition that the wise thing to do is not always determined by what is in one's self-interest nor always strictly in others' best interest. Further, the wise thing to do can only be determined by an impartial consideration of the situation. People must act virtuously in the moment, whatever that may entail, which often requires careful consideration and contemplation on what is Good (including both personal and social factors). See chapter 1 and also Bloomfield, *Virtues of Happiness*, 174. Scientists have debated the existence of an altruism gene. See, for example, Graham J.

Thompson, Peter L. Hurd, and Bernard J. Crespi, "Genes Underlying Altruism," *Biology Letters* 9, no. 6 (2013): 1–6.

98 The Christian tradition asserts that Jesus of Nazareth responded fully to the Sacred Insistence and so was recognized by his community as the Christ. See Paul Tillich's discussion of this Christology in his *Systematic Theology*, vol. 2, and Mesle, *Process Theology*, 104–9. To the extent that religious traditions support and encourage the ideals and practices of love, care, inclusion, diversity, beauty, goodness, and justice, they are worthy of our engagement. To the extent that they do not, they invite our resistance.

99 Pastoral theologian and Jungian scholar Margaret Kornfeld suggests that *wholeness* (her word, which I take to mean well-being) entails acknowledging and even embracing one's limits and that by so doing one feels a sense of freedom and acceptance. See Margaret Kornfeld, *Cultivating Wholeness: A Guide to Care and Counseling in Faith Communities* (2000; repr., New York: Continuum, 2012), 8.

100 "Morality" is defined as valuing what is rightly valued. Bloomfield, *Virtues of Happiness*, 125. This includes valuing ourselves as well as others, the earth, and "God." Pastoral theologian James Lapsley argues that participation in the life of God is a hallmark of flourishing and is something of a developmental achievement. See James Lapsley, *Salvation and Health: Interlocking Processes of Life* (Louisville, Ky.: Westminster John Knox, 1972). Pastoral theologian Rodney Hunter added nuance to the ability to participate in the Life of God, saying it involves active engagement but is also available for those who cannot actively participate: those who "suffer the limitation or destruction of their vital capacities" participate by offering themselves, their presence, and their ability to receive love as a mark of their participation in the Life of God, rather than a particular creation or achievement. Rodney J. Hunter, "Participation in the Life of God: Revisioning Lapsley's Salvation-Health Model," in *The Treasure of Earthen Vessels: Explorations in Theological Anthropology in Honor of James N. Lapsley*, ed. Brian H. Childs and David W. Waanders (Louisville, Ky.: Westminster John Knox, 1994), 13. See also McClure, *Moving beyond Individualism*, for my proposal of a synergistic anthropology that privileges participation in valuable, liberative activities rather than insight as the ultimate goal of psychotherapeutic practices.

101 Caputo, *Hope against Hope*, 79.

102 Sometimes flourishing of all means I must sacrifice my immediate happiness or contentment for that of another. But in order to flourish, I cannot do this continuously, only periodically and temporarily.

103 "Practical rationality" or *phronesis*—practical wisdom to Aristotle.

104 Bloomfield, *Virtues of Happiness*, 134. The authors of *Christian Practical Wisdom: What It Is, Why It Matters* argue that practical wisdom, the kind Aristotle thought was indispensable for eudaimonia, is the least understood and the most difficult to learn. See Dorothy C. Bass et al., *Christian Practical Wisdom: What It Is, Why It Matters* (Grand Rapids: Eerdmans, 2016).

105 *Phronesis* is a virtue insofar as acting rationally in practical contexts can be a well-developed character trait that aids and partly constitutes a well-lived life. Bloomfield, *Virtues of Happiness*, 224 and 134. See also the exploration of *phronesis* in the Christian life in Bass et al., *Christian Practical Wisdom*, 1.

106 Bloomfield, *Virtues of Happiness*, 225. Wisdom includes the recognition that complexity is at the heart of life and allows one to manage paradox. The wise know that "sometimes rules must be broken." Bloomfield, *Virtues of Happiness*, 229. For example, sometimes

justice errs on the side of mercy, and the guilty receive forgiveness. Courage might mean quitting, and sometimes the better thing is to break commitment to a commitment in the service of something richer or deeper—something that may lead to a more flourishing life for oneself and others too, if they follow the urgings of the Sacred Insistence. And, despite the fact that all one can really do is try, often and regularly, to do what is moral and virtuous in the moment, the wise rest in the knowledge that they could not have tried harder, could not have discerned more carefully in the moment, and could not have done better, given who they were at the time and the challenges they faced. See a discussion of this in Bloomfield, *Virtues of Happiness*, 230.

107 "Interpathy" is defined as "when empathy crosses cultural boundaries." See Emmanuel Y. Lartey, *In Living Color: An Intercultural Approach to Pastoral Care and Counseling* (Philadelphia: Jessica Kingsley, 2003), 93–94.

108 Of course, no one is infallible or perfect in practical reasoning; being practically wise, like all virtues, is an ideal that we may only approach with greater or lesser success.

109 Pastoral theologian Carrie Doehring suggests that emotions are a significant part of growing spiritually because they are "what connect our physical and embodied selves with our beliefs, values, and ways of coping," 585. See Carrie Doehring, "Emotions and Change in Spiritual Care," *Pastoral Psychology* 63, no. 5 (2014): 583–96. In this essay Doehring offers a useful pair of diagrams depicting the differences between life-limiting and life-giving interrelationships among emotions, values, beliefs, and practices, especially in relation to healing trauma. There are other examinations of emotions in relation to well-being in development and in spirituality. For example, for a helpful treatment of the emotion of shame among black men, see Jay-Paul Hinds, "Shame and Its Sons: Black Men, Fatherhood, and Filicide," *Pastoral Psychology* 63, no. 5 (2014): 641–58. In this essay Hinds explores the intergenerational phenomenon of shame among black men, reimagining it not as an "albatross" but as a "source of innovation that inspires new ways of enunciating and understanding [black men's] manhood." Hinds, "Shame and Its Sons," 644. Pastoral theologian Bonnie Miller-McLemore would likely applaud this idea; in what is now an almost classic essay, she has worried that part of the devaluation of religion and religious institutions is related to the "devaluation" of the feminine, which is often associated with emotion, care, nurture, and devotion. Bonnie Miller-McLemore, "The Living Human Web: Pastoral Theology at the Turn of the Century," in *Through the Eyes of Women: Insights for Pastoral Care*, ed. Jeanne Stevenson-Moessner (Minneapolis: Fortress, 1996), 28. On the problem of individualism in contemporary life, see also Pamela D. Couture, "Weaving the Web: Pastoral Care in an Individualistic Society," in *Through the Eyes of Women: Insights for Pastoral Care*, ed. Jeanne Stevenson-Moessner (Minneapolis: Fortress, 1996), 94–106.

110 This differs, of course, from the Stoic sage who is able to rid himself of all passions. See chapter 1 for more on this.

111 Theologian Wendy Farley argues that, echoing Augustine, we know the Good because it is an ontological part of who we are as human beings: it is our deepest desire. This deep desire, Farley asserts, tells us something about ourselves as human beings: that we long for the "great emptiness, which is beauty and love without limitation." Farley, *The Wounding and Healing of Desire*, 13. Desire for the "great emptiness" testifies to humans' need for the divine, and the great and precious beauty in each of us that is the root of that desire that "cannot be blotted out" (19). Farley asserts that we all have a deep desire for the sacred, for community, and love, something that religious systems—at their

best—provide some account of: their message is that we are, "deep, deep down," all knit together, and we cannot go so far astray that this solidarity is completely broken (3). Farley writes, "However far beneath our conscious experience, awareness of the preciousness of *home* remains alive because we are connected to others" (4, emphasis added). Farley, *The Wounding and Healing of Desire.*

I argue that we recognize virtues such as love, justice, and care because no human experience is monolithic; that is, because there are "gaps" and differences in and between all experience, there is leverage for agency. See McClure, *Moving beyond Individualism,* 243–54. Indeed, these are ideally experienced in one's earliest years and the sense of them is carried throughout our lives.

112 These are basic assumptions of developmental theorists such as Erik Erikson. There are credible critiques of classical developmental theory, often that developmental theories do not account adequately for the cultural and social environments in which people grow. See, for example, Erica Burman, *Deconstructing Developmental Psychology,* 2nd ed. (New York: Routledge, 2008), and Barbara Rogoff, *The Cultural Nature of Human Development* (Oxford: Oxford University Press, 2003). However, it is clear that humans are not born fully formed as human beings and the mere passage of time is insufficient in itself to ensure the development of full human personhood. Thus, while newborns should be deeply valued members of their communities, they do not possess qualities of ideal maturity such as the capacity for non-possessive love, nor are they already grounded in a reasonably understood, shared sense reality. Infants cannot have a clearly articulated set of values they can pursue that make life meaningful, nor can they exercise the fullest measure of their freedom of choice and creativity, deeply understand and respect others, have the capacity for reflection on their experience (and others'), or identify with all humans. Human beings differ in capacities such as cognition, moral reasoning, and emotional functioning. They differ in terms of the maturity of their ego development, the breadth and openness of their worldviews, their capacities for love, and their abilities to understand perspectives other than their own. Underlying all of these capacities are fundamental differences in the development of consciousness itself—the great evolving "ocean of awareness" on which all phenomena and experiences arise. (One psychologist suggests that everything that exists "floats on a stream that flows toward transcendence [or the Unconditional]." Benner, *Human Being and Becoming,* xii). Developmental psychologist Erik Erikson related wisdom to the last stage of his eight-stage theory of psychosocial development. Erik Erikson, *Identity: Youth and Crisis* (New York: W.W. Norton, 1968), 140–41. The Sacred Urge of Goodness Beyond Being presupposes growth and persistent change at the heart of the lifespan. What is distinctive about human beings is not that people are part of this flow but that they possess the possibility of consciously participating in it or ignoring it. And so often individuals resist it altogether. This developmental view of mature wisdom and other virtues should not lead to our devaluing children, the differently abled, etc. Rather, as Aristotle argued, each should be judged by his/her own capacities. On respecting children's agency, see, for example, pastoral theologians Bonnie Miller-McLemore, *Let the Children Come: Reimagining Childhood from a Christian Perspective* (San Francisco: Jossey-Bass, 2003), and Joyce A. Mercer, *Welcoming Children: A Practical Theology of Childhood* (St. Louis: Chalice Press, 2005).

113 Pastoral theologian James Lapsley argued this in his classic text *Salvation and Health.* As noted in note 105 of this chapter there are various levels and ways of "participating." Pastoral theologian Rodney Hunter argues that Lapsley focuses too heavily on the "giving"

kinds of participation and says that participation can include both activities of giving and also practices of receiving—for example, being "with" the other, "essentially, to suffer with and for the other." Hunter, "Participation in the Life of God," 22.

114 Caputo argues that the rose is as the rose is (and it is beautiful and right as it is), but a rose cannot participate in the same way to bring into existence justice and cannot love as a fully mature person can. Part of what differentiates us from a rock or a rose is the gift of consciousness. Like everything that is, the rose has both gifts and limits (for example, it is—as far as anyone knows—without consciousness.) Roses, then, are evidence of the Unconditional. Caputo, *Hope against Hope*, 106–14. Psychologist David Benner would likely agree. He writes, "Without consciousness we could never reflect on our lives, be absorbed by something that caught our attention or be fully present to others or ourselves. Without consciousness, we would be like rocks and trees—we would simply be what we do and do what we are." Benner, *Human Being and Becoming*, 2. Without consciousness we could not make sense of the experiences of our lives and could not respond as meaningfully to the Sacred Insistence toward love and justice; without consciousness we would be "destined to simply live in reaction to the events that happen to us. Without consciousness we would not have meaningfully organized perceptions, only scattered sensations. Without consciousness we would drift through life awash in stimulation and bereft of the most distinctive human resources for rising above the instinctual programming that was bequeathed to us by our evolutionary past." Benner, *Human Being and Becoming*, 2.

115 For good discussions on the developmental qualities of values, see Milton Rokeach, *Understanding Human Values: Individual and Societal* (New York: Free Press/Simon & Schuster, 1979), and Brian Hall, *Values Shift*.

116 As noted previously, while there are salient critiques of developmental theories, it is reasonable to present generally accepted stages or phases in the development of the ego as moving from a focus on survival (and physiological needs including food, warmth, shelter, comfort), in which one is interested primarily in the self and the ability to survive. Ideally, this individual eventually will develop into one who is interested in and capable of increasingly mutual relationship that considers the safety needs of self and those in close relationship (family, kin, tribe), to a capacity to hold one's own needs, goals, and values in interdependent relationship with all others' needs, goals, and values. If physiological and social needs are sufficiently met and skills for pursuing one's goals are well developed, developmental theories propose, people will likely have the self-esteem, confidence, competence, sense of belonging, trust, faith, and internal cohesion to live in a self-chosen but virtuous collaboration with others. Their desire to make a valuable difference and their capacities for doing so will be developed to the point that they will be able to engage the world meaningfully. On this, see, for example, Benner, *Human Being and Becoming*; Hall, *Values Shift*; Richard Barrett, *The New Leadership Paradigm: Leading Self, Leading Others, Leading an Organization, Leading in Society* (Lexington, Ky.: Barrett Values Centre, 2016); and Robert Kegan and Lisa Lahey, *An Everyone Culture: Becoming a Deliberately Developmental Organization* (Boston: Harvard Business Review Press, 2016), for accessible summaries of this argument.

117 See pastoral theologian Joretta Marshall's work on conditions for forgiveness and limits to as a practice. Marshall, *How Can I Forgive?*

118 Seligman argues that these strengths have been shown empirically to support and develop the virtues that describe and allow for the flourishing life. Seligman refers to his formula

as "PERMA": positive emotions, engagement, positive and deep relationships, complex meaning making, and accomplishments. Seligman, *Flourish*, 16 and 243. This is fundamentally a developmental argument, although adapting, learning, bonding, and cooperation, like all developmental processes, are tied less to age than to ability to handle complexity. Psychological maturity depends on our ability to individuate, self-actualize, and handle complexity, all of which "depends on our level of exposure to experience" and the ability to reflect on it with increasing wisdom. Benner, *Human Being and Becoming*, 89. Jewish and Christian theologians argue that human wisdom is different from godly wisdom. The goal is to align our wisdom with that of the wisdom of the Holy Other. Confucius said that wisdom can be learned through three methods: reflection (the most noble), imitation (the easiest), and experience (the bitterest).

119 Children need to be taught explicitly to experience, identify, and explore for understanding their own emotions and those of others and to develop their moral imaginations in light of the flourishing of all. Adults often need to be taught remedially, which is part of what I understand the role of psychodynamic psychotherapy to be.

120 As it turns out, people prefer being in an emotional state over not being in one. Keith Oatley and Jennifer M. Jenkins, "Psychotherapy, Consciousness, and Narrative," in Oatley and Jenkins, *Understanding Emotions*, 385–411.

121 There are, of course, situations when people are "not in their right minds." The opioid epidemic, for example, has made clear the deleterious effects certain substances can have on people's capacities to relate well, work, or otherwise engage themselves and the world. Traumatic experiences cloud people's judgment and their capacities to reason and relate. These examples clarify what is important for flourishing. However, Seligman's research with PTSD sufferers shows that difficult or unpleasant emotions tend not to last long in typically functioning people if those emotions are examined within a program of awareness, acceptance, understanding, and care. Seligman, *Flourish*, 143.

122 This extends even to the importance of understanding how our brains work. Pastoral theologian David Hogue argues the importance of this for developing good practices of care. See his essay "How the Brain Matters," in Ramsay, *Pastoral Theology and Care*, 31–53.

123 This is not to resort to a structural model. Rather, these emotions are, from a theological perspective, the result of something inborn in humans (e.g., *the imago dei*), as Wendy Farley argues. From a social constructive view, they are the result of being *taught* that one has value, is to be respected, and deserves dignity, and psychologist Christopher Bollas asserts they are developed in our earliest life experiences.

124 See chapter 6 for more on how categories relate to the generation of emotions.

125 For example, anger is typically a socially discouraged emotion for women in Western cultures, while love and tenderness are "prohibited" among "real" men. See, for example, Kay Deaux, "From Individual Differences to Social Categories: Analysis of a Decade's Research on Gender," *American Psychologist* 39, no. 2 (1984): 105–16. See also, for example, Ashley Montagu, ed., *The Learning of Nonaggression* (Oxford: Oxford University Press, 1987), and Leslie R. Brody and Judith A. Hall, "Gender and Emotion in Context," in Lewis, Haviland-Jones, and Barrett, 3rd ed., *Handbook of Emotion*, 395–408.

126 The righteous anger of Black Lives Matter activists has been deemed "excessive," "inappropriate," "unnecessary," "irresponsible," and more. See, for example, Kimberly Seals Allers, "Black Women Have Never Had the Privilege of Rage," *HuffPost*, October 14, 2008, https://www.huffingtonpost.com/entry/opinion-angry-black-women_us_5bbf7652e4b040bb4e800249.

127 Recall that Aristotle viewed people who never feel anger as "fools."

128 Civil rights attorney and activist Michelle Alexander suggests that our activities—even those that would purportedly support human flourishing—are for naught if they are not grounded in "revolutionary love." Michelle Alexander, presentation at the American Academy of Religion, November 20, 2016. See also Michelle Alexander, *The New Jim Crow: Mass Incarceration in the Age of Colorblindness* (New York: The New Press, 2012). There are other accounts of the challenges of living in a systemically racist society in the United States. See, for example, the work of Greg Ellison, *Cut Dead but Still Alive: Caring for African American Young Men* (Nashville: Abingdon, 2013); Lee Butler, *Liberating Our Dignity, Saving Our Souls* (St. Louis: Chalice Press, 2006); and Sandra L. Barnes and Anne S. Wimberly, *Empowering Black Youth of Promise: Education and Socialization in the Village-Minded Black Church* (New York: Routledge, 2016).

129 Remember, "negative" or unpleasant emotions are constructed in the moment when one's core affect is negative (e.g., unpleasant/high arousal) and when one interprets one's context as negative. If the memories of and beliefs that developed in the experience of similar core affect experiences are negative, then one's experiences in the moment are typically negative too. For example, a person often experiences impatience and frustration when he does not get what he wants when he wants it and expresses anger when such situations persist. Object-relations theorist D. W. Winnicott asserts, however, that we do not need (and in fact will never receive) "perfect" attention, but only "good enough" care, in order to develop well and to flourish. See Donald W. Winnicott, *Playing and Reality* (1971; repr., New York: Routledge Classics, 2005).

130 While one's core affect is not always pleasant (and can be very unpleasant), rather than using language of "positive" or "negative" emotions or adaptive or maladaptive emotions, it is more useful to use the language of "life-giving" versus "life-limiting." For example, while Martha Nussbaum accepts some of the early philosophical positions about the passions, such as the passions' tendencies to be unruly and disruptive, she does not go so far as to conflate "unpredictable" with "negative." She writes, "I proceed on the assumption that at least some things and people outside one's own control have real worth." Nussbaum, *Upheavals of Thought*, 11–12. Despite the fact that certain emotions are often referred to as adaptive or maladaptive evolutionarily speaking, sometimes what is most adaptive is most life-limiting, and vice versa, as Miguel De La Torre's work on hopelessness shows (see note 58, this chapter).

131 This implies, of course, that people's stories are significant entry points for understanding their emotions and feelings: stories are epistemological tools. It also implies that each of us needs "story companions" who can listen for ways our feelings are related to our developmental processes, memories of our past experiences, contextual challenges, needs, goals, values, and so on. For a good discussion of this, see Karen D. Scheib, *Pastoral Care: Telling the Stories of Our Lives* (Nashville: Abingdon, 2016), and David A. Hogue, *Remembering the Future, Imagining the Past: Story, Ritual, and the Human Brain* (Cleveland: Pilgrim Press, 2003). Australian pastoral theologian Neil Pembroke, too, writes about the exploration of emotions—particularly shame—in pastoral care. See Neil Pembroke, *The Art of Listening: Dialogue, Shame, and Pastoral Care* (New York: T&T Clark/Handsel, 2002). Accompanying one another in this work engenders hope, it has been argued, which emerges in relationship as we explore these things together. See Joretta L. Marshall, "Collaborating Hope: Joining the In-Between Spaces," *Journal of Pastoral Theology* 26, no. 2 (2016): 77–90.

132 There are, of course, other treatments that can be effective, such as EMDR (Eye Movement Desensitization and Reprocessing) and medications.

133 Trauma specialist Christy Sim suggests that certain practices can free survivors of the memories and trauma they wish not to relive. Sim, *Survivor Care*. The question of how completely one can be free of past trauma is a salient one, but out of the scope of this project.

134 While we will never have full control over our emotions, we can engage them in more informed, more intentional, more insightful, and wiser ways.

135 Peter Salovey, Brian T. Bedell, Jerusha B. Detweiler, and John D. Mayer, "Current Directions in Emotional Intelligence Research," in Lewis and Haviland-Jones, *Handbook of Emotions*, 2nd ed., 504–20.

Works Cited

Abu-Lughod, Lila, and Catherine Lutz. "Introduction: Emotion, Discourse, and the Politics of Everyday Life." In *Language and Politics of Emotion*, edited by Catherine Lutz and Lila Abu-Lughod, 1–23. Cambridge: Cambridge University Press, 1990.

Ahmed, Sara. *The Cultural Politics of Emotion*. Edinburgh, U.K.: Edinburgh University Press, 2014.

———. "Multiculturalism and the Promise of Happiness." *New Formations* 63, no. 63 (2007/2008): 121–38.

———. *The Promise of Happiness*. Chapel Hill, N.C.: Duke University Press, 2010.

Albers, Lisa H., Dana E. Johnson, and Margaret K. Hostetter. "Health of Children Adopted from the Soviet Union and Eastern Europe: Comparison with Preadoptive Medical Records." *Journal of the American Medical Association* 278, no. 11 (1997): 922–24.

Alexander, John M. *Capabilities and Social Justice: The Political Philosophy of Amartya Sen and Martha Nussbaum*. New York: Ashgate, 2008.

Alexander, Loveday C. A. "The Passions in Galen and the Novels of Chariton and Xenophon." In *Passions and Moral Progress in Greco-Roman Thought*, edited by John T. Fitzgerald, 175–97. New York: Routledge, 2008.

Alexander, Michelle. *The New Jim Crow: Mass Incarceration in the Age of Colorblindness*. New York: The New Press, 2012.

Allers, Kimberly Seals. "Black Women Have Never Had the Privilege of Rage." *HuffPost*, October 14, 2008. https://www.huffingtonpost.com/entry/opinion-angry-black-women_us_5bbf7652e4b040bb4e800249.

Allport, Floyd Henry. *Social Psychology*. Boston: Houghton Mifflin, 1924.

Aquinas, Saint Thomas. *Summa Theologica*. Translated by Anton Pegis. In *Basic Writings of Thomas Aquinas*. New York: Random House, 1945.

Aristotle. *Nichomachean Ethics*. Translated by W. D. Ross. Oxford: Clarendon, 1925. Reprint: Stillwell, KS: Digiread, 2005.

Armon-Jones, Claire. "The Social Functions of Emotion." In *The Social Construction of Emotions*, edited by Rom Harre, 57–82. Oxford: Basil Blackwell, 1986.

———. "The Thesis of Constructionism." In *The Social Construction of Emotions*, edited by Rom Harre, 32–56. New York: Blackwell, 1986.

Arnold, Magda. *Emotion and Personality*. 2 vols. New York: Columbia University Press, 1960.

———. "Neural Mediation of the Emotional Components of Action." In *The Nature of Emotions*, 318–65. London: Penguin, 1968.

Augustine, Saint. *The City of God*. In *The Basic Writings of St. Augustine* edited by Whitney Oates. New York: Random House, 1948.

———. *The Confessions*. Translated by Rex Warner. New York: New American Library, 1963.

Averill, James R. "A Constructivist View of Emotion." In *Emotion: Theory, Research and Experience*, edited by Robert Plutchik and Henry Kellerman, 305–39. Vol. 1. New York: Academic Press, 1980.

———. "The Emotions." In *Personality: Basic Aspects and Current Research*, edited by Ervin Staub, 134–99. Englewood Cliffs, N.J.: Prentice-Hall, 1980.

———. "Emotions in Relation to Systems of Behavior." In *Psychological and Biological Approaches to Emotion*, edited by Nancy L. Stein, Bennett Leventhal, and Tom Trabasso, 385–404. Hillsdale, N.J.: Erlbaum, 1990.

———. "Inner Feelings, Works of the Flesh, the Beast Within, Diseases of the Mind, Driving Force, and Putting on a Show: Six Metaphors of Emotion and Their Theoretical Extensions." In *Metaphors in the History of Psychology*, edited by David E. Leary, 104–32. Cambridge: Cambridge University Press, 1990.

Bakalar, Nicholas. "Childhood: A Little Sugar Does Seem to Ease the Pain." *New York Times*, December 17, 2012. https://well.blogs.nytimes.com/2012/12/17/childhood-a-little -sugar-does-seem-to-ease-the-pain/.

Bargh, John A., and Melissa J. Ferguson. "Beyond Behaviorism: On the Automaticity of Higher Mental Processes." *Psychological Bulletin* 126, no. 6 (2000): 925–45.

Barker-Benfield, G. J. *The Culture of Sensibility: Sex and Society in Eighteenth-Century Britain*. Chicago: University of Chicago Press, 1992.

Barnes, Sandra L., and Anne S. Wimberly. *Empowering Black Youth of Promise: Education and Socialization in the Village-Minded Black Church*. New York: Routledge, 2016.

Barrett, Lisa F. "Are Emotions Natural Kinds?" *Perspectives on Psychological Science* 1, no. 1 (2006): 28–58.

———. "Construction as an Integrative Framework for the Science of the Emotion." In *The Psychological Construction of Emotion*, edited by Lisa F. Barrett and James A. Russell, 448–58. New York: Guilford Press, 2015.

———. "Emotions Are Real." *Emotion* 12, no. 3 (2012): 413–29.

———. "The Future of Psychology: Connecting Mind to Brain." *Perspectives in Psychological Science* 4, no. 4 (1990): 326–39.

———. *How Emotions Are Made: The Secret Life of the Brain*. New York: Houghton Mifflin Harcourt, 2017.

———. "Psychological Construction: A Darwinian Approach to the Science of Emotions." *Emotion Review* 5, no. 4 (2013): 379–89.

———. "Solving the Emotion Paradox: Categorization and the Experience of Emotion." *Personality and Social Psychology Review* 10, no. 1 (2006): 20–46.

———. "Ten Common Misconceptions about Psychological Construction Theories of Emotion." In *The Psychological Construction of Emotion*, edited by Lisa F. Barrett and James A. Russell, 45–82. New York: Guilford Press, 2015.

———. "Your Emotions Are a Social Construct." *Tonic/Vice*, July 21, 2017. https://tonic.vice.com/en_us/article/qvpae5/would-someone-born-and-raised-in-solitary-have-any-emotions.

Barrett, Lisa F., and Ajay B. Satpute. "Large-Scale Brain Networks in Affective and Social Neuroscience: Towards an Integrative Functional Architecture of the Brain." *Current Opinion in Neurobiology* 23, no. 3 (2013): 361–72.

Barrett, Lisa F., and James A. Russell. *The Psychological Construction of Emotion*. New York: Guilford Press, 2015.

Barrett, Lisa Feldman, Michael Lewis, and Jeannette M. Haviland-Jones, eds. *Handbook of Emotions*. 4th ed. New York: Guilford Press, 2016.

Barrett, Lisa F., Batja Mesquita, Kevin N. Ochsner, and James J. Gross. "The Experience of Emotion." *Annual Review of Psychology* 58, no. 1 (2007): 373–403.

Barrett, Richard. *The New Leadership Paradigm: Leading Self, Leading Others, Leading an Organization, Leading in Society*. Lexington, Ky.: Barrett Values Centre, 2016.

Barsade, Sigal. "The Ripple Effect: Emotional Contagion and Its Influence on Group Behavior." *Administrative Quarterly* 47, no. 4 (2002): 644–75.

Barsade, Sigal G., Lakshmi Ramarajan, and Drew Westen. "Implicit Affect in Organizations." *ScienceDirect: Research in Organizational Behavior* 19 (2009): 135–62.

Barsade, Sigal G., and Olivia A. O'Neill. "What's Love Got to Do with It? The Influence of a Culture of Companionate Love and Employee and Client Outcomes in a Long-Term Care Setting." *Administrative Science Quarterly* 59 (2014): 551–98.

Barth, Karl. *Epistle to the Romans*. Translated from the 6th ed. by Edwin C. Hoskyns. 1933. Reprint, Oxford: Oxford University Press, 1968.

Bass, Dorothy C., Kathleen A. Cahalan, Bonnie J. Miller-McLemore, James R. Nieman, and Christian B. Scharen. *Christian Practical Wisdom: What It Is, Why It Matters*. Grand Rapids: Eerdmans, 2016.

Bauer, Jack J., and Dan P. McAdams. "Growth Goals, Maturity, and Well-Being." *Developmental Psychology* 40, no. 1 (2004): 114–27.

Bauman, Whitney. "Meaning-Making Practices and Environmental History: Toward an Ecotonal Theology." In *Routledge Companion to Religion and Science*, edited by James Haag, Gregory Peterson, and Michael Spezio, 370–71. Malden, Mass.: Routledge, 2014.

Beck, Aaron. *Cognitive Therapies and the Emotional Disorders*. Madison, Conn.: International Universities Press, 1976.

Bell, Charles. *The Anatomy and Philosophy of Expression as Connected with the Fine Arts*. 1840. Reprint, London: George Bell, 1877.

Bellah, Robert, and Richard Madsen, et al. *Habits of the Heart: Individualism and Commitment in American Life*. Berkeley: University of California Press, 1986.

Belliotti, Raymond Angelo. *Happiness Is Overrated*. Lanham, Md.: Rowman & Littlefield, 2004.

Benner, David G. *Human Being and Becoming: Living the Adventure of Life and Love*. Grand Rapids: Brazos, 2016.

———. *Identity: Youth and Crisis*. New York: W.W. Norton, 1968.

Berlant, Lauren. *Cruel Optimism*. Durham, N.C.: Duke University Press, 2011.

Berridge, Kent, and Piotr Wikielman. "What Is an Unconscious Emotion? (The Case for Unconscious 'Liking')." *Cognition & Emotion* 17, no. 2 (2003): 181–211.

Bidwell, Duane. *When One Religion Isn't Enough: The Lives of Spiritually Fluid People*. Boston: Beacon Press, 2018.

Birdwhistell, Raymond. *Kinesics and Context: Essays on Body Motion Communication*. Philadelphia: University of Philadelphia Press, 1970.

Black, John. "Darwin in the World of Emotions." *Journal of The Royal Society of Medicine* 95, no. 6 (2002): 311–13.

Blackson, Thomas A. *Ancient Greek Philosophy: From the PreSocratics to the Hellenistic Philosophers*. Malden, Mass.: Wiley-Blackwell, 2011.

Bloomfield, Paul. *The Virtues of Happiness: A Theory of the Good Life*. Oxford: Oxford University Press, 2014.

Bogdan, Radu J. *Interpreting Minds*. Cambridge, Mass.: Bradford Books, 1997.

Bollas, Christopher. *The Shadow of the Object: Psychoanalysis of the Unthought Known*. New York: Columbia University Press, 1987.

Bowlby, John. *A Secure Base: Parent-Child Attachment and Healthy Human Development*. New York: Basic Books, 1988.

Boylan, Michael. "Hippocrates." In the *Internet Encyclopedia of Philosophy*. http://www.iep.utm.edu/hippocrates/.

Brain, Peter. *Galen on Bloodletting*. Cambridge: Cambridge University Press, 2010.

Brennan, Tad. "The Old Stoic Theory of Emotions." In *The Emotions in Hellenistic Philosophy*, edited by Juha Sihvola and Troels Engberg-Pedersen, 21–70. Boston: Kluwer Academic Publishers, 1998.

Brenner, Charles. "On the Nature and Development of Affects: A Unified Theory." *Psychoanalytic Quarterly* 43 (1974): 532–56.

———. "A Psychoanalytic Theory of Affects." In *Emotion: Theory, Research, and Experience*, vol. 1, edited by Robert Plutchik and Henry Kellerman, 341–48. New York: Academic Press, 1980.

Breuer, Josef and Sigmund Freud. "Studies on Hysteria." *Standard Edition* 2 (1893–1895): 1–335.

Bridges, Katherine M. "Emotional Development in Early Infancy." *Child Development* 3 (1932): 324–34.

Brody, Leslie R., and Judith A. Hall. "Gender and Emotion in Context." In *Handbook of Emotion*, 3rd ed., edited by Michael Lewis, Jeannette M. Haviland-Jones, and Lisa Feldman Barrett, 395–408. New York: Guilford Press, 2008.

Brothers, Leslie. *Mistaken Identity*. New York: State University of New York Press, 2001.

Brown, Elspeth H. *The Corporate Eye: Photography and the Rationalization of American Commercial Culture, 1884–1929*. Baltimore: Johns Hopkins University Press, 2005.

Brown, Thomas. *Lectures on the Philosophy of the Human Mind*. 2 vols. 1828. Reprint, Miami: HardPress, 2017.

Browning, Don S. *Moral Context of Pastoral Care*. Louisville, Ky.: Westminster John Knox, 1983.

Bruce, Tina. *Learning Through Play: For Babies, Toddlers and Young Children*. 2nd ed. London: Hodder Education, 2011.

Burd, Larry. "Language and Speech in Tourette Syndrome: Phenotype and Phenomenology." *Current Developmental Disorders Reports* 1, no. 4 (2014): 229–35.

Burman, Erica. *Deconstructing Developmental Psychology*, 2nd ed. New York: Routledge, 2008.

Burnyeat, Myles F. "Aristotle on Learning to Be Good." In *Explorations in Ancient and Modern Philosophy*, vol. 2, 259–81. Cambridge: Cambridge University Press, 2012.

Butler, Lee. *Liberating Our Dignity, Saving Our Souls*. St. Louis: Chalice Press, 2006.

Cacioppo, John T., Gary G. Berntson, Jeff T. Larsen, Kirsten M. Poehlmann, and Tiffany A. Ito. "The Psychophysiology of Emotion." In *Handbook of Emotions*, 2nd ed., edited by Michael Lewis and Jeannette M. Haviland-Jones, 173–91. New York: Guilford Press, 2000.

Campbell, Sue. *Interpreting the Personal: Expression and the Formation of Feelings*. Ithaca, N.Y.: Cornell University Press, 1997.

Campos, Joseph J., Donna L. Mumme, Rosanne Kermoioan, and Rosemary G. Campos. "A Functionalist Perspective on the Nature of Emotion." *Monographs of the Society for Research in Child Development* 59, nos. 2–3 (1994): 284–303.

Cannon, Walter B. *Bodily Changes in Pain, Hunger, Fear, and Rage*. 2nd ed. New York: Appleton, 1929.

———. "The Interrelations of Emotions as Suggested by Recent Physiological Researches." *The American Journal of Psychology* 25, no. 2 (1914): 252–82.

———. "The James-Lange Theory of Emotions: A Critical Examination and an Alternative Theory." *The American Journal of Psychology* 39 (1927): 106–24. Reprinted in Walter B. Cannon, "The James-Lange Theory of Emotions: A Critical Examination and an Alternative Theory." *The American Journal of Psychology* 100, nos. 3–4, Special Centennial Issue (1987): 567–86.

Capps, Donald, and Richard K. Fenn. *Individualism Reconsidered: Readings Bearing on the Endangered Self in Modern America*. Monograph series 1. Princeton: Princeton Theological Seminary, Center for Religion, Self, and Society, 1993.

Caputo, John D. *Hope Against Hope: Confessions of a Postmodern Pilgrim*. Minneapolis: Fortress, 2015.

Cardinal, Rudolph N., John A. Parkinson, Jeremy Hall, and Barry J. Everitt. "Emotion and Motivation: The Role of the Amygdala, Ventral Striatum, and Prefrontal Cortex." *Neuroscience and Behavior Reviews* 26, no. 3 (2002): 321–52.

Carlin, Nathan, and Donald Capps. *100 Years of Happiness: Insights and Findings from the Experts*. New York: Praeger, 2012.

Carstensen, Laura L., Monisha Pasupathi, Ulrich Mayr, and John R. Nesselroade. "Emotional Experience in Everyday Life Across the Adult Life Span." *Journal of Personality and Social Psychology* 79, no. 4 (2000): 644–55.

Charmaz, Kathy and Melinda J. Milligan, "Grief." In *Handbook of the Sociology of Emotions*, edited by Jan E. Stets and Jonathan H. Turner, 516–43. New York: Springer, 2007.

Chavez, Nicole, Emanuela Grinberg, and Eliot C. McLaughlan. "Pittsburgh Synagogue Active Shooter." *CNN*, October 31, 2018. https://www.cnn.com/2018/10/28/us/pittsburgh -synagogue-shooting/index.html.

Clanton, Gordon. "Jealousy and Envy." In *Handbook of the Sociology of Emotions*, edited by Jan E. Stets and Jonathan H. Turner, 410–42. New York: Springer, 2007.

Clark, Elizabeth A. *Reading Renunciation: Asceticism and Scripture in Early Christianity*. Princeton, N.J.: Princeton University Press, 1999.

Clark, Margaret S. *Emotion*. Vol. 13 of *Review of Personality and Social Psychology*. Thousand Oaks, Calif.: SAGE, 1992.

Clark, Marilyn, and Kirsten Calleja. "Shopping Addiction: A Preliminary Investigation among Maltese Students." *Addiction Research & Theory* 16, no. 6 (2008): 633–49.

Clinebell, Howard. *Ecotherapy: Healing Ourselves, Healing the Earth*. Minneapolis: Fortress, 1996.

Clore, Gerald L. "Why Emotions Are Never Unconscious." In *The Nature of Emotion: Fundamental Questions*, edited by Paul Ekman and Richard J. Davidson, 285–90. Oxford: Oxford University Press, 1994.

———. "Why Emotions Require Cognition." In *The Nature of Emotion: Fundamental Questions*, edited by Paul Ekman and Richard J. Davidson, 181–91. Oxford: Oxford University Press, 1994.

Coan, James A., and Marlen Z. Gonzalez. "Emotions as Emergent Variables." In *The Psychological Construction of Emotion*, edited by Lisa F. Barrett and James A. Russell, 209–28. New York: Guilford Press, 2015.

Cooper, John M. "The Emotional Life of the Wise." *The Southern Journal of Philosophy*, 43 (2005): 176–218.

———. "Eudaimonism, the Appeal to Nature, and 'Moral Duty' in Stoicism." In *Aristotle, Kant, and the Stoics: Rethinking Happiness and Duty*, edited by Stephen Engstrom and Jennifer Whiting. New York: Cambridge University Press, 1996.

———. "Plato's Theory of Human Good in the Philebus." *Journal of Philosophy* 74, no. 11 (1977): 714–30.

———. *Pursuits of Wisdom: Six Ways of Life in Ancient Philosophy from Socrates to Plotinus*. Princeton, N.J.: Princeton University Press, 2012.

———. *Reason and Human Good in Aristotle*. Cambridge, Mass.: Harvard University Press, 1975.

Cooper-White, Pamela. *Shared Wisdom: Use of the Self in Pastoral Care and Counseling*. Minneapolis: Fortress, 2004.

Cornelius, Randolph R. *The Science of Emotion: Research and Tradition in the Psychology of Emotions*. Upper Saddle River, N.J.: Prentice Hall, 1996.

Cosmides, Leda, and John Tooby. "Evolutionary Psychology and the Emotions." In *Handbook of Emotions*, 2nd ed., edited by Michael Lewis and Jeannette M. Haviland-Jones, 91–115. New York: Guilford Press, 2000.

Couture, Pamela D. "Weaving the Web: Pastoral Care in an Individualistic Society." In *Through the Eyes of Women: Insights for Pastoral Care*, edited by Jeanne Stevenson-Moessner, 94–106. Minneapolis: Fortress, 1996.

Craig, A. D. "Interoception and Emotion: A Neuroanatomical Perspective." In *Handbook of Emotions*, 3rd ed., edited by Michael Lewis, Jeannette M. Haviland-Jones, and Lisa Feldman Barrett, 272–92. New York: Guilford Press, 2008.

Csikszentmihalyi, Mihaly. *Flow: The Psychology of Optimal Experience*. New York: Harper & Row, 1990.

Cushman, Philip. *Constructing the Self, Constructing America: A Cultural History of Psychotherapy*. Cambridge, Mass.: Perseus,1995.

Cvetkovich, Ann. *Depression: A Public Feeling*. Durham, N.C.: Duke University Press, 2012.

Damasio, Antonio R. *Descartes' Error: Emotion, Reason, and the Human Brain*. New York: G. P. Putnam, 1994.

———. *The Feeling of What Happens: Body and Emotion in the Making of Consciousness*. New York: Harcourt Brace, 1999.

———. *The Self Comes to Mind: The Construction of the Conscious Brain*. New York: First Vintage Books/Random House, 2010.

Darwin, Charles. *The Descent of Man*. 1871. Reprint, London: Penguin, 2004.

————. *The Expression of the Emotions in Man and Animals*. 2nd ed. Edited by Francis Darwin. In *The Works of Charles Darwin*, 1890, edited by Paul H. Barrett and R. B. Freeman, vol. 23. Reprint, New York: New York University Press, 1987–1989.

————. *On the Origin of Species*. Edited by Gillian Beer. Oxford: Oxford University Press, 2014 (1859).

Darwin, Francis, ed. *The Life and Letters of Charles Darwin*. New York: Appleton, 1896.

Davies, Paul. *The Cosmic Blueprint: New Discoveries in Nature's Ability to Order the Universe*. West Conshohocken, Pa.: Templeton, 2004.

Davies, William. *The Happiness Industry: How the Government and Big Business Sold Us Well-Being*. New York: Verso, 2015.

Davis, Michael, and Paul J. Whalen. "The Amygdala: Vigilance and Emotion." *Molecular Psychiatry* 6, no. 1 (2001): 13–34.

Deaux, Kay. "From Individual Differences to Social Categories: Analysis of a Decade's Research on Gender." *American Psychologist* 39, no. 2 (1984): 105–16.

De La Torre, Miguel. *Embracing Hopelessness*. Minneapolis: Fortress, 2017.

Denzin, Norman K. *On Understanding Emotion: With a New Introduction by the Author*. New Brunswick: Transaction Publishers, 2007.

Descartes, Rene. *Discourse on Method and Meditations of First Philosophy*. Translated by Elizabeth S. Haldane. Digireads.com Publishing, 2016 (1637).

————. *The Passions of the Soul*. Indianapolis: Hackett Classics, 1989 (1649).

Diener, Ed, Shigehiro Oishi, and Richard E. Lucas. "Personality, Culture, and Subjective Well-Being: Emotional and Cognitive Evaluations of Life." *Annual Review of Psychology* 54, no. 1 (2003): 403–25.

Dimas, Panos. "Epicurus on Pleasure, Desire, and Friendship." In *The Quest for the Good Life: Ancient Philosophers on Happiness*, edited by Oyvind Rabbas, Eyjolfur K. Emilsson, Hallvard Fossheim, and Miira Tuominen, 164–82. Oxford: Oxford University Press, 2015.

————. "Wanting to Do What Is Just in the *Gorgias*." In *The Quest for the Good Life: Ancient Philosophers on Happiness*, edited by Oyvind Rabbas, Eyjolfur K. Emilsson, Hallvard Fossheim, and Miira Tuominen, 66–87. Oxford: Oxford University Press, 2015.

Dixon, Thomas. *From Passions to Emotions: The Creation of a Secular Psychological Category*. Cambridge: Cambridge University Press, 2003.

Docter, Pete. "It's All in Your Head: Pete Docter Gets Emotional in *Inside Out.*" Interview by Terry Gross on NPR's *Fresh Air*, June 10, 2015. https://www.npr.org/2015/06/10/413273007/its-all-in-your-head-director-pete-docter-gets-emotional-in-inside-out.

Doehring, Carrie. "Emotions and Change in Spiritual Care." *Pastoral Psychology* 63, no. 5 (2014): 583–96.

————. *The Practice of Pastoral Care: A Postmodern Approach*. Rev. and expanded ed. Louisville, Ky.: Westminster John Knox, 2015.

Doi, Takeo. *The Anatomy of Dependence*. 1st ed., 1973. 2nd ed. Tokyo: Kodansha International, 1981.

Duchenne de Boulogne, G. B. *The Mechanism of Human Facial Expression*, edited and translated by R. Andrew Cuthbertson. 1862. Reprint, Cambridge: Cambridge University Press, 1990.

Durkheim, Emil. *The Elementary Forms of Religious Life*. Translated by Joseph W. Swain. London: Allen and Unwin, 1915.

————. *The Rules of Sociological Method*. 1895. Reprint, London: Macmillan, 1982.

Dykstra, Robert C. *Finding Ourselves Lost: Ministry in the Age of Overwhelm.* Eugene, Ore.: Cascade Books, 2018.

———. "Losers and the Struggle for Self-Awareness." In *Losers, Loners and Rebels: The Spiritual Struggles of Boys,* edited by Robert C. Dykstra, Allan Hugh Cole Jr., and Donald Capps, 27–73. Louisville, Ky.: Westminster John Knox, 2007.

Eberl, Jason T. *The Routledge Guidebook to Aquinas' Summa Theologiae.* New York: Routledge, 2016.

Edwards, Jonathan. "A Treatise Concerning Religious Affections." In *The Works of Jonathan Edwards,* vol. 1, 243–64. Peabody, Mass.: Hendrickson, 2000.

Ehrenreich, Barbara. *Smile or Die: How Positive Thinking Fooled America and the World.* London: Granta Books, 2010.

Ekman, Paul. "Are There Basic Emotions?" *Psychological Review* 99, no. 3 (1992): 550–53.

———. *Darwin and Facial Expression: A Century of Research in Review.* New York: Academic Press, 1973.

———. "Expression and the Nature of Emotion." In *Approaches to Emotion,* edited by Klaus Scherer and Paul Ekman, 319–43. Hillsdale, N.J.: Erlbaum, 1984.

———. "Universal Facial Expressions in Emotion." *Studia Psychologica* 15, no. 2 (1973): 140–47.

Ekman, Paul, and Wallace V. Friesen. "Constants across Cultures in the Face and Emotion." *Journal of Personality and Social Psychology* 17, no. 2 (1971): 124–29.

———. *Unmasking the Face: A Guide to Recognizing Emotions from Facial Clues.* Englewood Cliffs, N.J.: Prentice Hall, 1975.

Ekman, Paul, Wallace V. Friesen, and Phoebe C. Ellsworth. *Emotion in the Human Face.* New York: Pergamon Press, 1972.

Ekman, Paul, Wallace V. Friesen, Maureen O'Sullivan, Anthony Chan, Irene Diacoyanni-Tarlatzis, Karl Heider, Rainer Krause, William Ayhan LeCompte, Tom Pitcairn, Pio E. Ricci-Bitti, Klaus R. Scherer, Masatoshi Tomita, and Athanase Tzavaras. "Universals and Cultural Differences in the Judgments of Facial Expressions of Emotion." *Journal of Personality and Social Psychology* 53, no. 4 (1987): 712–17.

Elias, Norbert. *The Civilizing Process: Sociogenetic and Psychogenetic Investigations.* Rev. ed. Translated by Edmund Jephcott, edited by Eric Dunning, Johan Goudsblom, and Stephen Mennell. Malden, Mass.: Blackwell, 2000.

Ellison, Greg. *Cut Dead but Still Alive: Caring for African American Young Men.* Nashville: Abingdon, 2013.

Emory University Health Sciences Center. "Human Brain Loves Surprises, Research Reveals." *ScienceDaily* 16 (2001). https://www.sciencedaily.com/releases/2001/04/010415224316.htm.

Engstrom, Stephen, and Jennifer Whiting. *Aristotle, Kant and the Stoics: Rethinking Happiness and Duty.* New York: Cambridge University Press, 1996.

Erikson, Erik. *Identity: Youth and Crisis.* New York: W.W. Norton, 1968.

Farley, Wendy. *The Wounding and Healing of Desire: Weaving Heaven and Earth.* Louisville, Ky.: Westminster John Knox, 2005.

Fehr, Beverley, and James A. Russell. "Concept of Emotion Viewed from a Prototype Perspective." *Journal of Experimental Psychology: General* 113, no. 3 (1984): 464–86.

Feinstein, Howard M. "William James on the Emotions." *Journal of the History of Ideas* 31, no. 1 (1970): 133–42.

Feldman [Feldman Barrett], Lisa A. "Valence as a Basic Building Block of Emotional Life." *Journal of Research in Personality* 40, no. 1 (2006): 35–55.

———. "Valence Focus and Arousal Focus: Individual Differences in the Structure of Affective Experience." *Journal of Personality and Social Psychology* 69, no. 1 (1995): 153–66.

Feleky, Antoinette M. "The Expression of the Emotions." *Psychological Review* 21, no. 1 (1914): 33–41.

———. *Feelings and Emotions*. New York: Pioneer, 1924.

Fenner, William. *A Treatise of the Affections*. London: Rothwell, 1642.

Ferry, Luc. *What Is the Good Life?* Translated by Lydia G. Cochrane. Chicago: University of Chicago Press, 2005.

Fiorentini, Chiara. "Gender and Emotion Expression, Experience, Physiology and Well-Being: A Psychological Perspective." In *Gender and Emotion: An Interdisciplinary Approach*, edited by Ioana Latu, Marianne Scmid Mast, and Susanne Kaiser, 15–40. Bern: Peter Lang, 2013.

Fischer, Agneta H., and Antony S. R. Manstead. "Social Functions of Emotion and Emotion Regulation." In *Handbook of Emotions*, 4th ed., edited by Lisa Feldman Barrett, Michael Lewis, and Jeannette Haviland-Jones, 424–39. New York: Guilford Press, 2016.

Fonagy, Peter. *Attachment Theory and Psychoanalysis*. New York: Other Press, 2001.

———. "Psychoanalytic Theories." In *The Corsini Encyclopedia of Psychology*, 4th ed., edited by Irving B. Weiner and W. Edwards Craighead, 1–4. Hoboken, N.J.: John Wiley & Sons, 2010.

Fortenbaugh, William W. "Aristotle and Theophrastus on the Emotions." In *Passions and Moral Progress in Greco-Roman Thought*, edited by John T. Fitzgerald, 29–47. New York: Routledge, 2008.

Foucault, Michel. *The History of Sexuality*. Vol. 1, *An Introduction*. New York: Random House, 1978.

Franks, David D. "The Neuroscience of Emotions." In *Handbook of the Sociology of Emotions*, 3rd ed., edited by Jan E. Stets and Jonathan H. Turner, 38–62. New York: Springer, 2007.

Fredrickson, Barbara L. "The Role of Positive Emotions in Positive Psychology: The Broaden-and-Build Theory of Positive Emotions." *American Psychologist* 56, no. 3 (2001): 218–26.

Freud, Sigmund. *Beyond the Pleasure Principle*. Translated and edited by James Strachey, 1961. Reprint, New York: W. W. Norton, 1990.

———. *Civilization and Its Discontents*. 1930. Reprint, New York: W. W. Norton, 2010.

———. *Inhibitions, Symptoms and Anxiety*. 1926. Reprint, New York: W. W. Norton, 1959.

———. *New Introductory Lectures on Psychoanalysis*. Translated and edited by James Strachey. 1933. Reprint, New York: W. W. Norton, 1965.

———. "The Unconscious." In *Collected Papers*, vol. 4, translation supervised by Joan Riviere, 84–97. New York: The International Psycho-Analytical Press, 1924.

Fridlund, Alan J. "The Behavioral Ecology and Sociality of Human Faces." In *Review of Personality and Social Psychology*. Vol. 13, *Emotions*, edited by Margaret S. Clark, 90–121. Thousand Oaks, Calif.: SAGE, 1992.

———. *Human Facial Expression: An Evolutionary View*. San Diego: Academic Press, 1994.

Frijda, Nico H. "The Psychologists' Point of View." In *Handbook of Emotions*, 2nd ed., edited by Michael Lewis and Jeannette M. Haviland-Jones, 59–74. New York: The Guilford Press, 2000.

Frijda, Nico H., Peter Kuipers, and Ter Schure. "Relations among Emotion, Appraisal, and Emotional Action Readiness." *Journal of Personality and Social Psychology* 57, no. 2 (1989): 212–28.

Fulcher, J. R. "Puritans and the Passions: The Faculty Psychology in American Puritanism." *Journal of the History of the Behavioral Sciences* 9, no. 2 (1973): 123–29.

Furtak, Rick Anthony. *Wisdom in Love: Kierkegaard and the Ancient Quest for Emotional Integrity*. Notre Dame: University of Notre Dame Press, 2005.

"Galen." *Encyclopaedia Britannica Biography*. https://www.britannica.com/biography/Galen.

"Galen." *Greek Medicine*. http://www.greekmedicine.net/whos_who/Galen.html.

Gay, Peter. *Freud: A Life for Our Time*. New York: Norton, 1988.

Gendron, Maria, Kristen A. Lindquist, Lawrence Barsalou, and Lisa Feldman Barrett. "Emotion Words Shape Emotion Precepts." *Emotion* 12, no. 2 (2012): 314–25.

Gentner, Dedre, and Susan Goldin-Meadow, eds. *Language in Mind*. Cambridge, Mass.: MIT Press, 2003.

Gergen, Kenneth J. "Metaphors and Monophony in the 20th-Century Psychology of Emotions." *History of the Human Sciences* 8, no. 2 (1995): 1–23.

Gergen, Kenneth J., and Keith Davis. *The Social Construction of the Person*. New York: Springer-Verlag, 1985.

Giroux, Henry. *America on the Edge: Henry Giroux on Politics, Culture, and Education*. New York: Palgrave Macmillan, 2006.

Glenn, Jules. "Empathy, Countertransference, and Other Emotional Reactions of the Therapist." In *Psychotherapy: The Analytic Approach*, edited by Morton J. Aronson and Melvin A. Scharfman, 73–83. Northvale, N.J.: Jason Aronson, 1992.

Goldie, Peter. "Introduction." In *Oxford Handbook of Philosophy of Emotion*, edited by Peter Goldie, 1–13. Oxford: Oxford University Press, 2009.

Goldman, Linda. *Love and Loss: A Guide to Help Grieving Children*. 3rd ed. New York: Routledge, 2014.

Goldstein, Valerie Saiving. "The Human Situation: A Feminine View." *The Journal of Religion* 40, no. 2 (1960): 100–112.

Goleman, Daniel. *Emotional Intelligence: Why It Can Matter More Than IQ*. 1995. Reprint, New York: Bantam/Random House, 2006.

Gottman, John. *Why Marriages Succeed or Fail: And How You Can Make Yours Last*. New York: Simon & Schuster, 1994.

Graham, Larry K. *Care of Persons, Care of Worlds: A Psychosystems Approach to Pastoral Care and Counseling*. Nashville: Abingdon, 1992.

Greenberg, Elinor. *Borderline, Narcissistic, and Schizoid Adaptations: The Pursuit of Love, Admiration, and Safety*. New York: Greenbrooke Press, 2016.

Greenberg, Leslie S. "Emotion and Change Processes in Psychotherapy." In *Handbook of Emotions*, edited by Michael Lewis and Jeannette M. Haviland, 499–508. New York: Guilford Press, 1993.

———. "Emotion and Cognition in Psychotherapy: The Transforming Power of Affect." *Canadian Psychology* 49, no. 1 (2008): 49–59.

———. "Emotion-Focused Therapy." *Clinical Psychology and Psychotherapy* 11, no. 1 (2004): 3–16.

———. *Emotion-Focused Therapy: Coaching Clients to Work Through Their Feelings*. Washington, D.C.: American Psychological Association, 2002.

———. "On the Nature and Development of Affects: A Unified Theory." *Psychoanalytic Quarterly* 43 (1974): 532–56.

Greenberg, Leslie, and Jeremy D. Safran. "Emotion in Psychotherapy." *American Psychologist* 44, no. 1 (1989): 19–29.

Greenspan, Miriam. *Healing through the Dark Emotions: The Wisdom of Grief, Fear, and Despair.* Boston, Mass.: Shambhala Publications, 2003.

Griffiths, Paul. *What Emotions Really Are: The Problem of Psychological Categories.* Chicago: University of Chicago Press, 1997.

Hall, Brian P. *The Genesis Effect: Human and Organizational Transformations.* Reprint, Eugene, Ore.: Resource Publishing/Wipf and Stock, 2000.

———. *Values Shift: A Guide to Personal and Organizational Transformation.* Rockport, Mass.: Twin Lights Publishers, 1995.

Hamman, Jaco J. *A Play-Full Life: Slowing Down and Seeking Peace.* Cleveland: Pilgrim Press, 2011.

Hankinson, R. J. "Body and Soul in Galen." In *Common to Body and Soul: Philosophical Approaches to Explaining Living Behavior in Greco-Roman Antiquity*, edited by Richard A. H. King, 232–58. New York: de Gruyter, 2006.

Hanson, Ann Ellis. "Hippocrates: The 'Greek Miracle' in Medicine." *Medicina Antiqua.* http://www.ucl.ac.uk/~ucgajpd/medicina%20antiqua/sa_hippint.html.

Haraway, Donna J. *When Species Meet.* Minneapolis: University of Minnesota Press, 2007.

Harre, Rom. "An Outline of the Social Constructionist Viewpoint." In *The Social Construction of Emotions*, edited by Rom Harre, 1–14. Oxford: Basil Blackwell, 1986.

———, ed. *The Social Construction of Emotions.* Oxford: Basil Blackwell, 1986.

Harre, Rom, and Grant Gillett. *The Discursive Mind.* Thousand Oaks, Calif.: SAGE Publications, 1994.

Harre, Rom, and W. Gerrod Parrott, eds. *The Emotions: Social Cultural and Biological Dimensions.* Thousand Oaks, Calif.: SAGE Publications, 1996.

Heelas, Paul. "Emotion Talk Across Cultures." In *The Social Construction of Emotions*, edited by Rom Harre, 234–66. Oxford: Basil Blackwell, 1986.

Heimer, Lennart, Gary W. Van Hoesen, Michael Trimble, and Daniel S. Zahm. "The Eroding Relevance of the Limbic System." In *Anatomy of Neuropsychiatry: The New Anatomy of the Basal Forebrain and Its Implications for Neuropsychiatric Illness*, 15–26. Burlington, Mass.: Academic Press, 2008.

Herschbach, Mitchell, and William Bechtel. "Mental Mechanisms and Psychological Construction." In *The Psychological Construction of Emotion*, edited by Lisa Feldman Barrett and James A. Russell, 21–44. New York: Guilford Press, 2015.

Hillman, James. "Emotion as Energy." In *Emotion: A Comprehensive Phenomenology of Theories and Their Meanings for Therapy*, James Hillman, 66–86. Evanston, Ill.: Northwestern University Press, 1961.

———. *Emotions: A Comprehensive Phenomenology of Theories and Their Meanings for Therapy.* Evanston, Ill.: Northwestern University Press, 1961.

Hinds, Jay-Paul. "Shame and Its Sons: Black Men, Fatherhood, and Filicide." *Pastoral Psychology* 63, no. 5 (2014): 641–58.

Hochschild, Arlie. *The Commercialization of Intimate Life: Notes from Home and Work.* Berkeley: University of California Press, 2003.

———. "Emotion Work, Feeling Rules, and Social Structure." *American Journal of Sociology* 85, no. 3 (1979): 551–75.

———. *The Managed Heart: Commercialization of Human Feeling*. Berkeley: University of California Press, 1983.

Hogue, David A. "How the Brain Matters." In *Pastoral Theology and Care: Critical Trajectories in Theory and Practice*, edited by Nancy J. Ramsay, 31–53. Hoboken, N.J.: Wiley-Blackwell, 2018.

———. *Remembering the Future, Imagining the Past: Story, Ritual, and the Human Brain*. Cleveland: Pilgrim Press, 2003.

Holifield, E. Brooks. *A History of Pastoral Care in America: From Salvation to Self-Realization*. Nashville: Abingdon, 1983.

Hume, David. *A Treatise of Human Nature*, edited by L. A. Selby-Bigge. 1740. Reprint, Oxford: Clarendon, 1888.

Hume, Robert Ernest. *The Thirteen Principal Upanishads: Translated from the Sanskrit with an Outline of the Philosophy of the Upanishads*. Oxford: Oxford University Press, 1921. Classic Reprint, London: Forgotten Books, 2010.

Hunter, Rodney J. "Participation in the Life of God: Revisioning Lapsley's Salvation-Health Model." In *The Treasure of Earthen Vessels: Explorations in Theological Anthropology in Honor of James N. Lapsley*, edited by Brian H. Childs and David W. Waanders, 10–35. Louisville, Ky.: Westminster John Knox, 1994.

Ierodiakonou, Katerina. "How Feasible Is the Stoic Conception of *Eudaimonia*?" In *The Quest for the Good Life: Ancient Philosophers on Happiness*, edited by Oyvind Rabbas, Eyjolfur K. Emilsson, Hallvard Fossheim, and Miira Tuominen, 183–96. Oxford: Oxford University Press, 2015.

Illouz, Eva. *Cold Intimacies: The Making of Emotional Capitalism*. Cambridge, U.K.: Polity Press, 2007.

———. *Saving the Modern Soul: Therapy, Emotions, and The Culture of Self-Help*. Berkeley: University of California Press, 2008.

Irani, K. D., and Gerald E. Myers. *Emotions: Philosophical Studies*. New York: Haven Publications, 1983.

Irwin, T. H. "Kant's Criticism of Eudaemonism." In *Aristotle, Kant, and the Stoics: Rethinking Happiness and Duty*, 63–101. Cambridge: Cambridge University Press, 1996.

Isaacs, Kenneth S. *Uses of Emotion: Nature's Vital Gift*. New York: Praeger, 1998.

Isasi-Díaz, Ada María. *Mujerista Theology: A Theology for the Twenty-First Century*. Maryknoll, N.Y.: Orbis Books, 1996.

Izard, Carroll E. *Human Emotions*. New York: Plenum, 1977.

———. "Innate and Universal Facial Expressions: Evidence from Developmental and Cross-cultural Research." *Psychological Bulletin* 115, no. 2 (1994): 288–99.

Jackson, Stevi. "Even Sociologists Fall in Love: An Exploration in the Sociology of Emotions." *Sociology* 27, no. 2 (1993): 201–20.

Jacoby, Larry I., Andrew P. Yonellinas, and Janine M. Jennings. "The Relation between Conscious and Unconscious (Automatic) Influences: A Declaration of Independence." In *Scientific Approaches to Consciousness*, edited by Jonathan D. Cohen and Jonathan W. Schooner, 13–48. Hillsdale, N.J.: Erlbaum, 1997.

James, Susan. *Passion and Action: The Emotions in Seventeenth-Century Philosophy*. Oxford: Oxford University Press, 1997.

James, William. "The Physical Basis of Emotion." *Psychological Review* 101, no. 2, Special Centennial Issue (1994): 205–40.

———. *Principles of Psychology*. New York: Dover Publications, 1890.

————. *Talks to Teachers on Psychology: And to Students on Some of Life's Ideals*. 1899. Reprint, New York: Henry Holt, 1912.

————. "What Is an Emotion?" *Mind* 9, no. 34 (1884): 188–205.

Kagan, Jerome. *The Temperamental Thread: How Genes, Culture, Time and Luck Make Us Who We Are*. New York: Dana Press, 2010.

Kegan, Robert. *The Evolving Self: Problem and Process in Human Development*. Cambridge, Mass.: Harvard University Press, 1982.

Kegan, Robert, and Lisa Lahey. *An Everyone Culture: Becoming a Deliberately Developmental Organization*. Boston: Harvard Business Review Press, 2016.

Kelcourse, Felicity B., ed. *Human Development and Faith: Life-Cycle Stages of Body, Mind, and Soul*. St. Louis: Chalice Press, 2004.

Keller, Catherine. *On the Mystery: Discerning God in Process*. Minneapolis: Fortress, 2008.

————. *Political Theology of the Earth: Our Planetary Emergency and the Struggle for a New Public*. New York: Columbia University Press, 2018.

Kelly, Vernon C. "Affect and the Redefinition of Intimacy." In *Knowing Feeling: Affect, Script, and Psychotherapy*, edited by Donald L. Nathanson, 55–104. New York: W. W. Norton, 1996.

Keltner, Dacher, and Jonathan Haidt. "Social Functions of Emotions at Four Levels of Analysis." *Cognition and Emotion* 13, no. 5 (1999): 505–21.

Keltner, Dacher, and Paul Ekman. "Facial Expression of Emotion." In *Handbook of Emotions*, 2nd ed., edited by Michael Lewis and Jeannette M. Haviland-Jones, 236–49. New York: Guilford Press, 2000.

Kemper, Theodore D. "How Many Emotions Are There? Wedding the Social and the Autonomic Components." *American Journal of Sociology* 93, no. 2 (1987): 263–89.

————. "Power and Status and the Power-Status Theory of Emotions." In *Handbook of the Sociology of Emotions*, edited by Jan E. Stets and Jonathan H. Turner, 87–113. New York: Springer, 2007.

————. *A Social Interactional Theory of Emotions*. New York: Wiley, 1978.

————. "Social Models in the Explanation of Emotions." In *Handbook of Emotions*, 2nd ed., edited by Michael Lewis and Jeannette M. Haviland-Jones, 45–58. New York: Guilford Press, 2000.

————. "Sociological Models in the Explanation of Emotions." In *Handbook of Emotions*, 1st ed., edited by Michael Lewis and Jeannette M. Haviland, 41–51. New York: Guilford Press, 1993.

Knuuttila, Simo. *Emotions in Ancient and Medieval Philosophy*. Oxford: Oxford University Press, 2004.

Kohut, Heinz. *How Does Analysis Cure?* Chicago: University of Chicago Press, 1984.

————. *The Restoration of the Self*. Madison, Conn.: International Universities Press, 1977.

Konstan, David. *The Emotions of the Ancient Greeks: Studies in Aristotle and Classical Literature*. Toronto: University of Toronto Press, 2006.

————. *A Life Worthy of the Gods: The Materialist Psychology of Epicurus*. Las Vegas: Parmenides, 2008.

Kornfeld, Margaret. *Cultivating Wholeness: A Guide to Care and Counseling in Faith Communities*. 2000. Reprint, New York: Continuum, 2012.

Kovesces, Zoltan. *Emotion Concepts*. New York: Springer-Verlag, 1990.

Kreeft, Peter, ed. *Summa of the Summa*. San Francisco: Ignatius Press, 1990.

Krishna, Priya. "There Is a Free Lunch, after All. It's at the Office." *New York Times*. January 7, 2019. https://www.nytimes.com/2019/01/07/dining/free-food-employees.html.

Kupperman, Joel J. *Six Myths About the Good Life: Thinking about What Has Value*. Indianapolis: Hackett, 2006.

LaBarre, Weston. "The Cultural Basis of Emotions and Gestures." *Journal of Personality* 16, no. 1 (1947): 49–68.

Laird, Angela R., P. Mickle Fox, Simon B. Eickhoff, Jessica A. Turner, Kimberly L. Ray, D. Reese McKay, David C. Glahn, Christian F. Beckmann, Stephen M. Smith, Peter T. Fox. "Behavioral Interpretations of Intrinsic Connectivity Networks." *Journal of Cognitive Neuroscience* 23, no. 12 (2011): 4022–37.

LaMothe, Ryan. *Care of Souls, Care of Polis: Toward a Political Pastoral Theology*. Eugene, Ore.: Cascade Books, 2017.

———. *Pastoral Reflections on Global Citizenship*. New York: Lexington Books, 2018.

Lang, Peter J. "A Bio-informational Theory of Emotional Imagery." *Psychophysiology* 16, no. 6 (1979): 495–512.

Lange, Carl G. "The Emotions: A Psychophysiological Study." In *The Emotions*, edited by Carl G. Lange and William James, 33–90. 1922. Reprint, Baltimore: Williams and Wilkins, 1985.

Lange, Carl G., and William James. *The Emotions*. Baltimore: Williams and Wilkins, 1922.

Lapsley, James. *Salvation and Health: Interlocking Processes of Life*. Louisville, Ky.: Westminster John Knox, 1972.

Lartey, Emmanuel Y. *In Living Color: An Intercultural Approach to Pastoral Care and Counseling*. Philadelphia: Jessica Kingsley, 2003.

Lazarus, Richard. *Emotion and Adaptation*. Oxford: Oxford University Press, 1991.

———. "Thoughts on the Relations Between Emotion and Cognition." *American Psychologist* 37, no. 9 (1982): 1019–24.

Leary, David E. "Metaphor, Theory, and Practice in the History of Psychology." In *Metaphors in the History of Psychology*, edited by David E. Leary, 357–67. Cambridge: Cambridge University Press, 1990.

———, ed. *Metaphors in the History of Psychology*. Cambridge: Cambridge University Press, 1990.

LeDoux, Joseph E. "Afterword: Emotional Construction in the Brain." In *Psychological Construction of Emotion*, edited by Lisa Feldman Barrett and James A. Russell, 459–63. New York: Guilford Press, 2015.

———. *The Emotional Brain: The Mysterious Underpinnings of Emotional Life*. New York: Simon and Schuster, 1996.

———. "Emotional Memory Systems in the Brain." *Behavioural Brain Research* 58, no. 1 (1993): 69–79.

———. "In Search of an Emotional System in the Brain: Leaping from Fear to Emotion and Consciousness." In *The Cognitive Neurosciences*, edited by Michael S. Gazzaniga and George R. Mangun, 1049–61. Cambridge, Mass.: MIT Press, 1995.

———. "The Neurobiology of Emotion." In *Mind and Brain: Dialogues in Cognitive Neuroscience*, edited by Joseph E. LeDoux and William Hirst, 301–54. Cambridge: Cambridge University Press, 1986.

———. *Synaptic Self: How Our Brains Become Who We Are*. New York: Penguin, 2002.

LeDoux, Joseph E., and Elizabeth A. Phelps. "Emotional Networks in the Brain." In *Handbook of Emotions*, 1st and 2nd ed., edited by Michael Lewis and Jeannette M. Haviland-Jones, 157–72. New York: Guilford Press, 2001.

Leibniz, Gottfried. *New Essays on Human Understanding*, edited by Peter Remnant and Jonathan Bennett. Cambridge: Cambridge University Press, 1996.

Lester, Andrew D. *The Angry Christian: A Theology for Care and Counseling*. Louisville, Ky.: Westminster John Knox, 2003.

———. *Hope in Pastoral Care and Counseling*. Louisville, Ky.: Westminster John Knox, 1995.

Levy, Robert I. "Emotion, Knowing, and Culture." In *Culture Theory: Essays on Mind, Self, and Emotion*, edited by Richard A. Shweder and Robert A. LeVine, 214–37. Cambridge: Cambridge University Press, 1984.

Lewis, Michael. *The Rise of Consciousness and the Development of Emotional Life*. New York: Guilford Press, 2014.

Lewis, Michael, and Carolyn Saarni. "Culture and Emotions." In *The Socialization of Emotions*, edited by Michael Lewis and Carolyn Saarni, 1–17. New York: Plenum, 1985.

Lewis, Thomas, Fari Amini, and Richard Lannon. *A General Theory of Love*. New York: Vintage Books/Random House, 2001.

Lindquist, Kristen, A., Tor D. Wager, Hedy Kober, Eliza Bliss-Moreau, and Lisa Feldman Barrett. "The Brain Basis of Emotion: A Meta-Analytic Review." *Behavioral and Brain Sciences* 35, no. 3 (2012): 121–43.

Lloyd, Rachel. *Girls Like Us: Fighting for a World Where Girls Are Not for Sale—An Activist Finds Her Calling and Heals Herself*. New York: HarperCollins, 2011.

Loveday, C. A. Alexander. "The Passions in Galen and the Novels of Chariton and Xenophon." In *Passions and Moral Progress in Greco-Roman Thought*, edited by John T. Fitzgerald. New York: Routledge, 2008.

Luther, Martin. *What Luther Says: An Anthology*, vol. 1, compiled by Ewald M. Plass. St. Louis: Concordia, 1959.

Lutz, Catherine. "The Domain of Emotion Words on Ifaluk." In *The Social Construction of Emotions*, edited by Rom Harre, 267–88. Oxford: Basil Blackwell, 1986.

Mackey, John, and Rajendra Sisodia. *Conscious Capitalism: Liberating the Heroic Side of Business*. Cambridge, Mass.: Harvard Business School Publishing Corp., 2013.

MacLean, Paul. "Cerebral Evolution of Emotion." In *Handbook of Emotions*, edited by Michael Lewis and Jenneatte M. Haviland-Jones, 67–83. New York: Guilford Press, 1993.

———. *The Triune Brain in Evolution: Role in Paleocerebral Functions*. New York: Plenum Press, 1990.

Magai, Carol. "Long-Lived Emotions: A Life Course Perspective on Emotional Development." In *Handbook of Emotions*, 3rd ed., edited by Michael Lewis, Jeannette M. Haviland-Jones, and Lisa Feldman Barrett, 378–91. New York: Guilford Press, 2008.

Majdalani, Joelle F., and Bassem Maamari. "Emotional Intelligence: A Tool for Customer Satisfaction." *Journal for Global Business Advancement* 9, no. 3 (2016): 275–83.

Manson, Joseph H., Susan Perry, and Amy R. Parish. "Nonconceptive Sexual Behavior in Bonobos and Capuchins." *International Journal of Primatology* 18, no. 5 (1997): 767–86.

Manstead, Antony S. R., and Agneta H. Fischer. "Social Appraisal: The Social World as Object of and Influence on Appraisal Processes." In *Appraisal Processes in Emotion: Theory, Methods, Research*, edited by Klaus R. Scherer et al., 221–32. Oxford: Oxford University Press, 2001.

Marshall, Gary D., and Philip G. Zimbardo. "Affective Consequences of Inadequately Explained Physiological Arousal." *Journal of Personality and Social Psychology* 37, no. 6 (1979): 970–88.

Marshall, Joretta L. "Collaborating Hope: Joining the In-Between Spaces." *Journal of Pastoral Theology* 26, no. 2 (2016): 77–90.

————. *How Can I Forgive? A Study of Forgiveness*. Nashville: Abingdon, 2005.

"Martin Heidegger." *Stanford Encyclopedia of Philosophy*. https://plato.stanford.edu/entries/heidegger/.

Marx, Karl. *Selected Writings in Sociology and Social Philosophy*. Translated by T. B. Bottomore, edited by T. B. Bottomore and Maximillian Rubel. New York: McGraw-Hill, 1964.

Maslach, Christina. "Negative Emotional Biasing of the Unexplained Arousal." *Journal of Personality and Social Psychology* 37, no. 6 (1979): 953–69.

Maslow, Abraham. "A Preface to Motivation Theory." *Psychosomatic Medicine* 5, no. 1 (1943): 85–92.

————. "A Theory of Human Motivation." *Psychological Review* 50, no. 4 (1943): 370–96.

Mattern, Susan P. *The Prince of Medicine: Galen in the Roman Empire*. Oxford: Oxford University Press, 2013.

Mayr, Ernst. *What Makes Biology Unique? Considerations on the Autonomy of a Scientific Discipline*. New York: Cambridge University Press, 2007.

McClure, Barbara J. *Moving beyond Individualism in Pastoral Care and Counseling: Reflections on Theory, Theology and Practice*. Eugene, Ore.: Cascade Books, 2010.

————. "Pastoral Theology as the Art of Paying Attention: Widening the Horizons." *International Journal of Practical Theology* 12, no. 2 (2008): 189–209.

————. "The Social Construction of Emotions: A New Direction for the Pastoral Work of Healing." *Pastoral Psychology* 59, no. 6 (2010): 799–812.

McGill, V. J. *The Idea of Happiness*. New York: Praeger, 1967.

McKenna, James J., Sarah Mosko, Claibourne Dungy, and Jan McAninch. "Sleep and Arousal Patterns of Co-Sleeping Human Mother/Infant Pairs: A Preliminary Physiological Study with Implications for the Study of Sudden Infant Death Syndrome." *American Journal of Physical Anthropology* 83, no. 3 (1990): 331–47.

McNeill, John T. *A History of the Cure of Souls*. New York: Harper Torchbooks, 1951.

McNeill, William H. *Keeping Together in Time: Dance and Drill in Human History*. Cambridge, Mass.: Harvard University Press, 1995.

Menon, V. "Salience Network." In *Brain Mapping: An Encyclopedic Reference*, vol. 2, ed. Arthur W. Toga, 597–611. New York: Elsevier, 2015.

Mercer, Joyce A. *Welcoming Children: A Practical Theology of Childhood*. St. Louis: Chalice Press, 2005.

Mesle, C. Robert *Process Theology: A Basic Introduction*. St. Louis: Chalice Press, 1993.

Mesquita, Batja. "Emotions as Dynamic Cultural Phenomena." In *Handbook of Affective Sciences*, edited by Richard J. Davidson, Klaus R. Scherer, and H. Hill Goldsmith, 871–90. Oxford: Oxford University Press, 2003.

Mesquita, Batja, and Phoebe Ellsworth. "The Role of Culture in Appraisal." *Appraisal Processes in Emotion: Theory, Methods, Research*, edited by Klaus R. Scherer et al., 233–48. Oxford: Oxford University Press, 2001.

Mesquita, Batja, and Robert Walker. "Cultural Differences in Emotions: A Context for Interpreting Emotional Experiences." *Behaviour Research and Therapy* 41, no. 7 (2003): 777–93.

Mestrovic, Stjepan G. *Postemotional Society*. Thousand Oaks, Calif.: SAGE Publications, 1997.

Miles, Margaret Ruth. *Desire and Delight: A New Reading of Augustine's Confessions*. New York: Crossroad, 1992.

Mill, John Stuart. *Utilitarianism*. 1863. Reprint, Indianapolis: Hackett, 2001.

Miller-McLemore, Bonnie J. "Coming to Our Senses: Feeling and Knowledge in Theology and Ministry." *Pastoral Psychology* 63, no. 5/6 (2014): 689–704.

———. *Let the Children Come: Reimagining Childhood from a Christian Perspective.* San Francisco: Jossey-Bass, 2003.

———. "The Living Human Web: Pastoral Theology at the Turn of the Century." In *Through the Eyes of Women: Insights for Pastoral Care*, edited by Jeanne S. Moessner, 9–26. Minneapolis: Fortress, 1996.

Milne, A. A. *The Complete Tales of Winnie the Pooh.* New York: Dutton Children's Books/Penguin, 2016.

Moessner, Jeanne S., ed. *Through the Eyes of Women: Insights for Pastoral Care.* Minneapolis: Fortress, 1996.

Mohr, Richard D. "Plato's Theology Reconsidered." In *Essays in Ancient Greek Philosophy, vol. 3: Plato*, edited by John P. Anton and Anthony Preus, 293–307. Albany: State University of New York Press, 1989.

Montagu, Ashley, ed. *The Learning of Nonaggression.* Oxford: Oxford University Press, 1987.

Morsbach, H., and W. Tyler. "A Japanese Emotion: *Amae.*" In *The Social Construction of Emotions*, edited by Rom Harre, 289–307. Oxford: Basil Blackwell, 1986.

Moschella, Mary Clark. *Caring for Joy: Narrative, Theology, and Practice.* Boston: Brill Academic Publishers, 2016.

Myers, David G., and C. Nathan DeWall. "Theories of Emotion." In *Psychology*, 7th ed., 500–505. New York: Worth Publishers, 2004.

Nathanson, Donald L. *Knowing Feeling: Affect, Script, and Psychotherapy.* New York: W. W. Norton, 1996.

Nesse, Randolph. "Evolutionary Explanations of Emotions." *Human Nature* 1, no. 3 (1990): 268–69.

———. "Psychiatry." In *The Sociobiological Imagination*, edited by Mary Maxwell. New York: State University of New York Press, 1991.

Neuger, Christie. "Power and Difference in Pastoral Theology." In *Pastoral Care and Counseling: Redefining the Paradigms*, edited by Nancy J. Ramsay, 65–85. Nashville: Abingdon, 2004.

Niebuhr, Reinhold. *The Nature and Destiny of Man: A Christian Interpretation.* New York: Charles Scribner's Sons, 1941. Reprint, Louisville, Ky.: Westminster John Knox, 1996.

Niedenthal, Paula M., Lawrence W. Barsalou, Piotr Winkielman, Silvia Krauth-Gruber, and Francois Ric. "Embodiment in Attitudes, Social Perception, and Emotion." *Personality and Social Psychology Review* 9, no. 3 (2005): 184–211.

Nietzsche, Friedrich. *On the Genealogy of Morals.* Translated by Walter Kaufmann. 1887. Reprint, New York: Random House, 1967.

Nussbaum, Martha C. "Emotions as Judgments of Value and Importance." In *Thinking about Feeling: Contemporary Philosophers on Emotions*, edited by Robert C. Solomon, 183–99. Oxford: Oxford University Press, 2004.

———. "Eros and the Wise: The Stoic Response to a Cultural Dilemma." In *The Emotions in Hellenistic Philosophy*, edited by Juha Sihvola and Troels Engberg-Pederson, 271–304. Boston: Kluwer Academic Publishers, 1998.

———. *Fear: A Philosopher Looks at Our Political Crisis.* New York: Simon & Schuster, 2018.

———. *The Fragility of Goodness: Luck and Ethics in Greek Tragedy and Philosophy*, 2nd ed. New York: Cambridge University Press, 2001.

———. "Non-Relative Virtues: An Aristotelian Approach." In *The Quality of Life*, edited by Martha C. Nussbaum and Amartya Sen, 242–67. Oxford: Oxford University Press, 1993.

———. *Upheavals of Thought: The Intelligence of Emotions*. New York: Cambridge University Press, 2001.

Nussbaum, Martha C., and Amartya Sen. *The Quality of Life*. Oxford: Oxford University Press, 1993.

Oaklander, Mandy. "Why Do We Cry? Science Is Close to Solving the Mystery of Tears (and Why Some People Don't Shed Them)." In *Time* magazine, "The Science of Emotions—Love, Laughter, Fear, Grief, Joy," special edition (2017–2018): 28–33.

Oates, Whitney J. *The Stoic and Epicurean Philosophers: The Complete Extant Writings of Epicurus, Epictetus, Lucretius, Marcus Aurelius*. New York: Modern Library, 1957.

Oatley, Keith. *Emotions: A Brief History*. Malden, Mass.: Blackwell, 2004.

Oatley, Keith, and Jennifer M. Jenkins. *Understanding Emotions*. Malden, Mass.: Blackwell, 1996.

Ochs, Elinor, and Bambi Schieffelin. "Language Has a Heart." *Text* 9, no. 1 (1989): 7–25.

Oord, Thomas J. "Love and Cosmology." In *Defining Love: A Philosophical, Scientific, and Theological Engagement*, edited by Thomas J. Oord, 137–72. Grand Rapids: Brazos, 2010.

Oosterwijk, Suzanne, Alexandra Touroutoglou, and Kristen A. Lindquist. "The Neuroscience of Construction: What Neuroimaging Approaches Can Tell Us about How the Brain Creates the Mind." In *The Psychological Construction of Emotion*, edited by Lisa F. Barrett and James A. Russell, 111–43. New York: Guilford Press, 2015.

Ortony, Andrew, Gerald Clore, and Allan Collins. *The Cognitive Structure of Emotion*. New York: Cambridge University Press, 1988.

Owren, Michael J., and Jo-Anne Bachorowski. "Reconsidering the Evolution of Nonlinguistic Communication: The Case of Laughter." *Journal of Nonverbal Behavior* 27, no. 3 (2003): 183–200.

Paddock, Catharine. "Cursing Relieves Pain, But Not if Overused." *Medical News Today*, December 2, 2011. https://www.medicalnewstoday.com/articles/238525.php.

Panksepp, Jaak. "Emotions as Natural Kinds within the Mammalian Brain." In *Handbook of Emotions*, 2nd ed., edited by Michael Lewis and Jeannette M. Haviland-Jones, 137–56. New York: Guilford Press, 2000.

———. "The Quest for Long-Term Health and Happiness: To Play or Not to Play, That Is the Question." *Psychological Inquiry* 9, no. 1 (1998): 56–66.

Pargament, Kenneth I. *The Psychology of Religion and Coping: Theory, Research, Practice*. New York: Guilford Press, 1997.

———. *Spiritually Integrated Psychotherapy: Understanding and Addressing the Sacred*. New York: Guilford Press, 2007.

Parrott, W. Gerrod, ed. *Emotions in Social Psychology*. New York: Taylor & Francis Group, 2000.

———. *The Positive Side of Negative Emotions*. New York: Guilford Press, 2014.

Pawar, Sheela. "A Synopsis of Process Thought." *The Center for Process Studies*. http://www.ctr4process.org/about/what-process-thought/synopsis-process-thought.

Pembroke, Neil. *The Art of Listening: Dialogue, Shame, and Pastoral Care*. New York: T&T Clark/Handsel, 2002.

Pernau, Margrit, Helge Jordheim, Emmanuelle Saada, Christian Bailey, et al., eds. *Civilizing Emotions: Concepts in Nineteenth-Century Asia and Europe*. Oxford: Oxford University Press, 2015.

Pinch, Adela. "Emotion and History. A Review Article." *Comparative Studies in Society and History* 37, no. 1 (1995): 100–109.

Plamper, Jan. *The History of Emotions: An Introduction.* Translated by Keith Tribe. Oxford: Oxford University Press, 2012.

Plass, Ewald M., comp. *What Luther Says: An Anthology.* Vol. 1. St. Louis: Concordia, 1959.

Plato. *Dialogues.* In the *Dialogues of Plato.* Translated by Benjamin Jowett. 2 vols. New York: Random House, 1937.

Plutchik, Robert. *Emotion: A Psychoevolutionary Synthesis.* New York: Harper & Row, 1980.

———. "Emotions and the Brain." In *Emotions and Life: Perspectives from Psychology, Biology, and Evolution,* Robert Plutchik, 261–91. Washington, D.C.: American Psychological Association, 2003.

———. *Emotions in the Practice of Psychotherapy: Clinical Implications of Affect Theories.* Washington, D.C.: American Psychological Association, 2000.

———. "Landscapes of Emotion." In *Emotions and Life: Perspectives from Psychology, Biology, and Evolution,* by Robert Plutchik, 1–22. Washington, D.C.: American Psychological Association, 2003.

Plutchik, Robert, and H. R. Conte. "The Circumplex Structure of Personality Disorders: An Empirical Study." Paper presented at the Annual Meeting of the Society for Psychotherapy Research, York, England, 1994.

Powlison, David. "What Do You Feel?" *Journal of Pastoral Practice* 10, no. 4 (1991): 50–53.

Pryor, John B., Glenn D. Reeder, and Julie A. McManus, "Fear and Loathing in the Workplace: Reactions to AIDS-Infected Co-workers." *Personality and Social Psychology Bulletin* 17, no. 2 (1991): 133–39.

Quigley, Karen S., Lisa Feldman Barrett, and Suzanne Weinstein. "Cardiovascular Patterns Associated with Threat and Challenge Appraisals: A Within-Subjects Analysis." *Psychophysiology* 39, no. 3 (2002): 292–302.

Rabbas, Oyvind. "*Eudaimonia,* Human Nature, and Normativity." In *The Quest for the Good Life: Ancient Philosophers on Happiness,* edited by Oyvind Rabbas, Eyjolfur K. Emilsson, Hallvard Fossheim, and Miira Tuominen, 88–112. Oxford: Oxford University Press, 2015.

Rado, Sandor. *Adaptational Psychodynamics: Motivation and Control.* New York: Science House, 1969.

Rambo, Shelly. *Resurrecting Wounds: Living in the Afterlife of Trauma.* Waco: Baylor University Press, 2017.

Ramsay, Nancy J. "Where Race and Gender Collude: Deconstructing Racial Privilege." In *Women Out of Order,* edited by Jeanne S. Moessner and Theresa Snorton, 331–48. Minneapolis: Fortress, 2010.

Rank, Otto. *The Trauma of Birth.* Eastford, Conn.: Martino Fine Books, 2010.

Reber, Arthur S. *Penguin Dictionary of Psychology.* 3rd ed. London: Penguin, 2001.

Reddy, William M. "Against Constructionism." *Current Anthropology* 38, no. 3 (1997): 327–51.

———. *The Navigation of Feeling: A Framework for the History of Emotions.* Cambridge: Cambridge University Press, 2001.

Reevy, Gretchen M., Yvette Malamud Ozer, and Yuri Ito. *Encyclopedia of Emotion.* Santa Barbara, Calif.: Greenwood, 2010.

Reisenzein, Rainer. "The Schachter Theory of Emotion: Two Decades Later." *Psychological Bulletin* 94, no. 2 (1983): 239–64.

Rescorla, Robert A., and Allan R. Wagner. "A Theory of Pavlovian Conditioning: Variations in the Effectiveness of Reinforcement and Nonreinforcement." In *Classical Conditioning II: Current Theory and Research*, edited by Abraham Black and William F. Prokasy, 64–99. New York: Appleton-Century, 1972.

Ricci, Nicola. "The Behavior of Ciliated Protozoa." *Animal Behavior* 40 (1990): 1048–69.

Rick, Scott, and George Lowenstein. "The Role of Emotion in Economic Behavior." In *Handbook of Emotions*, 3rd ed., edited by Michael Lewis, Jeannette M. Haviland-Jones, and Lisa Feldman Barrett, 138–56. New York: Guilford Press, 2008.

Rieff, Philip. *The Triumph of the Therapeutic: Uses of Faith after Freud*. New York: Harper & Row, 1966.

Riesman, David. *The Lonely Crowd*. 1950. Reprint, New Haven: Yale University Press, 1965.

Riis, Ole, and Linda Woodhead. *Sociology of Religious Emotion*. Oxford: Oxford University Press, 2010.

Ritvo, Lucille B. *Darwin's Influence on Freud: A Tale of Two Sciences*. New Haven: Yale University Press, 1990.

Roberts, Robert C. *Emotions: An Essay in Aid of Moral Psychology*. Cambridge: Cambridge University Press, 2003.

———. "Emotions among the Virtues of the Christian Life." *The Journal of Religious Ethics* 20, no. 1 (1992): 37–68.

———. "What an Emotion Is: A Sketch." *The Philosophical Review* 97, no. 2 (1988): 183–209.

Robinson, Daniel N. *An Intellectual History of Psychology*. New York: MacMillan, 1976.

Roeser, Sabine, and Cain Todd. "Emotion and Value: Introduction." In *Emotion & Value*, edited by Sabine Roeser and Cain Todd, 1–14. Oxford: Oxford University Press, 2014.

Rogers, Carl. *Client-Centered Therapy, Its Current Practice, Implications, and Theory*. Boston: Houghton Mifflin, 1951.

———. "The Necessary and Sufficient Conditions of Therapeutic Personality Change." *Journal of Consulting and Clinical Psychology* 60, no. 6 (1992): 827–32.

———. *On Becoming a Person: A Therapist's View of Psychotherapy*. Boston: Houghton Mifflin, 1961.

———. "A Theory of Therapy, Personality, and Interpersonal Relationships, as Developed from the Client-Centered Framework." In *Psychology: A Study of Science*, edited by Sigmund Koch, vol. 3, 184–256. New York: McGraw-Hill, 1959.

Rogers-Vaughn, Bruce. *Caring for Souls in a Neoliberal Age*. New York: Palgrave Macmillan, 2016.

———. "Class Power and Human Suffering." In *Pastoral Theology and Care: Critical Trajectories in Theory and Practice*, edited by Nancy J. Ramsay, 55–77. Hoboken, N.J.: Wiley-Blackwell, 2018.

———. "Powers and Principalities: Initial Reflections toward a Post-Capitalist Pastoral Theology." *Journal of Pastoral Theology* 25, no. 2 (2015): 71–92.

Rogoff, Barbara. *The Cultural Nature of Human Development*. Oxford: Oxford University Press, 2003.

Rokeach, Milton. *Understanding Human Values: Individual and Societal*. New York: Free Press/Simon & Schuster, 1979.

Rorty, Amelie O. *Explaining Emotions*. Berkeley: University of California Press, 1980.

Rosch, Eleanor. "Cognitive Representations of Semantic Categories." *Journal of Experimental Psychology: General* 104, no. 3 (1975): 192–233.

Roseman, Ira. "Cognitive Determinants of Emotion." In *Review of Personality and Social Psychology*. Vol. 5, *Emotions, Relationships and Health*, edited by Phillip Shaver, 11–36. Thousand Oaks, Calif.: SAGE, 1984.

Roseman, Ira, and Craig A. Smith. "Appraisal Theory: Overview, Assumptions, Varieties, Controversies." In *Series in Affective Science: Appraisal Processes in Emotion: Theory, Methods, Research*, edited by Klaus R. Scherer, Angela Schorr, and Tom Johnstone, 3–19. Oxford: Oxford University Press, 2001.

Rosenblatt, Katariina, with Cecil Murphey. *Stolen: The True Story of a Sex Trafficking Survivor*. Grand Rapids: Revel/Baker, 2014.

Rosenthal, David M. "Emotions and the Self." In *Emotions: Philosophical Studies*, vol. 2, edited by K. D. Irani and Gerald E. Myers, 164–91. New York: Haven Publications, 1983.

Roth, Sheldon. *Psychotherapy: The Art of Wooing Nature*. Northvale, N.J.: Jason Aronson, 1990.

Rowe, Crayton E., Jr., and David S. MacIsaac. *Empathic Attunement: The "Technique" of Psychoanalytic Self Psychology*. Northvale, N.J.: Jason Aronson, 1995.

Russell, James A. "Core Affect and the Psychological Construction of Emotion." *Psychological Review* 110, no. 1 (2003): 145–72.

———. "Culture and the Categorization of Emotion." *Psychological Bulletin* 110, no. 3 (1991): 426–50.

———. "Is There Universal Recognition of Emotion from Facial Expression? A Review of the Cross-Cultural Studies." *Psychological Bulletin* 115, no.1 (1994): 102–41.

———. "My Psychological Constructionist Perspective, with a Focus on Conscious Affective Experience." In *The Psychological Construction of Emotion*, edited by Lisa F. Barrett and James A. Russell, 183–208. New York: Guilford Press, 2015.

Russell, James A., and Ghyslaine Lemay. "Emotion Concepts." In *Handbook of Emotions*, 2nd ed., edited by Michael Lewis and Jeannette M. Haviland-Jones, 491–503. New York: Guilford Press, 2000.

Saarni, Carolyn. "The Social Context of Emotional Development." In *Handbook of Emotions*, 3rd ed., edited by Michael Lewis and Jeannette M. Haviland-Jones, 307–22. New York: Guilford Press, 2008.

Sachs, Joe. "Aristotle: Poetics." *Internet Encyclopedia of Philosophy*. https://www.iep.utm.edu/aris-poe/#H3.

Salovey, Peter, and J. D. Mayer. "Emotional Intelligence." *Imagination, Cognition, and Personality* 9, no. 3 (1990): 185–211.

Salovey, Peter, Brian T. Bedell, Jerusha B. Detweiler, and John D. Mayer. "Current Directions in Emotional Intelligence Research." In *Handbook of Emotions*, 2nd ed., edited by Michael Lewis and Jeannette M. Haviland-Jones, 504–20. New York: Guilford Press, 2000.

Sandler, Joseph. *From Safety to the Superego: Selected Papers of Joseph Sandler*. New York: Guilford Press, 1987.

Sartre, Jean-Paul. *Sketch for a Theory of the Emotions*. 1962. Reprint, New York: Routledge, 1994.

Schachter, Stanley. "The Interaction of Cognitive and Physiological Determinants of Emotional State." In *Advances in Experimental Social Psychology*, edited by Leonard Berkowitz, 49–80. New York: Academic Press, 1964.

Schachter, Stanley, and Jerome Singer. "Cognitive, Social and Physiological Determinants of Emotional State." *Psychological Review* 69, no. 5 (1962): 379–99.

Scharfman, Melvin A. "The Therapeutic Relationship and the Role of Transference." In *Psychotherapy: The Analytic Approach*, edited by Morton J. Aronson and Melvin A. Scharfman, 53–71. Northvale, N.J.: Jason Aronson, 1992.

Scheib, Karen D. *Pastoral Care: Telling the Stories of Our Lives*. Nashville: Abingdon, 2016.

Scherer, Klaus. "Studying the Emotion-Antecedent Appraisal Process: An Expert System Approach." *Cognition and Emotion* 7, nos. 3–4 (1993): 325–55.

———. "What Are Emotions? And How Can They Be Measured?" *Social Science Information* 44, no. 4 (2005): 695–729.

Schleiermacher, Friedrich. *The Christian Faith*. Translated and edited by H. R. Mackintosh and J. S. Steward. 2 vols. 1821. Reprint, New York: Harper & Row, 1963.

Schmitter, Amy M. "17th and 18th Century Theories of Emotion." *Stanford Encyclopedia of Philosophy*. https://plato.stanford.edu/entries/emotions-17th18th/.

———. "Passions, Affections, Sentiments: Taxonomy and Terminology." In *The Oxford Handbook of British Philosophy in the Eighteenth Century*, edited by James A. Harris, 197–225. Oxford: Oxford University Press, 2013.

"The Science of Emotions: Love, Laughter, Fear, Grief, Joy." *Time* magazine, special edition (2017–2018).

Scruton, David L. "The Anthropology of an Emotion." In *Sociophobics: The Anthropology of Fear*, edited by David L. Scruton, 7–49. Boulder, Colo.: Westview Press, 1986.

Seeley, William. W., Vinod Menon, Alan F. Schatzbert, Jennifer Keller, Gary H. Glover, Heather Kenna, Allan L. Reiss, and Michael D. Greicius. "Dissociable Intrinsic Connectivity Networks for Salience Processing and Executive Control." *Journal of Neuroscience* 27, no. 9 (2007): 2349–56.

Seligman, Martin E. *Authentic Happiness: Using the New Positive Psychology to Realize Your Potential for Lasting Fulfillment*. New York: Atria/Simon & Schuster, 2002.

———. *Flourish: A Visionary New Understanding of Happiness and Well-Being*. New York: Free Press, 2011.

———. *Learned Optimism: How to Change Your Mind and Your Life*. 1990. Reprint, New York: Vintage Books/Random House, 2006.

Seligson, Hannah. "These Men Are Waiting to Share Some Feelings with You." *New York Times*, December 8, 2018. https://www.nytimes.com/2018/12/08/style/men-emotions-mankind-project.html.

Shane, Leo, III, and Patricia Kime. "New VA Study Finds 20 Veterans Commit Suicide Each Day." *MilitaryTimes,* July 7, 2016. https://www.militarytimes.com/veterans/2016/07/07/new-va-study-finds-20-veterans-commit-suicide-each-day/.

Shields, Christopher. "Aristotle." *Stanford Encyclopedia of Philosophy*. https://plato.stanford.edu/entries/aristotle/.

Shimer, David. "Yale's Most Popular Course Ever: Happiness." *New York Times*, January 26, 2018. https://www.nytimes.com/2018/01/26/nyregion/at-yale-class-on-happiness-draws-huge-crowd-laurie-santos.html.

Shoop, Marcia Mount. *Let the Bones Dance: Embodiment and the Body of Christ*. Louisville, Ky.: Westminster John Knox, 2010.

Siemer, Matthias, Iris Mauss, and James J. Gross. "Same Situation—Different Emotions: How Appraisals Shape Our Emotions." *Emotion* 7, no. 3 (2007): 592–600.

Sim, Christy. *Survivor Care: What Religious Professionals Need to Know About Healing Trauma*. Nashville, Tenn.: Wesley's Foundery Books, 2019.

Simon, Scott, and Jessica Purcell. "How Do Ants Survive Floods? Rafts of Course." *NPR*, April 23, 2016. http://www.npr.org/2016/04/23/475388734/how-do-ants-survive -floods-rafts-of-course.

Sisodia, Rajendra, and Michael J. Gelb. *The Healing Organization: Awakening the Conscience of Business to Help Save the World*. New York: HarperCollins Leadership, 2019.

Sisodia, Rajendra, Jagdish N. Seth, and David Wolfe. *Firms of Endearment: How World-Class Companies Profit from Passion and Purpose*. Upper Saddle River, N.J.: Pearson Education, 2014.

Smith, Craig A. "Emotion and Adaptation." In *Handbook of Personality: Theory and Research*, edited by Lawrence A. Pervin, 609–37. New York: Guilford Press, 1990.

Smith, Craig A., and Paul C. Ellsworth. "Patterns of Cognitive Appraisal in Emotion." *Journal of Personality and Social Psychology* 48, no. 5 (1985): 813–38.

Smith, Craig A., and Richard S. Lazarus. "Appraisal Components, Core Relational Themes, and the Emotions." *Cognition and Emotion* 7, no. 3–4 (1993): 233–69.

Solomon, Robert C. "Emotions in Continental Philosophy." Adapted from *Blackwell Companion to Phenomenology and Existentialism*, edited by Dreyfus and Wrathall, 413–31. *Philosophy Compass* 1, no. 5 (2006): 413–31.

———. *The Joy of Philosophy: Thinking Thin versus the Passionate Life*. Oxford: Oxford University Press, 1999a.

———. "Nietzsche and the Emotions." In *Nietzsche and Depth Psychology*, edited by Jacob Golomb, Weaver Santaniello, and Ronald L. Lehrer, 127–45. Albany: State University of New York, 1999b.

———. *The Passions: The Myth and Nature of Human Emotions*. Notre Dame: University of Notre Dame Press, 1983.

———. "The Philosophy of Emotions." In *Handbook of Emotions*, 2nd ed., edited by Michael Lewis and Jeannette M. Haviland-Jones, 3–29. New York: Guilford Press, 2000.

———. *Thinking about Feeling: Contemporary Philosophers on Emotions*. Oxford: Oxford University Press, 2004.

Sorabji, Richard. *Emotion and Peace of Mind: From Stoic Agitation to Christian Temptation*. Oxford: Oxford University Press, 2000.

Soupios, M. A. "Galen (A.D. 129–199): Physician, Scientist, Philosopher." In *The Greeks Who Made Us Who We Are: Eighteen Ancient Philosophers, Scientists, Poets and Others*, M.A. Soupios, 192–202. Jefferson, N.C.: McFarland & Company, 2013.

———. "Plotinus (A.D. 205–270): Mystic Philosopher." In *The Greeks Who Made Us Who We Are: Eighteen Ancient Philosophers, Scientists, Poets and Others*, M. A. Soupios, 203–29. Jefferson, N.C.: McFarland & Company, 2013.

———. "Zeno (335–263 BCE): Stoic Sage." In *The Greeks Who Made Us Who We Are: Eighteen Ancient Philosophers, Scientists, Poets and Others*. M. A. Soupios, 172–91. Jefferson, N.C.: McFarland & Company, 2013.

Spelke, Elizabeth S. "Core Knowledge." *American Psychologist* 55, no. 11 (2000): 1233–43.

Spitz, Rene A., and W. Godfrey Cobliner. *The First Year of Life: A Psychoanalytic Study of Normal and Deviant Development of Object Relations*. Madison, Conn.: International Universities Press, 1965.

Spretnak, Charlene. *Relational Reality: New Discoveries of Interrelatedness That Are Transforming the Modern World*. Topsham, Maine: Green Horizons, 2011.

Sroufe, L. Alan. "The Coherence of Individual Development: Early Care, Attachment, and Subsequent Developmental Issues." *American Psychologist* 34, no. 10 (1979): 834–41.

Stark, Judith Chelius, ed. *Feminist Interpretations of Augustine*. University Park: Pennsylvania State University Press, 2007.

Stearns, Carol Z. "'Lord Help Me Walk Humbly': Anger and Sadness in England and America, 1570–1750." In *Emotions: A Cultural Studies Reader*, edited by Jennifer Harding and E. Deidre Pribram, 170–90. New York: Routledge, 2009.

Stearns, Peter N. "History of Emotions: Issues of Change and Impact." In *Handbook of Emotions*, 2nd ed., edited by Michael Lewis and Jeannette M. Haviland-Jones, 17–31. New York: Guilford Press, 2000.

———. *Jealousy*. New York: New York University Press, 1989.

Steinhoffsmith, Roy H. "Infancy: Faith Before Language." In *Human Development and Faith: Life–Cycle Stages of Body, Mind, and Soul*, edited by Felicity B. Kelcourse, 129–46. St. Louis: Chalice Press, 2004.

Stets, Jan E., and Jonathan H. Turner. "The Sociology of Emotions." In *Handbook of Emotions*, 3rd ed., edited by Michael Lewis, Jeannette M. Haviland-Jones, and Lisa Feldman Barrett, 32–46. New York: Guilford Press, 2008.

Stocker, Michael. "How Emotions Reveal Value." In *Valuing Emotions*, edited by Michael Stocker with Elizabeth Hegeman, 56–87. Cambridge: Cambridge University Press, 1996.

Studtmann, Paul. "Aristotle's Categories." *Stanford Encyclopedia of Philosophy*. https://plato.stanford.edu/entries/aristotle-categories/.

Sullivan, Harry Stack. *Interpersonal Theory of Psychiatry*. New York: W. W. Norton, 1968.

Svavarsson, Svavar H. "On Happiness and Godlikeness before Socrates." In *The Quest for the Good Life: Ancient Philosophers on Happiness*, edited by Oyvind Rabbas, Eyjolfur K. Emilsson, Hallvard Fossheim, and Miira Tuominen, 28–48. Oxford: Oxford University Press, 2015.

Tamir, Maya. "What Do People Want to Feel and Why? Pleasure and Utility in Emotion Regulation." *Current Directions in Psychological Science* 18, no. 2 (2009): 101–5.

Thamm, Robert A. "The Classification of Emotions." In *Handbook of the Sociology of Emotions*, edited by Jan E. Stets and Jonathan H. Turner, 11–37. New York: Springer, 2006.

Thompson, Graham J., Peter L. Hurd, and Bernard J. Crespi. "Genes Underlying Altruism." *Biology Letters* 9, no. 6 (2013): 1–6.

Tillich, Paul. *The Courage to Be*. 3rd ed. New Haven: Yale University Press, 1963.

———. *Systematic Theology*. Vol. 1. Chicago: University of Chicago Press, 1951.

Tomaka, Joe, Jim Blascovich, Jeffrey Kibler, and John M. Ernst. "Cognitive and Physiological Antecedents of Threat and Challenge Appraisal." *Journal of Personality and Social Psychology* 73, no. 1 (1997): 63–72.

Tomaka, Joe, Jim Blascovich, Robert M. Kelsey, and Christopher L. Leitten. "Subjective, Physiological, and Behavioral Effects of Threat and Challenge Appraisal." *Journal of Personality and Social Psychology* 65, no. 2 (1993): 248–60.

Tomkins, Silvan. *Cognition*. Vol. 1 of *Affect, Imagery, and Consciousness*. New York: Springer, 1992.

Tooby, John, and Leda Cosmides. "The Past Explains the Present: Emotional Adaptations and the Structure of Ancestral Environments." *Ethology and Sociobiology* 11, nos. 4–5 (1990): 375–424.

Tornau, Christian. "Happiness in This Life? Augustine on the Principle That Virtue Is Self-Sufficient for Happiness." In *The Quest for the Good Life: Ancient Philosophers on Happiness*, edited by Oyvind Rabbas, Eyjolfur K. Emilsson, Hallvard Fossheim, and Miira Tuominen, 265–80. Oxford: Oxford University Press, 2015.

Torres, Monica. "4 Ways Elizabeth Holmes Manipulated Her Theranos Employees: And How Not to Get Fooled if Your Boss Tries This." *HuffPost Life*, March 2, 2019. https://www .huffpost.com/entry/elizabeth-holmes-office-employees_l_5c92abe3e4b01b140d351b6f ?ncid=engmodushpmg00000004.

Tracy, Phillip. "Study Relates Facebook Addiction to Snorting Cocaine." *The Daily Dot*, January 3, 2018. https://www.dailydot.com/debug/facebook-dopamine-addiction/.

Trible, Phyllis. "Adam and Eve: Genesis 2–3 Reread." Andover Newton Theological School, 1973. https://www.law.csuohio.edu/sites/default/files/shared/eve_and_adam-text_analysis -2.pdf.

Trower, Peter, and Paul Gilbert. "New Theoretical Conceptions of Social Anxiety and Social Phobia." *Clinical Psychology Review* 9, no. 1 (1989): 9–35.

Turkle, Sherry. *Alone Together: Why We Expect More from Technology and Less from Each Other*. New York: Basic Books, 2011.

Ulmner, Jeffrey T., Casey T. Harris, and Darrell Steffensmeier. "Racial and Ethnic Disparities in Structural Disadvantage and Crime: White, Black and Hispanic Comparisons." *Social Science Quarterly* 93, no. 3 (2012): 799–819.

Underwood, Emily. "Your Gut is Directly Connected to Your Brain, By a Newly Discovered Neuron Circuit." *Science*. September 20, 2018. https://www.sciencemag.org/news/2018/ 09/your-gut-directly-connected-your-brain-newly-discovered-neuron-circuit.

Vaillant, Leigh M. *Changing Character: Short-Term Anxiety-Regulating Psychotherapy for Restructuring Defenses, Affects, and Attachments*. New York: Basic Books, 1997.

Van Goozen, Stephanie, Nanne van de Poll, and Joseph A. Sergeant, eds. *Emotions: Essays on Emotion Theory*. Hillsdale, N.J.: Lawrence Erlbaum Associates, 1994.

Vohra, Sweta. "Documents Show Monitoring Black Lives Matter." *Al Jazeera News*, November 28, 2017. http://www.aljazeera.com/news/2017/11/documents-show-monitoring -black-lives-matter-171128110538134.html.

Volf, Miroslav. "The Crown of the Good Life: A Hypothesis." In *Joy and Human Flourishing: Essays on Theology, Culture, and the Good Life*, edited by Miroslav Volf and Justin E. Crisp, 127–36. Minneapolis: Fortress, 2015.

———. *Flourishing: Why We Need Religion in a Globalized World*. New Haven: Yale University Press, 2015.

Volf, Miroslav, and Justin E. Crisp, eds. *Joy and Human Flourishing: Essays on Theology, Culture, and the Good Life*. Minneapolis: Fortress, 2015.

Volkan, Vamik. *Immigrants and Refugees: Trauma, Perennial Mourning, Prejudice, and Border Psychology*. London: Karnak Books, 2017.

Wager, Tor D., Lisa Feldman Barrett, Eliza Bliss-Moreau, Kristen A. Lindquist, et al. "The Neuroimaging of Emotion." In *Handbook of Emotions*, 3rd ed., edited by Michael Lewis, Jeannette M. Haviland-Jones, and Lisa Feldman Barrett, 249–67. New York: Guilford Press, 2008.

Watson, John. M. "From Interpretation to Identification: A History of Facial Images in the Sciences of Emotion." *History of the Human Sciences* 17, no. 1 (2004): 29–51.

Weber, Max. *From Max Weber: Essays in Sociology*. Translated and edited by Hans H. Gerth and C. Wright Mills. Oxford: Oxford University Press, 1946.

"What Emotions Are (and Aren't)." *New York Times*, August 2, 2015, SR10.

White, Nicholas. *A Brief History of Happiness*. Malden, Mass.: Blackwell, 2006.

White, Richard. *The Heart of Wisdom: The Philosophy of Spiritual Life*. New York: Rowman & Littlefield, 2013.

Whitehead, James D., and Evelyn E. Whitehead. *Shadows of the Heart: A Spirituality of the Negative Emotions*. New York: Crossroad, 1994.

"Why Stress Causes People to Overeat." *Harvard Medical School Mental Health Letter*. https://www.health.harvard.edu/staying-healthy/why-stress-causes-people-to-overeat.

Widen, Sherri C. "The Development of Children's Concepts of Emotions." In *Handbook of Emotions*, 4th ed., edited by Lisa Feldman Barrett, Michael Lewis, and Jeannette Haviland-Jones, 307–18 (New York: Guilford Press, 2016).

Wierzbicka, Anna. *Emotions across Languages and Cultures: Diversity and Universals*. Cambridge: Cambridge University Press, 1999.

———. "Human Emotions: Universal or Culture-Specific?" *American Anthropologist* 88, no. 3 (1986): 584–94.

Williams, Sam. "Toward a Theology of Emotion." *The Southern Baptist Journal of Theology* 7, no. 4 (2003): 58–73.

Willingham, A. J. "A Mourning Orca Mom Carried Her Baby for Days Through the Ocean." *CNN*, July 27, 2018. https://www.cnn.com/2018/07/27/us/killer-whale-mother-dead-baby-trnd/index.html.

Wilson, Edward O. *Genesis: The Deep Origin of Societies*. New York: Liveright/W.W. Norton. 2019.

———. *The Meaning of Human Existence*. New York: W.W. Norton, 2014.

Wilson-Mendenhall, Christine D., Lisa F. Barrett, W. Kyle Simmons, and Lawrence W. Barsalou. "Grounding Emotion in Situated Conceptualization." *Neuropsychologia* 49, no. 5 (2011): 1105–27.

Winnicott, Donald W. *Playing and Reality*. 1971. Reprint, New York: Routledge Classics, 2005.

Wisco, Blair E., Brian P. Marx, Casey L. May, Brenda Martini, John H. Krystal, Steven M. Southwick, and Robert H. Pietrzak. "Moral Injury in U.S. Combat Veterans: Results from the National Health and Resilience in Veterans Study." *Depression and Anxiety* 34, no. 4 (2017): 340–47.

Young, Lidia. "Uber CEO Ousted Due to Low Emotional Intelligence and Hostile Company Culture." *ReThink Leadership Now*, June 30, 2017. http://rethinkleadershipnow.com/uber-ceo-ousted-due-to-low-emotional-intelligence-and-hostile-company-culture/.

Young, Paul Thomas. *Motivation and Emotion: A Survey of the Determinants of Human and Animal Activity*. New York: John Wiley & Sons, 1961.

Zajonc, Robert B. "Can Emotions Be Nonconscious?" In *The Nature of Emotion: Fundamental Questions*, edited by Paul Ekman and Richard Davidson, 293–97. Oxford: Oxford University Press, 1994.

———. "Emotion and Facial Efference: A Theory Reclaimed," *Science* 228, no. 4695 (1985): 15–21.

———. "Evidence for Nonconscious Emotions." In *The Nature of Emotion: Fundamental Questions*, edited by Paul Ekman and Richard Davidson, 293–97. Oxford: Oxford University Press, 1994.

———. "Feeling and Thinking: Preferences Need No Inferences." *American Psychologist* 35, no. 2 (1980): 151–75.

Zonta, Mauro. "Influence of Arabic and Islamic Philosophy on Judaic Thought." *Stanford Encyclopedia of Philosophy*. https://plato.stanford.edu/entries/arabic-islamic-judaic/.

Index